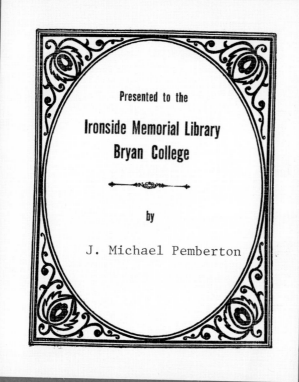

American & British Literature, 1945-1975

American & British Literature
1945-1975

An Annotated Bibliography
of Contemporary Scholarship

JOHN SOMER
and
BARBARA ECK COOPER

THE REGENTS PRESS OF KANSAS
LAWRENCE

Library of Congress Cataloging in Publication Data
Somer, John L
American & British literature, 1945-1975.
Bibliography: p.
Includes index.
1. American literature—20th century—History and criticism—Bibliography.
2. English literature—20th century—History and criticism—Bibliography.
3. Bibliography—Bibliography—American literature.
4. Bibliography—Bibliography—English literature.
I. Cooper, Barbara Eck, 1953-   joint author.
II. Title.
Z1227.S65   [PS221]   016.820′9′00914   79-19299
ISBN 0-7006-0195-3

TO

Teachers and students of contemporary literature

AND TO

Interlibrary loan librarians everywhere

Contents

There is every sign of a second great publishing revival the moment paper becomes abundant again.

Lawrence G. Green, 1947

Relativity, if not relativism, conceived not as the disappearance of standards but as the discernment of relationships, must be a premise whenever we consider literature.

Harry Levin, 1956

Introduction

This bibliography is designed to help the teacher solve the problems of researching contemporary literature, organizing classes, and leading students through a quantity of available material. We are concerned with books and monographs that study trends in American and British literature from 1945 to 1975. So many critical aids have appeared during this time that a good number are unknown to most students and to some teachers. By gathering this information, we hope to provide teachers and students a place to begin an inquiry into contemporary literature. Our main goal is to uncover important background studies and books not ordinarily highlighted in other bibliographies. Secondarily, our aim is to collect books and monographs that shed some light on contemporary issues and offer some insight into the contemporary *zeitgeist*.

Although this bibliography is designed as a tool for teachers, it may also help the general reader place favorite novels, poems, or plays in a critical context. It may help the specialist discover patterns, issues, and debates concerning contemporary literature. It may help the librarian purchase background studies. And we hope that through the bibliography, teachers, students, and librarians will find an awareness of the issues that shape American and British contemporary literature.

The annotation for each entry is generally composed of three parts: a brief statement of thesis and purpose, a description of special features, and a selected list of the writers studied to further clarify the book's focus. We have deliberately refrained from evaluating the studies because we thought it presumptuous to judge so many critical works in such a brief space. Occasionally, we include in the annotation brief quotations from the work if the author succinctly expressed his purpose. These quotations have the double advantage of allowing the author to speak for himself and of allowing our readers to sample the author's style. Naturally, the list of names, generally found at the end of the annotation, does not reflect every artist mentioned in a given work, but those artists who are listed received substantial attention in the work. (Of course, what is substantial for one work is not for another.) Moreover, the authors listed generally wrote after 1945 in American or British literature. Sometimes, however, earlier names or foreign names are listed when their presence reflects more accurately the emphasis of the work.

The annotated books are grouped into five categories: General Studies, Drama, Fiction and Prose, Poetry, and Critical Theory. We hope that the first four sections are reasonably complete because we have gleaned the Modern Language Association, the Modern Humanities Research Association, and thirty-five specialized bibliographies, plus advertisements and reviews. We used four standards for inclusion in these four categories: the books must deal with more than one author; they must have been published in English between 1945 and 1975; and they must deal with writers who began their careers after 1944 (Vonnegut) or who wrote important work both before and after 1944 (Faulkner). The first category, General Studies, was designed to cover studies of two or more genres. It serves this function well, but it also contains books that are important but difficult to categorize, such as W. H. Auden's *The Dyer's Hand and Other Essays*. Our fifth section, Critical Theory, is a selected list of theoretical studies that seem to us pertinent to the study of contemporary literature. The studies listed in this section do not always cover specific writers.

We have two observations for the professional student. We saw no need to track down every edition of a work since our task was to survey the general trends in contemporary criticism, not to establish editions. In general, when there were multiple editions, we used the one our library or Interlibrary Loan Office at Emporia State University could provide. Moreover, we decided to include some entries in the unannotated sections even though we had not verified the bibliographical information with their title pages. (We used this practice sparingly and have noted each instance with an asterisk. Many entries in the section entitled Studies Published after 1975 are asterisked because we used information from publishers' advertisements.) Finally, we included some Monarch and Cliff study guides because they were as responsible in their coverage of contemporary literature as many works published by scholarly presses.

A number of materials have been formally excluded. First, primary materials—novels, short stories, plays, and poems—were omitted because they are included in other bibliographies. Second, we omitted books devoted to a single author because they are easily located in a card catalogue or the *Library of Congress Catalogs*. Also, dissertations were omitted because there are several bibliographies devoted to them, the

INTRODUCTION

most recent being Lawrence McNamee's *Dissertations in English and American Literature* (1969). Finally, we omitted articles and essays because the annual bibliographies of the MLA and the MHRA adequately index them. Moreover, Howard Harper's "General Studies of Recent American Fiction: A Selected Checklist" (*Modern Fiction Studies,* Spring 1973) solves more specific problems in the listing of articles.

In addition to the five annotated categories, we have compiled five other lists that should prove helpful to a teacher or student of contemporary literature. The first is a list of books on contemporary literature that were published after 1975. This list completes Part 1 of the bibliography. Part 2, Study Guides, includes: Abstract, Summary, and Excerpt Collections; Bibliographies and Indexes; Biographical Guides and Directories; and Handbooks and Guides. Because there are so many bibliographies, we subdivided that section as follows: Bibliographies of Bibliographies; General Bibliographies; Drama Bibliographies; Fiction Bibliographies; Poetry Bibliographies; and Bibliographies by Topic (Specialized Bibliographies, Minority Bibliographies, Regional Bibliographies, and Science Fiction Bibliographies). These sections should lead our readers to other materials not listed here.

While this bibliography contains many entries, it can serve only as an introduction to the period. Before the beginning student uses it, we want to note the types of helpful items we generally omitted and to mention a representative few. The student of contemporary literature will find that there are a great variety of annuals, works that appear once a year, that contain valuable information: *The American Theatre; Broadway's Best; Documents of American Theatre History; International Literary Annual; International Theatre Annual; Yearbook of Comparative Criticism; Theatre Annual; Theatre: The Annual of the Repertory Theatre of Lincoln Center; Theater Book of the Year;* and *Theatre World.*

In addition to the annuals, there are a great many series that are helpful: *Approaches to the Study of Twentieth-Century Literature;* the English Association's *Essays and Studies; English Institute Essays; English Studies Today; Literature in the Modern World: Lectures Delivered at George Peabody College for Teachers;* and *World Perspectives.*

There are also a great number of periodicals, journals, and newspapers that students of contemporary literature read frequently. We can mention only a few: *The American Poetry Review; Chicago Review; Contemporary Literature; Fiction International; Modern Fiction Studies; New Left Review; Oyez Review; Partisan Review; Perspective; Seems; Southern Review; TLS: The Times* (London) *Literary Supplement;* and *Wisconsin Studies in Contemporary Literature.*

Finally, there are many excellent studies of the various literary

INTRODUCTION

genres: *Approaches to the Novel: Materials for a Poetics* (Robert E. Scholes); *The Context and Craft of Drama: Critical Essays on the Nature of Drama and Theatre* (Robert W. Corrigan and James L. Rosenberg); *The Novel: Modern Essays in Criticism* (Robert M. Davis); *Perspectives on Drama, Perspectives on Fiction,* and *Perspectives on Poetry* (James L. Calderwood and Harold E. Toliver); and *The Theory of the Novel* (Philip Stevick). In addition, the Critical Idiom Series contains many helpful studies. All of these sources only point to the great amount of material that awaits the student of contemporary literature.

We wish to thank the following people for their support and help: Charles E. Walton, who was our chairperson when we began this project; Mary Reeves Bain for her early work on the bibliography; the staffs of the Kansas State University and the Wichita State University libraries; the staff of the University of Kansas library, especially Susan Ketzner and David Bauer; the staff of the William Allen White Library at Emporia State University, Barbara Robins, Alan Doolittle, Ann Birney, Neal Van Der Voorn, and especially Kathy Mitchum of the Interlibrary Loan Office (for without her persistence there would have been no bibliography); members of the Faculty Research and Creativity Committee at Emporia State University for a grant to begin this project; Arlene Guhr and Kate Weigand for typing the manuscript; James Woodress for letting us read manuscript pages of *ALS 1975* prior to its publication; James Gunn for letting us work in his private collection; Ruth Clements for indexing the annotations; and special thanks to Connie Somer and David Cooper for consistent sacrifices and support.

Part 1

Studies of
Contemporary Literature

A
General Studies

A1   Abbs, Peter, ed. *The Black Rainbow: Essays on the Present Breakdown of a Culture.* London: Heineman, 1975. A study of the impact of nihilism upon various facets of our culture: art, poetry, fiction, language, pop music, architecture, philosophy, and science. Herbert Read's "The Limits of Permissiveness" informs, first, the collection's call for an identification and a rejection of nihilism and, second, the collection's call for a culture based on creativity and trust. Ted Hughes, Samuel Beckett, T. S. Eliot, Ezra Pound, and brief references to many others.

A2   Aiken, Conrad. *A Reviewer's ABC: Collected Criticism of Conrad Aiken from 1916 to the Present.* [New York:] Meridan, 1958. In his introduction, Rufus H. Blanshard states that Aiken wanted an art that could reflect "the sensibility of modern man in a modern world and yet still be *art*, art that might take its place in richness beside that of the past, and perhaps even surpass it in subtlety." Aiken's criticism reflects his vision of an age. Reissued as *Collected Criticism.*

A3   Allen, Walter. *The Urgent West: The American Dream and Man.* New York: Dutton, 1969. From his perspective as an Englishman, Allen studies the theme of the American dream in literature from Crèvecoeur through James Fenimore Cooper, Mark Twain, John Dos Passos, William Faulkner, John Steinbeck, Allen Ginsberg, Norman Mailer, William Carlos Williams, and others. Bibliography.

A4   Allsop, Kenneth. *The Angry Decade: A Survey of the Cultural Revolt of the Nineteen-fifties.* Port Washington, N.Y.: Kennikat, 1964. A "social bulletin" about the "angry cult" of writers who "share a quality which has been misread and misnamed anger." Allsop contends that a more accurate word is "dissentience." His study examines the origins, both social and intellectual, of these writers and their attitudes. In addition, Allsop evaluates "the quality of their despair" or the hope that their anger may contain. John Wain, Kingsley Amis, John Osborne, Colin Wilson, Iris Murdoch, John Braine, Hugh Thomas, and others.

A5 —————. *Scan.* London: Hodder & Stoughton, 1965. Twenty-one character sketches focusing on the writer behind the writing: Brendan Behan, William S. Burroughs, John Betjeman, Robert Graves, Christopher Isherwood, James Thurber, Eugène Ionesco, Frank Richards, C. S. Forester, William Faulkner, Alan Sillitoe, Patience Strong, Ignazio Silone, Irving Stone, Raymond Chandler, Mrs. Robert Henrey, Tennessee Williams, C. P. Snow, Edith Sitwell, W. Somerset Maugham, and Evelyn Waugh.

A6 Alter, Robert. *After the Tradition: Essays on Modern Jewish Writing.* New York: Dutton, 1969. Alter focuses upon the "Jewish renaissance" of the 1950s and '60s and the connections between the literature of American and Israeli Jews. Whole essays on Franz Kafka, Saul Bellow, Bernard Malamud, S. Y. Agnon, Elie Wiesel, and others.

A7 Alvarez, Alfred. *Beyond All This Fiddle: Essays 1955–1967.* New York: Random House, 1968. Essays on poetry, novels, criticism, and philosophy. Sylvia Plath, Edith Sitwell, Robert Lowell, Richard Eberhart, Hugh MacDiarmid, Philip Larkin, John Berryman, W. H. Auden, Louis MacNeice, Ronald Firbank, Dashiell Hammett, Norman Mailer, Patrick White, and others.

A8 —————. *The Savage God: A Study of Suicide.* New York: Random House, 1972. Alvarez looks at suicide in literature "to see how and why it colors the imaginative world of creative people." He examines the reasons why suicide is so central to contemporary writing and how the theme developed during the past five hundred to six hundred years. In addition, he attempts to counterbalance two prejudices: suicide as a moral crime and the scientific reduction of suicide to statistics. Sylvia Plath, Samuel Beckett, John Berryman, T. S. Eliot, Ted Hughes, Robert Lowell, Norman Mailer, and others.

A9 Anderson, David. *The Tragic Protest: A Christian Study of Some Modern Literature.* Richmond, Va.: John Knox,

1969. Anderson states that the writers he has selected for study "have deepened and extended [his] awareness of what it means to be a human being, and that in so doing they have raised questions about humanness concerning which Christianity has some comments to make and some explanations to offer." United by a Christian perspective, these diverse essays study Albert Camus, Kingsley Amis, T. S. Eliot, Saul Bellow, and others. Bibliography.

A10   Atkins, John. *Sex in Literature: The Erotic Impulse in Literature*. London: Calder & Boyars, 1970. A study of eroticism in literature in English. Nelson Algren, James Baldwin, Samuel Beckett, J. P. Donleavy, Lawrence Durrell, Mary McCarthy, Norman Mailer, Henry Miller, Vladimir Nabokov, John O'Hara, and others. Bibliography.

A11   Auden, W. H. *The Dyer's Hand and Other Essays*. New York: Random House, 1962. Criticism commissioned for diverse occasions on reading and writing, drama, the American scene, music, poetry, Robert Frost, and Marianne Moore.

A12   Bader, A. L., ed. *To the Young Writer: Hopwood Lectures, Second Series*. Ann Arbor: University of Michigan Press, 1965. Collection of essays about technique, literary genres, the problems of the writer's training, and gaining recognition. Also includes criticism of individual authors. Contributors include Stephen Spender, John Gassner, Archibald MacLeish, Philip Rahv, Malcolm Cowley, John Ciardi, Howard Nemerov, Theodore Roethke, Saul Bellow, Mark Schorer, Arthur Miller, and Alfred Kazin. Bibliography.

A13   Berthoff, Warner. *American Literature: Traditions and Talents*. Oberlin, Ohio: Press of the Times, 1960. Berthoff contends that American literature is not the result of a literary tradition, but of "provinciality, disconnectedness, watchful self-consciousness, civil and sectarian idealism, democratic anonymity, an uneasy measure of parish vanity or of populist spleen, capitalist libertarianism, Puritan conscientiousness, Utopian anticipation." Still, Berthoff sees some hope for the future in this brief address.

A14   ————. *Fictions and Events: Essays in Criticism and Literary History*. New York: Dutton, 1971. Literature expresses the way we participate in life and clarifies the form and manner of this participation. Berthoff writes: "A shared fiction of 'literature' and its uses underlies every particular literary performance, every new venture at fictive creation." Includes essays on "the unnerving disturbances of present history" and American literary subjects. Wallace Stevens, Iris Murdoch, Norman Mailer, and many earlier writers.

A15 Bewley, Marius. *The Complex Fate: Hawthorne, Henry James and Some Other American Writers.* New York: Gordian, 1967. Essays not only on Hawthorne and James, but also on modern American poetry, Wallace Stevens, H. L. Mencken and the American language, Kenneth Burke, and T. S. Eliot.

A16 Bier, Jesse. *The Rise and Fall of American Humor.* New York: Holt, Rinehart & Winston, 1968. "A serious treatment of humor" in popular forms, mass media, and formal literature. Surveys early American humor to the 1960s. Includes such modern figures as J. D. Salinger, Saul Bellow, Joseph Heller, Robert Gover, Edward Albee, Robert Benchley, e. e. cummings, William Faulkner, Robert Frost, Ernest Hemingway, Ogden Nash, Dorothy Parker, James Thurber, E. B. White, Tennessee Williams, John Barth, William Burroughs, Norman Mailer, Bernard Malamud, Vladimir Nabokov, and others. Bibliography.

A17 Bigsby, C. W. E., ed. *The Black American Writer.* Vol. 1, *Fiction.* Vol. 2, *Poetry and Drama.* Deland, Fla.: Everett/ Edwards, 1969. Bigsby's purpose is "to examine the achievement of some of the major talents to emerge from the black community, to analyze and assess the difficulties facing the black writer, and to examine the problem of criticism in a field so fraught with social, cultural, and political prejudices." Volume 1: P. L. Dunbar, Charles Chesnutt, Richard Wright, Ralph Ellison, and James Baldwin. Volume 2: Harold Cruse, Langston Hughes, Gwendolyn Brooks, Loften Mitchell, Ossie Davis, Douglas Turner Ward, Lorraine Hansberry, James Baldwin, LeRoi Jones (Imamu Amiri Baraka), and Lonne Elder III.

A18 Bode, Carl. *The Half-World of American Culture: A Miscellany.* Carbondale: Southern Illinois University Press, 1965. Bode writes: "In this book I have brought together my

essays and notes on several things in American culture
which seem to me worth talking about." This study of
American writing includes both "investigations of high culture and mass culture." Bode's unifying interest is "in the
social surroundings of a printed work and in the possible
motivations of both the writer and the reader." Henry
David Thoreau, Walt Whitman, Nathaniel Hawthorne,
Erskine Caldwell, Lloyd Douglas, J. D. Salinger, Katherine
Anne Porter, e. e. cummings, and others.

A19 ————, ed. *The Great Experiment in American Literature.*
New York: Praeger, 1961. Essays on experimentation in
American literature, the search for fresh literary forms, and
exploration of new possibilities of the language. From a
series of public lectures arranged by the cultural section of
the American embassy in Great Britain. Edgar Allan Poe,
Walt Whitman, Emily Dickinson, e. e. cummings, Wallace
Stevens, and Ernest Hemingway.

A20 ————, ed. *The Young Rebel in American Literature.*
New York: Praeger, 1959. A series of lectures at the Amer-
ican embassy in London on the American tradition of non-
conformity in the lives and works of American authors.
Henry David Thoreau, Walt Whitman, Sinclair Lewis, F.
Scott Fitzgerald, H. L. Mencken, John Steinbeck, and
William Faulkner.

A21 Bogan, Louise. *Selected Criticism: Prose, Poetry.* New York:
Noonday, 1955. Selections of Louise Bogan's criticism that
appeared in the *New Yorker* between 1931 and 1954. Section 1, "Modernism in American Literature," contains
essays on T. S. Eliot, James Joyce, Ezra Pound, Marianne
Moore, and W. H. Auden. Section 2, "Young Poets: 1944–
1954," includes essays on Robert Penn Warren, Robert
Fitzgerald, Elizabeth Bishop, Robert Lowell, Richard Wilbur, W. S. Merwin, Peter Viereck, Karl Shapiro, and Barbara Howes.

A22 Bowen, Elizabeth; Graham Greene; and V. S. Pritchett. *Why
Do I Write?* London: Percival Marshall, 1948. Letters
exchanged between the three writers. Of these letters, V. S.
Pritchett states, "Three writers talk of themselves and for
themselves in their own terms."

A23   Bradbury, John M. *Renaissance in the South: A Critical History of the Literature, 1920–1960*. Chapel Hill: University of North Carolina Press, 1963. Recognizes the important literary contribution made by the South. Bradbury groups and classifies southern literature to display its range and depth as well as its larger trends and individual deviations within the movement. In the process, he rediscovers "authors whose enduring qualities have been buried in the avalanche of more recent writing." Bradbury studies poetry, drama, fiction, the Negro in literature, social realism, and traditionalists. List of authors. Over six hundred writers are mentioned.

A24   Brady, Frank; John Palmer; and Martin Price, eds. *Literary Theory and Structure*. New Haven: Yale University Press, 1973. A collection of essays in honor of William K. Wimsatt on the general theme of literary theory and structure. About half of the nineteen essays deal with topics and figures of interest to students of contemporary literature: Saussure's concepts, art as a form of biological adaption, John Crowe Ransom, T. S. Eliot, Wallace Stevens, and postsymbolist structures.

A25   Brashers, Howard C. *An Introduction to American Literature for European Students*. Stockholm: Svenska Blkförlaget, 1965. A historical and "introductory survey of the important authors and principal works of American literature" for the beginning European university student. "I have tried to present the ordinary vocabulary that American scholars use and their usual critical judgments." The final chapter is on contemporary authors. Bibliography.

A26   Breit, Harvey. *The Writer Observed*. Cleveland: World, 1956. "Talks" with T. S. Eliot, Robert Sherwood, Evelyn Waugh, J. P. Marquand, E. M. Forster, Arnold Toynbee, Albert Schweitzer, Christopher Morley, Angela Thirkell, Robert Hillyer, John O'Hara, Nelson Algren, Alan Paton, Robert Frost, William Carlos Williams, Henry Green, Elizabeth Bowen, Christine Weston, Charles Jackson, Robert Nathan, Dylan Thomas, Aldous Huxley, Robert Penn Warren, Wilbur Daniel Steele, Budd Schulberg, John Dos Passos, W. Somerset Maugham, Francis Parkinson Keyes, Conrad Aiken, e. e. cummings, James Norman Hall, Joyce Cary,

Noel Coward, Cecil Woodham-Smith, James Jones, Arthur Koestler, Helen MacInnes, Gilbert Highet, J. B. Priestly, Frank Yerby, Norman Mailer, Malcolm Cowley, Ray Bradbury, Phyllis McGinley, Christopher Isherwood, Van Wyck Brooks, Jean Stafford, Mary Roberts Rinehart, Truman Capote, Ralph Ellison, C. S. Forester, George Jean Nathan, Carl Sandburg, James Thurber, Frank O'Connor, Ernest Hemingway, Edmund Wilson, Saul Bellow, and William Faulkner.

A27 Brodbeck, May; James Gray; and Walter Metzler. *American Non-Fiction, 1900–1950*. Chicago: Regnery, 1952. American nonfiction writers have "ignored traditional assumptions about the nature of the literary essay." They have "merged biography with history, social theory, or literary criticism." A general survey of writers of social theory, philosophy, and literary journalism. Bibliography.

A28 Brooks, Cleanth. *The Hidden God: Studies in Hemingway, Faulkner, Yeats, Eliot, and Warren*. New Haven: Yale University Press, 1963. "One looks for an image of a man, attempting in a world increasingly dehumanized to realize himself as a man—to act like a responsible moral being, not to drift like a mere thing." Brooks studies the problems of Christian as well as unorthodox literature. Five lectures given in 1955 at the Conference on Theology for College Faculty, held at Trinity College, Hartford, Connecticut.

A29 Brooks, Van Wyck. *The Writer in America*. New York: Dutton, 1953. A personal account of the literary life in America. The last chapter deals primarily with contemporary authors.

A30 Brophy, Brigid. *Don't Never Forget: Collected Views and Reviews*. New York: Holt, Rinehart & Winston, 1967. Journalistic writing published in periodicals or from broadcasts. Evelyn Waugh, George Bernard Shaw, Katherine Mansfield, Jean-Paul Sartre, Jean Genet, and others.

A31 Brown, Francis, ed. *Opinions and Perspectives from the New York Times Book Review*. Boston: Houghton Mifflin, 1964. Sixty-two essays on contemporary writing, the American classics, and the experience of the writer as well as reviews, reappraisals, and historical essays. Contributors include Saul Bellow, Stephen Spender, Karl Shapiro, M. L. Rosenthal, James Baldwin, Angus Wilson, Elizabeth Bowen, Lawrence Durrell, Robert Penn Warren, Mark Schorer, and John Knowles.

A32   Brown, John Mason. *Seeing Things.* New York: McGraw-Hill, 1946. Short essays on literary and newsworthy topics reprinted from the *Saturday Review of Literature*'s "Seeing Things" department. *Seeing More Things* (1948); *Still Seeing Things* (1950); *As They Appear* (1952).

A33   Bruns, Gerald L. *Modern Poetry and the Idea of Language: A Critical and Historical Study.* New Haven: Yale University Press, 1974. "The purpose of this book is to inquire, by diverse means, into two broadly antithetical conceptions of poetic or literary language: the idea of the 'pure expressiveness' of literary speech . . . and the idea of poetic speech as the ground of all signification." Bruns calls the first idea "hermetic" because the poet's activity is towards "the work as a self-contained object." The second, he calls "Orphic," after Orpheus, "the primordial singer whose sphere of activity is governed by a mythological or ideal unity of word and being." The study deals with poetry and fiction. Roland Barthes, Samuel Beckett, James Joyce, Stéphane Mallarmé, Gustave Flaubert, Wallace Stevens, William Carlos Williams, and others.

A34   Buchen, Irving, ed. *The Perverse Imagination: Sexuality and Literary Culture.* New York: New York University Press, 1970. A collection of essays on pornography. Includes essays written by Ihab Hassan, Joseph Bentley, Geoffrey Gorer, Wayland Young, Richard Schechner, Robert Brustein, Gore Vidal, William Phillips, Benjamin DeMott, Stanton Hoffman, George Plimpton, Robert Boyers, Strother Purdy, Kate Millet, Norman O. Brown, Georges Bataille, Lawrence Lipton, and Anthony Burgess. Subjects range from homosexuality and incest to authors such as Philip Roth and Norman Mailer. Bibliography.

A35   Burgess, Anthony. *Urgent Copy: Literary Studies.* New York: Norton, 1968. A collection of journalistic essays on a wide variety of topics. Graham Greene, Evelyn Waugh, C. S. Lewis, Arthur Koestler, and many others.

A36   Burrows, David J.; Lewis M. Dabney; Milne Holton; and Grosvenor E. Powell. *Private Dealings: Modern American Writers in Search of Integrity*. Rockville, Md.: New Perspectives, 1974. First published in Sweden (1969), these eight essays focus upon American writers who "aggressively maintained their sense of self in a society where personal integrity is increasingly difficult." Robert Frost, Wallace Stevens, William Carlos Williams, Edmund Wilson, Bernard Malamud, Ralph Ellison, J. D. Salinger, and Robert Lowell.

A37   Cahill, Susan and Thomas. *A Literary Guide to Ireland*. New York: Scribner's, 1973. A guidebook to points of literary interest in Ireland. It treats all the literary giants and "their relationship to Irish history and to the Irish landscape." The authors discuss "the ancient sources of Irish imagination: the myths and legends of the countryside." Samuel Beckett, Brendan Behan, Elizabeth Bowen, J. P. Donleavy, Frank O'Connor, George Bernard Shaw, and many earlier figures.

A38   Caldwell, Erskine. *Call It Experience*. London: Hutchinson, 1952. Caldwell's aim is "to set forth some of the experiences of an author which may be of interest to curious readers and would-be writers who seek visions of the wonderland in which all authors are believed to exist." Caldwell writes a personal history of the literary experience.

A39   Carpenter, Frederic I. *American Literature and the Dream*. New York: Philosophical Library, 1955. "American literature has differed from English because of the constant and omnipresent influence of the American dream upon it." Carpenter suggests that American literature is a symbolic and experimental projection of the dream. Considered in this light, American literature falls into new patterns, for this interpretation emphasizes "the ideal attitudes of American writers toward the dream." Carpenter redefines traditional categories of American literature and reinterprets major writers. Thomas Wolfe, John Steinbeck, William Saroyan, Ernest Hemingway, Robinson Jeffers, and earlier writers.

A40   Carr, John, ed. *Kite-Flying and Other Irrational Acts: Conversations with Twelve Southern Writers*. Baton Rouge:

Louisiana State University Press, 1972. Interviews with Shelby Foote, Walker Percy, Marion Montgomery, Reynolds Price, Willie Morris, Larry L. King, Doris Betts, George Garrett, Jessie Hill Ford, Fred Chappell, Guy Owen, and James Whitehead.

A41   Chassman, Neil A., ed. *Poets of the Cities New York and San Francisco, 1950–1965*. New York: Dutton, 1974. A collection of pictures, paintings, essays, and biographies that speaks to the life of contemporary art in two cities. This catalogue prepared for the Dallas Museum of Fine Arts and the Meadows School of the Arts draws "together related currents in various arts of the 1950s and early '60s." Chassman, Robert Creeley, and John Clellon Holmes contributed essays about the literary figures of the times. Bibliography.

A42   Clark, D. Waldo. *Writers of Today*. London: Longmans, 1956. A volume in the Essential English Library, a series intended for foreign students. The style and content are aimed at the "serious adult student." Ends with a glossary of difficult words. This brief study introduces today's literature with chapters on six authors, one on poets, and one on dramatists. James Joyce, T. S. Eliot, Virginia Woolf, Aldous Huxley, Charles Morgan, Graham Greene, and others.

A43   Clough, Wilson O. *The Necessary Earth: Nature and Solitude in American Literature*. Austin: University of Texas Press, 1964. An essay, not "an exercise in research scholarship," with three divisions: first, the "initial impact of the New World upon Old World men"; second, "the gradual awareness that the frontier might furnish American writers with a native source of metaphor"; and third, "the degree to which echoes of this native metaphor . . . may have lingered into the twentieth century." The implied political theme of the essay is that "the American writer . . . had to keep in touch with this source—this simple, democratic man—and at the same time, extend himself to consider the larger implications for self, for the American, for mankind." An implied intellectual theme is that as Americans lost the past, they learned to speak from experience. Wallace Stevens, Robinson Jeffers, William Faulkner, Thomas Hornsby Ferril, and Robert Frost. Bibliography.

A44   Collins, A. S. *English Literature of the Twentieth Century.*
       London: University Tutorial Press, 1951. "An introduc-
       tory guide to the major writers and the main tendencies of
       our century." W. B. Yeats through T. S. Eliot, Aldous
       Huxley, Graham Greene, Elizabeth Bowen, George Bern-
       ard Shaw, and others. Bibliography.

A45   Committee on Trends in Research, American Literature Group,
       MLA. *Report of the Committee on Trends in Research in
       American Literature.* Edited by James D. Hart, et al.
       N.p.: MLA, 1951. A statistical study of the research "un-
       dertaken in the years 1940–50 inclusive." The information
       is divided into five historical periods; the final one covers
       the literature of 1885 through 1950. The study focuses
       upon major figures, minor figures, and subjects.

A46   Connolly, Cyril. *Previous Convictions.* New York: Harper &
       Row, 1963. Journalistic essays that "communicate my en-
       thusiasm for literature and throw a little light on my favor-
       ite authors." Ezra Pound, James Joyce, Ernest Hemingway,
       e. e. cummings, George Orwell, Louis MacNeice, Denton
       Welch, Edith Sitwell, and earlier writers.

A47   Cook, Albert. *Prisms: Studies in Modern Literature.* Bloom-
       ington: Indiana University Press, 1967. A study of "the
       philosophical bases of the literary use of language" and the
       ways modern literary practice has revealed and extended
       them. Cook's book rests upon the assumption that "func-
       tional categories are often also historical ones, that a way
       of handling verbal material artistically not only entails a
       way of seeing the world but also appears at a characteristic
       moment of time." Eugenio Montale, Samuel Beckett,
       Robert Lowell, Henrik Ibsen, and others.

A48   Cook, Bruce. *The Beat Generation.* New York: Scribner's,
       1971. A literary history of the beat generation from its
       beginnings to the scene at Woodstock. Supplies biograph-
       ical and literary information about all the leading figures.
       Richard Brautigan, William S. Burroughs, Paul Carroll,
       Neal Cassady, Gregory Corso, Robert Creeley, Robert Dun-
       can, William Everson (Brother Antoninus), Lawrence
       Ferlinghetti, Allen Ginsberg, John Clellon Holmes, LeRoi
       Jones (Imamu Amiri Baraka), Jack Kerouac, Philip La-
       mantia, Michael McClure, Norman Mailer, Charles Olson,

Peter Orlovsky, Kenneth Rexroth, Gary Snyder, Jack Spicer, Philip Whalen, William Carlos Williams, and others.

A49   Cowley, Malcolm. *The Literary Situation*. New York: Viking, 1954. "A social history of literature" during the '50s in contrast with the author's "memories" of what happened after the Second World War. Discusses war novels, new fiction, critical influence, naturalism, the publishing industry, and the writing profession. Saul Bellow, Nelson Algren, Erskine Caldwell, Truman Capote, T. S. Eliot, Ralph Ellison, William Faulkner, Ernest Hemingway, James Jones, Norman Mailer, and Mickey Spillane.

A50   Cox, C. B., and A. E. Dyson, eds. *Word in the Desert: The Critical Quarterly Tenth Anniversary Number*. London: Oxford University Press, 1968. Essays collected "to oppose cultural pessimism." The editors state: "Great literature helps to keep alive our most subtle and delicate feelings, our capacity for wonder, and our faith in human individuality. The artist contributes to the vitality of language, to the preservation of the Word in the desert." New formalism, French new criticism, poems of the fifties, Boris Pasternak, J. R. R. Tolkien, Bernard Malamud, and current novel criticism.

A51   Creeley, Robert. *A Quick Graph: Collected Notes & Essays*. Edited by Donald Allen. San Francisco: Four Seasons Foundation, 1970. Nearly ninety short essays on prose and poetry. Includes essays on Ezra Pound, William Carlos Williams, Louis Zukofsky, Charles Olson, Kenneth Patchen, D. H. Lawrence, John Hawkes, Ramón Sender, and many others.

A52   Cronin, Anthony. *A Question of Modernity*. London: Secker & Warburg, 1966. Essays that define the attribute of "modernity." Rather than a criticism of individual works, these essays examine matters "of importance to both criticism and creation." Cronin traces modernity through the 1940s. He discusses numerous writers, especially James Joyce and Samuel Beckett.

A53   Cruise O'Brien, Conor. *Maria Cross: Imaginative Patterns in a Group of Modern Catholic Writers*. London: Burns &

Oates, 1962. A book about the "imaginative worlds" created by eight writers who happen to be Catholics. An attempt to follow "the actual patterns of several exceptionally vivid imaginations which are permeated by Catholicism." François Mauriac, Georges Bernanos, Graham Greene, Sean O'Faoláin, Evelyn Waugh, Charles Péguy, Paul Claudel, and Léon Blau.

A54 ————. *Writers and Politics.* New York: Pantheon, 1965. Essays concerning writers and the visions of society we have through them. For Cruise O'Brien, the functions of the critics are to chip away at the distorting façades of propaganda and to analyze contemporary culture. Writings from America, England, France, and Ireland are studied. Brief references to numerous writers.

A55 Cunliffe, Marcus, ed. *American Literature since 1900.* Vol. 9 of *History of Literature in the English Language.* London: Barrie & Jenkins, 1975. A collection of articles that studies the evolution of the literature of the United States from a "defensive position . . . to one of superpower magnitude and ease." The essays are arranged chronologically and deal with "thematic units," such as the theatre since 1945, the poetry of the sixties, and the nature of "modernism" and "post-modernism." Edward Albee, John Ashbery, James Baldwin, Saul Bellow, John Berryman, Robert Bly, Robert Creeley, e. e. cummings, Robert Duncan, T. S. Eliot, William Faulkner, Robert Frost, Allen Ginsberg, Ernest Hemingway, Randell Jarrell, LeRoi Jones (Imamu Amiri Baraka), Robert Lowell, Norman Mailer, Arthur Miller, Charles Olson, Ezra Pound, Theodore Roethke, Jerome Rothenberg, Karl Shapiro, Gary Snyder, Wallace Stevens, Richard Wilbur, William Carlos Williams, Yvor Winters, and others. Table of dates. Bibliography.

A56 Dahlberg, Edward, and Herbert Read. *Truth Is More Sacred: A Critical Exchange on Modern Literature.* New York: Horizon, 1961. Letters in which Dahlberg and Read discuss and compare James Joyce, D. H. Lawrence, Henry James, Robert Graves, T. S. Eliot, and Ezra Pound.

A57 Daiches, David. *The Present Age, after 1920.* London: Cresset, 1958. Studies British literature between 1920 and 1950. Includes five introductory chapters on the historical and cultural background and the major genres. Primary bibliography.

A58   ———. *The Present Age in British Literature.* Blooming-ton: Indiana University Press, 1958. Daiches examines the effects of World War II on British culture, imagist litera-ture, Anglo-American literary relations, and the British scene as viewed from America. W. H. Auden, T. S. Eliot, Christopher Fry, and James Joyce. Bibliography.

A59   Davenport, F. Garvin. *The Myth of Southern History: His-torical Consciousness in Twentieth-Century Southern Liter-ature.* Nashville: Vanderbilt University Press, 1967. Be-cause southerners have had more experience than people from other parts of the United States in trying to "create consciously a relevant approach to their history," they are the focus of this study. Davenport tries "to examine the existence of the idea of historical consciousness within American society and the importance of that idea to Amer-ica in the 1970s." William Faulkner, Martin Luther King, Jr., Robert Penn Warren, and brief references to others. Bibliography.

A60   Davidson, Donald. *Still Rebels, Still Yankees and Other Essays.* [Baton Rouge:] Louisiana State University Press, 1957. Essays and articles "concerned with the impact of the mod-ern regions upon 'tradition.'" Specifically, Davidson exam-ines the Southern scene, past and present, which "naturally affords examples of the clash between tradition and anti-tradition." Five sections deal with poetry, fiction, oral tra-dition, the South, and regionalism and nationalism. Robert Penn Warren, T. S. Eliot, William Faulkner, Robert Frost, and others.

A61   Davies, Robertson. *A Voice from the Attic.* New York: Knopf, 1960. A convivial discussion of "the world of books today," designed to provide "diversion for the reader."

A62   Davis, Arthur P. *From the Dark Tower: Afro-American Writers, 1900–1960.* Washington, D.C.: Howard University Press, 1974. "This volume has been designed to serve as a supple-mentary text or reference book for courses in Negro Amer-ican literature or black studies." Authors included range from W. E. B. Du Bois, Jean Toomer, and Langston

Hughes to Richard Wright, Saunders Redding, Chester Himes, Melvin B. Tolson, Robert Hayden, Margaret Walker, Gwendolyn Brooks, Ann Petry, Julian Mayfield, Lorraine Hansberry, Ralph Ellison, and James Baldwin. Primary and secondary bibliography.

A63   Dembo, L. S., and Cyrena N. Pondrom, eds. *The Contemporary Writer: Interviews with Sixteen Novelists and Poets.* Madison: University of Wisconsin Press, 1972. Interviews concerned not only with the "craft of fiction" but with "specific philosophical, ethical, and aesthetic issues" raised in the work of each. John Hawkes, John Barth, Saul Bellow, Vladimir Nabokov, Isaac Bashevis Singer, Jorge Luis Borges, Sara Lidman, Per Olof Sundman, James Merrill, Kenneth Rexroth, George Oppen, Carl Rakosi, Charles Reznikoff, Louis Zukofsky, Gwendolyn Brooks, and George Barker.

A64   Dillard, R. H. W.; George Garrett; and John Rees Moore, eds. *The Sounder Few: Essays from the Hollins Critic.* Athens: University of Georgia Press, 1971. A new form of literary journalism that provides more than a book review, yet does something less than "deliver a verdict" on a work's place in literary history. J. P. Donleavy, John Cheever, William Golding, Richard Eberhart, Brendan Behan, Flannery O'Connor, James Baldwin, Vladimir Nabokov, Kurt Vonnegut, Jr., John Barth, Robert Lowell, Louis MacNeice, Wright Morris, Colin Wilson, William Styron, Norman Podhoretz, and Howard Nemerov. Index to Hollins Critics. Bibliography.

A65   Donoghue, Denis. *The Ordinary Universe: Soundings in Modern Literature.* New York: Macmillan, 1968. Donoghue studies "literature and the attitudes that get into it." Concerned with content and not form, Donoghue is interested in "resuscitating the relation between the tongue and the heart"—in restoring emphasis upon the writer's commitment to the human event. Saul Bellow, T. S. Eliot, William Carlos Williams, Wallace Stevens, Ezra Pound, and Samuel Beckett.

A66   Duberman, Martin. *Black Mountain: An Exploration in Community.* New York: Dutton, 1972. A history of a "now defunct experimental community located in the foothills of

North Carolina" from 1933 to 1956. Black Mountain was "the forerunner and exemplar of much that is currently innovative in art, education and life style." In its later years, the following people were associated with it in some way: John Cage, Robert Creeley, Edward Dahlberg, Robert Duncan, Charles Olson, Ezra Pound, Kenneth Rexroth, William Carlos Williams, and many others.

A67   Duncan, Robert. *The Truth and Life of Myth: An Essay in Essential Autobiography.* Fremont, Mich.: Sumac, 1968. An investigation into myth, stories, intellectual heritage, art, and the individual life.

A68   Dupee, F. W. *"The King of the Cats" and Other Remarks on Writers and Writing.* New York: Farrar, Straus & Giroux, 1965. "Literary portraits" based on letters and memoirs that give a conception of the particular writer's mind and culture. James Agee, Thomas Mann, Vladimir Nabokov, Bernard Malamud, Robert Lowell, Kenneth Koch, F. R. Leavis, James Baldwin, and others.

A69   Durant, Will and Ariel. *Interpretations of Life: A Survey of Contemporary Literature.* New York: Simon & Schuster, 1970. The "confessions of an amateur who has been philandering among a variety of loves these last eighty years." The authors' personal responses to William Faulkner, Ernest Hemingway, John Steinbeck, Upton Sinclair, Eugene O'Neill, Robinson Jeffers, Ezra Pound, James Joyce, T. S. Eliot, W. Somerset Maugham, Marcel Proust, André Gide, Ludwig Wittgenstein, Søren Kierkegaard, Edmund Husserl, Martin Heidegger, Jean-Paul Sartre, Simone de Beauvoir, Albert Camus, Thomas Mann, Franz Kafka, Nikos Kazantzakis, Mikhail Sholokov, Boris Pasternak, Alexander Solzhenitsyn, and Yevgeni Yevtushenko. Bibliography.

A70   Durr, R. A. *Poetic Vision and the Psychedelic Experience.* Syracuse: Syracuse University Press, 1970. Durr finds similarities between the world of psychedelic vision and the world of imaginative literature. Psychedelic substances and elements in literature "share a mode of being and of apprehension, a constellation of values and a view of life. Through the psychedelics it is possible to experience the world as many of our great writers have experienced it." Durr's primary focus is what Timothy Leary calls "the extroverted experience" in which the self fuses with an external object. Discusses imagination, ego, self, and the cosmos in terms of literature. T. S. Eliot, Robert Frost, Aldous Huxley, Henry Miller, and many earlier writers.

A71   Eagleton, Terence. *Exiles and Emigrés: Studies in Modern Literature.* New York: Schocken, 1970. Eagleton's aim is "not to provide an exhaustive or systematic account of the theme of expatriotism in modern literature, but rather to offer a series of critical explorations, at once autonomous and interrelated, which centre around a number of general problems raised by the 'émigré' theme." He focuses upon "social exile"—when social attitudes limit or shape a writer's ability to achieve a sense of interrelation with his culture. Joseph Conrad, Evelyn Waugh, George Orwell, Graham Greene, T. S. Eliot, W. H. Auden, and D. H. Lawrence.

A72   Elliott, George P. *Conversations: Literature and the Modernist Deviation.* New York: Dutton, 1971. A book of essays on modernism. Includes "Kicking Some Modern Habits," "Science and the Profession of Literature," "Teaching Writing," "The Novelist as Meddler," "Against Pornography," and other essays.

A73 _ Elliott, Robert C. *The Power of Satire: Magic, Ritual, Art.* Princeton: Princeton University Press, 1960. Discusses the connection between satire and magic. Elliott describes the magical efficacy attributed to satire and the way literary satire developed out of magical roots. Wyndham Lewis, Roy Cambell, W. H. Auden, T. S. Eliot, and many earlier writers.

A74   Ellison, Ralph, and Karl Shapiro. *The Writer's Experience.* Washington, D.C.: Library of Congress, 1964. Pamphlet that includes two lectures presented under the auspices of the Gertrude Clark Whittal Poetry and Literature Fund: "Hidden Name and Complex Fate: A Writer's Experience" by Ralph Ellison and "American Poet?" by Karl Shapiro.

A75   Ellmann, Richard. *Eminent Domain: Yeats among Wilde, Joyce, Pound, Eliot, and Auden.* New York: Oxford University Press, 1967. Discusses Yeats's influence upon Oscar Wilde, James Joyce, Ezra Pound, T. S. Eliot, and W. H. Auden.

A76   ————, and Charles Feidelson, Jr., eds. *The Modern Tradition: Backgrounds of Modern Literature.* New York: Oxford University Press, 1965. By collecting statements by writers, artists, philosophers, and scientists, Ellmann and Feidelson represent various facets of modernism. Their arrangement of the book by themes guides the reader through the world of modernism: symbolism, realism, nature, cultural history, the unconscious, myth, the self-conscious, existence, and faith.

A77   English Association. *Essays and Studies, 1971.* Edited by Bernard Harris. London: Cox & Wyman, 1971. Essays on Sean O'Casey, Brendan Behan, and Samuel Beckett.

A78   Enright, D. J. *Conspirators and Poets.* London: Chatto & Windus, 1966. "The majority of the essays and reviews here collected were originally written . . . for weekly or monthly publications of a not specifically scholarly nature. Some of these pieces can scarcely be called 'literary criticism.'" W. H. Auden, Lawrence Durrell, Dylan Thomas, T. S. Eliot, Robert Graves, Mary McCarthy, C. P. Snow, John Updike, Cyril Connolly, Henry Miller, Philip Larkin, and others.

A79   Evans, B. Ifor. *Literature and Science.* London: Allen & Unwin, 1954. "My aim is to explore the position of the artist, and here more particularly the writer in our modern scientific society." Evans studies the effects of technology upon literature, the cultural *zeitgeist*, and "the historical relationship between literature and science. Evans points to a "new humanism" as the goal of our literature; and finally, he interprets "the place of the new humanism in our contemporary civilization."

A80   Fadiman, Clifton. *Party of One: The Selected Writings of Clifton Fadiman.* Cleveland: World, 1955. Previously published essays on cartoonists, scientists, conversationalists, actors, comedians, musical comedy, radio and TV, teaching, language, and writers and books. John O'Hara, William Faulkner, and Gertrude Stein.

A81   Fairman, Marion A. *Biblical Patterns in Modern Literature.* Cleveland: Dillon/Liederbach, 1972. Discusses literature in the light of Biblical patterns: the Fall, after the Fall,

Jonah in the belly of the whale, the sorrowing compromises, the prodigal way, and the promise. T. S. Eliot, Graham Greene, Dorothy L. Sayers, Charles Williams, William Golding, Robert Lowell, W. H. Auden, William Faulkner, Flannery O'Connor, and others. Bibliography.

A82 Farrell, James T. *Literature and Morality*. New York: Vanguard, 1947. Farrell contends that the problem of the American writer is fear of the words he uses. If the words "are not used to describe and reveal the discoveries which come from an honest and relentless effort to explore to the bitter end the nature of our experience, then we will come to despise our own words."

A83 Feidelson, Charles, Jr., and Paul Brodtkorb, Jr., eds. *Interpretations of American Literature*. London: Oxford University Press, 1959. A collection of interpretive essays on major works, writers, and major strains of American literature. The essays are "designed to serve the student and inquiring reader as a running commentary on texts." Hawthorne through William Faulkner and Ernest Hemingway.

A84 Fiedler, Leslie A. *The Collected Essays of Leslie Fiedler*. 2 vols. New York: Stein & Day, 1971. Essays that record "impressions and responses" to the twenty-year period from 1948 to 1970. Fiedler writes on politics, cultural changes, and literature as they are influenced by public events. Includes *An End to Innocence* and *No! In Thunder*. Bernard Malamud, William Faulkner, Robert Penn Warren, Saul Bellow, Philip Roth, Norman Mailer, John Hawkes, Ernest Hemingway, and earlier writers.

A85 ————. *No! In Thunder: Essays on Myth and Literature*. Boston: Beacon Press, 1960. Fiedler's essays are "an autobiography, a confession: the continuing record of my sentimental education, as well as an account of the world in which I am being educated." Fiedler discusses literary theory, literary works, and the role of myth in art and society. The book is organized around three issues: the artist and his work in terms of myth, specific problems of race and generation that have mythic resonance, and the deliverance of the Negro and the Jew through literature— "where myth and dream are made flesh." I. L. Peretz,

Franz Kafka, Bernard Malamud, Robert Penn Warren, James Baldwin, and others.

A86   ————. *The Return of the Vanishing American.* New York: Stein & Day, 1968. Fiedler examines the American Indian in the process of rediscovering his identity out of his tribal lore and the science created by the white man. "Just as the Indian is becoming more visible to himself, he is also becoming more visible to White writers, who think of themselves as being on his side." Fiedler studies the basic myths concerning the Indian as well as "the creation of the New Western, a form which not so much redeems the Pop Western as exploits it with irreverence and pleasure." Ernest Hemingway, Ken Kesey, and earlier writers.

A87   ————. *Waiting for the End.* New York: Stein & Day, 1964. Fifteen essays including "The Death of the Old Men," "Jewish-Americans, Go Home!," "Indian or Injun?," "The Alteration of Consciousness," "The End of the Novel," "Towards the Suburbs: The Fear of Madness, and The Death of the 'I.' "

A88   Finkelstein, Sidney. *Existentialism and Alienation in American Literature.* New York: International Publishers, 1965. A study of existentialism's "rise as a philosophy in Europe" and "its influence on literature, particularly that of the United States today." Finkelstein tries "to show that the philosophical development and the literary expression make up one continuous history." Søren Kierkegaard, Friedrich Nietzche, Albert Camus, Jean-Paul Sartre, Eugene O'Neill, T. S. Eliot, William Faulkner, John Dos Passos, Henry Miller, William Styron, J. D. Salinger, Edward Albee, John Updike, James Purdy, Arthur Miller, Saul Bellow, Norman Mailer, James Baldwin, and others.

A89   Firchow, Peter, ed. *The Writer's Place: Interviews on the Literary Situation in Contemporary Britain.* Minneapolis: University of Minnesota Press, 1974. Interviews with Kingsley Amis, Victor Bonham-Carter, Alan Burns, John Calder, Maurice Callard, Margaret Drabble, Roy Fuller, Giles Gordon, Ian Hamilton, L. P. Hartley, Bill Hopkins, Ted Hughes, Pamela Hansford Johnson, Melvin Lasky, Thomas Michael Maschler, Charles Osborne, V. S. Pritchett, William Sansom, Anthony Thwaite, William Trevor, John Wain, and Angus Wilson.

A90   Fisch, Harold. *The Dual Image: The Figure of the Jew in English and American Literature*. New York: KTAV Publishing House, 1971. A historical survey of the Jew as he appears in literature from the medieval period to the present. Fisch writes that the "Jew is seen as both noble and ignoble, black and white; from one angle he is a paragon, from another, he is a worm and no man. Different authors may see the contradictions in different terms, but they are always there, not only for the non-Jew, but for the Jewish writer also as he views himself through the prism of his self-awareness." Bibliography.

A91   Fischer, John, and Robert B. Silvers, eds. *Writing in America*. New Brunswick, N.J.: Rutgers University Press, 1960. Essays collected from a special supplement to the October 1959 issue of *Harper's*. Contributors include Mason W. Gross, Alfred Kazin, Stanley Kunitz, Robert Brustein, Elizabeth Hardwick, Kingsley Amis, C. P. Snow, Archibald MacLeish, Budd Schulberg, Vance Bourjaily, Frank Yerby, and John Fischer.

A92   Fishman, Soloman. *The Disinherited of Art: Writer and Background*. Berkeley: University of California Press, 1953. Essays that study "the impact of culture on literature," contemporary American criticism of American literature, "the writer's sense of alienation from his culture," "literary theory relating . . . to the whole body of American literature," and "the status of literary art in contemporary culture."

A93   Foerster, Norman. *Image of America: Our Literature from Puritanism to the Space Age*. Notre Dame, Ind.: University of Notre Dame, 1962. Foerster's objective is "to increase the general reader's understanding—and hence enjoyment—of our national literature." Sketches the profound changes from colonial days to the present.

A94   Ford, Boris, ed. *The Modern Age*. Vol. 7 of *The Pelican Guide to English Literature*. Baltimore: Penguin, 1964. This guide offers "an account of the social context of literature in the period," "a literary survey of this period," "detailed studies of some of the chief writers and works in this period," and "an appendix of essential facts for reference purposes." From Henry James to W. H. Auden, Graham Greene, and Dylan Thomas. Bibliographies.

A95   Foster, Joseph R. *Contemporary Christian Writers.* New York: Hawthorn, 1963. Seventy brief essays on writers from England, America, France, Germany, Italy, Spain, and Eastern European countries. Generally each essay focuses upon a figure and his career. Bibliography.

A96   Fowlie, Wallace. *The Clown's Grail: A Study of Love in Its Literary Expression.* London: Dennis Dobson, 1948. Examines the three orders of love in modern literature: philosophic love, divine love, and human love and passion. Fowlie argues that "the dualism of any profound love is resolved in the unity of great art. The history of modern symbolism is nothing more or less than the history of the secularization of medieval Christian man." Only in symbolic literature does Fowlie find "the meaning of the trial in which man is engaged." T. S. Eliot, Djuna Barnes, and earlier writers.

A97   Fraser, G. S. *The Modern Writer and His World.* London: Derek Verschoyle, 1953. Fraser's aim is "to provide Japanese students of English literature, who had been cut off from contact with us during the war, with a fairly clear guide-book to modern tendencies."

A98   Frazer, John. *Violence in the Arts.* New York: Cambridge University Press, 1974. A "personal essay" that examines the significance of violence in a number of genres. Frazer first studies the use of violence in the arts and how "violences seem to make for intellectual clarity and a more civilized consciousness." Second, he creates "an informal poetics with respect to the victims and the perpetrators of violence." Finally, he closely examines "protest" art. W. H. Auden, William Burroughs, Ernest Hemingway, George Orwell, and brief references to others.

A99   French, Warren, ed. *The Fifties: Fiction, Poetry, Drama.* DeLand, Fla.: Everett/Edwards, 1970. Essays that survey the literary activity of the beat movement, black and Jewish-American literature, and the off-Broadway theater.

J. D. Salinger, Ernest Hemingway, William Faulkner, John Steinbeck, Norman Mailer, Saul Bellow, Mary McCarthy, Elizabeth Spenser, Flannery O'Connor, James Agee, Bernard Malamud, James Purdy, Wallace Stevens, Richard Eberhart, Theodore Roethke, Richard Wilbur, Archibald MacLeish, and others.

A100   ————, ed. *The Forties: Fiction, Poetry, Drama*. DeLand, Fla.: Everett/Edwards, 1969. Essays on the fiction, poetry, and drama engendered by World War II and other events that influenced literature. Carson McCullers, Eudora Welty, Thornton Wilder, Richard Rodgers, Oscar Hammerstein, Theodore Dreiser, Wallace Stevens, Robert Penn Warren, Eugene O'Neill, Malcolm Lowry, Lionel Trilling, Tennessee Williams, Truman Capote, Arthur Miller, Ezra Pound, Nelson Algren, and others. Bibliography.

A101   ————, and Walter E. Kidd, eds. *American Winners of the Nobel Literary Prize*. Norman: University of Oklahoma Press, 1968. A collection of essays about the seven American winners of the Nobel literary award between 1901 and 1962. "This book is concerned with these American winners of the prize, an assessment of the literary value of their writing both before and after receiving it, and a consideration of other close contenders or candidates." Sinclair Lewis, Eugene O'Neill, Pearl Buck, T. S. Eliot, William Faulkner, Ernest Hemingway, and John Steinbeck. Bibliographical notes.

A102   Frenz, Horst, ed. *Nobel Lectures Including Presentation Speeches and Laureates' Biographies: Literature, 1901–1967*. Amsterdam: Elsevier Publishing, 1969. Lectures by the Nobel Prize winners in literature.

A103   Friedman, Maurice. *To Deny Our Nothingness: Contemporary Images of Man*. New York: Delacorte, 1967. Friedman uses the image of man as a focus to study literature, philosophy, psychotherapy, and religious thought. André Gide, T. S. Eliot, Arthur Koestler, John Steinbeck, Carlo Levi, Aldous Huxley, Graham Greene, Hermann Hesse, Albert Camus, Samuel Beckett, and others.

A104   Friedman, Melvin J., and John B. Vickery, eds. *The Shaken Realist: Essays in Modern Literature in Honor of Freder-*

ick J. Hoffman. Baton Rouge: Louisiana State University Press, 1970. Includes essays on writers and texts, themes and motifs, and the contemporary scene. Ernest Hemingway, William Carlos Williams, T. S. Eliot, Flannery O'Connor, Anthony Burgess, and Vance Bourjaily. Bibliography.

A105   Frohock, W. M. *Strangers to This Ground: Cultural Diversity in Contemporary American Writing.* Dallas: Southern Methodist University Press, 1961. Frohock argues that there is cultural variety in American life and that it exerts a shaping force on the entire spectrum of literature. He finds evidence in literature that the process of conformity has a long way to go. Ezra Pound, Jack Kerouac, and earlier writers.

A106   Frye, Roland Mushat. *Perspective on Man: Literature and the Christian Tradition.* Philadelphia: Westminster, 1961. Frye's premise is that all literature gives us insight "into human nature and eternal truth that stands in close relationship to the heart of the Biblical message." In part 1, Frye examines the way "literature treats history and conveys truth." Part 2 is "concerned with literary affirmations and questionings that are universally important." Finally, part 3 is an application of Christian themes to great books. Robert Frost, J. D. Salinger, Tennessee Williams, T. S. Eliot, William Faulkner, Christopher Fry, John Osborne, George Bernard Shaw, Robert Sherwood, and others. Bibliography.

A107   Fuller, Edmund. *Books with Men behind Them.* New York: Random House, 1962. Fuller considers a good writer to have not only talent, but also a ripened, rational vision of life. The writer's work is this vision. Fuller, then, explores the work of a number of writers who have in common "a balanced, comprehensive, realistic, authentically compassionate and mature vision of man." Thornton Wilder, Gladys Schmitt, Alan Paton, C. P. Snow, C. S. Lewis, J. R. R. Tolkien, and Charles Williams.

A108   Gardiner, Harold C. *In All Conscience: Reflections on Books and Culture.* Garden City, N.Y.: Hanover House, 1959*; rpt. Freeport, N.Y.: Books for Libraries Press, 1972. A collection of "fugitive pieces" that "appeared in the issues since 1940 of *America*" of which Gardiner was the literary editor. "The pieces have, therefore, been written in large part to meet immediate needs: controversies of the moment, trends that may since have stopped trending, certain books, motion pictures, and the like which may seem very dead indeed by now. . . . My criticism has always intended to be . . . a comment on how books and our culture generally mirror that basic craving for happiness, for fulfillment, that underlies and girds all our human hopes and fears, loves and aspirations."

A109 Garrett, George, ed. Conducted by John Graham. *The Writer's Voice: Conversations with Contemporary Writers.* New York: William Morrow, 1973. Conversations between John Graham and contemporary authors R. V. Cassill, William Peden, Margaret Sayers Peden, Fred Chappell, Brian Moore, Richard Wilbur, Shelby Foote, Henry Taylor, Michael Mewshaw, William Manchester, James Seay, James Whitehead, Sylvia Wilkinson, Jonathan Baumbach, Ralph Ellison, James Dickey, David Slavitt, William Harrison, and R. H. W. Dillard.

A110 Gayle, Addison, Jr., ed. *The Black Aesthetic.* Garden City, N.Y.: Doubleday, 1971. Includes essays on theory, music, poetry, drama, and fiction by such contributors as Hoyt W. Fuller, Alain Locke, Addison Gayle, Jr., Langston Hughes, Loften Mitchell, Richard Wright, Ishmael Reed, and others.

A111 ————, ed. *Black Expressionism: Essays by and about Black Americans in the Creative Arts.* New York: Weybright & Talley, 1969. Black literature and criticism remains "an unwanted and unacknowledged appendage to the vast body of American literature." To combat this problem Gayle collects these essays on folk culture, poetry, drama, and fiction. Contributors include Arna Bontemps, Alain Locke, Loften Mitchell, LeRoi Jones (Imamu Amiri Baraka), Richard Wright, Hugh M. Gloster, Langston Hughes, Nathan A. Scott, Jr., Ralph Ellison, James Baldwin, Eldridge Cleaver, and others. Suggested readings.

A112 Geismar, Maxwell. *American Moderns: From Rebellion to Conformity.* New York: Hill & Wang, 1958. A collection of articles and reviews written during the forties and fifties. This collection takes the shape of an "informal daybook or journal of the times." Includes general essays as well as essays on Theodore Dreiser, Ernest Hemingway, John Dos Passos, William Faulkner, Sinclair Lewis, Thomas Wolfe, James Gould Cozzens, John Steinbeck, J. P. Marquand, Norman Mailer, John Hersey, Nelson Algren, J. D. Salinger, Saul Bellow, James Jones, William Styron, and John Howard Griffin.

A113   Gibson, Donald B., ed. *Five Black Writers: Essays on Wright, Ellison, Baldwin, Hughes, and LeRoi Jones* [Imamu Amiri Baraka]. New York: New York University Press, 1970. Gibson collects essays "to encourage further study of these writers." The last section of the volume, "The Writer and Social Responsibility," is intended "to elicit further thinking about what constitutes value in literature and about the relation of the writer to his society."

A114   Gierow, Karl Ragnar, ed. *Problems of International Literary Understanding: Proceedings of the Sixth Nobel Symposium, Stockholm, September 1967.* Stockholm: Almqvist & Wiksell, 1968. Essays in search of the ways in which literature can bridge national differences.

A115   Gilman, Richard. *The Confusion of Realms.* New York: Random House, 1969. A collection of essays and reviews written between 1963 and 1969. Includes essays on Norman Mailer, Henrik Ibsen, August Strindberg, Marshall McLuhan, Susan Sontag, Donald Barthelme, John Updike, "The Living Theatre," and "Art and History."

A116   Glicksberg, Charles I. *Literature and Society.* The Hague: Martinus Nijhoff, 1972. A study of how literature affects society. This large work studies three literary-social stances: asocial absurdists, the social critics, and the literature of social commitment. Numerous European authors are covered along with Samuel Beckett, Henry Miller, Jack Kerouac, John Steinbeck, Ernest Hemingway, and C. P. Snow.

A117   ————. *Modern Literary Perspectivism.* Dallas: Southern Methodist University Press, 1970. While the relativists and the absolutists have been quarreling for centuries, Einstein's theories of the nature of the universe and new notions of time gave the relativists a formal platform for the first time in history. Glicksberg studies the idea of relativism, its history and nature, and then outlines various perspectives that have evolved to orient man in a relative world: the Marxist, utopian, mechanistic, scientific, mythic, and inhumanist perspectives. Although the work focuses mainly upon early modern writers and European writers, Samuel Beckett, Aldous Huxley, and Robinson Jeffers are also studied.

A118　————. *Modern Literature and the Death of God.* The Hague: Martinus Nijhoff, 1966. A study of the ways that modern literature was altered by the "traumatic loss of the religious absolute." Glicksberg focuses upon the Tillichian paradox: man continues to quest for God despite believing Him to be dead. While Glicksberg deals mainly with European writers, he also treats Samuel Beckett, T. S. Eliot, William Faulkner, Graham Greene, Ernest Hemingway, and Aldous Huxley.

A119　————. *The Self in Modern Literature.* University Park: Pennsylvania State University Press, 1963. "The brooding, intellectual hero of modern literature frequently becomes a solipsist and eventually learns to distrust his perceptions, his thoughts, the language he employs, and the beliefs he once cherished." Glicksberg studies the self in relation to the death of God in Søren Kierkegaard; to the threat of science in Henrik Ibsen; to biology in Franz Kafka; to the machine in George Orwell and Aldous Huxley; to the doctrine of relativity in Luigi Pirandello, André Gide, and Lawrence Durrell; and to the shattering of all myths in Eugène Ionesco and Samuel Beckett.

A120　————. *The Sexual Revolution in Modern American Literature.* The Hague: Martinus Nijhoff, 1971. Glicksberg analyzes and evaluates the sexual revolution that took place in American literature. Theodore Dreiser, Sherwood Anderson, Ernest Hemingway, F. Scott Fitzgerald, William Faulkner, Eugene O'Neill, Henry Miller, Jack Kerouac, Norman Mailer, Katherine Anne Porter, James Purdy, John Barth, Vladimir Nabokov, and James Jones.

A121　Goodman, Paul. *Utopian Essays and Practical Proposals.* New York: Random House, 1962. Includes "Utopian Thinking," "Pornography and the Sexual Revolution," "On Writer's Block," "Dr. Reich's Banned Books," "Advance-guard Writing in America: 1900–1950," "Good Interim Writing—1954," "Underground Writing—1960," and other essays.

A122   Graef, Hilda. *Modern Gloom and Christian Hope.* Chicago: Regnery, 1959. This brief study analyzes "the works of some representatives" of contemporary pessimism and shows "its opposition to an authentic Christian outlook, with its emphasis on hope and its rejection of 'dread' and despair. . . . But this criticism of the contemporary literary scene from the Catholic point of view implies no literary judgments." John Osborne, Colin Wilson, Graham Greene, T. S. Eliot, and many French authors.

A123   Grant, Douglas. *Purpose and Place: Essays on American Writers.* London: Macmillan, 1965. Studies "American" writers to understand America as a "condition" that affects the rest of the world. Edward Taylor through Robert Frost, Sinclair Lewis, Ernest Hemingway, and William Faulkner.

A124   Green, Lawrence G. *Authors' Post-War Guide.* London: Allen & Unwin, 1947. A practical guide aimed at the beginning writer. It quickly surveys the period immediately after the Second World War and asserts that "there is every sign of a second great publishing revival the moment paper becomes abundant again."

A125   Green, Martin. *Re-Appraisals: Some Commonsense Readings in American Literature.* New York: Norton, 1965. "A protest against a literary taste and method which seems to me to sacrifice even logic and common sense in its search for early patrons of the alienated mind." These essays argue against alienation and despair. William Faulkner, J. D. Salinger, Vladimir Nabokov, and earlier writers. Selected bibliography.

A126   ————. *Science and the Shabby Curate of Poetry: Essays about the Two Cultures.* New York: Norton, 1961. Essays based upon the ideas in C. P. Snow's lecture, "The Two Cultures." Green discusses the split between the two cultures, science and literature. Includes "Two Defenses of 'The Two Cultures,'" essays on science, humanism, the literary culture, a liberal education, science fiction, and "science non-fiction."

A127 ————. *Yeats's Blessings on von Hügel: Essays on Litera-ture and Religion.* London: Longmans, Green, 1967. Green calls Baron von Hügel the great hero "of liberal humanism, one of the synthesizers of modern Western cul-ture." Using von Hügel to inform his argument, Green studies the humanism, psychology, and sensibility of the Catholic mind. In his critical discussions of novels, he dis-cusses the relationship between Catholicism, humanism, and literature. J. F. Powers, Vladimir Nabokov, Boris Pasternak, Fyodor Dostoevsky, T. S. Eliot, James Joyce, D. H. Lawrence, W. B. Yeats, and others. Bibliography.

A128 Grigson, Geoffrey. *The Contrary View: Glimpses of Fudge and Gold.* Totowa, N.J.: Rowman & Littlefield, 1974. A col-lection of essays and reviews on a wide range of topics. Includes essays on Boris Pasternak, Henry Miller, A. E. Housman, Lytton Strachey, Robert Lowell, and many others.

A129 Gross, Seymour, and John Edward Hardy, eds. *Images of the Negro in American Literature.* Chicago: University of Chicago Press, 1966. Essays by black and white critics who trace the evolution of Negro stereotypes from colonial times to the literary characters of James Baldwin. Ralph Ellison, Eudora Welty, William Faulkner, Richard Wright, Langston Hughes, and earlier writers. Bibliography.

A130 Grosshans, Henry, ed. *To Find Something New: Studies in Contemporary Literature.* Pullman: Washington State University Press, 1969. A collection of comments about the significant literature of the 1960s with a particular focus "upon contemporary, as differentiated from what is com-monly called modern literature." These essays examine the characteristics of contemporary literature and what sepa-rates it from the past. Plays of protest, Hispano-American literature, new village literature in Russia, Peter Weiss, Gabriel Fielding, the Brazilian short story, and other topics.

A131 Gunn, Drewey Wayne. *American and British Writers in Mex-ico, 1556–1973.* Austin: University of Texas Press, 1974. Studies writers who crossed the border and confronted the Mexican culture. As a symbol for writers, Mexico repre-sents "a prison," "a possible answer," or "demonic or at best purgatorial forces." Saul Bellow, Ray Bradbury, William Burroughs, Lawrence Ferlinghetti, Allen Ginsberg, Graham Greene, Jack Kerouac, Norman Mailer, W. Somerset Maugham, Wright Morris, Katherine Anne Porter, Tennessee Williams, and William Carlos Williams. Bibliography.

A132   Gurian, Jay. *Western American Literature: Tradition and Promise*. Deland, Fla.: Everett/Edwards, 1975. An attempt to define "western writing." Gurian shows the relationships between the themes and styles of western literature and Frederick Jackson Turner's frontier thesis. Jack London, Mary Austin, Thomas Berger, Jack Kerouac, John Neihardt, and others. Bibliography.

A133   Guttmann, Allen. *The Jewish Writer in America: Assimilation and the Crisis of Identity*. New York: Oxford University Press, 1971. A study of Jews in a country "that combined new freedoms with more than a trace of old hostilities. . . . It is a *literary* study of the conversions to 'Americanism' (and even to Christianity), to political radicalism, and—on the part of those who had abandoned or never known Judaism—to some form of the faith of their fathers." Mary Antin, Saul Bellow, Abraham Cahan, Allen Ginsberg, Paul Goodman, Meyer Levin, Ludwig Lewisohn, Norman Mailer, and Philip Roth. Primary bibliography.

A134   Hahn, Emily. *Romantic Rebels: An Informal History of Bohemianism in America*. Boston: Houghton Mifflin, 1967. A historical survey of Bohemianism. Henri Murger, Edgar Allan Poe, Walt Whitman, and Allen Ginsberg. Bibliography.

A135   Hall, James B., and Barry Ulanov, eds. *Modern Culture and the Arts*. New York: McGraw-Hill, 1967. A collection of essays on the various arts by critics and practitioners. Six essays on the novel and poetry and seven essays on drama. They address the status of the genres, their natures, and their futures.

A136   Hardwick, Elizabeth. *Seduction and Betrayal: Women and Literature*. New York: Random House, 1974. Essays from the *New York Review of Books* on Henrik Ibsen's women, Zelda Fitzgerald, Sylvia Plath, Virginia Woolf, and earlier figures.

A137   ————. *A View of My Own: Essays in Literature and Society.* New York: Farrar, Straus & Cudahy, 1962. Articles written between 1951 and 1961 on the subjugation of women, books about poverty, British and American plays, living in Italy, Mary McCarthy, Christine Stead, Graham Greene, Dylan Thomas, David Riesman, Eugene O'Neill, and earlier writers.

A138   Hassan, Ihab. *Contemporary American Literature, 1945–1972: An Introduction.* New York: Ungar, 1973. An introductory survey of the period. Hassan provides a critical sense of the literature and a historical view of the period. In addition to discussing the three genres, Hassan explains the various schools and trends in American literature since 1945. Saul Bellow, Norman Mailer, Wright Morris, Bernard Malamud, J. D. Salinger, Kurt Vonnegut, Jr., James Purdy, Truman Capote, John Hawkes, William Styron, John Barth, John Updike, Theodore Roethke, John Berryman, Allen Ginsberg, Tennessee Williams, Arthur Miller, Edward Albee, and many others. Bibliography.

A139   ————. *The Dismemberment of Orpheus: Toward a Postmodern Literature.* New York: Oxford University Press, 1971. "Radical questions engage the total quality of our life; they are questions of being. Often, they arouse large hopes: to change consciousness, to banish death from our midst. They have a radical innocence. This work may imply such questions." Hassan writes about authors "who give themselves to silence," writers who realize that "literature does not suffice." They seek, instead, to "transcend themselves in a complex silence." This "dialogue of silence" is concerned with questions of being, nothingness, and changing awareness. Essays on the Marquis de Sade, Ernest Hemingway, Franz Kafka, Jean Genet, and Samuel Beckett. Also discussed are William Burroughs, Nathalie Sarraute, Alain Robbe-Grillet, Jean-Paul Sartre; brief references to others.

A140   ————. *The Literature of Silence: Henry Miller and Samuel Beckett.* New York: Knopf, 1968. Hassan argues that literature has adopted a new attitude toward itself. Silence is its metaphor. Language, states Hassan, is in a state of entrophy; the result is an anti-literature. "The attitude this kind of literature expresses is a judgment on ourselves in a time of outrage and apocalypse." Hassan discusses Henry Miller and Samuel Beckett as exemplary figures of this anti-literature.

A141   Haydn, Hiram. *Words & Faces.* New York: Harcourt Brace Jovanovich, 1974. An account of Haydn's career and life in the publishing industry beginning in 1944. Publishing houses, editors, writers, "the nature of the work, and the people I have come to know in the pursuit of the work" are Haydn's topics. Loren Eiseley, Ralph Ellison, William Faulkner, John Fowles, Ernest Hemingway, Aldous Huxley, Norman Mailer, Wright Morris, Vladimir Nabokov, John O'Hara, Ayn Rand, William Styron, and many others briefly mentioned.

A142   Heiney, Donald W. *Essentials of Contemporary Literature.* Great Neck, N.Y.: Barron's Educational Series, 1954. An attempt to survey the major writers of the twentieth century in brief essays. The discussions are arranged under general headings that reflect schools and tendencies. Heiney attempts to present the diversity of the century in an ordered way. Over a hundred and fifty writers discussed. Bibliography.

A143   ————, and Lenthiel H. Downs. *Recent American Literature after 1930.* Vol. 4. Woodbury, N.Y.: Barron's Educational Series, 1974. Heiney and Downs look at contemporary American literature by examining movements—realism, naturalism, expressionism, and the theater of the absurd. Pearl Buck, William Faulkner, William Saroyan, John O'Hara, J. D. Salinger, Truman Capote, Richard Wright, Ralph Ellison, Carson McCullers, Tennessee Williams, Edward Albee, Theodore Roethke, Ezra Pound, and many others.

A144   Heppenstall, Rayner. *The Fourfold Tradition: Notes on the French and English Literatures, with Some Ethnological and Historical Asides.* London: Barrie & Rockliff, 1961. Studies the literary relationship between France and England from 1400 through 1955, noting similarities and differences.

A145   Highet, Gilbert. *People, Places and Books.* New York: Oxford

University Press, 1953. Thirty talks that Highet gave in 1952 on radio broadcasts. T. S. Eliot, Christopher Fry, John Masefield, Donald Tover, and earlier writers.

A146   Hill, Herbert, ed. *Anger, and Beyond: The Negro Writer in the United States.* New York: Harper & Row, 1966. Hill argues that there must be a connection between artistic means and "a recognition of the significant relationship between freedom and social necessity." Literature by Negroes has become a "literature of necessity" in which writers are transmitting their awareness of the racial situation into literature. But protest and anger are not enough; therefore, Negro writers are now moving into new areas of involvement, "into an awareness of the tragedy, irony and absurdity of American and twentieth century life." Ralph Ellison, Richard Wright, and James Baldwin.

A147   Hoffman, Frederick J., ed. *Perspectives on Modern Literature.* Evanston, Ill.: Row, Peterson, 1962. Essays from several "areas and levels of discourse in twentieth-century British and American writing": "pieces of journalism," "reactions to cultural and intellectual situations of peculiar and special interest," and critical essays. "I have chosen these because they are above all another kind of 'perspective.' " Contributors include Randolph Bourne, H. L. Mencken, D. H. Lawrence, T. E. Hulme, Ezra Pound, Joseph Wood Krutch, T. S. Eliot, I. A. Richards, Hart Crane, Norman Foerster, Yvor Winters, Christopher Caudwell, Michael Gold, Kenneth Burke, William Faulkner, Daniel Bell, John Wain, and Norman Mailer.

A148   Hoggart, Richard. *Speaking to Each Other.* Vol. 1, *About Society.* Vol. 2, *About Literature.* New York: Oxford University Press, 1970. In volume 1, Hoggart investigates "how one understands, interprets and evaluates cultural change." Volume 2 is on particular authors, the "subjective" literary imagination, and teaching. W. H. Auden, Graham Greene, Henry Miller, George Orwell, and Tom Wolfe.

A149   Hopper, Stanley Romaine. *Spiritual Problems in Contemporary Literature: A Series of Addresses and Discussions.* New York: Institute for Religious and Social Studies, 1952. Lectures presented at the Institute for Religious and Social Studies of the Jewish Theological Seminary of America.

The purpose is to clarify the hiatus between men of letters and men of faith and to bridge this gulf between artist and student of religion. Part 1 explores the place of the artist in the modern world; part 2 outlines the artist's aesthetic options; and part 3 examines religious orientation in literature. W. H. Auden, T. S. Eliot, Aldous Huxley, George Bernard Shaw, Wallace Stevens, Allen Tate, and others.

A150   Hough, Graham. *The Dream and the Task: Literature and Morals in the Culture of Today.* London: Duckworth, 1963. BBC talks "on the place of literature in our intellectual economy," morality and the novel, the function of criticism, and literary education.

A151   Howe, Irving. *The Critical Point: On Literature and Culture.* New York: Horizon, 1973. Howe's essays deal with figures who represent or reflect some of the less attractive elements of this recent cultural period. Howe states: "It is toward this end, the recreation of a vital democratic radicalism in America, that much of my political-cultural criticism is directed." Discusses the literature of suicide, Gandhi, and sexual politics. Ezra Pound, Saul Bellow, Philip Roth, Sylvia Plath, Kate Millet, and earlier writers.

A152   ————. *Decline of the New.* New York: Harcourt, Brace & World, 1970. "Literary culture of the last century has been dominated by a style of perception and composition —a style at once iconoclastic, difficult, and experimental— that we call modernist." Howe contends that we are now living through "the unsettling moral and intellectual consequences of the breakup of modern culture, or the decline of the new." His essays contain approaches to this problem. T. E. Lawrence, Isaac Bashevis Singer, Louis-Ferdinand Céline, Martin du Gard, George Orwell, Ignazio Silone, and earlier writers.

A153   ————. *A World More Attractive: A View of Modern Literature and Politics.* New York: Horizon, 1963. Essays that range "from literary criticism to political analysis, from intellectual portraiture to cultural polemic." Howe's focus is on problems and ideas, having to do with the strife of experience called "modern." Includes literary essays, political essays from a Socialist perspective, and a study of T. E. Lawrence that forms the centerpiece of the book.

Edith Wharton, Norman Mailer, Robert Frost, Wallace Stevens, George Gissing, Louis-Ferdinand Céline, Sholom Aleichem, and Edmund Wilson.

A154 ————, ed. *Literary Modernism*. Greenwich, Conn.: Fawcett, 1967. A study of modernism as a sensibility, a way of viewing life and literature that is a reflection of recent history. Contains essays by writers, critics, philosophers, and historians who analyze the preoccupations, attitudes, styles, and values of modern writers. Discusses movements such as symbolism and surrealism and such major figures as Marcel Proust, Thomas Mann, T. S. Eliot, Wallace Stevens, and W. B. Yeats. Howe's extensive introduction provides an overview to the collection.

A155 Hoyle, Bernadette. *Tar Heel Writers I Know*. Winston-Salem, N.C.: Blair, 1956. Sketches of thirty-five writers that attempt "to explore the thoughts and feelings of the people involved." The writers have made names for themselves in the fields of fiction, history, biography, nonfiction, poetry, drama, and juvenile literature. Each sketch is designed to give the "reader a visit with the writer."

A156 Hubbell, Jay B. *Who Are the Major American Writers? A Study of the Changing Literary Canon*. Durham, N.C.: Duke University Press, 1972. Hubbell's study of the literary canon is based on critical polls, literary histories, anthologies, reviews of books, magazine articles on individual authors, results of elections to the Hall of Fame, and Pulitzer, Nobel, and other literary prizes. He illustrates the changes in literary taste over the last century and a half.

A157 Huttar, Charles A., ed. *Imagination and the Spirit: Essays in Literature and the Christian Faith Presented to Clyde S. Kilby*. Grand Rapids, Mich.: William B. Eerdmans, 1971. A collection of essays that seeks to theorize about the nature of the artistic endeavor, examines the artistic techniques "by which an imaginative moral vision was given local habitation and a name," and studies the ideas of individual authors. The essays center around themes of mystery and paradox, sin, incarnation, redemption, providence, myth, destiny, love, and self-knowledge. C. S. Lewis, Howard Nemerov, Bernard Malamud, and earlier writers. Bibliography.

A158   Hyman, Stanley Edgar. *The Promised End: Essays and Reviews, 1942–1962.* Cleveland: World, 1963. Essays and reviews that appeared in magazines. Topics include images of the American writer, psychology and anthropology, dictionaries, folk literature, literature and culture, Isaac Babel, John Steinbeck, and earlier writers.

A159   ————. *Standards: A Chronicle of Books for Our Time.* New York: Horizon, 1966. Includes essays on Henry Miller, James Baldwin, Bernard Malamud, Philip Roth, W. H. Auden, John Updike, Thomas Pynchon, Truman Capote, Günter Grass, John Barth, William Golding, James Purdy, Norman Mailer, and many more.

A160   International Congress of the P.E.N. Clubs. *The Author and the Public: Problems of Communication.* London: Hutchinson, 1957. Speeches on "Criticism, History and Biography, Contemporary Techniques in Poetry, the Technique of the New Mass-Communication Media, Minority Literature, and Contemporary Techniques in Fiction."

A161   Ivask, Ivar, and Gero von Wilpert, eds. *World Literature since 1945: Critical Surveys of the Contemporary Literature of Europe and the Americas.* New York: Ungar, 1973. A survey of the developments in literature of the Western world since the end of World War II that gives "some idea of the supranational correlations in Western literature as a whole." Numerous figures mentioned.

A162   James, Clive. *The Metropolitan Critic.* London: Faber & Faber, 1974. A collection of reviews written for the *New Statesman,* the *Listener,* and the *Times Literary Supplement.* They cover a variety of contemporary authors, reflect contemporary tastes, and contain all sorts of information.

A163   Jameson, Storm. *The Writer's Situation and Other Essays.* London: Macmillan, 1950. Concerns the crisis of the spirit that resulted from the situation of the writer between 1939 and 1949. Essays on the form of the novel, the situation in Paris, and the responsibilities of a writer.

A164   Kampf, Louis. *On Modernism: The Prospects for Literature and Freedom.* Cambridge, Mass.: M.I.T. Press, 1967. "The critical attitudes which control this book derive from a personal sense of current needs: not the needs of criticism,

38

but those of life." Consequently, Kampf does not deal with the clichés of modernism but with "the states of mind from which our feelings, thoughts, and actions proceed." Jack Gelber, Denis Diderot, Alexander Herzen, Doris Lessing, other authors and topics.

A165 Kaplan, Charles, ed. *The Overwrought Urn: A Potpourri of Parodies of Critics Who Triumphantly Present the Real Meaning of Authors from Jane Austen to J. D. Salinger.* New York: Pegasus, 1969. "In the hope that parody, itself a form of criticism, can provide a salutary gust of fresh air, this collection has been assembled to blow a few academic minds. It is no accident that most of the authors in this collection are themselves critics and teachers of literature; it is a hopeful sign when the professional literati can laugh at themselves."

A166 Kazin, Alfred. *Contemporaries.* Boston: Little, Brown, 1962. Essays on the background of modern literature, the American past, literature before 1945, literature since World War II, European literature, Freud and his influence, modern society, and the critic's task. William Faulkner, Graham Greene, Nelson Algren, James Agee, Lawrence Durrell, Bernard Malamud, Saul Bellow, Robert Lowell, J. D. Salinger, Brendan Behan, Norman Mailer, James Baldwin, Philip Roth, and many others.

A167 —————. *The Inmost Leaf: A Selection of Essays.* New York: Noonday, 1955. Essays on e. e. cummings, Sherwood Anderson, William Faulkner, and earlier writers.

A168 Kenner, Hugh. *Gnomon: Essays on Contemporary Literature.* New York: McDowell, Obolensky, 1958. A report on ten years of watching contemporary literature. Kenner uses exegetical criticism to discuss the methods of W. B. Yeats, Ezra Pound, William Carlos Williams, Wyndham Lewis, Marianne Moore, and Ford Madox Ford.

A169 Kermode, Frank. *Continuities.* New York: Random House, 1968. A sequel to *Puzzles and Epiphanies.* This book includes pieces written between 1962 and 1967 on the cultural problem of schism and continuity. Wallace Stevens, Allen Tate, Edmund Wilson, Northrop Frye, Colette, Ernest Hemingway, Samuel Beckett, Jean-Paul Sartre, J. D.

Salinger, Muriel Spark, Bernard Malamud, Saul Bellow, and Alan Sillitoe.

A170 ————. *Puzzles and Epiphanies: Essays and Reviews, 1958–1961*. New York: Chilmark Press, 1962. Essays concerned with modern criticism and fiction. David Jones, Paul Valéry, Edmund Wilson, Mario Praz, Northrop Frye, James Joyce, Lawrence Durrell, Vladimir Nabokov, Boris Pasternak, Christopher Isherwood, Anthony Powell, Allen Tate, Samuel Beckett, C. P. Snow, Evelyn Waugh, Graham Greene, J. D. Salinger, and William Golding.

A171 Killinger, John. *The Failure of Theology in Modern Literature*. New York: Abingdon, 1963. Examines "certain areas of contemporary literature as they are related to several recurrent themes in the theology of the Christian faith" and raises the question of whether Christian art is possible.

A172 ————. *The Fragile Presence: Transcendence in Modern Literature*. Philadelphia: Fortress, 1973. Our ability to see the reality of God "is directly related to our ability to perceive him in the outrageously new and secular aspects of our existence." Experimental forms of writing, then, are evidence of the poet's search "for the stillness about which the world moves." His search is a quest for a "new transcendence *in* and *through* the materialities of human existence." Albert Camus, James Baldwin, Samuel Beckett, Eugène Ionesco, LeRoi Jones (Imamu Amiri Baraka), Henry Miller, Alain Robbe-Grillet, Richard Wright, and earlier writers.

A173 Kolodny, Annette. *The Lay of the Land: Metaphor as Experience and History in American Life and Letters*. Chapel Hill: University of North Carolina Press, 1975. Kolodny expresses distress at what we have done to our continent and explores the continued land-as-woman symbolization in American life and letters. Her emphasis is upon the historical and literary consequences of this symbol. She intentionally explores this metaphor only in masculine materials because women's writings have continually offered an alternative means of expression. Kolodny surveys literature from colonial to present times.

A174   Kostelanetz, Richard. *The End of Intelligent Writing: Literary Politics in America.* New York: Sheed & Ward, 1973. A study of how the "literary-industrial complex" came into being and how it works. "It focuses upon the intermediary agencies that lie between writers and readers" that affect "what is read by selecting what one is advised to read or what is available to be read." The second part of the book outlines the alternative to "the New York gang"—the new periodicals, publishers, and critics. This is a discussion of the business of literature. Bibliography.

A175   ————, ed. *The New American Arts.* New York: Horizon, 1965. Critics, all under thirty-five and qualified in their field, "attempt to distinguish and define new trends in their areas of interest and to describe and evaluate the individual artists within these trends, to identify and analyze the intelligible forms and expressed content of the major works, . . . to set the new achievements in their historical and esthetic contexts; so as to provide a full, discriminating picture of the most original and significant activity today." Includes essays on film, theater, painting, poetry, dance, fiction, and music. Bibliography.

A176   ————, ed. *On Contemporary Literature.* New York: Avon, 1969. This collection includes essays on important aspects of contemporary literature with the purpose of providing students with general criticism on movements and writers. Includes essays on American, British, Canadian, French, German, Italian, Russian, and Spanish writing. James Agee, John Barth, Saul Bellow, Ralph Ellison, Joseph Heller, Doris Lessing, Norman Mailer, Vladimir Nabokov, Boris Pasternak, Alain Robbe-Grillet, J. D. Salinger, Dylan Thomas, Robert Penn Warren, Harold Pinter, and twenty-five others.

A177   Kunkel, Francis L. *Passion and the Passion: Sex and Religion in Modern Literature.* Philadelphia: Westminster, 1975. The combination of theology and erotica in literature stems from an ancient tradition. Kunkel examines writers "who have wrestled with either the significance of Christ or some other aspect of religion and then coupled their concern with the mystery of sex." William Golding, John Updike, Tennessee Williams, Jean Genet, Nathanael West,

41

Flannery O'Connor, and nine European Roman Catholic writers.

A178   LaFrance, Marston, ed. *Patterns of Commitment in American Literature*. Toronto: University of Toronto Press, 1967. A series of lectures and essays that offer "common-sense criticism helpful to students of American literature." These essayists study thematic patterns and "compare and contrast the cultures of Europe and America." Includes "Recent Southern Fiction" and Contemporary American Poetry." Wallace Stevens, William Faulkner, and others.

A179   Langbaum, Robert. *The Modern Spirit: Essays on the Continuity of Nineteenth- and Twentieth-Century Literature*. New York: Oxford University Press, 1970. Lectures and essays presented since 1965 on various subjects and themes such as "post-Enlightenment that connects the nineteenth and twentieth centuries," a "new nineteenth-century concept of literature," "the nineteenth-century concept of history as involving development or evolutionary process," "changing ideas about nature, . . . self and identity," and "the cyclical view of history." T. S. Eliot, Robert Frost, Norman Mailer, Theodore Roethke, Wallace Stevens, and Richard Wilbur.

A180   Langer, Lawrence L. *The Holocaust and the Literary Imagination*. New Haven: Yale University Press, 1975. Langer studies the literature that grew out of the "holocaust experience." He examines a number of themes that illustrate the problem of "reconciling normalcy with horror." Ilse Aichinger, Samuel Beckett, Heinrich Böll, Albert Camus, Fyodor Dostoevsky, Pierre Gascar, Franz Kafka, Jerzy Kosinski, José Ortega y Gassett, and others.

A181   Langford, Richard E., et al., eds. *Essays in Modern American Literature*. Deland, Fla.: Stetson University Press, 1963. Twelve essays by as many authors, generally on a literary figure. Arranged chronologically, the essays begin with Melville and end with Purdy. Tennessee Williams, Jack Kerouac, James Gould Cozzens, and James Purdy.

A182   Leary, Lewis, ed. *Contemporary Literary Scholarship: A Critical Review*. New York: Appleton-Century-Crofts, 1958. "An informal discussion of trends and the specific achievements in the study of literature during the past thirty years." Leary's goal is "to present a useful guide for teachers through which their own specialization or their absorption in other duties has not allowed them to roam." Includes comments on the scholar and critic, historical periodicals, literary genres, the literary audience and popular arts, and a bibliography of fifty "outstanding literary studies."

A183   Lehmann, John, ed. *The Craft of Letters in England*. London: Cresset, 1956. The historical focus of this edition is on the second quarter of this century with special emphasis on the "post-war scene." These essays have two common themes: first, that "we are living in an age without giants," and second, that "it is impossible not to write about the human condition in our time." The essays address all genres and major movements of the period in England. W. H. Auden, T. S. Eliot, Christopher Isherwood, Ezra Pound, George Bernard Shaw, and earlier figures.

A184   Lessing, Doris. *A Small Personal Voice: Essays, Reviews, Interviews*. Edited by Paul Schlueter. New York: Vintage, 1975. Includes "The Small Personal Voice," "Preface to *The Golden Notebook*," "A Talk with Doris Lessing by Florence Howe," "Vonnegut's Responsibility," and others.

A185   Levi, Albert William. *Literature, Philosophy and the Imagination*. Bloomington: Indiana University Press, 1962. Levi's theme is *"the imagination,"* his purpose is *"a defense of the humanities,"* and his "point of origin [is] *the philosophy of Kant."* He demonstrates the function of the imagination in "the epic and the novel, in the modes of poetic perception, and in the varieties of the tragic drama." T. S. Eliot, Graham Greene, Aldous Huxley, John O'Hara, Alain Robbe-Grillet, Wallace Stevens, and earlier figures.

A186   Levin, Harry. *Contexts of Criticism*. Cambridge, Mass:. Harvard University Press, 1957. A series of papers informed by humanistic scholarship. Levin's approach is contextual because "it centers upon the exact relation between form and meaning." He argues that "relativity, if not relativism, conceived not as the disappearance of standards but as the discernment of relationships" is important to literature. "The historical and comparative approaches enable us to place a given work precisely by relating it to other works

43

and to other manifestations of culture." Levin's essays study the "texture of language" as "surrogate for reality," "the sphere of prose fiction," the definition of terms, specific novelists, traditions, Honoré de Balzac, Marcel Proust, James Joyce, Ernest Hemingway, e. e. cummings, T. S. Eliot, William Faulkner, and others.

A187   Lewald, H. Ernest, ed. *The Cry of Home: Cultural Nationalism and the Modern Writer.* Knoxville: University of Tennessee Press, 1972. A comparative study of cultural nationalism "endorsed as an official project of the MLA." "The mature and technologically advanced countries of the Western World seem to be undergoing a process of losing some national essence, while the younger and underdeveloped nations of the so-called Third World are still destined to search for a national identity." Minority cultures "continue to draw on their cultural resources in an effort to avoid social absorption."

A188   Lingner, Erika, et al., eds. *Essays in Honour of William Gallacher: Life and Literature of the Working Class.* Berlin: Humboldt University, 1966. A collection of works by "scholars, writers, workers and students" in Great Britain and the German Democratic Republic. Contains memoirs of Gallacher's labor and political activities and "studies of working-class literature." Raymond Williams, Arnold Wesker, Herbert Smith, and Alan Sillitoe.

A189   Lipton, Lawrence. *The Holy Barbarians.* New York: Julian Messner, 1959. A three-hundred-page study of the beat generation. Includes pictures, discussions of most of the cultural aspects of the beat movement, and a glossary. Allen Ginsberg, Michael McClure, Kenneth Rexroth, Henry Miller, Jack Kerouac, J. D. Salinger, William Carlos Williams, Charles Olson, Kenneth Patchen, Gregory Corso, Lawrence Ferlinghetti, Lawrence Lipton, Gary Snyder, and John Clellon Holmes.

A190   Liptzin, Sol. *The Jew in American Literature.* New York: Bloch, 1966. A study of what it means to be a Jew in America as revealed in American literature.

A191   Littlejohn, David. *Black on White: A Critical Survey of Writing by American Negroes.* New York: Grossman, 1966.

Littlejohn argues that "the works of recent American Negro authors evoke a closed, colorless, nonexistensive world that the most despairing white existentialist will never know." He examines black writing by discussing what the white reader can learn about the Negro. Littlejohn concludes that there is no "Negro experience" and no "Negro writer." James Baldwin, Ralph Ellison, Langston Hughes, LeRoi Jones (Imamu Amiri Baraka), and Richard Wright.

A192 ——————. *Interruptions.* New York: Grossman, 1970. A collection of Littlejohn's essays covering the years from 1962 to 1969: "it seemed important to sum up and declare myself now, as the decade changes." Includes "On Reading Black Authors," "The Anti-realists," essays on Henry Miller, Lawrence Durrell, F. Scott Fitzgerald, Jean Genet, William Faulkner, and others.

A193 *The Little Magazine and Contemporary Literature: A Symposium Held at the Library of Congress, 2 and 3 April 1965.* Manaska, Wisc.: George Banta Co. for the Modern Language Association, 1966. Editors of about sixty small magazines and a "handful of college teachers of contemporary literature and a few observers from the worlds of foundations and commercial publishing" discuss three topics: the present state and the future state of literary publishing and the teaching of contemporary literature.

A194 McCarthy, Mary. *On the Contrary.* New York: Farrar, Straus & Cudahy, 1961. Essays reprinted from journals spanning the period from 1946 to 1961. Topical concerns as well as essays on Arthur Miller, "Realist Playwrights," "Characters in Fiction," and others.

A195 ——————. *The Writing on the Wall and Other Literary Essays.* New York: Harcourt, Brace & World, 1970. Essays on Vladimir Nabokov, J. D. Salinger, William Burroughs, Ivy Compton-Burnett, George Orwell, and others.

A196 MacIver, R. M., ed. *New Horizons in Creative Thinking: A Survey and Forecast.* New York: Institute for Religious and Social Studies, 1954. A series of essays on various facets of the arts and contemporary life. Some discuss the novel, poetry, and recent literature.

A197   MacNeice, Louis. *Varieties of Parable.* Cambridge: Cambridge University Press, 1965. MacNeice traces the parable—what he calls "double-level writing"—from Spenser and Bunyan to contemporary poetry, fiction, and drama. Franz Kafka, Samuel Beckett, Harold Pinter, and William Golding. Bibliography.

A198   McNeir, Waldo, and Leo B. Levy, eds. *Studies in American Literature.* Baton Rouge: Louisiana State University Press, 1960. Essays on writers from Edward Taylor through T. S. Eliot, e. e. cummings, William Faulkner, Carson Mc-Cullers, and others.

A199   Madden, Charles, ed. *Talks With Authors.* Carbondale: Southern Illinois University Press, 1968. Transcribed telephone conversations with John Dos Passos, Horace Gregory, Arthur Mizener, Carvel Collins, Warren Beck, Carlos Baker, James T. Farrell, Karl Shapiro, Muriel Rukeyser, Anne Sexton, Richard Wilbur, Vance Bourjaily, and Kay Boyle.

A200   Madden, David, ed. *American Dreams, American Nightmares.* Carbondale: Southern Illinois University Press, 1970. "The American experiment has produced *both* dreams and nightmares, and what we achieve or fail to achieve happens within the tensions, conflicts, and contraries between these polar conceptions of our experiences." A collection of essays on Abraham Cahan, William Faulkner, Henry Miller, Thomas Wolfe, Eugene O'Neill, Arthur Miller, Ralph Ellison, Norman Mailer, and earlier writers. Selective bibliography.

A201   Major, Clarence. *The Dark and Feeling: Black American Writers and Their Work.* New York: Third Press/Josephy Okpaku, 1974. Interviews, self-interviews, essays on black criteria, on censorship, "The Tribal Terrain and the Technological Beast," and "The Explosion of Black Poetry." Addison Gayle, Jr., June Jordan, Ishmael Reed, George Cain, Ernest J. Gaines, Richard Wright, James Baldwin, John A. Williams, Willard Motley, Frank London Brown, Eldridge Cleaver, and Victor Hernandez Cruz.

A202   Malin, Irving. *Jews and Americans.* Carbondale: Southern Illinois University Press, 1965. In this book, Malin discusses seven writers "who deal with the Jew in America." "They would not readily admit that their art is 'parochial,' but I hope to demonstrate that there is an American-Jewish context, a *'community of feeling' which transcends individual style and different genres*. Because our writers flee from orthodox commitments, rebelling against the God of their ancestors, they belong to a 'deceptive' community; but in an ironic way they mirror their ancestors." Karl Shapiro, Delmore Schwartz, Isaac Rosenfeld, Leslie Fiedler, Saul Bellow, Bernard Malamud, and Philip Roth.

A203 ————, ed. *Contemporary American-Jewish Literature: Critical Essays*. Bloomington: Indiana University Press, 1975. Malin argues that American-Jewish literature must be approached from a "theological framework," for it dramatizes the heritage it cannot escape. "Only when a Jewish (by birth) writer, moved by religious tensions, shows 'ultimate concern' in creating a new structure of belief, can he be said to create 'Jewish' literature." Malin presents these essays in an attempt to "invent being a Jew." Each critic who contributes to the collection defines Jewishness. Philip Roth, Norman Mailer, Saul Bellow, Leslie Fiedler, Lionel Trilling, Bernard Malamud, Karl Shapiro, Edward Lewis Wallant, Bruce Jay Friedman, and Isaac Bashevis Singer. Bibliography by Jackson R. Bryer.

A204 Mander, John. *The Writer and Commitment*. London: Secker & Warburg, 1961. An inquiry into the meaning of commitment "in relation to certain English writers of the last thirty years." Mander questions the nature of this commitment and its source. W. H. Auden, George Orwell, Angus Wilson, Arthur Miller, Thom Gunn, John Osborne, Arnold Wesker, and others.

A205 Margolies, Edward. *Native Sons: A Critical Study of Twentieth-Century Negro American Authors*. Philadelphia: Lippincott, 1968. Margolies examines writing that exposes the direction in which "unassimilated" Negro culture seems to be moving. He finds that the black writer's work is more intensely American than that of his white counterparts. W. E. B. DuBois, Charles Waddell Chesnutt, James Weldon Johnson, Paul Laurence Dunbar, Langston Hughes, Jean Toomer, Claude McKay, Countee Cullen, William Attaway, Richard Wright, Chester Himes, James Baldwin, Ralph Ellison, Malcolm X, William Demby, and LeRoi Jones (Imamu Amiri Baraka). Bibliography.

A206   Martin, F. David. *Art and the Religious Experience: The "Language" of the Sacred.* Lewisburg, Pa.: Bucknell University Press, 1972. Music, painting, literature, and architecture approached from religious and aesthetic perspectives. W. H. Auden, Samuel Beckett, T. S. Eliot, Ralph Ellison, William Faulkner, Ernest Hemingway, and others. Bibliography.

A207   Maschler, Tom. *Declaration.* London: MacGibbon & Kee, 1959. Maschler's aim is to help the public understand what is happening in British thought and literature. For this reason, he collects essays in which the authors define their position in relation to society. Contributors include Doris Lessing, Colin Wilson, John Osborne, John Wain, Kenneth Tynan, Bill Hopkins, Lindsay Anderson, and Stuart Holroyd.

A208   Matthews, Honor. *The Hard Journey: The Myth of Man's Rebirth.* London: Chatto & Windus, 1968. Matthews explores the myth of man's Fall—"the journey downward from created light and order, the world of the Sun and the heavens, into chaos and darkness, the world of the Earth, as it was without form and void, before the Spirit of the creator brooded upon it." He examines this journey first in *Oedipus Tyrannus* and *The Inferno*; then, he looks at the journey in contemporary society. Henrik Ibsen, T. S. Eliot, Jean-Paul Sartre, Albert Camus, Franz Kafka, Samuel Beckett, and Bertolt Brecht.

A209   Maugham, W. Somerset. *Selected Prefaces and Introductions of W. Somerset Maugham.* Garden City, N.Y.: Doubleday, 1963. Includes "The Art of Fiction—Chapter One," "A Writer's Notebook—Preface," "Of Human Bondage—Foreword," "Traveler's Library—General Introduction," "Tellers of Tales—Introduction," "Maugham's Choice of Kipling's Best—Introduction," and others.

A210   Mauriac, Claude. *The New Literature.* Translated by Samuel I. Stone. New York: Braziller, 1959. Mauriac studies "aliterature"—literature that is freed from conventions.

Franz Kafka, Antonin Artaud, Henry Miller, Michel Leiris, Samuel Beckett, Georges Bataille, Albert Camus, Henri Michaux, Georges Simenon, Vladimir Weidlé, Jean Rostand, Roger Caillois, Roland Barthes, Dionys Mascolo, E. M. Cioran, Alain Robbe-Grillet, and Nathalie Sarraute.

A211   Melchiori, Giorgio. *The Tightrope Walkers: Studies of Mannerism in Modern English Literature.* London: Routledge & Kegan Paul, 1956. Melchiori's aim is to find out the common characteristics of the style of an age full of contradictions and uncertainties. He takes the position of T. S. Eliot as a vantage point for viewing the modern period. T. S. Eliot, Christopher Fry, Henry Green, and Dylan Thomas.

A212   Mendelson, Moris O. *Current Soviet Thought: Soviet Interpretation of Contemporary American Literature.* Translated by Deming B. Brown and Rufus W. Mathewson. Washington, D.C.: Public Affairs Press, 1948. A public lecture delivered in Moscow and published "by the 'Pravda' Publishing House in Moscow." In thirty large pages it fulfills its title—examining American literature at the end of the Second World War from the Soviet point of view.

A213   Miller, Henry. *Stand Still like the Hummingbird.* New York: New Directions, 1962. A collection of essays, prefaces, and reviews that presents "America seen through the eyes of an American." The dominant theme is the plight of the individual in society. Kenneth Patchen, Eugène Ionesco, Albert Cossery, and earlier writers.

A214   Miller, James E., Jr. *Quests Surd and Absurd: Essays in American Literature.* Chicago: University of Chicago Press, 1967. Miller's study is "a volume of essays loosely related by their recurring concern with the quest theme in American literature." The "Quest Absurd" deals with the existential hero in an irrational land; as for the "Quest Surd," the irrationality lies within the speaker. J. D. Salinger, William Faulkner, T. S. Eliot, and earlier writers.

A215   Moore, Marianne. *Predilections.* New York: Viking, 1955. A collection of essays representing Moore's "predilections" over two decades. Wallace Stevens, T. S. Eliot, Ezra Pound, W. H. Auden, and William Carlos Williams.

A216   Moorman, Charles. *Arthurian Triptych: Mythic Materials in Charles Williams, C. S. Lewis, and T. S. Eliot.* Berkeley: University of California Press, 1960. Moorman formulates "a theory of the function of myth in literature," tests the theory in terms of the Arthurian myth, and applies it to "three contemporary British writers." He feels these writers, because they experienced the chaos of the First World War, have a special need for the order of myth. He hopes that this study will clarify the direction and value of myth criticism.

A217   ————. *The Precincts of Felicity: The Augustinian City of the Oxford Christians.* Gainesville: University of Florida Press, 1966. A "study of the literary influence" of the Oxford Christians. Moorman discusses them in terms of shared images and major themes. Charles Williams, C. S. Lewis, J. R. R. Tolkien, T. S. Eliot, and Dorothy L. Sayers.

A218   Moss, Howard. *Writing against Time: Critical Essays and Reviews.* New York: William Morrow, 1969. Includes essays on Dylan Thomas, Katherine Anne Porter, Nathalie Sarraute, Denis Devlin, Glenway Wescott, and earlier writers.

A219   Mudrick, Marvin. *On Culture and Literature.* New York: Horizon, 1970. Reprinted essays on George Orwell, Arthur Koestler, Oscar Lewis, George Bernard Shaw, Ernest Hemingway, T. S. Eliot, Norman Mailer, William Styron, Bernard Malamud, Saul Bellow, Philip Roth, Harold Rosenberg, and others.

A220   Murray, Albert. *The Hero and the Blues.* Columbia: University of Missouri Press, 1973. Three public lectures that illustrate, with a discussion of numerous novels, "The Social Function of the Story Teller," "The Dynamics of Heroic Action," and "The Blues and the Fable in the Flesh." All three lectures are concerned with action and experience.

A221   Nemerov, Howard. *Poetry and Fiction: Essays.* New Brunswick, N.J.: Rutgers University Press, 1963. Essays, lectures, and reviews written between 1948 and 1962. Wallace Stevens, Karl Shapiro, Theodore Roethke, Yvor Winters, Reed Whittemore, Weldon Kees, Thomas Mann, James Gould Cozzens, William Faulkner, and earlier writers.

A222   Newport, John P. *Theology and Contemporary Art Forms.* Waco, Tex.: Word Books, 1971. A discussion of art and theology and a survey of literature, drama, and painting from the perspective of theology. Many figures briefly discussed.

A223   Newquist, Roy. *Conversations.* New York: Rand McNally, 1967. Interviews with contemporary figures such as Lerone Bennett, Jr., Gwendolyn Brooks, Rachel Carson, Laura Z. Hobson, Rona Jaffe, James Michener, Ogden Nash, Katherine Anne Porter, Jacqueline Susann, Arnold Toynbee, Irving Wallace, Robert Penn Warren, and P. G. Wodehouse. Issues discussed are the problems of the Negro, young writers, the process of research, the Catholic press, writer's block, success, the nuclear world, censorship, and best sellers.

A224   ————. *Counterpoint.* New York: Rand McNally, 1964. Sixty-three interviews "with authors, columnists, and publishers." Four basic topics: "(a) the writer's obligation to his material and to his readers; (b) advice to a beginning writer; (c) the interviewer's attitudes toward, his opinions of, contemporary culture; and (d) the writer's ultimate ambitions insofar as his own career is concerned. . . . I hope to capture the working philosophies of the writer, his own life and attitudes toward life, his own work and the reason for that work." Louis Auchincloss, Erskine Caldwell, Truman Capote, John Ciardi, Maxwell Geismar, Herbert Gold, William Inge, James Jones, Harper Lee, Doris Lessing, Lillian Ross, C. P. Snow, Diana Trilling, Mark Van Doren, and others.

A225   Nott, Kathleen. *The Emperor's Clothes.* Bloomington: Indiana University Press, 1958. Attacks "the dogmatic orthodoxy of T. S. Eliot, Graham Greene, Dorothy Sayers, C. S. Lewis, and others."

A226   Oates, Joyce Carol. *New Heaven, New Earth: The Visionary Experience in Literature.* New York: Vanguard, 1974. Art, for visionary artists, is a means "by which they communicate their truths." Oates finds that the conflict between the intellectual and the mystic in Western civilization provides a possible generating source for communication. Samuel

Beckett, Harriette Arnow, Sylvia Plath, Flannery O'Connor, Norman Mailer, James Dickey, and others.

A227   O'Brien, John, ed. *Interviews with Black Writers.* New York: Liveright, 1973. Interviews with Arna Bontemps, Cyrus Colter, William Demby, Owen Dodson, Ralph Ellison, Ernest J. Gaines, Michael Harper, Robert Hayden, Clarence Major, Julian Mayfield, Ann Petry, Ishmael Reed, Alice Walker, John Wideman, John A. Williams, Charles Wright, and Al Young. Brief biographies, centering upon each writer's peculiar interests, precede each interview. Bibliographies.

A228   O'Connor, William Van. *The Grotesque: An American Genre and Other Essays.* Carbondale: Southern Illinois University Press, 1962. A collection of essays—some reprinted, some written for this collection. "Although the various pieces have been written at different times, I believe the collection has a certain homogeneity . . . the American-ness of American literature." William Faulkner, Ernest Hemingway, T. S. Eliot, Wallace Stevens, Robert Frost, and Caroline Gordon.

A229   ————. *The New University Wits and the End of Modernism.* Carbondale: Southern Illinois University Press, 1963. O'Connor writes that "the situation of writers in England after World War II has been distinctly different from what it was after World War I." The writers whom he discusses, "sometimes called the Movement and sometimes called the New University Wits, have experienced the social and cultural shifts of the Welfare State, and their writings reflect and interpret these changes." This group, argues O'Connor, represents "a new class in English literary life." Philip Larkin, John Wain, Iris Murdoch, Kingsley Amis, and others.

A230   Orwell, George. *The Collected Essays, Journalism and Letters of George Orwell.* 4 vols. Edited by Sonia Orwell and Ian Angus. New York: Harcourt, Brace & World, 1968. Volume 4, *In Front of Your Nose: 1945–50,* contains 167 essays, reviews, and letters on contemporary events.

A231   Padovano, Anthony T. *The Estranged God: Modern Man's Search for Belief.* New York: Sheed & Ward, 1966. Padovano studies existentialism and literature from the view-point of Catholic theology. Fyodor Dostoevsky, Thomas Wolfe, Franz Kafka, Albert Camus, J. D. Salinger, William Golding, and George Orwell. Bibliography.

A232   Panichas, George A., ed. *Mansions of the Spirit: Essays in Literature and Religion.* New York: Hawthorn, 1967. Panichas explores "the connections between literature and religion." In the process, he shows the inadequacy of the formalistic approach and the limitations imposed by schools of literary criticism. Panichas argues that the critic must direct his attention to "those universals in human life that are religious in origin: the meaning of the human predicament, the nature of evil, the fact of death, the concept of redemption." William Faulkner, Aldous Huxley, John Masefield, Albert Camus, Jean Genet, Saul Bellow, Flannery O'Connor, J. D. Salinger, T. S. Eliot, David Gascoyne, Dylan Thomas, and others.

A233   Parkinson, Thomas, ed. *A Casebook on the Beat.* New York: Crowell, 1961. Parkinson's aim is "to present a body of material essential to understanding the writing placed under the rubric 'Beat Generation.'" Section 1 contains selections of poetry and fiction as well as pieces of expository prose in which the writers clarify their motives. Section 2 presents comments on the beats, ranging from partisan viewpoints to aggressive attacks. Allen Ginsberg, Jack Kerouac, Gregory Corso, William S. Burroughs, Lawrence Ferlinghetti, Gary Snyder, Philip Whalen, Michael McClure, and John Wieners. Bibliography.

A234   Pearce, Roy Harvey. *Historicism Once More: Problems and Occasions for the American Scholar.* Princeton: Princeton University Press, 1969. "The essays reprinted here are informed by a conviction that works of literature, precisely as they are events occasioned at a particular time and in a particular place, have the power to carry with them, beyond their time and place into ours, a continuing sense of the occasion." Pearce's study is an exegetical preparation to meet the text on its own terms. Includes theoretical essays and studies on writers from James Fenimore Cooper to Wallace Stevens and Theodore Roethke.

A235   P.E.N. English Centre. *Mightier Than the Sword: The P.E.N.*

Herman Ould Memorial Lectures, 1953–1961. London: Macmillan, 1964. Includes "Dialogue in Novels and Plays" by Charles Morgan, "History as an Art" by Bertrand Russell, "The Writer in a Changing Society," by J. B. Priestley, "Young Poets" by Edith Sitwell, "The Role of the Intellectuals in Society" by A. L. Rowse, "Tolstoy and Enlightenment" by Isaiah Berlin, and "Breaking the Barrier—The Writer's Problems and Opportunities" by C. V. Wedgwood.

A236   Phelps, Robert, and Peter Deane. *The Literary Life: A Scrapbook Almanac of the Anglo-American Literary Scene from 1900 to 1950.* New York: Farrar, Straus & Giroux, 1968. A year-by-year collection of literary facts and details, "Comprising Pictures, Gossip, Homage, Warnings and Clues—Together with Laurels, Letters, Lists, and Whispered Asides—The Whole Reverently Garnered and Arranged."

A237   Pitt, Valerie. *The Writer and the Modern World: A Study in Literature and Dogma.* London: S.P.C.K., 1966. Because the "welfare state" challenges the "Christian social theology," Christians are drawn "to an inverted Christianity" where they tend to speak to themselves and be ignored by the world at large. Focusing upon writers who made their reputations after the Second World War, the work studies the theological implications of numerous novelists, poets, and dramatists, most of whom are not generally thought to be religious. William Golding, Muriel Spark, Angus Wilson, and brief references to many others.

A238   Podhoretz, Norman. *Doings and Undoings: The Fifties and After in American Writing.* New York: Noonday, 1964. "A collection of occasional essays" written "in hot response to a particular event and out of a highly specific context." Podhoretz examines the effects of the new conditions of the postwar period on the writer's vision of the world and demonstrates that the effects were damaging. William Faulkner, Nathanael West, Mary McCarthy, Norman Mailer, Saul Bellow, Philip Roth, James Baldwin, and John Updike.

A239   Porter, Katherine Anne. *The Collected Essays and Occasional Writings of Katherine Anne Porter.* New York: Delacorte, 1970. Criticism, personal essays, biographical essays, essays on Mexico, on writing, and on poetry.

A240   Powell, Lawrence Clark. *Books, West Southwest: Essays on Writers, Their Books, and Their Land.* Los Angeles: Ritchie, 1957. Essays written "because I was moved by what I read and saw of the Southwest to communicate my thoughts and feelings to others." Powell's primary subject is the land.

A241   Price, Lawrence Masden. *The Reception of United States Literature in Germany.* Chapel Hill: University of North Carolina Press, 1966. A history of the German-American literary relationship between 1775 and 1965. Bibliography.

A242   Priestley, J. B. *Thoughts in the Wilderness.* New York: Harper & Brothers, 1957. "Polemical pieces" that were "originally written to challenge and provoke readers of a weekly review." Priestley writes about mass communication, education, novels, the popular press, television, F. R. Leavis, "The Writer in a Changing Society," and other topics.

A243   Pritchett, V. S. *Books in General.* New York: Harcourt, Brace & World [1953]. Reprinted essays from the *New Statesman* and the *Nation,* dealing with numerous literary topics.

A244   Rahv, Philip. *Image and Idea: Twenty Essays on Literary Themes.* London: Weidenfeld & Nicolson, 1957. A collection of essays on Nathaniel Hawthorne, Henry James, Leo Tolstoy, Franz Kafka, William Carlos Williams, Henry Miller, Virginia Woolf, Arthur Koestler, Herman Melville, Ernest Hemingway, T. S. Eliot, and others.

A245   ————. *Literature and the Sixth Sense.* Boston: Houghton Mifflin, 1969. Studies based upon Nietzsche's theory of historical insight functioning as a sixth sense. Rahv's essays ask his readers "to recognize and . . . restore a proper perspective on what has transpired in American literary culture during the past thirty years." Henry Miller, Bernard Malamud, William Carlos Williams, T. S. Eliot, Ernest Hemingway, Arthur Miller, Saul Bellow, Norman Mailer, and others.

246   ————. *The Myth and the Powerhouse.* New York: Farrar, Straus & Giroux, 1965. A collection of sixteen pieces published between 1949 and 1964 on the changing tastes of "literary intellectuals." Discusses myth, religion, criticism,

European writers and the following: T. S. Eliot, Ernest Hemingway, Saul Bellow, Arthur Miller, Norman Mailer, and others.

A247   Ransom, John Crowe, ed. *The Kenyon Critics: Studies in Modern Literature from the Kenyon Review.* Port Washington, N.Y.: Kennikat, 1951. Essays by thirty-three critics who "are professionally sensitive to what is latent in the [literary] work, therefore likely to be difficult, and will not content themselves with what is manifest and for everybody to see." "It is the critic who must teach us to find the thing truly authoritative but hidden; the critic trying and judging the literary work which has one content that is visible and another content which is not so visible." Evelyn Waugh, William Faulkner, Allen Tate, Robert Penn Warren, Aldous Huxley, William Carlos Williams, T. S. Eliot, and others. Bibliography.

A248   Reilly, R. J. *Romantic Religion: A Study of Barfield, Lewis, Williams, and Tolkien.* Athens: University of Georgia Press, 1971. Deals with one crosscurrent of the time: "the fusion of a certain literary form with a certain subject matter, the romantic manner applied to religious matter." Reilly shows "that the work of these four men reveals itself, on analysis, as a deliberate and conscious attempt to revive certain well-known doctrines and attitudes by showing that they have not merely literary but religious validity." Owen Barfield, C. S. Lewis, Charles Williams, and J. R. R. Tolkien.

A249   Rexroth, Kenneth. *Assays.* New York: New Directions, 1961. Twenty essays on various topics important to the author: translation, Indian songs, nineteenth-century painting, China, Gnosticism, French poetry, new poetry, and various literary figures, especially Lawrence Durrell and William Carlos Williams.

A250   —————. *Bird in the Bush: Obvious Essays.* New York: New Directions, 1959. Rexroth protests the institutionalized art of the dominant mindless and what he calls "The Pre-Frontal Lobotomy Movement." He writes that "art is a weapon. After millions of well-aimed blows, someday perhaps it will break the stone heart of the mindless cacodemon called Things As They Are. Everything else has failed." Samuel Beckett, Kenneth Patchen, Henry Miller, and earlier writers.

A251 ————. *With Eye and Ear*. New York: Herder & Herder, 1970. A collection of forty-three essays on British and European literature, on the Far East, on religion, on the past, and on American writing. William Golding, William Carlos Williams, Henry Miller, Isaac Bashevis Singer, Leslie Fiedler, Allen Ginsberg, Philip Whalen, and others.

A252 Richardson, Robert. *Literature and Film*. Bloomington: Indiana University Press, 1969. A study of the relationships between literature and the film, historically and technically. Chapters on the similarities of the two forms and the "impact of the film upon modern literature," especially modern poetry. Ends with a discussion of the humanistic implications of both forms. Jean Cocteau, T. S. Eliot, Ezra Pound, Alain Robbe-Grillet, Wallace Stevens, William Carlos Williams, and others. Bibliography.

A253 Richman, Robert, ed. *The Arts at Mid-Century*. New York: Horizon, 1954. A collection of forty-one essays on the arts in France, Italy, Germany, England, and the United States. Topics studied are criticism, the novel, poetry, painting, music, film, and the theater.

A254 Robinson, Cecil. *With the Ears of Strangers: The Mexican in American Literature*. Tucson: University of Arizona Press, 1963. Includes an early history of the border and a study of the Mexican influence upon the literary imagination. Saul Bellow, Ernest Hemingway, Jack Kerouac, Oliver LaFarge, Henry Miller, Katherine Anne Porter, John Steinbeck, William Carlos Williams, and others. Bibliography.

A255 Robson, W. W. *Crtical Essays*. London: Routledge & Kegan Paul, 1966. A collection of essays on such figures as F. R. Leavis, T. S. Eliot, C. S. Lewis, W. H. Auden, William Empson, and many earlier writers.

A256 Rogers, Robert. *A Psychoanalytic Study of the Double in Literature*. Detroit: Wayne State University Press, 1970. Often the literary artist creates comparable figures, doubles, for some of his characters. Rogers attempts "to provide an account of the psychological framework of doubling—more for its heuristic value than its intrinsic interest." Thus, he analyzes the incidence of doubling in a number of works "to suggest that it is a basic literary process reflecting fundamental tendencies of the human mind and not just an aberration on the part of a few authors." John Barth, Leslie A. Fiedler, Vladimir Nabokov, and earlier novelists, dramatists, and poets.

A257   Rosenfeld, Isaac. *An Age of Enormity: Life and Writing in the Forties and Fifties.* Edited by Theodore Solotaroff. Cleveland: World, 1962. Solotaroff states: "His [Rosenfeld's] 'ephemeral' book reviews and articles offer, it seems to me, the most sustained example of the human use of literature in recent American letters." Arranged in chronological order, the essays reflect "the development of Rosenfeld's career as a critic and . . . the changing climate of the age." A collection of fifty pieces on a variety of literary topics and figures such as Richard Wright, Anaïs Nin, Kenneth Patchen, Henry Miller, Christopher Isherwood, Henry Green, Ernest Hemingway, William Faulkner, and others.

A258   Rubin, Louis D., Jr. *William Elliott Shoots a Bear: Essays on the Southern Literary Imagination.* Baton Rouge: Louisiana State University Press, 1975. Essays concerning the problem: "why do southern writers write the way they do?" Rubin discusses writers of the antebellum South, southern writers after the Civil War, and southern writers of the twentieth century. William Elliott, Mark Twain, George W. Cable, Joel Chandler Harris, Sidney Lanier, Allen Tate, John Crowe Ranson, Robert Penn Warren, William Faulkner, Thomas Wolfe, Eudora Welty, William Styron, and others.

A259   ————, ed. *The Comic Imagination in American Literature.* New Brunswick, N.J: Rutgers University Press, 1973. Thirty-two introductory papers originally prepared for broadcast over the Voice of America. "The objective was to sketch out the modes of American comedy, ranging from the journalistic and the subliterary on through the reaches of artistic achievement" and to discuss comedy's social significance. John Barth, Erskine Caldwell, Langston Hughes, William Faulkner, Eudora Welty, Paul Goodman, Isaac Bashevis Singer, Bernard Malamud, Flannery O'Connor, Walker Percy, and Ralph Ellison.

A260   ————, and Robert D. Jacobs, eds. *South: Modern Southern Literature in Its Cultural Setting*. Garden City, N.Y.: Doubleday, 1961. Twenty-one essays that study "most of the major figures in what has been called the Southern Literary Renaissance." "A critical analysis and an effort . . . to understand something of the complex relationship between the individual work of art and the region." James Agee, Hamilton Basso, Erskine Caldwell, Truman Capote, Donald Davidson, Ralph Ellison, William Faulkner, Shelby Foote, George Garrett, Lillian Hellman, Randall Jarrell, Andrew Nelson Lytle, Carson McCullers, Merrill Moore, Flannery O'Connor, Katherine Anne Porter, Elizabeth Spencer, William Styron, Peter Taylor, Robert Penn Warren, Eudora Welty, and Tennessee Williams. Bibliography.

A261   Scherman, David E. *Literary America: A Chronicle of American Writers from 1607–1952 with 173 Photographs of the American Scene that Inspired Them*. New York: Dodd, Mead, 1952. A pictorial history.

A262   Schwartz, Delmore. *Selected Essays of Delmore Schwartz*. Edited by Donald A. Dike and David H. Zucker. Chicago: University of Chicago Press, 1970. Essays on poetry, fiction, criticism, and other topics. Thomas Hardy, Ezra Pound, T. S. Eliot, W. H. Auden, Allen Tate, John Crowe Ransom, Wallace Stevens, Ring Lardner, John Dos Passos, André Gide, Ernest Hemingway, William Faulkner, Yvor Winters, R. P. Blackmur, Edmund Wilson, and others. Includes "Bibliography of Publications by Delmore Schwartz."

A263   Scott-James, R. A. *Fifty Years of English Literature: 1900–1950*. London: Longmans, Green, 1951. A survey of British poetry, novels, drama, essayists, and literary movements. Includes George Bernard Shaw, Enoch Arnold Bennett, John Galsworthy, Gilbert Keith Chesterton, T. S. Eliot, and others.

A264   Scott, Nathan A., Jr. *The Broken Center: Studies in the Theological Horizon of Modern Literature*. New Haven: Yale University Press, 1966. Scott's aim is "to search out and explore those areas of interrelationship in the modern period that unite the literary and the religious imagination, whether in a state of accord or of tension." What underlies modern poetry, drama, and fiction "is a sense that the anchoring center of life is broken and that the world is therefore abandoned and adrift." Modern literature initiates theological inquiry. Samuel Beckett, Saul Bellow, T. S. Eliot, Ralph Ellison, William Faulkner, Ernest Hemingway, Ezra Pound, James Purdy, J. D. Salinger, William Styron, Allen Tate, Lionel Trilling, John Updike, Robert Penn Warren, and William Carlos Williams.

A265 ————. *Modern Literature and the Religious Frontier.* New York: Harper & Brothers, 1958. Scott contends that "outside theology itself, the literary intelligence is by far the best intelligence of our time." It has ventured to ask the hard questions. Scott's book is a historical study of literature and religion in the modern world, an analysis of modern critics, and "a summary of the modern consciousness." Samuel Beckett, T. S. Eliot, William Faulkner, Graham Greene, Ezra Pound, J. D. Salinger, Allen Tate, Robert Penn Warren, and others. Bibliography.

A266 ————. *Negative Capability: Studies in the New Literature and the Religious Situation.* New Haven: Yale University Press, 1969. The "rage for order" of the moderns—Eliot, Yeats, Kafka, etc—prevented them from using Keats's negative capability; Beckett, Robbe-Grillet, Grass, Burroughs, Godard use negative capability and, therefore, do not try to order the chaos of our time. Scott contends that negative capability is "distinctively characteristic of our contemporary situation." Samuel Beckett, Saul Bellow, T. S. Eliot, William Faulkner, Ezra Pound, Alain Robbe-Grillet, Wallace Stevens, and others.

A267 ————, ed. *The Climate of Faith in Modern Literature.* New York: Seabury, 1964. Scott's premise is that the distinctions between holy and profane, religious and secular, are false, for "the whole world is God's world." Includes ten essays illustrating the new union of theologians and literary critics. On all aspects of contemporary literature. Bibliography.

A268 Shapiro, Karl. *In Defense of Ignorance.* New York: Random House, 1960. An attack on the "dictatorship of intellectual 'modernism,' the sanctimonious ministry of 'the Tradition,' the ugly programmatic quality of twentieth-century criticism," which has destroyed poetry. Aimed at the public, at the young poets and at teachers, the book hopes "to restore the respect of the ordinary reader for his own judgment." Such subjects as Jewish writers, psychology, poetry, and cosmic consciousness. Randall Jarrell, T. S. Eliot, Ezra Pound, W. B. Yeats, W. H. Auden, William Carlos Williams, Dylan Thomas, Henry Miller.

A269 Sheed, Wilfred. *The Morning After: Selected Essays and Reviews*. New York: Farrar, Straus & Giroux, 1971. Journalistic essays on Norman Mailer, Walker Percy, James Jones, John Updike, Gore Vidal, James Agee, Bernard Malamud, James Baldwin, Robert Coover, William Styron, Kurt Vonnegut, Jr., William Golding, Iris Murdoch, the theatre, films, and other topics.

A270 Slote, Bernice. *Literature and Society by Germaine Bree and Others: A Selection of Papers Delivered at the Joint Meeting of the Midwest Modern Language Association and the Central Renaissance Conference, 1963*. Lincoln: University of Nebraska Press, 1964. Includes essays on George Bernard Shaw, Clifford Odets, Graham Greene, "Theater of the Absurd," "The New Novel in France," and "Recent Trends in French Poetry."

A271 Snodgrass, W. D. *In Radical Pursuit: Critical Essays and Lectures*. New York: Harper & Row, 1975. Snodgrass's "aim is to broaden the reader's experience of the work of art, not to limit or control it." Includes four "Personal Lectures" on poetry, studies on Theodore Roethke, John Crowe Ransom, D. H. Lawrence, Fyodor Dostoevsky, and four "Studies in the Classics."

A272 Solotaroff, Theodore. *The Red Hot Vacuum and Other Pieces on the Writing of the Sixties*. New York: Atheneum, 1970. Essays and reviews written during the 1960s. Solotaroff is concerned with the literary climate, "the new initiatives and options, the new problems and perplexities that marked the writing and thought of the Sixties." Isaac Rosenfeld, Henry Miller, Seymour Krim, Harry Golden, Bernard Malamud, Katherine Anne Porter, Irving Howe, James Purdy, Flannery O'Connor, Jean-Paul Sartre, R. D. Laing, William Burroughs, Susan Sontag, J. D. Salinger, Saul Bellow, Philip Roth, and others.

A273   Sontag, Susan. *Against Interpretation and Other Essays.* New York: Farrar, Straus & Giroux, 1966. A collection of articles, reviews, and critical pieces written between 1961 and 1966. Includes essays on Simone Weil, Albert Camus, Georg Lukács, Jean-Paul Sartre, Eugène Ionesco, Nathalie Sarraute, Rolf Hochhuth, tragedy, science fiction, films, "camp," and other topics. Also includes "Against Interpretation," "The Imagination of Disaster," "A Note on Novels and Films," and "One Culture and the New Sensibility."

A274   —————. *Styles of Radical Will.* New York: Farrar, Straus & Giroux, 1969. A collection of essays that includes "The Aesthetics of Silence," "The Pornographic Imagination," " 'Thinking Against Oneself': Reflections on Cioran," "Theatre and Film," "Bergman's Persona," "Godard," "What's Happening in America," and "Trip to Hanoi."

A275   Spender, Stephen. *Love—Hate Relations: English and American Sensibilities.* New York: Random House, 1974. Based on the Clark Lectures delivered at Columbia University in 1965, the book describes the interaction of literary figures of England and America, focusing especially on Henry James. Robert Graves, John Berryman, Robert Lowell, T. S. Eliot, Wallace Stevens, Ezra Pound, and others.

A276   Spiller, Robert E., ed. *A Time of Harvest: American Literature, 1910–1960.* New York: Hill & Wang, 1962. Spiller's collection tells the story of "the flowering and the decline of naturalism in American literature." Numerous authors are discussed.

A277   Stanford, Donald E., ed. *Nine Essays in Modern Literature.* Baton Rouge: Louisiana State University Press, 1965. A collection of nine essays "indicative of the cosmopolitan nature of twentieth-century literature." Eleven writers are studied: five Americans, two English, one Irish, one Spanish, one French, and one Greek. The critics "found it appropriate to examine their writers in relation to European antecedents or to Western civilization as a whole." James Joyce, Constantine Cavafy, John Dos Passos, William Faulkner, Lawrence Ferlinghetti, Alain Robbe-Grillett, Muriel Spark, Allen Tate, Yvor Winters, Pio Baroja, and Ezra Pound.

A278   Stein, Walter. *Criticism and Dialogue.* Cambridge: Cambridge University Press, 1969. From the standpoint of "a radical Christian humanism," Stein creates a dialectic through which he examines T. S. Eliot, Samuel Beckett, Albert Camus, Anton Chekhov, Henrik Ibsen, D. H. Lawrence, William Shakespeare, and W. B. Yeats.

A279   Stone, Edward. *A Certain Morbidness: A View of American Literature.* Carbondale: Southern Illinois University Press, 1969. Stone investigates the irrational and the morbid in Herman Melville, Henry James, Stephen Crane, Robert Frost, William Faulkner, and J. D. Salinger.

A280   —————. *Voices of Despair: Four Motifs in American Literature.* Athens: Ohio University Press, 1966. Stone attempts "to write a history of despair in the literature of the United States: of the conflict between optimism and pessimism, between the concepts of design and chaos." Each chapter studies a different motif of that history. Chapters 1 and 2 treat the whole "range of American literature"; the first uses an animal motif, the second a color motif. Chapter 3 is concerned with the "post–Civil War generation," and chapter 4 "is on the present century." William Faulkner, Robert Frost, Ernest Hemingway, Robert Penn Warren, and many earlier figures.

A281   Straumann, Heinrich. *American Literature in the Twentieth Century.* London: Hutchinson's University Library, 1951. Straumann studies the attitudes underlying the literature of the twentieth century. The purpose of his study is to arrive at an understanding of "the apparent contradictions and puzzling complexities of the modern American outlook." Straumann studies writers from William James to George Santayana, Eugene O'Neill, Maxwell Anderson, Thornton Wilder, William Saroyan, Tennessee Williams, and Arthur Miller.

A282   —————. *Contexts of Literature: An Anglo-Swiss Approach.* Bern: Francke, 1973. Twelve essays published over a period of forty-four years. Discussions on William Faulkner, James Gould Cozzens, contemporary American criticism, best sellers in the United States of the 1960s, and other topics.

A283   Symons, Julian. *Critical Occasions*. London: Hamish Hamilton, 1966. Reprinted essays and reviews. Anthony Trollope, George Eliot, Arthur Machen, Saki, George Orwell, Wyndham Lewis, C. P. Snow, Evelyn Waugh, Anthony Powell, Edmund Wilson, Mary McCarthy, Nathanael West, Carson McCullers, Saul Bellow, Robert Penn Warren, Henry Miller, and a variety of topics.

A284   Sypher, Wylie. *Literature and Technology: The Alien Vision*. New York: Random House, 1968. "During the last century technology, limited in its aims and methods, contaminated both science and art, interdicting each by its law of parsimony, its principle of minimal expenditure, its fallacies of specification and exactitude, its manipulation of techniques." Sypher is optimistic, however, "because the arts seem to be a continuing revolt against the tyranny of techniques. Although the results of technological imperatives have not always been rewarding in literature, there is convincing evidence that literature and other arts can, at least on occasions, adapt the technological method and divert it to nontechnological purposes." Bibliography.

A285   —————. *Loss of Self in Modern Literature and Art*. New York: Random House, 1962. Sypher contrasts the "romantic" self of the nineteenth century and the self in our own day, which he calls "an anonymous self." He contends that our interpretation of twentieth-century literature "will be better if we look back to the romanticisms of the nineteenth century to see how the romantic affirmation of the self was followed by a rejection of the self." Sypher writes on the theme "that the romantic-liberal tradition created an idea of the self we have not only rejected but destroyed." References to numerous artists document and illustrate Sypher's thesis. Bibliographical note.

A286   Tate, Allen. *Memoirs and Opinions, 1926–1974*. Chicago: Swallow, 1975. Ten memoirs about his life and his generation, including pieces on William Faulkner and T. S. Eliot. Nine essays on a variety of themes and writers, including Robert Frost and William Faulkner. "Humanism and Naturalism" is also included.

A287   Thorp, Willard. *American Writing in the Twentieth Century*. Cambridge, Mass.: Harvard University Press, 1960. Chronological survey of American writing between 1912 and the 1950s. "Beginning about 1912 and continuing through the second World War a new generation of writers brought about an extraordinary renaissance in fiction, poetry, the drama, and criticism." Thorp's survey attempts to put this renaissance in writing into perspective. Numerous writers discussed.

A288   Toliver, Harold E. *Pastoral Forms and Attitudes.* Berkeley: University of California Press, 1971. An expansion of "the principles of the old shepherd poem . . . to literature that abandons many of its conventions while illustrating its theme and attitudes." These literary forms "do not develop in a vacuum but respond continuously to pressures of a complex kind, from social history to discoveries in science to the impact of individual poets who have reconceived inherited conventions in the light of their own experience." Edmund Spenser through Saul Bellow, Wallace Stevens, and Robert Frost. Bibliography.

A289   *Tradition and Innovation in Contemporary Literature / Tradition et modernité dans la littérature de notre tempe.* Budapest: Corvina, 1964. A round table conference of the International P.E.N. in Budapest in 1964. W. H. Auden, William Cooper, Mary McCarthy, Walter Allen, and Péter Veres contributed.

A290   Trilling, Diana. *Claremont Essays.* New York: Harcourt, Brace & World, 1964. "Diverse essays" unified by a "social" point of view. Edith Wharton, Virginia Woolf, Norman Mailer, Edward Albee, and others.

A291   Trilling, Lionel. *A Gathering of Fugitives.* Boston: Beacon Press, 1956. A collection of reprinted essays. Includes "The Great-Aunt of Mr. Forster," "In Defense of Zola," "The Morality of Inertia," "Edmund Wilson: A Backward Glance," "The Situation of the American Intellectual at the Present Time," "A Novel in Passing," "Dr. Leavis and the Moral Tradition," "The Novel Alive or Dead," and others.

A292   Trimmer, Joseph F. *Black American Literature: Notes on the Problem of Definition.* Muncie, Ind.: Ball State University Press, 1971. A discussion of the themes of the black writer as he relates to the human experience of being black in a white society, and a discussion of the aesthetic problems of the black artist. Ralph Ellison, Don L. Lee, James Baldwin, LeRoi Jones (Imamu Amiri Baraka), Eldridge Cleaver, and others.

A293   Turner, Darwin T., ed. *Black Literature: Essays.* Columbus, Ohio: Merrill, 1969. A collection of essays that reflects a search for black identity. Contributors include Langston Hughes, George S. Schuyler, Saunders Redding, Ralph Ellison, James Baldwin, John O. Killens, LeRoi Jones (Imamu Amiri Baraka), Eldridge Cleaver, and earlier writers. Bibliography.

A294   —————, and Barbara Dodds Stanford. *Theory and Practice in the Teaching of Literature by Afro-Americans.* Urbana, Ill.: NCTE, 1971. A "state-of-the-art" paper based on the ERIC data system which assesses the published and unpublished material relevant to the topic. This knowledge could be "a necessary foundation for reviewing existing curricula and planning new beginnings." Bibliography.

A295   Ulanov, Barry. *The Two Worlds of American Art: The Private and the Popular.* New York: Macmillan, 1965. A "study of the American Imagination during the first half of the twentieth century" and of America's "two cultures." Ulanov probes "into the American arts: literature, the popular novel, the avant-garde theater, jazz, classical music, musical comedy, abstract painting, movies, television, and so on."

A296   Vahanian, Gabriel. *Wait without Idols.* New York: Braziller, 1964. Vahanian's aim is "to illustrate the significance of theological insights into the nature of man and their rich relevance to an investigation of the domain of literature." Three points inform his study: first, "What makes the religious tradition of Western culture is also what accounts for the *Christian* quality of our literary tradition"; second, both literature and the Christian tradition are iconoclastic; and third, "the line of demarcation between God and the idol is a thin one." William Faulkner, T. S. Eliot, W. H. Auden, Fyodor Dostoevsky, Pär Lagerkvist, and earlier writers.

A297   Val Baker, Denys, ed. *Writers of To-Day*. London: Sidgwick
        & Jackson, 1946. Introductory essays containing bio-
        graphical and bibliographical information on the follow-
        ing: Aldous Huxley, Graham Greene, André Gide, James
        Joyce, Edith Sitwell, J. P. Priestley, Arthur Koestler, Fred-
        erico García Lorca, Dorothy Sayers, John Steinbeck, T. S.
        Eliot, and E. M. Forster.

A298   —————, ed. *Writers of To-Day: 2*. London: Sidgwick &
        Jackson, 1948. Introductory essays containing biographical
        and bibliographical information on the following: Ernest
        Hemingway, Jean-Paul Sartre, W. Somerset Maugham,
        Mulk Raj Anand, Virginia Woolf, Ignazio Silone, W. H.
        Auden, John Cowper Powys, Evelyn Waugh, H. E. Bates,
        Liam O'Flaherty, and Thomas Mann.

A299   Van Nostrand, A. D. *Everyman His Own Poet: Romantic
        Gospels in American Literature*. New York: McGraw-Hill,
        1968. Van Nostrand's topic is a group of writings that
        "dramatize a characteristic way of looking at one's self in
        the world that is generally called romantic." These writers
        "reveal a persistent overstatement of a romantic world
        view" that is peculiarly American, evangelical, and sounds
        like gospels or manuals of instruction. Each work "ex-
        presses its author's attempt to build a universal system out
        of words and make it function in fact." These cosmologies
        are dramatic fictions in which the writer uses a paradigm
        to convey the whole subject in all of its complexity. Wil-
        liam Faulkner, William Carlos Williams, and earlier
        writers.

A300   Vernon, John. *The Garden and the Map: Schizophrenia in
        Twentieth-Century Literature and Culture*. Urbana: Uni-
        versity of Illinois Press, 1973. "A significant shift in con-
        sciousness in the twentieth century" is the "realization that
        'reality' is simply one structure, one mode of experiencing
        the world, among many. The literature of fantasy in this
        century . . . can be fully understood only in terms of this
        shift." Western civilization is schizophrenic "in that it
        chooses to fragment its experience and seal certain areas
        off from each other." Schizophrenia, then, is a map of the
        world, the garden, that is reality. Culturally, we are mov-
        ing from the map to the garden, from "insane sanity to

sane insanity." Not a history, but an interpretative analysis. Theodore Roethke and William S. Burroughs, plus John Barth, Samuel Beckett, James Dickey, T. S. Eliot, R. D. Laing, Thomas Pynchon, Alain Robbe-Grillet, and Wallace Stevens. Bibliography.

A301   Vidal, Gore. *Rocking the Boat.* Boston: Little, Brown, 1962. Journalistic essays on "politics and writing and the theater." Eugene O'Neill, George Bernard Shaw, John Dos Passos, Norman Mailer, Ayn Rand, Carson McCullers, Friedrich Dürrenmatt, Robert Penn Warren, and others.

A302   Vogel, Dan. *The Three Masks of American Tragedy.* Baton Rouge: Louisiana State University Press, 1974. A study of the nature of tragedy, its continuity in theme and method, in a democratic culture. In addition to democracy, the pressures of the twentieth century have diminished the stature of the tragic figure. Yet the American tragic hero is based on three large models: Oedipus Tyrannos, Christ, and Satan. One chapter per model. Bibliography.

A303   Wager, Willis. *American Literature: A World View.* New York: New York University Press, 1968. Wager examines the "natural environment" of American literature and the "relationship between American-Indian and American-European literature." Columbus through T. S. Eliot, Eugene O'Neill, William Faulkner, Richard Wilbur, Edward Albee, Wright Morris, and others.

A304   Wain, John. *Essays on Literature and Ideas.* London: Macmillan, 1963. A collection of essays that originally appeared as book reviews. Includes "The Conflict of Forms in Contemporary English Literature," "T. S. Eliot," "Edmund Wilson," "R. P. Blackmur," "Cyril Connolly," "George Orwell," and others.

A305   Warren, Robert Penn. *Selected Essays.* New York: Random House, 1958. A collection of Warren's essays written between 1935 and 1950. Joseph Conrad, Samuel Taylor Coleridge, William Faulkner, Ernest Hemingway, Robert Frost, Katherine Anne Porter, Eudora Welty, Thomas Wolfe, and Herman Melville.

A306   Watkins, Floyd C. *The Flesh and the Word: Eliot, Hemingway, Faulkner.* Nashville: Vanderbilt University Press,

1971. "The embodiment or incarnation of meaning in image has been a chief element in style, in the struggle of literature to come to terms with life, and in the ultimate questions of religion. This book is the result of years of labor to understand the phenomenon in modern literature."

A307   Watts, Alan W. *Beat Zen, Square Zen, and Zen.* San Francisco: City Lights, 1959. A brief, disinterested discussion of the Zen of the beat writers, the Zen of the official Zen schools in Japan, and the spirit of Zen. Allen Ginsberg, Philip Whalen, Gary Snyder, and Jack Kerouac.

A308   Weimer, David R. *The City as Metaphor.* New York: Random House, 1966. "Designed as a critical introduction to major American writers on the city, this book has both the broad and narrow aims which that description implies." Covers the "neglected features of that native poetry and fiction in which the city figures prominently as theme or image." Stresses "the figurative uses to which the metropolis has been put, with the language in which it has been fixed." Walt Whitman, Henry James, Stephen Crane, Theodore Dreiser, e. e. cummings, F. Scott Fitzgerald, William Carlos Williams, and W. H. Auden. Suggested readings.

A309   West, Anthony. *Principles and Persuasions: The Literary Essays of Anthony West.* New York: Harcourt, Brace, 1957. Essays reprinted from the *New Yorker* on George Orwell, Graham Greene, Denis Johnston, Ralph Ellison, and many earlier writers.

A310   West, Ray B., Jr. *The Writer in the Room: Selected Essays.* East Lansing: Michigan State University Press, 1968. Essays, reprinted from literary journals, on Ezra Pound, Ernest Hemingway, William Faulkner, Katherine Anne Porter, Thomas Mann, Eudora Welty, and other earlier writers.

A311   Whitbread, Thomas B., ed. *Seven Contemporary Authors: Essays on Cozzens, Miller, West, Golding, Heller, Albee, and Powers.* Austin: University of Texas Press, 1966. Seven essays, originally delivered as the English Department Public Lectures for 1964–65 at the University of Texas. James Gould Cozzens, Henry Miller, Nathanael

West, William Golding, Joseph Heller, Edward Albee, and J. F. Powers.

A312 Whitlow, Roger. *Black American Literature: A Critical History with a 1,520-title Bibliography of Works Written by and about Black Americans.* Chicago: Nelson Hall, 1973. A historical approach divided into seven periods from the oral tradition to the present. Because the black tradition was formed outside the white tradition, "black writing can best be understood and appreciated when studied separately from other American literature." Richard Wright, Ralph Ellison, James Baldwin, Gwendolyn Brooks, Ossie Davis, Ishmael Reed, Imamu Amiri Baraka (LeRoi Jones), Nikki Giovanni, John A. Williams, and others.

A313 Wilder, Amos N. *Theology and Modern Literature.* Cambridge, Mass.: Harvard University Press, 1958. Examines the contributions that secular art can make to faith. Wilder argues that "all imaginative creations from the oldest myth and ritual to the most recent poem . . . offer 'news of reality.' It is in this respect that modern literature opens itself to theological and moral scrutiny."

A314 Williams, Duncan. *Trousered Apes.* New Rochelle, N.Y.: Arlington House, 1971. Traces the fall of contemporary society—"when men lose sight of their eternal significance, and of their dependence on God"—from the security of the eighteenth century. Through a study of literature, Williams shows what happens to man when he forgets his God. Mostly European and early authors. T. S. Eliot and John Osborne; brief discussions of others. Bibliography.

A315 Williams, Raymond. *Modern Tragedy.* Stanford: Stanford University Press, 1966. A history and criticism of tragedy followed by an examination of modern tragic literature. Henrik Ibsen, Arthur Miller, August Strindberg, Eugene O'Neill, Tennessee Williams, Samuel Beckett, T. S. Eliot, Boris Pasternak, Albert Camus, Bertolt Brecht, and others.

A316 Williams, William Carlos. *Selected Essays of William Carlos Williams.* New York: New Directions, 1969. Critical essays written between 1920 and 1954. Includes "Prologue to Kora in Hell," "A Point for American Criticism," "The Simplicity of Disorder," "Marianne Moore," "Pound's

Eleven New 'Cantos,' " "The Poem as a Field of Action,"
and thirty-six others.

A317   Wilson, Colin. *The Strength to Dream: Literature and the
        Imagination.* London: Victor Gollancz, 1962. Studies a
        great many writers in an attempt to define the imagination.
        Wilson attempts to develop general laws apart from "the
        eccentricities and imprecisions of different imaginations."
        H. P. Lovecraft, W. B. Yeats, Oscar Wilde, August Strind-
        berg, Nathanael West, William Faulkner, Evelyn Waugh,
        Graham Greene, Jean-Paul Sartre, Alain Robbe-Grillet,
        Nathalie Sarraute, Leonid Andreyev, Samuel Beckett, H. G.
        Wells, E. T. A. Hoffman, J. R. R. Tolkien, D. H. Law-
        rence, and others.

A318   Wilson, Edmund. *The Bit between My Teeth: A Literary
        Chronicle of 1950–1965.* New York: Farrar, Straus &
        Giroux, 1966. A collection of Wilson's critical essays. Top-
        ics include John Peale Bishop, George Bernard Shaw, Max
        Beerbohm, Mario Praz, W. H. Auden, T. S. Eliot, Boris
        Pasternak, Dawn Powell, and many others.

A319   Wright, George T., ed. *Seven American Stylists from Poe to
        Mailer: An Introduction.* Minneapolis: University of
        Minnesota, 1973. Reprints of University of Minnesota
        Pamphlets on American Writers. All seven writers tend to
        "look to style as a resource against what seems to some
        of them the meaninglessness or the prison of history." "As
        the external world grows more uncertain, as experience
        seems more and more the only guide we have, and our own
        experience the only reliable guide, writers of talent . . . re-
        member and record the turns and tremors of consciousness."
        Focuses upon the connections between writers' lives and
        their styles. Vladimir Nabokov, Robert Penn Warren,
        Norman Mailer, and others. Bibliography.

A320   *Writers at Work: The Paris Review Interviews.* Edited by
        Malcolm Cowley. New York: Viking, 1958. Authors inter-
        viewed: E. M. Forster, François Mauriac, Joyce Cary,
        Dorothy Parker, James Thurber, Thornton Wilder, Wil-
        liam Faulkner, Georges Simenon, Frank O'Connor, Robert
        Penn Warren, Alberto Moravia, Nelson Algren, Angus Wil-
        son, William Styron, Truman Capote, and Françoise Sagan.

A321   *Writers at Work: The Paris Review Interviews.* Second Series. Edited by George Plimpton. New York: Viking, 1963. Authors interviewed are Robert Frost, Ezra Pound, Marianne Moore, T. S. Eliot, Boris Pasternak, Katherine Anne Porter, Henry Miller, Aldous Huxley, Ernest Hemingway, S. J. Perelman, Lawrence Durrell, Mary McCarthy, Ralph Ellison, and Robert Lowell.

A322   *Writers at Work: The Paris Review Interviews.* Third Series. Edited by George Plimpton. New York: Viking, 1967. Authors interviewed are William Carlos Williams, Blaise Cendrars, Jean Cocteau, Louis-Ferdinand Céline, Evelyn Waugh, Lillian Hellman, William Burroughs, Saul Bellow, Arthur Miller, James Jones, Norman Mailer, Allen Ginsberg, Edward Albee, and Harold Pinter.

A323   *Writers on Themselves.* London: British Broadcasting Corporation, 1964. Talks originally broadcast in the BBC Home Service in which the authors describe their first "awareness of a vocation." Norman Nicholson, Rebecca West, William Sansom, Emanual Litvinoff, Vernon Scannell, Thomas Hinde, John Bowen, Richard Murphy, Michael Baldwin, Julian Mitchell, Ted Hughes, David Storey, and Sylvia Plath.

A324   Zolla, Elémire. *The Writer and the Shaman: A Morphology of the American Indian.* Translated by Raymond Rosenthal. New York: Harcourt Brace Jovanovich, 1969. "The history of the many images of the Indian that appear in the course of American literature sets a whole series of works . . . in an unusual, revelatory perspective." Because the works are linked by forms rather than chronology, this is "not so much a history as a morphology." Concludes with a discussion of the emergence of an Indian literature. William Faulkner, Carlos Castaneda, William Eastlake, John Barth, Leonard Cohen, Thomas Berger, Walter van Tilburg Clark, and Ken Kesey.

A325   Zukofsky, Louis. *Prepositions: The Collected Essays of Louis Zukofsky.* New York: Horizon, 1967. Essays on poetry, William Carlos Williams, Lewis Carroll, Ezra Pound, Henry Adams, and other topics.

B

Drama

B1   Abramson, Doris E. *Negro Playwrights in the American The-
      atre, 1925–1959.* New York: Columbia University Press,
      1969. A thematic and topical study of plays written by
      American Negroes and produced in the New York profes-
      sional theater between 1925 and 1959. A study of the Ne-
      gro's vision of himself, dealing with such figures as Langston
      Hughes, Richard Wright, James Baldwin, Alice Childress,
      Joseph S. Cotter, Ossie Davis, Marc Connelly, Lorraine
      Hansberry, Adrienne Kennedy, LeRoi Jones (Imamu
      Amiri Baraka), and others. Bibliography.

B2   Ansorge, Peter. *Disrupting the Spectacle: Five Years of Ex-
      perimental and Fringe Theatre in Britain.* London: Pit-
      man, 1975. Ansorge began watching the experimental
      theater in 1972 and now feels these writers are different
      from their predecessors. "It is the purpose of this short
      book to describe the directions in which many of our fresh-
      est theatrical talents have moved over the past five years."
      Brief essays on Howard Brenton, David Hare, Snoo Wil-
      son, Nancy Meckler, Pip Simmons, Charles Marowitz, John
      McGrath, Trevor Griffiths, David Edgar. Also discussed:
      John Arden, Ed Berman, Edward Bond, Peter Handke,
      John Osborne, Harold Pinter, Sam Shepard, Arnold
      Wesker, Chris Wilkinson, Heathcote Williams, and others.
      Bibliography.

B3   Armstrong, William A., ed. *Experimental Drama.* London:
      Bell, 1963. A collection of essays based upon a series of
      lectures on "Experimental Drama, 1945–1961" given at the
      University of London. Christopher Fry, T. S. Eliot, Sean
      O'Casey, Brendan Behan, Thomas Murphy, Robert Bolt,
      John Whiting, Samuel Beckett, Harold Pinter, John Os-
      borne, Arnold Wesker, Keith Waterhouse, Willis Hall,
      John Arden, N. F. Simpson, and others.

B4   *Aspects of Drama and the Theatre: Five Kathleen Robinson Lectures Delivered in the University of Sydney, 1961–63.* Sydney: Sydney University Press, 1965. Five selections from the twenty-one Kathleen Robinson lectures. Each essay deals with a central theme of the following authors: Eugène Ionesco, Jean-Paul Sartre, Bertolt Brecht, Antonin Artaud, Samuel Beckett, Harold Pinter, and John Osborne.

B5   Atkinson, J. Brooks. *Broadway.* New York: Macmillan, 1970. A pictorial history of the Broadway theater from 1900 to 1970. Covers the plays produced, the actors, the influence of the theater, critical reception, attitudes towards Broadway, world events, and the fall of legitimate theater.

B6   —————. *Broadway Scrapbook.* New York: Theatre Arts, 1947. Selected reviews of plays that appeared on Broadway between 1935 and 1947. Contains satiric drawings of actors by Al Hirschfeld.

B7   —————, and Albert Hirschfeld. *The Lively Years: 1920–1973.* New York: Association Press, 1973. Reviews "of the plays that have given the modern theatre a new dimension" and made it a "part of our cultural life since World War I." Atkinson contends that the war experience influenced the theater to take an adversary role; the war era produced plays "that criticize life, that wrestle with the dilemmas of civilized life." For Atkinson, plays should draw people out of themselves "into an imagined world in which wit, humor, romance, excitement, and audacity are as valid as reality."

B8   Aylen, Leo. *Greek Tragedy and the Modern World.* London: Methuen, 1964. Aylen challenges Fergusson's *The Idea of a Theater* and Steiner's *The Death of Tragedy* and then corrects the false notions we have about Greek tragedy. Finally, he examines the possibilities of modern tragic writing. Henry Miller, Jean Cocteau, André Gide, Jean Giraudoux, Jean Anouilh, Jean-Paul Sartre, Henri Ghéon, and T. S. Eliot. Bibliography.

B9   Baxter, Kay M. *Contemporary Theatre and the Christian Faith.* New York: Abingdon, 1964. "The aim of this short book is to observe the points at which the 'new' theatre can illuminate some of the problems which Christians face in understanding and communicating their faith." Edward Albee, Samuel Beckett, T. S. Eliot, Graham Greene, Arthur Miller, Archibald MacLeish, John Osborne, George Bernard Shaw, and Tennessee Williams.

B10 Bentley, Eric. *In Search of the Theater*. New York: Knopf, 1953. Responses and appraisals of the theaters in several countries. Bentley also pays tribute to the outstanding careers of George Bernard Shaw, Stark Young, Jacques Copeau, and Henrik Ibsen. Other essays are about Tennessee Williams, Eugene O'Neill, Jean-Louis Barrault, Martha Graham, and others.

B11 —————. *The Theatre of Commitment and Other Essays on Drama in Our Society*. New York: Atheneum, 1967. A collection of essays on Ibsen, American drama (1944–1954), the political theater, the theater of commitment, and other topics.

B12 —————. *Theatre of War: Comments on 32 Occasions*. New York: Viking, 1972. Bentley's reviews record his responses to the "great stage" of the world and "the little stage of the theatre." He contends that "the two are one." Reviews are divided into three sections: "The Life of Modern Drama," "The Drama of Modern Life," "Living Theatre in a Dying World."

B13 —————. *What is Theatre? A Query in Chronicle Form*. London: Dennis Dobson, 1957. A collection of Bentley's play reviews from 1954 to 1956.

B14 —————. *What is Theatre? Incorporating the Dramatic Event and Other Reviews, 1944–1967*. New York: Atheneum, 1968. Journalistic reviews on drama.

B15 Bermel, Albert. *Contradictory Characters: An Interpretation of the Modern Theatre*. New York: Dutton, 1973. Each chapter of this work focuses on "the theatrical nature" of a given play. It attempts to escape the recent traps of biography and philosophy that drama critics have fallen into. Instead, its primary concern is how characterization determines the structure and the content of a play. From Henrik Ibsen and August Strindberg through Bertolt Brecht and Antonin Artaud to Samuel Beckett, Harold Pinter, LeRoi Jones (Imamu Amiri Baraka), and George Bernard Shaw.

B16   Bigsby, C. W. E. *Confrontation and Commitment: A Study of Contemporary American Drama, 1959–1966.* [Columbia:] University of Missouri Press, 1968. The dramatists of confrontation believe in the need to confront a nihilistic vision of the world and to accept its freedom. With this renewal of social commitment, dramatists experimented with metaphysical drama. Bigsby contends that these new dramatists turned away from the traditions of Ibsen and Chekhov and, with their willingness to experiment, liberated the American theater. Arthur Miller, Edward Albee, James Baldwin, LeRoi Jones (Imamu Amiri Baraka), Lorraine Hansberry, Jack Gelber, and Kenneth Brown. Bibliography.

B17   Blau, Herbert. *The Impossible Theater: A Manifesto.* New York: Macmillan, 1964. "The purpose of this book is to talk up a revolution." The first part is a series of chapters of "more or less invidious comparisons, complaints, warnings, exordia, and exhortations" relating to the American theater and the world. In the second part, Blau uses the San Francisco theater and its milieu as his main example in the discussion of the theater against the backdrop of the Cold War.

B18   Bogard, Travis, and William I. Oliver, eds. *Modern Drama: Essays in Criticism.* New York: Oxford University Press, 1965. Essays that "offer the reader a sense of the central direction of the important writers for the modern theatre and of major contemporary critical interpretations of their immediate forerunners." Arthur Miller, Eugene O'Neill, Luigi Pirandello, Jean-Paul Sartre, George Bernard Shaw, Thornton Wilder, Tennessee Williams, Jean Anouilh, Bertolt Brecht, Jean Genet, Jean Giraudoux, Frederico García Lorca, and others.

B19   Brockett, Oscar G. *History of the Theatre.* 2nd ed. Boston: Allyn & Bacon, 1974. Traces the development of the European and American theater from its beginning until 1973. Brief treatment of numerous figures. Bibliography.

B20 ——————. *Perspectives on Contemporary Theatre.* Baton Rouge: Louisiana State University Press, 1971. The result of a series of lectures delivered at a conference held by the Department of Speech at Louisiana State University. Designed for the generalist, not the specialist, the book attempts to explain the contemporary theater, first, by studying "current practices and issues," and second, by explaining the background forces that produced today's theater. Antonin Artaud, Samuel Beckett, Bertolt Brecht, Arthur Miller, and others.

B21 ——————, and Robert R. Findlay. *Century of Innovation: A History of European and American Theatre and Drama since 1870.* Englewood Cliffs, N.J.: Prentice-Hall, 1973. An eight-hundred-page history of modern drama that focuses on societal influences, dramaturgy, dramatists, theoreticians, and audiences. Discusses hundreds of authors, among them: Arthur Adamov, Edward Albee, Robert Anderson, Jean Anouilh, John Arden, Fernando Arrabal, Antonin Artaud, Jacques Audiberti, Jean-Louis Barrault, Samuel Beckett, Ugo Betti, François Billetdoux, Robert Bolt, Antonion Buero Vallejo, Ed Bullins, Albert Camus, Noel Coward, Friedrich Dürrenmatt, T. S. Eliot, Paul Foster, Christopher Fry, Jean Genet, Günter Grass, Eugène Ionesco, LeRoi Jones (Imamu Amiri Baraka), Arthur Kopit, Arthur Miller, Henry de Montherlant, René Obaldia, John Osborne, Harold Pinter, Terence Rattigan, Jean-Paul Sartre, Alfonso Sastre, Georges Schehadé, Neil Simon, Norman Frederick Simpson, Martin Sperr, Tom Stoppard, Jean Tardieu, Peter Terson, Peter Weiss, and Tennessee Williams. Bibliography.

B22 Broussard, Louis. *American Drama: Contemporary Allegory from Eugene O'Neill to Tennessee Williams.* Norman: University of Oklahoma Press, 1962. Broussard's book proposes, first, "to establish the attitude of American drama towards contemporary man," second, to trace "the evolution of the allegorical play in America, [third,] to suggest the influences which went into its creation, and [fourth,] to relate the example in question to other works by the same author and to other forms of contemporary expression with the same theme." Eugene O'Neill, Elmer Rice, John Howard Lawson, Philip Barry, T. S. Eliot, Thornton Wilder,

Robert E. Sherwood, Tennessee Williams, Arthur Miller, and Archibald MacLeish. Bibliography.

B23   Brown, John Mason. *Dramatis Personae: A Retrospective Show*. New York: Viking, 1963. Includes a historical survey (from 1820 to 1920), essays about the theater, and essays about the violently changing decades after 1920. Clifford Odets, Maxwell Anderson, Thornton Wilder, Tennessee Williams, Arthur Miller, T. S. Eliot, Edward Albee, and others.

B24   Brown, John Russell. *Theatre Language: A Study of Arden, Osborne, Pinter and Wesker*. New York: Taplinger, 1972. Brown studies four dramatists and examines "how they have made the theatre speak." "*Theatre Language* is . . . no 'Guide' or 'Survey' to new English theatre. It looks closely . . . at important contemporary plays by authors who have sustained a writing career for more than ten years in a changing world." Primary bibliography.

B25   ————, ed. *Modern British Dramatists: A Collection of Critical Essays*. Englewood Cliffs, N.J.: Prentice-Hall, 1968. Essays on the breakthrough and establishment of new modes of playwriting in the 1950s and '60s and on the influence of Beckett and Whiting. Brown collects these essays to "relate new works to each other and to our understanding of man, society, and history." John Osborne, Harold Pinter, John Arden, and Arnold Wesker. Bibliography.

B26   ————, and Bernard Harris, eds. *American Theatre*. Stratford-upon-Avon Studies 10. New York: St. Martin's, 1967. Ten essays by five American and five British authors on general themes in the American theater: realism, European influence, theatrical writing of poets, economic and social pressures on dramatists. "The aim is to provide not one view but several, to use different approaches, to concentrate attention on individual writers, on influences, on ideological and social conditions, on theatrical idioms and on theatrical history." Essays on Edward Albee, Eugene O'Neill, Arthur Miller, and Tennessee Williams. Also studied are Samuel Beckett, Paddy Chayefsky, Harold Churman, T. S. Eliot, William Inge, Archibald MacLeish, Harold Pinter, and Thornton Wilder. Bibliography.

B27   ————, and Bernard Harris, eds. *Contemporary Theatre*.

Stratford-upon-Avon Studies 4. London: Edward Arnold, 1962. Nine authors deal with the theater historically, technically, and thematically. Specifically, they deal with such issues as verse theater, the long career of George Bernard Shaw, the influence of "romantic and Existentialist ideas on some plays," comparisons between British and European dramatists, and the Irish theater. Arnold Wesker, Harold Pinter, Bertolt Brecht, John Arden, George Bernard Shaw, Samuel Beckett, Brendan Behan, Robert Bolt, Paddy Chayefsky, T. S. Eliot, Christopher Fry, Sean O'Casey, and John Osborne.

B28   Brustein, Robert. *The Culture Watch: Essays on Theatre and Society, 1969–1974.* New York: Knopf, 1975. Brustein sees the theater as the fundamental metaphor of American life. Thus, he watches culture through "the prism of the theatre." The focus of these essays is upon the symptoms of "culture leveling," for the theater, music, dance, and literature are falling prey to popularization. Brustein expresses alarm concerning what he calls "cultural Schizophrenia: the simultaneous desire of the artists to be serious and respected and, at the same time, stars on the celebrity circuit." John Arden, Samuel Beckett, Robert Brustein, T. S. Eliot, Arthur Miller, John Osborne, George Bernard Shaw, Sam Shephard, and others.

B29   ————. *Seasons of Discontent: Dramatic Opinions, 1959–1965.* New York: Simon & Schuster, 1965. A collection of reviews and articles written for the *New Republic.* Because of the "absence of distinguished drama on the American stage," Brustein was unable to fulfill his role as critic— evaluating and elucidating works—and found himself trying to identify the "obstacles in the way of a genuine dramatic art." Over seventy pieces on performances from 1959 to 1965.

B30   ————. *The Third Theatre.* New York: Knopf, 1969. A collection of essays written between 1957 and 1968 on the theater, literature, culture, and the movies. The book takes its title from the new theater that developed in opposition to the Broadway theater. Brustein argues that this new theater has taken a wrong turn, abandoning language, form, and accomplishment "in favor of an easy instant culture." Edward Albee, Arthur Miller, John Osborne, Jean-Paul Sartre, and others.

B31   Chiari, J. *Landmarks of Contemporary Drama*. London: Herbert Jenkins, 1965. Delineates the main aspects of the drama performed since World War II. Chiari relates these plays to one another and to Western civilization. Jean-Paul Sartre, Jean Anouilh, Paul Claudel, Eugène Ionesco, Arthur Adamov, Samuel Beckett, T. S. Eliot, Christopher Fry, Bertolt Brecht, John Obsorne, Arnold Wesker, Harold Pinter, John Whiting, John Arden, Eugene O'Neill, Tennessee Williams, Arthur Miller, and Edward Albee.

B32   Clurman, Harold. *Lies like Truth: Theatre Reviews and Essays*. New York: Macmillan, 1958. Theater reviews written between 1947 and 1957 on American, English, French, and German playwrights.

B33   —————. *The Naked Image: Observations on the Modern Theatre*. New York: Macmillan, 1966. For Clurman, "the primary obligation of the critic is *to define* the character of the object he is called upon to judge." Reviews and essays on Edward Albee, Jean Anouilh, James Baldwin, Samuel Beckett, Brendan Behan, Saul Bellow, Robert Bolt, Bertolt Brecht, Albert Camus, Shelagh Delaney, Jean Genet, Jean Giraudoux, Rolf Hochhuth, Eugène Ionesco, Ann Jellicoe, LeRoi Jones (Imamu Amiri Baraka), Robert Lowell, Eugene O'Neill, John Osborne, Harold Pinter, Murry Schisgal, Peter Weiss, and Tennessee Williams.

B34   Cohn, Ruby. *Currents in Contemporary Drama*. Bloomington: Indiana University Press, 1969. A study of contemporary drama in English, French, and German. After tracing the "cross-national currents," Cohn studies several trends: dialogue of cruelty, heroes, myths, anti-heroes, mixed modes, and the stage as a metaphor for life. Numerous authors; some are: Edward Albee, Jean Anouilh, Fernando Arrabal, Antonin Artaud, Samuel Beckett, Paul Claudel, T. S. Eliot, Jean Genet, Eugène Ionesco, Arthur Miller, John Osborne, Harold Pinter, Jean-Paul Sartre, Peter Weiss, and Tennessee Williams. Bibliography.

B35   —————. *Dialogue in American Drama*. Bloomington: Indiana University Press, 1971. Even though Antonin Artaud's rejection of dialogue as a dramatic device seems to dominate the American stage, Cohn takes a "backward glance" at the Aristotelian notion that "dialogue furthers plot and reveals character." She studies the work of four dramatists who have "written original and distinctive dramatic dialogue": Eugene O'Neill, Arthur Miller, Tennessee Williams, and Edward Albee. Bibliography.

B36   Cole, Toby, ed. *Playwrights on Playwriting: The Meaning and Making of Modern Drama from Ibsen to Ionesco.* New York: Hill & Wang, 1960. Essays by playwrights who have addressed themselves to the art and craft of playwriting. Includes essays that reflect the modern dramatist's search for form toward and away from realism, as well as notes on their own plays. Henrik Ibsen, Emile Zola, August Strindberg, Anton Chekhov, Maurice Maeterlinck, W. B. Yeats, George Bernard Shaw, Frederico García Lorca, Jean Giraudoux, Eugene O'Neill, Bertolt Brecht, Thornton Wilder, Jean-Paul Sartre, Christopher Fry, Friedrich Dürrenmatt, John Osborne, Eugène Ionesco, William Synge, Luigi Pirandello, Ernst Toller, Jean Cocteau, Sean O'Casey, T. S. Eliot, Arthur Miller, and Tennessee Williams. Bibliography.

B37   Corrigan, Robert W. *The Theatre in Search of a Fix.* New York: Delacorte, 1973. The title refers to the drug culture of the '60s. Corrigan contends that this period presents issues that the theater must face up to. The book is organized in four parts: the "Classical Solution," the "Modernist Dilemma," the "Theatre in a Collective Society," and contemporary possibilities. Henrik Ibsen, August Strindberg, Anton Chekhov, Bertolt Brecht, Ugo Betti, Thornton Wilder, John Arden, Arthur Miller, and others.

B38   ————, ed. *Theatre in the Twentieth Century.* New York: Grove, 1963. A guide to the complexities of the modern theater. Essays deal with the writing, producing, and criticizing of plays. Contributors are Eugène Ionesco, Christopher Fry, Jean Vilar, Theodore Hoffman, Bertolt Brecht, Ugo Betti, Ronald Peacock, Arthur Miller, Hugo von Hofmannsthal, Jean-Paul Sartre, Robert W. Corrigan, Sigmund Freud, John Gassner, Martin Esslin, Eric Bentley, and others.

B39   Croyden, Margaret. *Lunatics, Lovers, and Poets: The Contemporary Experimental Theatre.* New York: McGraw-Hill, 1974. This book is intended to give the "theatregoer and student of the theatre a historical and social perspective as well as an aesthetic evaluation and description of a phenomenon of the 1960's—a theatre that did not depend on the playwright." Croyden delineates influences from the past on the modern avant-garde authors and analyzes their work. Antonin Artaud, Julian Beck, Peter Brook, Joseph Chaikin, and Jerzy Grotowski. Bibliography.

B40   Dane, Clemence, *pseud.* [Winifred Ashton]. *Approaches to Drama.* London: Oxford University Press, 1961. Studies drama since the development of cinema, radio, and television. Dane examines historical forces as influences upon drama, and contemporary drama's tendency to encourage audience passivity.

B41   Dennis, Nigel. *Dramatic Essays.* London: Weidenfeld & Nicolson, 1962. A series of essays from *Encounter* that deal with plays, playwrights, productions, and actors. Dennis bases these essays upon the assumption that imaginative presentation is better than imitative theater. Tennessee Williams, Harold Pinter, Eugène Ionesco, Samuel Beckett, N. F. Simpson, George Bernard Shaw, Noel Coward, Kenneth Tynan, T. S. Eliot, Jean-Paul Sartre, John Osborne, and others.

B42   Dickinson, Hugh. *Myth on the Modern Stage.* Urbana: University of Illinois Press, 1969. Studies ten dramatists who wrote plays based on classical myths of Greece and Rome: André Gide, Jean Cocteau, Robinson Jeffers, Eugene O'Neill, Jean Giraudoux, T. S. Eliot, Jean-Paul Sartre, Jean Anouilh, Tennessee Williams, and Eugène Ionesco. Bibliography.

B43   Donoghue, Denis. *The Third Voice: Modern British and American Verse Drama.* Princeton: Princeton University Press, 1959. Poetic drama reveals the relationship between the "scene" and the moral "act" because such relationships are "the immediate, local manifestations of the unity which is the 'poetry' of the play. A play is 'poetic,' then, when its concrete elements (plot, agency, scene, speech, gesture) continuously exhibit in their internal relationships those qualities of mutual coherence and illumination required of the words of a poem." Donoghue contends that modern writers fail to grasp this unity. W. H. Auden, e. e. cummings, T. S. Eliot, Christopher Fry, Wallace Stevens, Richard Eberhart, Archibald MacLeish, and Ezra Pound.

B44   Downer, Alan S. *Fifty Years of American Drama: 1900–1950.* Chicago: Regnery, 1951. A survey of drama that analyzes "where it came from, how it developed, and where it arrived." Describes American theater as an art grown out of a people and its customs through an assertion of independence from transatlantic forms and conventions. Suggested readings.

B45   ————. *Recent American Drama.* Minneapolis: University of Minnesota Press, 1961. Downer's pamphlet surveys the dramatic techniques in, and subjects of, plays since World War II. Bibliography.

B46   ————, ed. *American Drama and Its Critics: A Collection of Critical Essays.* Chicago: University of Chicago Press, 1965. Essays selected "to illustrate the variety of critical experiences that accompanied the development of the modern American theater." Clifford Odets, Maxwell Anderson, Tennessee Williams, Arthur Miller, Edward Albee, and earlier writers.

B47   ————, ed. *The American Theater Today.* New York: Basic Books, 1967. A collection of essays on the background of the American theater, Broadway, playwrights, off-Broadway, and the future of the American theater.

B48   Driver, Tom F. *Romantic Quest and Modern Query: A History of the Modern Theatre.* New York: Delacorte, 1970. A historical survey that illuminates "the struggle of the modern" in the theater, and its meaning for modern culture. Driver states his historical thesis: "the modern theatre can best be interpreted as a paradigm of the development of modern consciousness in Europe and America." Henrik Ibsen, Anton Chekhov, George Bernard Shaw, Luigi Pirandello, Bertolt Brecht, Jean Genet, Samuel Beckett, Tennessee Williams, Arthur Kennedy, Jack Gelber, Edward Albee, Christopher Fry, Graham Greene, T. S. Eliot, Thornton Wilder, and others. Bibliography.

B49   Duprey, Richard A. *Just off the Aisle: The Ramblings of a Catholic Critic.* Westminster, Md.: Newman, 1962. A thematic discussion of contemporary drama and motion pictures from the perspective of Catholicism. Duprey explains what the Catholic "position" is; then, he applies it to various issues, such as the quest, violence, sex, and comedy. In the process he discusses Edward Albee, Robert Bolt, T. S. Eliot, Jean Genet, Eugène Ionesco, Archibald MacLeish, Arthur Miller, Eugene O'Neill, George Bernard Shaw, Thornton Wilder, Tennessee Williams, and others.

B50   Dusenbury, Winifred L. [Frazer]. *The Theme of Loneliness in Modern American Drama.* Gainesville: University of Florida Press, 1960. Playwrights today use the theme of loneliness "as a reflection of present-day American Life." Dusenbury divides her analysis into eight categories: "Personal Failure," "Homelessness," "An Unhappy Family," "The Failure of a Love Affair," "Socioeconomic Forces," "In the South," "Conflict between the Material and Spiritual," and "The Lonely Hero." William Inge, Arthur Miller, Eugene O'Neill, Carson McCullers, Philip Barry, Elmer Rice, Maxwell Anderson, Lillian Hellman, William Saroyan, and others. Bibliography.

B51   Eliot, T. S. *The Aims of Poetic Drama: The Presidential Address to the Poets' Theatre Guild.* London: Galleon, 1949. Discusses poetic drama in contemporary terms.

B52   ————. *Poetry and Drama.* Cambridge, Mass.: Harvard University Press, 1951. In this short work Eliot studies the aesthetic and rhetorical dimensions of poetic drama. He also views his own career as a playwright.

B53   Ellison, Jerome. *God on Broadway.* Richmond, Va.: Knox, 1971. A study of how man's "sense of strangeness" informs the "twentieth-century American commercial theater." Each essay contains biographical information about the playwright, an overview of his work, an analysis of one play that illustrates man's "relation to Deity," and a "classification of the playwright's view of Deity according to the history of religion, and according to the psychology of C. G. Jung." Eugene O'Neill, Thornton Wilder, Archibald MacLeish, Tennessee Williams, Arthur Miller, Edward Albee, Paddy Chayefsky, and others.

B54   Elsom, John. *Erotic Theatre.* New York: Taplinger, 1974. A contrast of the sexual morals in plays and entertainments during two periods of time: 1890 to 1910 and 1950 to 1972. While the book deals with changing social patterns, it is primarily a book on theater. Edward Albee, Antonin Artaud, Bertolt Brecht, Jean Genet, Arthur Miller, Harold Pinter, Paul Raymond, G. A. Redford, and Tennessee Williams.

B55   Esslin, Martin. *Brief Chronicles: Essays on Modern Theatre.* London: Temple Smith, 1970. A collection of articles, lectures, contributions, introductions, and interviews on the theater. Deals mainly with European dramatists, but all discussions pertain to the theater in general. Discusses such topics as violence, nudity, absurdity, the happening, and the mass media. Edward Albee, John Arden, Samuel Beckett, Robert Bolt, T. S. Eliot, and others.

B56   ————. *Reflections: Essays on Modern Theatre.* Garden City, N.Y.: Doubleday, 1969. A collection of Esslin's articles, lectures, essays, introductions to volume of plays, and interviews. His critical emphasis is upon drama as it "sheds light" on the whole of society. Henrik Ibsen, Luigi Pirandello, Bertolt Brecht, Max Frisch, Eugène Ionesco, Friedrich Dürrenmatt, Rolf Hochhuth, Günter Grass, Peter Weiss, and Samuel Beckett.

B57   ————. *The Theatre of the Absurd.* Rev. ed. Woodstock, N.Y.: Overlook Press, 1973. Esslin shows the development of the contemporary theater, defines the theater of the absurd, and provides an analysis and elucidation of the meaning of major plays. He contends that an understanding of the theater of the absurd sheds light on science, psychology, and philosophy, for the theater is the point of intersection of many fields. Samuel Beckett, Arthur Adamov, Eugène Ionesco, Jean Genet, Jean Tardieu, Boris Vian, Dino Buzzati, Ezio d'Errico, Günter Grass, Harold Pinter, Jack Gelber, Edward Albee, Norman Frederick Simpson, and others. Primary bibliography.

B58   Falb, Lewis W. *American Drama in Paris, 1945–1970: A Study of Its Critical Reception.* Chapel Hill: University of North Carolina Press, 1973. A history of the reception of American drama in France. Falb's study is an attempt "to document the French reaction to post–World War II American drama." Eugene O'Neill, Tennessee Williams, Arthur Miller, and a survey of many others. Bibliography.

B59 Fergusson, Francis. *The Human Image in Dramatic Literature.* Gloucester, Mass.: Peter Smith, 1969. Fergusson studies drama as it reflects "the human image" and the writer as he is engaged with human life. For Fergusson, the "life" of the play reflects the poet's vision, that which is derived from many experiences. Hence, we can only hold a writer responsible for what he really and intimately sees. Essays on the modern theater, Shakespeare, and critical attitudes. Kenneth Burke, Bertolt Brecht, Thornton Wilder, T. S. Eliot, James Joyce, and others.

B60 Findlater, Richard. *The Unholy Trade.* London: Victor Gallancz, 1952. A study of the British theater with emphasis upon "the influence of economic facts." Findlater describes the scope of his work: "The book attempts to show the evils of the theatre today and to suggest remedies; to outline the theory and practice of the component parts; to consider them in their social and historical setting; and to provide detailed criticism of some contemporary dramatists." W. H. Auden, T. S. Eliot, Christopher Fry, W. Somerset Maugham, Arthur Miller, Tennessee Williams, and others. Bibliography.

B61 Freedman, Morris. *American Drama in Social Context.* Carbondale: Southern Illinois University Press, 1971. Eight essays on drama and its social context. Essays on T. S. Eliot, LeRoi Jones (Imamu Amiri Baraka), and the "new Senecanism." Edward Albee, Jean Genet, Arthur Miller, Eugene O'Neill, John Osborne, Tennessee Williams, and others. Bibliography.

B62 —————. *The Moral Impulse: Modern Drama from Ibsen to the Present.* Carbondale: Southern Illinois University Press, 1968. Freedman sees the modern theater as one of moral ideas. Absurdist drama is the descendant of the moral impulse which characterized Henrik Ibsen, George Bernard Shaw, and Anton Chekhov. Freedman's study is both a treatment of individual playwrights and a survey of the modern theater. Edward Albee, Samuel Beckett,

Arthur Miller, Harold Pinter, George Bernard Shaw, Tennessee Williams, and earlier figures.

B63   ————, ed. *Essays in the Modern Drama*. Boston: D. C. Heath, 1964. Freedman puts emphasis upon drama as literature. This collection presents "an exhibition of the immensely varied, infinitely layered nature of our repsonse to drama." Henrik Ibsen, Anton Chekhov, George Bernard Shaw, Luigi Pirandello, Eugene O'Neill, Oscar Wilde, Sean O'Casey, Bertolt Brecht, Clifford Odets, Jean-Paul Sartre, Friedrich Dürrenmatt, John Osborne, Samuel Beckett, Arthur Miller, T. S. Eliot, Tennessee Williams, Christopher Fry, Thornton Wilder, and others.

B64   Frenz, Horst, ed. *American Playwrights on Drama*. New York: Hill & Wang, 1965. Twentieth-century American playwrights discuss the various problems of the American theater and give their impressions of the contemporary state of drama. Contributors include Eugene O'Neill, Maxwell Anderson, John Howard Lawson, Thornton Wilder, Tennessee Williams, Paul Green, Arthur Miller, William Inge, Robinson Jeffers, S. N. Behrman, Archibald MacLeish, Elmer Rice, Lorraine Hansberry, and Edward Albee.

B65   Gard, Robert E.; Marson Balch; and Pauline B. Temkin. *Theater in America: Appraisal and Challenge*. Madison, Wisc.: Dembar Educational Research Services, 1968. A "critical overview" of the theater in the 1960s. "Its panorama takes in current developments and trends in the theater's main sectors of commercial, community, educational, children's, and regional professional repertory." Bibliography.

B66   Gardner, R. H. *The Splintered Stage: The Decline of the American Theater*. New York: Macmillan, 1965. The theater of the absurd marks the end of the deterioration of man's image. "This process can be carried no further, since the dramatization of nothingness is a prologue to silence." Gardner argues that a new approach to drama is needed. This book is "an expression of one man's hope as to what that approach will be." Tennessee Williams, Arthur Miller, Eugène Ionesco, Edward Albee, William Inge, Eugene O'Neill, Thornton Wilder, and others.

B67   Gascoigne, Bamber. *Twentieth-Century Drama*. New York:

Barnes & Noble, 1962. Beginning with the premise that Pirandello is the father of contemporary drama, Gascoigne is concerned with "the continuing development of drama in the twentieth century, and of the forces that have influenced not only the thinking of the playwright but also the art and method of the actor." Luigi Pirandello, Eugene O'Neill, Bertolt Brecht, Jean Giraudoux, Jean Anouilh, Jean-Paul Sartre, T. S. Eliot, Tennessee Williams, Arthur Miller, and others.

B68   Gassner, John. *Directions in Modern Drama*. New York: Holt, Rinehart & Winston, 1966. (An expanded edition of *Form and Idea in Modern Theatre*.) The "modern theatre appears as an enterprise strongly marked by instability, eclecticism, and a mélange of genres." Gassner traces the history of drama since 1870 and attempts to make sense of this "chaos of contrary winds." Includes a collection of articles on drama since 1945 and a "Chronology of Modern Theatre."

B69   ————. *Dramatic Soundings: Evaluations and Retractions Culled from Thirty Years of Dramatic Criticism*. New York: Crown, 1968. Critical essays dating from 1935 to 1966, which are organized around six areas of concern: 1) surveys and judgments of "the work of masters from the distant and the recent past"; (2) "the craft of writing plays and evaluating them"; (3) a "chronology of American drama"; (4) the theater of the thirties; (5) the "productions of the sixties"; and (6) new movements "in thinking about and writing for the theatre."

B70   ————. *Form and Idea in Modern Theatre*. New York: Dryden, 1956. Examines "the paths hitherto followed by those who have sought to modernize dramatic art in conformity with some idea or ideal." Gassner discusses the realistic phase, the movement from realism to expressionism, and theatricalism and crisis. Finally, he argues that the future of the stage depends upon "the reconciliation of the polarities of realism and theatricalism." Bibliography.

B71   ————. *Masters of the Drama*. 3rd rev. and enl. ed. New York: Dover, 1954. Gassner provides a humanistic and historical context for drama from its beginnings to the 1950s—written for the general reader, not the specialist.

George Bernard Shaw, Eugene O'Neill, Bertolt Brecht, Jean Giraudoux, Jean Anouilh, Jean-Paul Sartre, Albert Camus, T. S. Eliot, Christopher Fry, Tennessee Williams, Arthur Miller, and others. Bibliography.

B72 —————. *Theatre at the Crossroads: Plays and Playwrights of the Mid-Century American Stage.* New York: Holt, Rinehart & Winston, 1960. An optimistic and pessimistic assessment of the Broadway and off-Broadway stage at mid century. The collection begins with eleven essays that treat general issues of the stage from the beginnings of modern drama. The rest of the book is a collection of reviews that chronicle the "New York stage during the 1950–1960 period."

B73 —————. *The Theatre in Our Times: A Survey of the Men, Materials and Movements in the Modern Theatre.* New York: Crown, 1954. A collection of essays that deals with history, dramatic criticism, and dramatic theory. Henrik Ibsen, George Bernard Shaw, Jean Cocteau, Luigi Pirandello, William Synge, Sean O'Casey, Eugene O'Neill, T. S. Eliot, Clifford Odets, Jean-Paul Sartre, Tennessee Williams, Arthur Miller, and others.

B74 —————, and Ralph G. Allen, eds. *Theatre and Drama in the Making.* Boston: Houghton Mifflin, 1964. A collection of "major essays, documents, and critical accounts" of the theatre. Surveys Western drama from the classical theater to the present. William Synge, Luigi Pirandello, Jean-Paul Sartre, Eugène Ionesco, Eugene O'Neill, Tennessee Williams, Arthur Miller, and others.

B75 Gilman, Richard. *Common and Uncommon Masks: Writings on Theatre, 1961–1970.* New York: Random House, 1971. Gilman's reviews of drama during the sixties fall into five categories. They contain ideas about criticism, classics such as *Saint Joan* by George Bernard Shaw, contemporary drama such as *The Caretaker* by Harold Pinter, phenomena, and theaters.

B76 Gottfried, Martin. *A Theater Divided: The Postwar American Stage.* Boston: Little, Brown, 1967. Gottfried argues that the stage has been divided since World War II. He describes the nature of the Right and Left wings and what formed them. Each wing has its own "identities, theatres, playwrights, performers, audiences," attitudes, and critics. Edward Albee, Samuel Beckett, Bertolt Brecht, Eugene O'Neill, Harold Pinter, Christopher Plummer, Richard Rodgers, Tennessee Williams, and Arthur Miller.

B77   Gould, Jean. *Modern American Playwrights.* New York: Dodd, Mead, 1966. A historical survey that begins with Elmer Rice and ends with Edward Albee. Gould's focus is on playwrights and their theatrical life, rather than on criticism. Lillian Hellman, Clifford Odets, Thornton Wilder, Tennessee Williams, Arthur Miller, William Inge, Edward Albee, and earlier writers.

B78   Guthrie, Tyrone. *In Various Directions: A View of Theatre.* New York: Macmillan, 1965. Essays on the theater that "add up to some coherent statement of A Point of View." Guthrie is concerned primarily with trends on the stage. He compares the New York theater to the London theater and the theater to television and the university stage.

B79   Heilman, Robert Bechtold. *The Iceman, the Arsonist, and the Troubled Agent: Tragedy and Melodrama on the Modern Stage.* Seattle: University of Washington Press, 1973. The iceman, an allusion to *The Iceman Cometh,* is a metaphor for a wide range of characters who find it difficult to face the world or themselves. The arsonist, an allusion to *The Firebugs,* is a metaphor for a wide range of strong and aggressive characters. The troubled agent is "the vigorous man with enough moral sensitivity to be troubled by what he does." Through these metaphors, Heilman discusses our thoughts and feelings in relation to the writing of tragedy, and makes a distinction between tragedy and melodrama. Eugene O'Neill, Tennessee Williams, Arthur Miller, Bertolt Brecht, and Max Frisch.

B80   ——————. *Tragedy and Melodrama: Versions of Experience.* Seattle: University of Washington Press, 1968. A generic study of tragedy and melodrama based upon "the notion that experience . . . affords a perspective on drama." What is more important, however, is that drama and experience interact: "The artist may forge the conscience of his race, or the race temper the imagination of the artist." Heilman examines a number of plays "from Aeschylus to the present." His business is with "the constants of generic form that reflect basic attitudes to human conduct and that nourish certain kinds of aesthetic experience." Samuel Beckett, T. S. Eliot, Christopher Fry, Arthur Miller, John Osborne, Thornton Wilder, Tennessee Williams, and many earlier figures.

B81 Henn, T. R. *The Harvest of Tragedy*. New York: Barnes & Noble, 1966. Henn's aim is "to examine certain facts, theories, and assumptions regarding the nature of the form which we term, loosely, Tragedy." He examines tragedy as "a highly complex, composite and active substance and form; with characteristic effects which can best be apprehended, because of their very nature, in religious or mystical terms." Then, he projects these conclusions into some relationship with life and death. T. S. Eliot, Henrik Ibsen, Sean O'Casey, George Bernard Shaw, William Synge, and earlier writers.

B82 Hobson, Harold. *The Theatre Now*. London: Longmans, Green, 1953. A discussion of sixty-nine performances of plays in England from May 1949 to March 1952. An entire chapter on T. S. Eliot and a half chapter on Christopher Fry. Numerous other playwrights briefly discussed. Hobson writes from the perspective of a reviewer and many of his ideas first appeared in the *Sunday Times*.

B83 ⸺. *Verdict at Midnight: Sixty Years of Dramatic Criticism*. London: Longmans, Green, 1952. A "history of the modern English theatre as that theatre appears to dramatic critics." Hobson writes that his method "is to take nearly forty of the most important theatrical productions [in English] of the last . . . sixty years" and to study "what their first night critics thought about them with the considered judgment, in most cases, of posterity." Sir James Barrie, Noel Coward, T. S. Eliot, Christopher Fry, W. Somerset Maugham, George Bernard Shaw, Clement Scott, and others.

B84 Hogan, Robert. *After the Irish Renaissance: A Critical History of the Irish Drama since The Plough and The Stars*. Minneapolis: University of Minnesota Press, 1967. "An informal critical account of Irish dramatic writing since about 1926." Michael Molloy, Denis Johnston, George

Fitzmaurice, Brendan Behan, John B. Keane, and others.

B85   Houghton, Norris. *The Exploding Stage: An Introduction to Twentieth Century Drama.* New York: Weybright & Talley, 1971. "This primer was developed from a series of twenty-five one-hour lectures delivered on Educational Television." It is not entirely a history, nor a book of criticism, but an attempt to encourage "readers to extend their playgoing" and expand their theatrical and literary knowledge. Edward Albee, Julian Beck, Samuel Beckett, Robert Brustein, T. S. Eliot, Jerzy Grotowski, George S. Kaufman, Arthur Miller, Thornton Wilder, Tennessee Williams, and other earlier and European figures.

B86   Hughes, Catharine. *Plays, Politics, and Polemics.* New York: Drama Book Specialists, 1973. "Although all plays in the theatre of controversy are in a sense protest plays—expressions of discontent over a situation, an action, or a failure to act—many are as interested in revolution as in alteration." Hughes argues that the protest is not of prime importance to the play; unless the writer looks beyond politics, his play does no more than to reinforce the beliefs of the converted. Daniel Berrigan, Jules Feiffer, Donald Freed, Charles Gordone, Günter Grass, Joseph Heller, Rolf Hochhuth, Heinar Kipphardt, Arthur Kopit, Arthur Miller, Conor Cruise O'Brien, Sean O'Casey, David Rabe, Robert Shaw, Peter Weiss, and Richard Wesley. Bibliography.

B87   Kennedy, Andrew K. *Six Dramatists in Search of a Language: Studies in Dramatic Language.* Cambridge: Cambridge University Press, 1975. This book is a study of "language as one of several interacting elements in drama," with emphasis upon both the structure and texture of dialogue. Kennedy uses only the stylistic methods that help in "understanding the specific dramatic effects of language." George Bernard Shaw, T. S. Eliot, Samuel Beckett, Harold Pinter, John Osborne, and John Arden. Bibliography.

B88   Kernan, Alvin B., ed. *The Modern American Theater: A Collection of Critical Essays.* Englewood Cliffs, N.J.: Prentice-Hall, 1967. Kernan collects articles which examine some crucial area of the theater and suggest its strengths and its weaknesses. The basic premise behind each of these essays is that drama is part of civilization. The essayists discuss the peculiarities of modern theater, five successful playwrights, the range of the theatrical community, and the problems of the theater. Arthur Miller, Tennessee Williams, Thornton Wilder, William Inge, and Edward Albee. Bibliography.

B89   Kerr, Walter. *God on the Gymnasium Floor and Other Theatrical Adventures.* New York: Simon & Schuster, 1970. Essays on contemporary theater, the death of the theater, open theater, experimental theater, audience involvement, despair in the theater, illusion on the stage, the theater of fact, nudity, the playwright as existentialist, the revival of plays, financial problems, the problems of the playwright, and the problems of the actor.

B90   —————. *The Theater in Spite of Itself.* New York: Simon & Schuster, 1963. A collection of "first-night reviews, Sunday pieces, and magazine articles" that "suggest the contrary energies that do clash by night" on the Broadway and off-Broadway stages. John van Druten, Brendan Behan, Edward Albee, Harold Pinter, Jean Genet, John Osborne, Lillian Hellman, Tennessee Williams, William Inge, Eugene O'Neill, and others.

B91   —————. *Thirty Plays Hath November: Pain and Pleasure in the Contemporary Theatre.* New York: Simon & Schuster, 1968. Journalistic essays and reviews. Anton Chekhov, Edward Albee, Arthur Miller, Tennessee Williams, Bertolt Brecht, Eugène Ionesco, Eugene O'Neill, and Harold Pinter.

B92   Kershaw, John. *The Present Stage: New Directions in the Theatre Today.* London: Collins, 1966. With the success of John Osborne's *Look Back in Anger* in 1956, plays were no longer written "in the styles admired by scholars and literary people." Kershaw examines the changes in the drama of John Osborne, Arnold Wesker, Max Frisch, Harold Pinter, Eugène Ionesco, and Samuel Beckett. Bibliography.

B93   Killinger, John. *World in Collapse: The Vision of Absurd Drama.* New York: Dell/Delta, 1971. Based on the premise that the death of God generates "anarchy and madness,"

Killinger's survey evaluates the development of the theater of the absurd. Edward Albee, Fernando Arrabal, Antonin Artaud, Samuel Beckett, Jack Gelber, Jean Genet, Eugène Ionesco, Harold Pinter, and others. Bibliography.

B94   Kirby, Michael, ed. *The New Theatre: Performance Documentation.* New York: New York University Press, 1974. Because performances are perishable and seen by a few people, this collection tries to record objectively "fine art" productions. It moves from the drama to the dance, recording twenty-four performances in nine countries. Norman Taffel, Red Grooms, Peter Schumann, Richard Foreman, Robert Wilson, Richard Gallo, Robert Israel, Marjorie Strider, John Perreault, David Gordon, Joan Jonas, Trisha Brown, and other dramatists from the world stage.

B95   Kitchin, Laurence. *Drama in the Sixties: Form and Interpretation.* London: Faber & Faber, 1966. A study of the professional theater in the sixties with an emphasis upon the theme of war and violence. It is "a book about dramatic form and the principles of production, revealed or restated in terms of current practice. Form, as the envelope of communication, needs to be understood before any meaningful criticism can be made. Production depends on a confluence of the author's assumptions with those of his director." Discusses the theater of the absurd, the theater of cruelty, Eugene O'Neill, Sean O'Casey, Edward Albee, and earlier writers. Bibliography.

B96   ————. *Mid-Century Drama.* London: Faber & Faber, 1962. Kitchin's aim is "to find some shape in recent theatrical events." He discusses a new style of writing and the decline of classical acting. His ideas are based on interviews and his personal assessment as a member of the audience. Tennessee Williams, Bertolt Brecht, Samuel Beckett, Eugène Ionesco, Harold Pinter, and others.

B97   Kostelanetz, Richard. *The Theatre of Mixed Means: An Introduction to Happenings, Kinetic Environments, and Other Mixed-Means Performances.* New York: Dial, 1968. This introduction to the theater of mixed means contains: first, "an essay that characterizes the new art form, identifies its various genres, traces the diverse strains of its artistic ancestry, ascertains its significances, and discerns its ultimate purposes"; second, "conversations with the leading practitioners"; third, a "conclusion in which the critical questions the new movement raises are broached"; and fourth, a "four-part bibliography listing statements and scripts by the practitioners, critical essays about the new movement, reviews of individual performers, and background materials. . . ." John Cage, Ann Halprin, Robert Rauschenberg, Allen Kaprow, Claes Oldenburg, Ken Dewey, LaMonte Young, and Robert Whitman.

B98   Kronenberger, Louis. *The Thread of Laughter: Chapters on English Stage Comedy from Jonson to Maugham.* New York: Hill & Wang, 1952. A survey of three hundred years of English stage comedy. Ben Jonson through George Bernard Shaw, William Synge, and W. Somerset Maugham.

B99   Lahr, John. *Acting out America: Essays on Modern Theatre.* Baltimore: Penguin, 1972. In these essays written from 1968 to 1970, Lahr attempts "to probe the American consciousness by looking at its theatre." He studies the "underground" theater and its dramatists, stressing common themes, the American musical, the open theater, and Broadway comedy. Edward Albee, Woody Allen, Joseph Chaikin, Jules Feiffer, Arthur Kopit, Howard Sackler, Richard Schechner, Neil Simon, and others.

B100   —————. *Astonish Me: Adventures in Contemporary Theater.* New York: Viking, 1973. Lahr focuses upon current drama as it astonishes and as it is connected to tradition. He studies pageants, playwrights, and performers. Harold Pinter, Anton Chekhov, Joe Orton, Jules Feiffer, Sam Shepard, Neil Simon, Woody Allen, Heathcote Williams, and others.

B101   —————. *Up against the Fourth Wall: Essays on Modern Theater.* New York: Grove Press, 1970. Lahr studies the emphasis of modern dramatists. Essays on playwrights, theatrical movements, and the stage from 1968 to 1970. Edward Albee, Jules Feiffer, Arthur Kopit, Harold Pinter, John Osborne, Samuel Beckett, T. S. Eliot, Jerzy Grotowski, and others.

B102   Lambert, J. W. *Drama in Britain, 1964–1973.* Burnt Mill, Eng.: Longman, 1974. The fourth book in the British

Council's brief histories of the British theater from 1939 to 1964 (see B143, B144, B145). "This account gives a detailed view not only of Britain's major theatrical enterprises, subsidized and commercial, but of the still continuing expansion of the theatre's role in the country . . . and the increasing involvement—which originally sprang from the English Stage Company in 1956—of its dramatists in contemporary life." John Arden, Samuel Beckett, John Mortimer, John Osborne, Harold Pinter, Tom Stoppard, and many others briefly discussed. Bibliography.

B103   Laufe, Abe. *Anatomy of a Hit: Long-Run Plays on Broadway from 1900 to the Present Day.* New York: Hawthorn, 1966. Laufe discusses ninety-nine plays that ran five hundred or more consecutive performances. He does not offer a formula for writing a hit; instead, he presents a factual study of authors, stars, and the contexts of the hits. Bibliography.

B104   Leaska, Mitchell A. *The Voice of Tragedy.* New York: Robert Speller, 1963. Leaska writes that "the purpose of this volume is two-fold: to point out the major philosophical attitudes . . . that have prevailed and must prevail in periods of tragic drama; and, secondly, to locate and define that condition basic to tragedy and to the distinctive values of Western civilization." Leaska studies the relationship between world events and the tragic theater. Discusses writers from Aeschylus through T. S. Eliot, Eugene O'Neill, Arthur Miller, and Tennessee Williams.

B105   Lewis, Allan. *American Plays and Playwrights of the Contemporary Theatre.* Rev. ed. New York: Crown, 1970. A critical analysis of plays and playwrights in which Lewis attempts "to judge our theatre in its historical and cultural context." Lewis states: "Though the theatre of this decade may have been preoccupied with the trivial and the personal, there are strong indications that absorption with the self has grown too threadbare for continued use." Eugene O'Neill, Arthur Miller, Tennessee Williams, Thornton Wilder, William Saroyan, Edward Albee, Paddy Chayefsky, William Inge, and others.

B106   ————. *The Contemporary Theatre: The Significant Playwrights of Our Time.* New York: Crown, 1962. Lewis

DRAMA

studies playwrights in all Western languages beginning with Ibsen. He discusses the subtopics that make up modernism: realism, naturalism, romanticism, symbolism, social conflict, and psychology. The study also includes topics from dadaism to the theater of the absurd. A guide for the general reader. Sean O'Casey, George Bernard Shaw, T. S. Eliot, Samuel Beckett, Tennessee Williams, Arthur Miller, and others.

B107   Lumley, Frederick. *New Trends in 20th Century Drama: A Survey since Ibsen and Shaw.* New York: Oxford University Press, 1967. Lumley's aim is to assess the important playwrights who appeared after Ibsen and Shaw in Britain, the U.S., and Europe. Luigi Pirandello, Jean Giraudoux, Paul Claudel, Bertolt Brecht, Eugene O'Neill, T. S. Eliot, Samuel Beckett, Eugène Ionesco, Jean Genet, Arthur Adamov, John Osborne, Max Frisch, Peter Weiss, and many others. Bibliography.

B108   McCarthy, Mary. *Mary McCarthy's Theatre Chronicles, 1937–1962.* New York: Farrar, Straus, 1963 (originally published in 1956 as *Sights and Spectacles*). Written for the *Partisan Review*, these drama reviews reflect McCarthy's attitudes for over two decades. William Inge, Tennessee Williams, Arthur Miller, John Osborne, Eugene O'Neill, Kenneth Tynan, William Saroyan, George Bernard Shaw, Thornton Wilder, and others.

B109   Marowitz, Charles. *Confessions of a Counterfeit Critic: A London Theatre Notebook, 1958–1971.* London: Methuen, 1973. A personal introduction to the author and over forty of his reviews.

B110   ————, and Simon Trussler. *Theatre at Work: Playwrights and Productions in the Modern British Theatre.* London: Methuen, 1967. A collection of interviews and essays on the theater in Britain, designed for the generalist who has a familiarity with the theater. The pieces deal with all aspects of stagecraft, technical and aesthetic. Interviews are with John Whiting, John Arden, Robert Bolt, Arnold Wesker, and Harold Pinter.

B111   ————; Tom Milne; and Owen Hale, eds. *The Encore Reader: A Chronicle of the New Drama.* London: Methuen, 1965. Essays reprinted from the drama magazine, *Encore*. The editors collect these essays to show the development of what they call the English "new drama." The period covered is 1956 to 1963. John Arden, Samuel Beckett, Bertolt Brecht, Shelagh Delaney, Jean Genet, Eugène Ionesco, Joan Littlewood, Arthur Miller, John Osborne, Harold Pinter, Jean-Paul Sartre, N. F. Simpson, Kenneth Tynan, Arnold Wesker, and others.

B112   Matthews, Honor. *The Primal Curse: The Myth of Cain and Abel in the Theatre*. New York: Schocken, 1967. Dramatic art has reflected man's consciousness of guilt, fear of punishment, and hope of redemption. Matthews first studies the primordial myth of Cain and Abel in Shakespeare, *A Spanish Tragedy*, and Jacobean revenge plays; then, he looks at contemporary theater and the myth of the warring brothers. Henrik Ibsen, August Strindberg, Jean-Paul Sartre, Samuel Beckett, Franz Kafka, Jean Genet, Edward Albee, T. S. Eliot, Harold Pinter, and others.

B113   Merchant, W. Moelwyn. *Creed and Drama: An Essay in Religious Drama*. Philadelphia: Fortress, 1966. Chapters on religious drama from Sophocles to Christopher Fry and T. S. Eliot. Includes "A Short Book List."

B114   Meserve, Walter J., ed. *Discussions of Modern American Drama*. Boston: D. C. Heath, 1966. A collection of essays with the intent "to present in chronological sequence those essays which most effectively evaluate some of the major aspects and the principal dramatists of modern American drama." These essays suggest the beginnings and progress of modern drama. Eugene O'Neill, Lillian Hellman, Thornton Wilder, Arthur Miller, Tennessee Williams, and Edward Albee.

B115   Nannes, Caspar H. *Politics in the American Drama*. Washington, D.C.: Catholic University of America Press, 1960. A survey of the plays on the New York Broadway stage between 1890 and 1959 that provides insight into the changing attitudes of Americans towards politicians and political society. Nannes's aim is "to point out that playwrights and theatrical producers were alert during these years to the dramatic possibilities of contemporary events." Bibliography.

B116   Nathan, George Jean. *The Magic Mirror: Selected Writings on the Theatre by George Jean Nathan.* Edited by Thomas Quinn Curtiss. New York: Knopf, 1960. Curtiss writes: "To Nathan both art and life were forms of metamorphosis, and in mirroring the drama of his work, he demonstrated the rich development that transformation ever brings." Includes essays on critical theory, theatrical personalities, playwrights, and performances. George Bernard Shaw, Edmond Rostand, Sean O'Casey, Jim Tully, John Galsworthy, William Saroyan, Eugene O'Neill, Tennessee Williams, Arthur Miller, and earlier writers.

B117   —————. *The Theatre in the Fifties.* New York: Knopf, 1953. "The purpose of this book is not a complete record of the New York theatre in the early years of the 1950's, but rather simply a detailed impression of the overall picture." Maxwell Anderson, Elmer Rice, John van Druten, Lillian Hellman, Paul Osborn, Clifford Odets, S. N. Behrman, Mary Chase, Moss Hart, George S. Kaufman, Arthur Carter, William Inge, N. Richard Nash, Joseph Kramm, Truman Capote, Stanley Young, Arthur Miller, Christopher Fry, Terence Rattigan, Frederick Knott, Hugh Hastings, Aimée Stuart, George Bernard Shaw, and many other writers.

B118   *New York Theatre Critics' Reviews.* New York: Critics' Theatre Reviews, 1940–. A compilation of reviews written each year by New York theater critics.

B119   *The New York Times Theater Reviews, 1920–1970.* 10 vols. New York: The New York Times & Arno Press, 1971. A reprint of "every *Times* notice and every *Times* theater story from 1920 to 1970."

B120   *The New York Times Theater Reviews, 1971–1972.* New York: The New York Times & Arno Press, 1973. A reprint of "all the *Times* theater reviews published in 1971–72." In addition, it contains articles, lists of important dramatic events, and awards.

B121   Olson, Elder. *Tragedy and the Theory of Drama.* Detroit: Wayne State University Press, 1961. An "inquiry into dramatic principles." Olson attempts "to see tragedy—indeed, as much as possible of the whole of drama—from a point of view which is seldom taken: the point of view of the working dramatist." "The problems of the dramatist, the technical means for their solution, the principles governing the different methods of solution comprise the subject of this book." Eugene O'Neill, Arthur Miller, T. S. Eliot, and others.

B122   Peacock, Ronald. *The Art of Drama*. London: Routledge & Kegan Paul, 1957. The critic must define "the nature of drama as an art form." Only then, "can a theory be worked out to explain the variety of drama, the main types of plays, the relation between acting, scene and dialogue, the varying use of verse and prose, and the creation of style and poetic effect." Peacock bases his argument on a "view of *images* and *imagery*" in relation to aesthetics. T. S. Eliot, George Bernard Shaw, and many earlier writers. Selected bibliography.

B123   Phillips, Elizabeth C., and David Rogers. *Modern American Drama*. New York: Monarch, 1966. A Monarch study guide dealing with nineteenth-century background and twentieth-century authors such as Eugene O'Neill, Lillian Hellman, William Inge, Maxwell Anderson, T. S. Eliot, Arthur Miller, Tennessee Williams, Edward Albee, and others.

B124   Porter, Thomas E. *Myth and Modern American Drama*. Detroit: Wayne State University Press, 1969. Porter uses mythic and ritualistic Greek drama as a point of departure to "examine American drama in the light of its cultural milieu." This study is an examination of patterns that "express attitudes that characterize the American group mind." T. S. Eliot, Eugene O'Neill, Archibald MacLeish, Tennessee Williams, Arthur Miller, and Edward Albee. Bibliography.

B125   Price, Julia S. *The Off-Broadway Theater*. New York: Scarecrow, 1962. A chronological study of the off-Broadway theater, beginning in 1905 and ending in 1960. In each historical section, Price studies the tone of the drama, the playhouses and their productions, and the socio-economic forces working on the theater. Bibliography.

B126   Roberts, Patrick. *The Psychology of Tragic Drama*. London: Routledge & Kegan Paul, 1975. A critical rather than a historical study of the relationship between psychology and the tragic mode. Roberts explains the connections between psychoanalysis and literature, the way psychoanalysis informs the tragic drama, and he explores recurrent psychological themes. T. S. Eliot, Eugène Ionesco, Eugene O'Neill, Harold Pinter, Peter Weiss, and others. Bibliography.

B127   Roy, Emil. *British Drama since Shaw.* Carbondale: Southern Illinois University Press, 1972. A study of two waves of "innovative, rebellious drama" beginning with Shaw and Wilde. The last chapter focuses on contemporary dramatists. George Bernard Shaw, Oscar Wilde, W. B. Yeats, J. M. Synge, Sean O'Casey, T. S. Eliot, Christopher Fry, John Osborne, John Arden, Harold Pinter, Arnold Wesker, John Whiting. Bibliography.

B128   Sainer, Arthur. *The Radical Theatre Notebook.* New York: Avon, 1975. An overview of the theater from the 1950s to the present, focusing upon the radical changes in theatrical assumptions. "A compelling perspective on the events and personalities" that shaped the radical theater. It does not study authors as much as "experimental ensembles." It analyzes their work and includes their "notes, logs, correspondence, articles and, where possible, actual scripts." Studies the Living Theatre, the San Francisco Mime Troupe, the Bread & Puppet Theater, the Performance Group, and others.

B129   ————. *The Sleepwalker and the Assassin: A View of the Contemporary Theatre.* New York: Bridgehead Books, 1964. Sainer writes: "The present volume reflects a collusion between evaluator, conscience-holder and transformer (myself) and theatre works of varying distinction, produced in New York between the beginning of 1962 and the latter half of 1963." Most of these essays were written for the *Village Voice.*

B130   Schechner, Richard. *Environmental Theater.* New York: Hawthorn, 1973. As a basis for his book, Schechner uses his association with the Performance Group to describe the phenomenon of environmental theater during the last fifteen years. Bibliography.

B131 —————. *Public Domain: Essays on the Theatre.* Indianapolis: Bobbs-Merrill, 1969. Includes "Exit Thirties, Enter Sixties," "Ford, Rockefeller, and Theatre," "Approaches," "In Warm Blood: The Bacchae," "There's Lots of Time in Godot," "Megan Terry: The Playwrite as Wrighter," "Pornography and the New Expression," "Happenings," "Six Axioms for Environmental Theatre," "Negotiations with Environment," "Public Events for the Radical Novel," and "The Politics of Ecstasy."

B132 Schevill, James. *Breakout: In Search of New Theatrical Environments.* Chicago: Swallow, 1973. For Schevill, the theater has "the ability to center the word in a physical context." His book records his search for "new theatrical visions and spaces," spaces in which we can act out realities and fantasies. Schevill says his "aim is to investigate the breakout from conventional theatres of entertainment. . . . " Lawrence Ferlinghetti, Bertolt Brecht, Norman Mailer, Eric Bentley, Eugene O'Neill, Sonia Sanchez, Jerzy Grotowsky, Robert Brustein, Joan Littlewood, and many others.

B133 Sievers, W. David. *Freud on Broadway: A History of Psychoanalysis and the American Drama.* New York: Hermitage House, 1955. This study is not an attempt to judge plays by Freudian dogma, nor an attempt to psychoanalyze dramatists, but an attempt to detail the influence of Freud on the drama. In addition to conventional literary evidence, Sievers obtained answers from thirty-three dramatists to a questionnaire that he designed in order to document his work. Sievers explains Freudian theory and traces its influence historically. Eugene O'Neill, Philip Barry, many early moderns, Arthur Laurents, William Inge, Mary Chase, John Patrick, Richard Rodgers, Oscar Hammerstein, Tennessee Williams, and Arthur Miller. Bibliography.

B134 Simon, John. *Singularities: Essays on the Theater, 1964–1973.* New York: Random House, 1975. A collection of journalistic essays on Edward Albee, Samuel Beckett, Bertolt Brecht, Jerzy Grotowsky, Henrik Ibsen, Clifford Odets, and topical concerns.

B135 —————. *Uneasy States: A Chronicle of the New York Theater, 1963–1973.* New York: Random House, 1975. A season-by-season account of New York drama.

DRAMA

B136   Simpson, Alan. *Beckett and Behan and a Theatre in Dublin.* London: Routledge & Kegan Paul, 1962. Simpson states: "I have done very little research and have just set down what I know, believe and think about the two playwrights, the Ireland from which they sprang and the theatre of the fifties in general."

B137   Spanos, William V. *The Christian Tradition in Modern British Drama: The Poetics of Sacramental Time.* New Brunswick, N.J.: Rutgers University Press, 1967. Spanos argues that Christian critical theory and art are unfortunately "viewed from the traditional humanistic perspective" and, therefore, misinterpreted "as embodiments of the poet's contemptuous rejection of the concrete life of man." Spanos makes his study an attempt to "reorient an outmoded critical perspective on Christian art." His approach to verse plays is to accept "the *donnée* of the Christian poet-dramatist" and to define his strategies. T. S. Eliot, Gordon Bottomly, Charles Williams, Dorothy Sayers, John Masefield, Anne Ridler, Christopher Fry, and Ronald Duncan. Bibliography.

B138   Stevens, David H., ed. *Ten Talents in the American Theatre.* Norman: University of Oklahoma Press, 1957. Essays by ten persons who "have spent their lives in the American theatre." Robert E. Gard, Paul Baker, Alan Schneider, Margo Jones, Frederic McConnell, Barclay Leathem, Gilmor Brown, Leslie Cheek, Jr., George C. Izenour, and Paul Green write on the origins, development, and new growth of the theater.

B139   Taylor, John Russell. *The Angry Theatre: New British Drama.* Rev. ed. New York: Hill & Wang, 1969. (British title: *Anger and After.*) After the success of John Osborne's *Look Back in Anger,* "theatres began to feel differently about young writers, and with a new willingness to consider staging plays by new and unknown writers came, not surprisingly, the new and unknown writers to supply the plays." These new writers have two distinguishing features: "their tremendous variety and patent unwillingness to fall behind any one standard or one leader; and the fact that the great majority of them have working-class origins." Denis Cannan, John Whiting, Giles Cooper, John Osborne, N. F.

Simpson, Ann Jellicoe, John Arden, Joan Littlewood, Brendan Behan, Shelagh Delaney, Arnold Wesker, Bernard Kops, David Campton, David Turner, Alun Owen, Clive Sexton, John Mortimer, Peter Shaffer, Henry Livings, Johnny Speight, David Rudkin, and Harold Pinter.

B140 ————. *The Second Wave: British Drama for the Seventies.* New York: Hill & Wang, 1971. A study of the writers "who began to come to prominence towards the middle of the 1960s." Peter Nichols, David Mercer, Charles Wood, Edward Bond, Tom Stoppard, Peter Terson, Joe Orton, David Storey, Alan Ayckbourn, David Cregan, Simon Gray, John Hopkins, Alan Plater, Cecil P. Taylor, William Corlett, Kevin Laffan, Christopher Hampton, Barry England, Anthony Shaffer, Robert Shaw, David Caute, Peter Barnes, Colin Spenser, David Pinner, David Selbourne, David Hare, Roger Milner, David Halliwell, Howard Brenton, and Heathcote Williams. Bibliography of playscripts.

B141 Taylor, Karen Malpede. *People's Theatre in Amerika: Documents by the People Who Do It.* New York: Drama Book Specialists, 1972. "This book is a pioneering attempt to deal with avant-garde movements in the American Theatre from the early twenties to the seventies. This history is diverse, fragmented, contradictory, but always rich in promise, always concerned with fundamental questions of dramatic art." Numerous essays on all aspects of the avant-garde theater in America.

B142 Taylor, William E., ed. *Modern American Drama: Essays in Criticism.* Deland, Fla.: Everett/Edwards, 1968. A collection of essays that show dramatic advances as being "as vital and as important to our literature as the advances of poetry and fiction." Many of the essays raise questions of the validity of the dramatic mode as well as the thematic concerns of modern drama. Eugene O'Neill, Clifford Odets, Maxwell Anderson, Tennessee Williams, Arthur Miller, Edward Albee, James Baldwin, Carson McCullers, Saul Bellow, and others. Bibliography.

B143 Trewin, J. C. *Drama, 1945–1950.* London: Longmans, Green, 1951. Discusses the "renaissance" that took place in British drama between 1945 and 1950. George Bernard Shaw, Terence Rattigan, J. B. Priestley, James Bridie, Oscar

Hammerstein II, Sir Alan Herbert, Christopher Fry, T. S. Eliot, and others. Primary and secondary bibliography.

B144   ————. *Drama in Britain 1951–1964.* London: Longmans, Green, 1965. A discussion of the developments in "dramatic writing, in acting, in staging, in administration," the National Theatre, the Royal Shakespeare Company, the West End of London, and the repertory theaters. Bibliography.

B145   ————. *Dramatists of Today.* New York: Staples Press, 1953. Not an academic study, but a personal view of the impressions the dramatists made upon the stage. Trewin is more concerned with the effect of plays in "the theatre for which they were written," than in the literary value of each play. T. S. Eliot, Noel Coward, Christopher Fry, Terence Rattigan, Peter Ustinov, George Bernard Shaw, John Masefield, Sean O'Casey, and Wynyard Browne. Play lists.

B146   Tynan, Kenneth. *Curtain: Selections from the Drama Criticism and Related Writings.* New York: Atheneum, 1961. "A self-compiled anthology of theatre pieces" that Tynan contributed to newspapers and magazines both in the United States and Britain. Includes articles on the theater in Britain, the United States, the Soviet Union, and Germany.

B147   Von Szeliski, John. *Tragedy and Fear: Why Modern Tragic Drama Fails.* Chapel Hill: University of North Carolina Press, 1971. Von Szeliski studies the background of the pessimism-optimism debate, weaknesses in modern attempts at tragedy, and "just what 'fear' (or pessimism) does to tragic expression." Paul Green, Elmer Rice, Arthur Miller, Eugene O'Neill, Maxwell Anderson, Clifford Odets, DuBose Heyward, Lillian Hellman, Lynn Riggs, Robert Turney, Tennessee Williams, Archibald MacLeish, Robert Sherwood, and others. Bibliography.

B148   Wager, Walter, ed. *The Playwrights Speak.* New York: Delacorte, 1967. Interviews of contemporary dramatists on their work. Arthur Miller, Edward Albee, Friedrich Dürrenmatt, John Osborne, William Inge, Eugène Ionesco, Harold Pinter, Peter Weiss, Tennessee Williams, John Arden, and Arnold Wesker.

B149   Weales, Gerald. *American Drama since World War II.* New

York: Harcourt, Brace & World, 1962. "A critical description of the American plays that have been produced since 1945." Survey treatment of many playwrights.

B150 ————. *The Jumping-Off Place: American Drama in the 1960's.* London: Macmillan, 1969. "A critical description of American plays." Tennessee Williams, Arthur Miller, Edward Albee, Robert Lowell, Saul Bellow, and many others.

B151 ————. *Religion in Modern English Drama.* Philadelphia: University of Pennsylvania Press, 1961. Weales examines "the ways in which religion has been used on the commercial stage," "the history of the church drama movement," and the "religious drama since World War II." Survey of plays from 1879 through 1953. Bibliography.

B152 Wellwarth, George. *The Theatre of Protest and Paradox: Developments in the Avant-Garde Drama.* New York: New York University Press, 1967. "A critical study of the extraordinary outburst of drama in the French, German, English, and American theaters since the end of the second World War." Wellwarth's purpose is "to explain the meanings of these plays, set them in their proper place in the history of dramatic literature, and point out their basic similarities. These similarities consist of a common theme (protest) and a common technique (paradox)." Harold Pinter, N. F. Simpson, John Osborne, Arnold Wesker, Bernard Kops, Doris Lessing, Shelagh Delaney, John Mortimer, Brendan Behan, Nigel Dennis, John Arden, Edward Albee, Jack Richardson, Arthur Kopit, Jack Gelber, and French and German playwrights. Bibliography.

B153 Whiting, John. *On Theatre.* London: Alan Ross, 1966. Reviews reprinted from the *London Magazine.*

B154 Wickham, Glynne. *Drama in a World of Science and Three Other Lectures.* Toronto: University of Toronto Press, 1962. Five lectures on the crisis in the professional theater: "The Post-War Revolution in British Drama," "Poets and Playmakers," "Drama in a World of Science," "University Theatre," and "L'Envoye."

B155 Williams, Raymond. *Drama from Ibsen to Brecht.* New York: Oxford University Press, 1969. Williams finds "a general historical development, from Ibsen to Brecht, from dramatic naturalism to dramatic expressionism." What he attempts "is a more general statement, based on the particular studies, of the history and significance of the main dramatic forms—the conventions and structures of feeling —of this remarkable hundred years." Henrik Ibsen, W. B. Yeats, T. S. Eliot, Christopher Fry, Eugene O'Neill, Arthur Miller, Bertolt Brecht, Eugène Ionesco, Samuel Beckett, John Whiting, John Osborne, Harold Pinter, John Arden, and others.

B156   Williamson, Audrey. *Contemporary Theatre, 1953–1956.* London: Rockliff [1956]. A survey of plays produced in England between 1953 and 1956. T. S. Eliot, John Whiting, Christopher Fry, George Bernard Shaw, Samuel Beckett, Shakespeare, Eugene O'Neill, and many others.

B157   Wilson, Garff. *Three Hundred Years of American Drama and Theatre: From Ye Bear and Ye Cubb to Hair.* Englewood Cliffs, N.J.: Prentice-Hall, 1973. A history of the theater in America from 1665 through the 1960s, designed for the beginning student. Organized chronologically, the work discusses drama, the theater and its internal aspects (styles of acting, playhouses, stagecraft, and management), and the social context of drama in each period discussed. It also treats motion pictures. Lillian Hellman, Arthur Miller, Eugene O'Neill, George Bernard Shaw, Tennessee Williams, and others. Bibliography.

B158   Worsley, T. C. *The Fugitive Art: Dramatic Commentaries, 1947–1951.* London: Lehmann, 1952. A collection of reviews of plays performed in England between 1947 and 1952.

C

Fiction and Prose

C1   Aichinger, Peter. *The American Soldier in Fiction, 1880–1963: A History of Attitudes toward Warfare and the Military Establishment.* Ames: Iowa State University Press, 1975. "This work constitutes an examination of the attitudes toward warfare and the military establishment that can be detected in a representative number of the war novels written by American authors in the period from 1880 to 1963." Not a work of literary criticism, but a discussion of "the American war novels in relation to historical, economic, and political events that accompanied or preceded their appearance." Historically structured, the book studies four periods: 1880–1917; 1917–1939; 1939–1952; 1952–1963. Saul Bellow, e. e. cummings, William Faulkner, Mark Harris, Joseph Heller, John Hersey, James Jones, Norman Mailer, John Marquand, James Michener, William Styron, Leon Uris, Kurt Vonnegut, Jr., and Philip Wylie. Bibliography.

C2   Aldiss, Brian W. *Billion Year Spree: The True History of Science Fiction.* Garden City, N.Y.: Doubleday, 1973. A history of science fiction from Mary Shelley to Kurt Vonnegut, Jr., from its origin through its emergence as a genre. Science fiction is the place where "private fantasy and public event meet," dignifying fantasy and humanizing technology. This blend of technology and fantasy accounts for the endurance of science fiction as a genre. C. S. Lewis, George Orwell, Isaac Asimov, Robert A. Heinlein, Ray Bradbury, and J. R. R. Tolkien. Bibliography.

C3   Aldridge, John W. *After the Lost Generation: A Critical Study of the Writers of Two Wars.* New York: Noonday, 1958. Traces some of the changes in the world since the time of Fitzgerald and Hemingway in the work of the "younger novelists of the 1940's." Aldridge contrasts two generations that grew up under the influence of war and concludes that the first generation had greater "moral resources" than the second. When Aldridge and his friends returned from World War II, they found that their world had been destroyed and no new one was being born. This book attempts to discover "what had happened." Ernest Hemingway, F. Scott Fitzgerald, John Dos Passos, Vance Bourjaily, Norman Mailer, Irwin Shaw, Merle Miller, Gore Vidal, Paul Bowles, Truman Capote, and Frederick Buechner.

C4   ————. *The Devil in the Fire: Retrospective Essays on American Literature and Culture, 1951–1971.* New York: Harper's Magazine Press, 1972. Essays that study the literary and cultural issues that make up our contemporary intellectual climate. The essays "represent a kind of running commentary on the social and literary developments of a period we can now recognize as having had a distinctive beginning, middle, and end." They focus both on a body of literature in the process of being born and on the historical form of the postwar period from 1945 to 1971. Saul Bellow, Norman Mailer, Donald Barthelme, William Faulkner, Ernest Hemingway, James Joyce, Mary McCarthy, William Styron, and John Updike are covered.

C5   ————. *In Search of Heresy: American Literature in an Age of Conformity.* New York: McGraw-Hill, 1956. A collection of essays that argues writers have lost the ability to reject convention. In losing the platform of dissent, the American intellectual has lost the way to suggest alternative visions to mass society. The "absence of an active alternative to conformism is attested to not only by the emptiness of some recent novels of dissent but by others which affirm conformism the most strongly." The essays offer a study of the relation between this cultural problem and the quality of the culture's fiction. James T. Farrell, Malcolm Cowley, Saul Bellow, Carson McCullers, William Styron, and Ernest Hemingway are studied.

C6   ————. *Time to Murder and Create: The Contemporary Novel in Crisis.* New York: McKay, 1966. The dilemma of the contemporary novel is that it fails to hold the attention of its audience. The novelist, rather than making what is known to him a viable factor of his imagination, deals in stereotypes inherited from the modern classics. "If the novel is to survive, it must begin now to murder its dependency upon the dead literary formulations of the past and create new formulations to express its understanding of the vital present." Saul Bellow, John Cheever, William Faulkner, Ernest Hemingway, Norman Mailer, Mary McCarthy, John O'Hara, Katherine Anne Porter, Alan Sillitoe, William Styron, John Updike, and P. G. Wodehouse.

C7 —————, ed. *Critiques and Essays on Modern Fiction, 1920–1951: Representing the Achievement of Modern American and British Critics.* New York: Ronald, 1952. Thirty-four essays. Designed as a text for a course in modern criticism, it also illustrates formalistic criticism and contains much insight on modern fiction. William Faulkner, Robert Penn Warren, Katherine Anne Porter, Aldous Huxley, E. M. Forster, Virginia Woolf, Graham Greene, and others. Bibliography.

C8 Allen, L. David. *Science Fiction: An Introduction.* Lincoln, Neb.: Cliff Notes, 1973. Includes discussions of the categories and definitions of sciene fiction and guidelines for reading it. Also contains analyses of representative novels. Jules Verne, H. G. Wells, Isaac Asimov, Alfred Bester, Arthur C. Clarke, Fritz Leiber, Hal Clement, Walter M. Miller, Jr., Frank Herbert, Robert A. Heinlein, Alexei Panshin, Ursula K. LeGuin, and Larry Niven. Bibliography.

C9 —————. *Science Fiction Reader's Guide.* Lincoln, Neb.: Centennial, 1974. Analyzes representatives of "hard" science fiction, "soft" science fiction, and fantasy. Jules Verne, H. G. Wells, Isaac Asimov, Alfred Bester, Arthur C. Clarke, Fritz Leiber, Hal Clement, Walter M. Miller, Jr., Frank Herbert, Robert A. Heinlein, Alexei Panshin, Ursula K. LeGuin, and Larry Niven. Primary and secondary bibliography.

C10 Allen, Walter. *The Modern Novel in Britain and the United States.* New York: Dutton, 1964. Covers the period from 1920 to 1960 but is primarily focused on the twenties and thirties, with two chapters on war and postwar fiction.

a transparent container of 'real' contents." For Alter, a Does not cover authors who started writing after 1955. The difference between American and British literary consciousness is that the British is more traditional and the American more ambitious and daring. The British novel deals with the working class, and the American novel has shifted emphasis from the southern writer to the Jewish writer. Saul Bellow, William Faulkner, Graham Greene, James Joyce, Carson McCullers, John Steinbeck, Bernard Malamud, Alan Sillitoe, David Storey, and Keith Waterhouse.

C11   ————. *The Novel To-Day.* London: Longmans, Green, 1955. A selective assessment of the contemporary novel. In this booklet, Allen studies Elizabeth Bowen, Ivy Compton-Burnett, Joyce Cary, Wyndham Lewis, Evelyn Waugh, and others.

C12   ————. *Reading a Novel.* London: Phoenix House, 1949; rev. ed., 1956. Assumes that the "novel is the most important vehicle of imaginative writing in our time." Because it is focused mainly on people, the novel satisfies our needs to be entertained and informed about human nature. Fiction offers the opportunity of knowing representations of human beings intimately, thereby making the unknowable comprehensible. Once the writer's part is finished, the reader must begin to work: "real reading . . . is a creative act," a "collaboration between the reader and the novelist." This study outlines such collaboration and applies it to seven novels. Graham Greene, Virginia Woolf, George Eliot, C. P. Snow, Joyce Cary, François Mauriac, and Kingsley Amis.

C13   Alter, Robert. *Partial Magic: The Novel as a Self-Conscious Genre.* Berkeley: University of California Press, 1975. Alter writes that "in many important novelists from Renaissance Spain to contemporary France and America the realistic enterprise has been enormously complicated and qualified by the writer's awareness that fictions are never real things, that literary realism is a tantalizing contradiction in terms." In this light, Alter discusses "the purposeful experiments with form undertaken by the novelists, experiments intended in various ways to draw our attention to fictional form as a consciously articulated entity rather than

112

"self-conscious novel" is a "novel that systematically flaunts its own condition of artifice and that by so doing probes into the problematic relationship between real-seeming artifice and reality." Miguel de Cervantes, Denis Diderot, Henry Fielding, Vladimir Nabokov, James Joyce; brief references to John Barth, Donald Barthelme, William Faulkner, John Fowles, Flann O'Brien, Martha Robert, and others.

C14   ————. *Rogue's Progress: Studies in the Picaresque Novel.* Cambridge, Mass.: Harvard University Press, 1964. Studies the tradition of the picaresque narrative, the picaresque vision of the world, the picaroon's relationship to society, and how these elements are dependent upon the historical situation in which they were created. Primary emphasis is upon novels of the eighteenth century, but the last chapter discusses recent developments. Thomas Mann, Saul Bellow, Joyce Cary, and earlier writers.

C15   Amis, Kingsley. *New Maps of Hell: A Survey of Science Fiction.* New York: Harcourt, Brace & World, 1960. A survey of science fiction from Verne and Wells to the 1960s that examines the current state of the genre, its relationship to the unconsciousness, and science fiction as a medium "of social diagnosis and warning." It concludes with an analysis of the strengths and weaknesses of the genre. Ray Bradbury, Arthur C. Clarke, Robert A. Heinlein, George Orwell, Kurt Vonnegut, Jr., Frederik Pohl, C. M. Kornbluth, John Updike, and Philip Wylie.

C16   Ash, Brian. *Faces of the Future—The Lessons of Science Fiction.* London: Elek/Pemberton, 1975. The purpose of this study is "to examine the social implications, whether intended or accidental, of those science fiction stories which can be deemed of serious content—and to draw what lessons we will." Ash studies "the outpourings of realists who have seen little of comfort ahead." Historical treatment of themes in science fiction that ranges from the writings of Lucian to Kurt Vonnegut, Jr. Bibliography.

C17   Auchincloss, Louis. *Pioneers and Caretakers: A Study of Nine American Women Novelists.* Minneapolis: University of Minnesota Press, 1965. American women writers see America discriminatingly; they are concerned with preserving our national heritage; and they penetrate deeply into the ailments of our time. Auchincloss calls these women "caretakers" of the American dream. Mary McCarthy, Carson McCullers, Jean Stafford, Katherine Anne Porter, and earlier writers.

C18   Axthelm, Peter. *The Modern Confessional Novel.* New Haven: Yale University Press, 1967. Explores the origins of the confessional novel and its characteristic techniques. For Axthelm, a confessional novel "presents a hero, at some point in his life, examining his past as well as his innermost thoughts, in an effort to achieve some form of perception." Fyodor Dostoevsky, André Gide, Jean-Paul Sartre, Albert Camus, Arthur Koestler, William Golding, and Saul Bellow. Bibliography.

C19   Bailey, J. O. *Pilgrims through Space and Time: Trends and Patterns in Scientific and Utopian Fiction.* New York: Angus, 1947. A chronological study of scientific romances. Bailey contends that the atomic bomb makes the study of science fiction necessary because it has already dealt with the future. Bibliography.

C20   Balakian, Nona, and Charles Simmons, eds. *The Creative Present: Notes on Contemporary American Fiction.* Garden City, N.Y.: Doubleday, 1963. Recognizes writers whose identities have been blurred by the enormity of Faulkner and Hemingway and studies post–World War II writers distinguished by their accomplishments and potentiality. James Baldwin, J. D. Salinger, Vladimir Nabokov, Carson McCullers, Truman Capote, Saul Bellow, William Styron, Norman Mailer, Eudora Welty, James Jones, Jack Kerouac, Bernard Malamud, John Updike, Mary McCarthy, and others. Primary bibliography.

C21   Baldwin, Kenneth H., and David K. Kirby, eds. *Individual and Community: Variation on a Theme in American Fiction.* Durham, N.C.: Duke University Press, 1975. Baldwin's and Kirby's aim was to select "essays which point to the continuity of an important theme in American fiction and to offer insight into the variety of philosophical and literary strategies utilized in the significant works of significant authors dealing with the question of the individual and the community." Ernest Hemingway, William Faulkner, Djuna Barnes, Thomas Pynchon, and earlier writers.

C22 Baumbach, Joseph. *The Landscape of Nightmare: Studies in the Contemporary American Novel.* New York: New York University Press, 1965. Baumbach's focus is upon the themes of guilt and redemption. Our novelists, states Baumbach, "have tried to make sense—to make an art—of what it's like to live in this nightmare." The works discussed are not studied "as nightmare news reports of our culture, but as works of the imagination, as works that preserve the possibility of consciousness. As works of art." Robert Penn Warren, Saul Bellow, J. D. Salinger, Ralph Ellison, Flannery O'Connor, Bernard Malamud, William Styron, E. L. Wallant, and Wright Morris. Primary bibliography.

C23 Beachcroft, T. O. *The English Short Story, II.* London: Longmans, Green, 1964. This monograph begins with Robert Louis Stevenson and Rudyard Kipling and concludes with a final section on contemporary writers. Most writers are treated in a paragraph.

C24 Beja, Morris. *Epiphany in the Modern Novel.* Seattle: University of Washington Press, 1971. This book examines the part that spiritual manifestations play in the modern novel. Beja studies the traditional and present context of Epiphany, the purpose of Epiphany, representative novelists, and the way Epiphanic moments are essential to these writers' views of art and experience. James Joyce, Virginia Woolf, Thomas Wolfe, and William Faulkner. Brief references to Djuna Barnes, John Barth, Lawrence Durrell, John Galsworthy, William Golding, Ernest Hemingway, Nathalie Sarraute, William Styron, and others. Bibliography.

C25 Bellamy, Joe David. *The New Fiction: Interviews with Innovative American Writers.* Urbana: University of Illinois Press, 1974. The last ten years of American writing have been drastically different from the time of the modernists. "The purpose of this book has been to try to find out why this change has taken place and what, in specific terms, has characterized the transformations of sensibility, language, and formal and technical modes of the present and immediately upcoming periods." Taped interviews with American writers involved in the change. John Barth, Joyce Carol Oates, William H. Gass, Donald Barthelme, Ronald Sukenick, Tom Wolfe, John Hawks, Susan Sontag, Jerzy Kosinski, John Gardner, Kurt Vonnegut, Jr., and others.

C26 Bellow, Saul. *Recent American Fiction: A Lecture Presented under the Auspices of the Gertrude Clarke Whittall Poetry and Literature Fund.* Washington, D.C.: Library of Congress, 1963. Bellow examines "the view taken by recent American novelists and short-story writers of the individual and his society." Wylie Sypher's *Loss of Self in Modern Literature and Art* provides the springboard for Bellow's discussion of the self in American literature.

C27 Bergonzi, Bernard. *The Situation of the Novel.* Pittsburgh: University of Pittsburgh Press, 1970. Concerned "with the contemporary novel as the product of a particular phase of history, in a particular culture." Studies the present state and possible future of fiction and cultural attitudes implicit in the recent English novel. Contrasts the American and British novel. Kingsley Amis, John Barth, Anthony Burgess, Nigel Dennis, Doris Lessing, Anthony Powell, C. P. Snow, Evelyn Waugh, and Angus Wilson.

C28 Berry, Thomas Elliott. *The Newspaper in the American Novel, 1900–1969.* Metuchen, N.J.: Scarecrow, 1970. Discusses the portrayal of the twentieth-century American newspaper in the American novel. Berry's study is based on two premises: first, "the complex nature and the far-reaching significance of the American newspaper can be explained only by a competent interpretation of the total institution of American newspaper journalism"; and second, "because the novelists' interpretations of institutions often exert a strong impact on the conclusions held by society, the interpretations of the American newspaper by American novelists merit a careful examination." Berry discusses numerous novels.

C29 Blish, James, ed. *The Issue at Hand: Studies in Contemporary Magazine Science Fiction by William Atheling, Jr.* Chicago: Advent, 1964. A collection of criticism Blish wrote under the name William Atheling, Jr., on magazine science fiction. Poul Anderson, Isaac Asimov, Anthony Boucher, Ray Bradbury, John W. Campbell, Jr., Robert A. Heinlein,

116

Damon Knight, Cyril M. Kornbluth, Theodore Sturgeon, and others.

C30   ——————, ed. *More Issues At Hand: Critical Studies in Contemporary Science Fiction by William Atheling, Jr.* Chicago: Advent, 1970. A collection of essays Blish wrote under the name William Atheling, Jr. Brian Aldiss, Kingsley Amis, Poul Anderson, J. G. Ballard, Ray Bradbury, John W. Campbell, L. Sprague de Camp, Harry Harrison, Robert A. Heinlein, Damon Knight, Judith Merril, Sam Moskowitz, Theodore Sturgeon, H. G. Wells, and many others.

C31   Blotner, Joseph L. *The Modern American Political Novel, 1900–1960.* Austin: University of Texas Press, 1966. "The principal purpose of this study is to discover the image of American politics presented in American novels over the sixty-year span from 1900 through 1960." Blotner continues: "The purpose is actually twofold in that it is concerned with the artist's conception of this aspect of the American experience and also with the nature and quality of the fictional art itself." Survey of 138 novels. Primary and secondary bibliography.

C32   ——————. *The Political Novel.* Garden City, N.Y.: Doubleday, 1955. Written for the political scientist, this study makes "available an original classification of political novels and politically relevant summaries." In a series of brief segments, the work studies the novel as a political instrument, as a political history, as a mirror of national character, as an analysis of group behavior and of individual behavior. Numerous novelists from America, Britain, the Continent, and elsewhere. Norman Mailer, George Orwell, Arthur Koestler, Joyce Cary, and others. Bibliography.

C33   Bluefarb, Sam. *The Escape Motif in the American Novel: Mark Twain to Richard Wright.* Columbus: Ohio State University Press, 1972. Discusses eight novels that "form a paradigmatic parabola of the escape motif." Traces the appearance of the flight or escape motif from Mark Twain through Carson McCullers, Ernest Hemingway, John Steinbeck, and Richard Wright. Primary bibliography.

C34   Bone, Robert A. *The Negro Novel in America.* New Haven:

Yale University Press, 1966. Bone finds two poles in the Negro novel, assimilation and Negro nationalism, which he uses to interpret the consciousness of individual authors and whole periods. His ultimate aim is "to measure the contribution of the Negro novelist to American letters." This study traces Negro fiction from 1890 through William Gardner Smith, Chester Himes, Richard Wright, Ralph Ellison, William Demby, Dorothy West, Owen Dodson, Ann Petry, and Willard Motley. Primary and secondary bibliography.

C35   Bova, Ben. *Through Eyes of Wonder: Science Fiction and Science.* Reading, Mass.: Addison-Wesley, 1975. Explanation of the ways that "science and science fiction have affected" Bova's life. He also discusses "the interplay between science and science fiction," which is "important for an understanding of the world."

C36   Bowden, Edwin T. *The Dungeon of the Heart: Human Isolation and the American Novel.* New York: Macmillan, 1961. "The problem of human isolation is one of the great and pressing ones in American life and so is one of the great themes of the American novel." J. D. Salinger, Sherwood Anderson, William Faulkner, John Steinbeck, and earlier writers.

C37   Bradbury, Malcolm. *Possibilities: Essays on the State of the Novel.* New York: Oxford University Press, 1973. Studies "the novel as a form and the novel as a history" from its "rise" in the eighteenth century to the present day. Bradbury examines the novel's form, history, criticism, and possibilities. His concentration is on "the relation between individual authors and works and phases of style, the question of the novel's realism and its fictiveness, its humanism and its formalism." Malcolm Lowry, William Cooper, C. P. Snow, Angus Wilson, Iris Murdoch, Muriel Spark, and John Fowles.

C38   Bretnor, Reginald, ed. *Modern Science Fiction: Its Meaning and Its Future.* New York: Coward-McCann, 1953. Essays collected to give readers a general picture of science fiction. Contributors include John W. Campbell, Jr., Anthony Boucher, Don Fabun, Fletcher Pratt, Rosalie Moore, L.

Sprague de Camp, Isaac Asimov, Arthur C. Clarke, Philip Wylie, Gerald Heard, and Reginald Bretnor.

C39 —————, ed. *Science Fiction, Today and Tomorrow: A Discursive Symposium*. New York: Harper & Row, 1974. This volume represents an "examination of science fiction in our contemporary world, which means of course that it looks at science fiction as a life process." Includes essays by Ben Bova, Frederik Pohl, George Zebrowski, Frank Herbert, Alan E. Nourse, Thomas N. Scortia, Reginald Bretnor, James Gunn, Alexei and Cory Panshin, Hal Clement, Anne McCaffrey, Gordon R. Dickson, and Jack Williamson. Bibliography.

C40 Broes, Arthur T., et al. *Lectures on Modern Novelists*. Pittsburgh: Department of English, Carnegie Institute of Technology, 1963. Lectures on William Golding, J. D. Salinger, Jack Kerouac, Thomas Wolfe, Henry James, and David Michael Jones.

C41 Bryant, Jerry H. *The Open Decision: The Contemporary American Novel and Its Intellectual Background*. New York: Free Press, 1970. Bryant writes: "I have tried to construct the logic of the larger intellectual climate to be found in present-day physics, philosophy, sociology, psychology, and other disciplines of study. This climate is unified by a particular view of reality, and one of this book's main assumptions is that this view of reality forms the foundations of contemporary morality and that the novels studied herein examine that foundation and dramatize the dilemmas of that morality." Elliott Baker, James Baldwin, John Barth, Saul Bellow, William Burroughs, Albert Camus, J. P. Donleavy, Ralph Ellison, Alfred Grossman, Joseph Heller, James Jones, Jack Kerouac, and many others.

C42 Burgess, Anthony. *The Novel Now: A Guide to Contemporary Fiction*. New York: Norton, 1967. A survey of British novels up to 1966. For Burgess, the novel is concerned "with interpreting, through the imagination, though not with the cold deliberation of the scientist, the nature of the external world and the mind that surveys it." Kingsley Amis, Elizabeth Bowen, Anthony Burgess, Joyce Cary, Graham Greene, Aldous Huxley, Doris Lessing, Vladimir

Nabokov, Anthony Powell, C. P. Snow, Evelyn Waugh, and others.

C43   Butterfield, Stephen. *Black Autobiography in America.* Amherst: University of Massachusetts Press, 1974. In black autobiography, wounds heal and pride develops. It is a representation of objective facts and subjective awareness. "Black writers offer a model of the self which is different from white models, created in response to a different perception of history and revealing divergent, often completely opposite meanings of human actions." Butterfield states that the purpose of his study is "to read the books closely, to evaluate their importance, to trace the development of the genre over a period of time, to discuss the books as embodiments of the black American experience, to relate them where possible to the literature of the mainstream." Studies writers in the "Slave Narrative Period" (1831–1895) to Richard Wright, James Baldwin, Ida Wells, Maya Angelou, Anne Moody, and others. Bibliography.

C44   Calder, Jenni. *Chronicles of Conscience: A Study of George Orwell and Arthur Koestler.* Pittsburgh: University of Pittsburgh Press, 1968. Essays that compare Orwell and Koestler through an analysis of their fiction. Calder's focus is the relationship between conscience and political allegiance and between words and deeds. She writes that Koestler will be remembered as the spokesman of an era, while Orwell's significance lies in the quality of his writing. Bibliography.

C45   Carter, Lin. *Imaginary Worlds: The Art of Fantasy.* New York: Ballantine, 1973. A critical and technical analysis of "the major fantasy writers of the past three quarters of a century" and their tradition of creating alternate worlds. In order to study fantasy as literature, Carter studies how fantasy is made, how the authors "create the illusion of a genuine historical reality," and how they influence their readers. Poul Anderson, L. Sprague de Camp, Lord Dunsany, E. R. Eddison, Robert E. Howard, C. S. Lewis, H. P. Lovecraft, Clark Ashton Smith, J. R. R. Tolkien, Jack Vance. Bibliography.

C46   Church, Margaret. *Time and Reality: Studies in Contemporary Fiction.* Chapel Hill: University of North Carolina Press,

1963. Church's purpose is "to indicate how an author's concept of time influences the value and meaning of his novels." She contends that an understanding of the form, content, thought, and motif of fiction depends on an understanding of an author's attitude toward time and space. Henri Bergson, Marcel Proust, James Joyce, Virginia Woolf, Aldous Huxley, Thomas Mann, Franz Kafka, Thomas Wolfe, William Faulkner, and Jean-Paul Sartre. Bibliography.

C47   Clareson, Thomas D., ed. *SF: The Other Side of Realism: Essays on Modern Fantasy and Science Fiction.* Bowling Green, Ohio: Bowling Green University Press, 1971. Clareson brings together "a sampling of essays and notes, primarily but not exclusively, from the 1960's and from academic, popular, and specialist sources in order to indicate the diversity with which the genre may be approached." Includes essays by Thomas D. Clareson, Julius Kagarlitski, Judith Merril, Lionel Stevenson, Robert B. Schmerl, Brian Aldiss, Samuel R. Delany, Patrick J. Callahan, Michel Butor, James Blish, I. F. Clarke, Mark R. Hillegas, Alexei Panshin, Susan Glicksohn, and others. Lists "Award-Winning Science Fiction Novels." Bibliography.

C48   Collins, R. G., ed. *The Novel and Its Changing Form.* Winnipeg: University of Manitoba Press, 1972. Traces the novel from the early sixteenth-century picaresque romance to the "new" new novel. Among the contributors are E. F. Sterling, Wendell V. Harris, David Ketterer, Jacques Barzun, John Fowles, Philip Stevick, and ten others.

C49   ————, and Kenneth McRobbie, eds. *New Views of the English and American Novel.* Winnipeg: University of Manitoba Press, 1971. A collection of essays that discusses various facets of the novel. Joseph Heller, Bernard Malamud, William Faulkner, and C. P. Snow.

C50   Colmer, John, ed. *Approaches to the Novel.* Edinburgh: Oliver & Boyd, 1967. Colmer's purpose is "to awaken interest in the problems of reading a novel, and to offer different approaches to this literary form." Discusses the relationship between matter and form, the relationship between tale and teller, techniques of multiple narration, the relationship between social commentary and narrative technique, the importance of recognizing dominant modes or genres in a novel, and reading for pleasure. Joseph Heller, Evelyn Waugh, and earlier writers.

C51   Comfort, Alex. *The Novel in Our Time*. London: Phoenix, 1948. Examines "critical and technical problems arising out of the novel in its present setting." Comfort's position is romanticism, which "implies a belief that humanity" is in "a constant state of conflict with the external universe." Brief references to many writers, among them Graham Greene and Ernest Hemingway.

C52   Cooke, M. G., ed. *Modern Black Novelists: A Collection of Critical Essays*. Englewood Cliffs, N.J.: Prentice-Hall, 1971. Fifteen essays on black writing in the U.S., Africa, and the West Indies. Ralph Ellison, Richard Wright, James Baldwin, Chinua Achebe, Wilson Harris, V. S. Naipaul, and others. Bibliography.

C53   Core, George, ed. *Southern Fiction Today: Renascence and Beyond*. Athens: University of Georgia Press, 1969. A collection of essays. In the southern writer's depiction of moral, ethical, and cosmic truth, Core sees the South as a metaphor for the fate of man. Thomas Wolfe, Robert Penn Warren, William Styron, Flannery O'Connor, William Faulkner, Erskine Caldwell, and others.

C54   Cornillon, Susan Koppleman, ed. *Images of Women in Fiction: Feminist Perspectives*. Bowling Green, Ohio: Bowling Green University Popular Press, 1972. This collection of essays illustrates "the beginnings of new directions for women in reading and understanding fiction, and therefore new directions and depths for women in their personal paths." The essays are divided into four sections: "Woman as Heroine," "The Invisible Woman," "The Woman as Hero," and "Feminist Aesthetics." James Baldwin, Sylvia Plath, Kate Chopin, Kate Millet, Joyce Carol Oates, and others. Primarily earlier authors.

C55   Davenport, Basil. *Inquiry into Science Fiction*. New York: Longmans, Green, 1955. An analysis of science fiction, space operas, mad scientists, bug-eyed monsters, scientific science fiction, and speculative science fiction. Ends with a discussion of the effect of science fiction on the emotions. Suggested readings.

C56 —————, et al. *The Science Fiction Novel: Imagination and Social Criticism.* Chicago: Advent, 1964. Includes "Science Fiction: Its Nature, Faults, and Virtues" by Robert A. Heinlein, "The Failure of the Science Fiction Novel as Social Criticism" by C. M. Kornbluth, "Science Fiction and the Renaissance Man" by Alfred Bester, and "Imagination and Modern Social Criticism" by Robert Bloch.

C57 Davies, Horton. *A Mirror of the Ministry in Modern Novels.* New York: Oxford University Press, 1959. Davies's study contains "estimates of the ministry and the priesthood in the last hundred years" in the novel. James Gould Cozzens, Graham Greene, Sinclair Lewis, Alan Paton, James Hawck Street, Peter de Vries, and others. Bibliography.

C58 Detweiler, Robert. *Four Spiritual Crises in Mid-Century American Fiction.* University of Florida Monographs 14 (Fall 1963). Freeport, N.Y.: Books for Libraries, 1970. Includes "Religion in Postwar American Fiction," "William Styron and the Courage to Be," "John Updike and the Indictment of Culture-Protestantism," "Philip Roth and the Test of Dialogic Life," and "J. D. Salinger and the Quest for Sainthood."

C59 Dyson, A. E. *The Crazy Fabric: Essays in Irony.* London: Macmillan, 1965. Studies irony in prose writers, from Jonathan Swift through Lytton Strachey, Aldous Huxley, Evelyn Waugh, and George Orwell. Select bibliography.

C60 Edel, Leon. *The Modern Psychological Novel.* New York: Grove Press, 1959*; rpt. New York: Grosset & Dunlap, 1964. Edel writes about "the literary representation of thought in its flowing and evanescent state" and "the representation within consciousness of sensory experience." His study includes the stream-of-consciousness novel, the internal monologue novel, and the twentieth-century search for inner reality. C. P. Snow, Lawrence Durrell, Edouard Dujardin, Arthur Miller, William Faulkner, Henry James, James Joyce, Dorothy Richardson, Virginia Woolf, and others.

C61 Eisinger, Chester E. *Fiction of the Forties.* Chicago: University of Chicago Press, 1963. Defines the fiction of the forties within its cultural and literary background. Eisinger contends that this period changed the face of our total literature. Nelson Algren, Budd Schulberg, Irwin Shaw, John Dos Passos, Granville Hicks, Mary McCarthy, Lionel Trilling, James Gould Cozzens, William Faulkner, Caroline Gordon, Andrew Lytle, Peter Taylor, Robert Penn Warren, Truman Capote, Carson McCullers, Eudora Welty, Paul Bowles, Jean Stafford, Walter van Tilburg Clark, Wallace Stegner, Wright Morris, and Saul Bellow. Primary bibliography.

C62   Eshbach, Lloyd Arthur, ed. *Of Worlds Beyond: The Science of Science Fiction Writing.* Reading, Pa.: Fantasy Press, 1947. (Reissued by Advent Press in 1964.)* One of the first studies of the genre of science fiction. Seven practitioners write on aspects relevant to their own fiction. Robert A. Heinlein, John Taine, Jack Williamson, A. E. Van Vogt, L. Sprague de Camp, Edward E. Smith, John W. Campbell, Jr.

C63   Federman, Raymond, ed. *Surfiction: Fiction Now . . . and Tomorrow.* Chicago: Swallow, 1975. Essays gathered "in an effort to determine, define, analyze what is the present state of fiction—FICTION NOW—and, to some extent, in an effort to suggest, project, propose what will be the future of fiction— . . . AND TOMORROW." Federman discusses authors whose work is recognized "as having disrupted the tradition on which fiction has been functioning." William Burroughs, John Hawkes, J. M. G. LeClezio, and others. Contributors include John Barth, Ronald Sukenick, Richard Kostelanetz, Jerome Klinkowitz, Marcus Klein, Jacques Ehrmann, and others.

C64   Fiedler, Leslie A. *The Jew in the American Novel.* New York: Herzl Institute Pamphlet, no. 10, 1959. "This essay is intended to be not exhaustive but representative. The few writers who are discussed at any length are those who seem to me . . . both most rewarding as artists and most typical as actors in the drama of Jewish cultural life in America." Fiedler tries for "a general notion of the scope and shape of the Jewish American tradition in fiction—useful to Gentile and Jew, reader and writer alike, not merely as history but as a source of pleasure and self-knowledge." Norman Mailer, Irwin Shaw, Herman Wouk, J. D. Salinger, Bernard Malamud, and Saul Bellow.

C65   ————. *Love and Death in the American Novel.* Cleveland: World, 1964. Fiedler's aim is "to emphasize the neglected contexts of American fiction, largely depth-psychological and anthropological, but sociological and formal as well." By concentrating on the themes of love and death, Fiedler demonstrates the fate and character of the American novel. "There is a pattern imposed both by writers of our past and the very conditions of life in the United States from which no American novelist can escape, no matter what philosophy he consciously adopts or what themes he thinks he pursues." The time span studied is from 1789 to 1959. William Faulkner, Ernest Hemingway and earlier writers.

C66   Folsom, James K. *The American Western Novel.* New Haven, Conn.: College & University Press, 1966. Folsom examines the themes, motifs, and implications inherent in the literature of the West. He asks for a new evaluation of the western story, one that is not historical in orientation, but one that sees the West as a "fable" that "must be interpreted in terms of a parable." James Fenimore Cooper through Walter van Tilburg Clark and A. B. Guthrie. Bibliography.

C67   French, Warren. *Season of Promise: Spring Fiction 1967.* Columbia: University of Missouri Press, 1968. In the spring of 1967, the appearance of five novels signaled new life for the genre. For French, these novels represent the rediscovery of the American experience. Elia Kazan, Thornton Wilder, R. K. Narayan, William Goldman, Don Asher, and James Purdy protest "the complacency and self-delusion that cause human relationships to deteriorate." Bibliography.

C68   Friedman, Alan Warren, ed. *Forms of Modern British Fiction.* Austin: University of Texas Press, 1975. Friedman arranges the essays in this collection to formulate this thesis: "Hardy—the first of the modern British novelists—and Joyce and Woolf—the last—are framed by Galsworthy and his like (who were dismissed by Woolf as 'materialists,' anachronistic, premodern) and by self-conscious postmoderns like Durrell, Beckett, and Henry Green who may, thereby, be seen as just as anachronistic in their own way

—writing after the period we call modern and yet writing as though the radical innovation we associate with the moderns remained the novel's hallmark."

C69   Friedman, Melvin J., ed. *The Vision Obscured: Perceptions of Some Twentieth Century Catholic Novelists.* New York: Fordham University Press, 1970. A collection of essays that reassesses "the roles of a distinguished group of twentieth-century Catholic writers, of American, English, French, Spanish, Italian, and German origin." The literary climate as well as individual novels are discussed by J. F. Powers, Flannery O'Connor, Evelyn Waugh, Muriel Spark, Graham Greene, François Mauriac, Elizabeth Langgässer, Carmen Laforet, Giovanni Papini, and others. Bibliography compiled by Jackson R. Bryer and Nanneska N. Magie.

C70   Frohock, W. M. *The Novel of Violence in America.* 2nd ed. Dallas: Southern Methodist University Press, 1957. Frohock studies the American novels of violence and the climate which makes violence acceptable. He sees time as the factor which is the real agent or active force that stands between man and happiness. Novelists, then, combine violence of action with a feeling of time as corrosive. John Dos Passos, Thomas Wolfe, James T. Farrell, Robert Penn Warren, Erskine Caldwell, John Steinbeck, William Faulkner, and James Agee.

C71   Fuller, Edmond. *Man in Modern Fiction: Some Minority Opinions on Contemporary American Writing.* New York: Vintage, 1958. Many writers can write an articulate novel but few can "think" a novel. It is in this area that contemporary fiction is anemic. Fuller argues that contemporary literature presents a corrupted and debased image of man, and he explores the work of writers who have this vision. John Aldridge, James Joyce, and Jack Kerouac.

C72   Gado, Frank, ed. *First Person: Conversations on Writers and Writing with Glenway Wescott, John Dos Passos, Robert Penn Warren, John Updike, John Barth, Robert Coover.* Schenectady, N.Y.: Union College Press, 1973. A collection of tape-recorded interviews. This series of interviews reflects "the evolution of fiction in the post-war years."

C73   Galloway, David D. *The Absurd Hero in American Fiction:*

Updike, Styron, Bellow, Salinger. Austin: University of Texas Press, 1966. According to Camus, man can create a heroism in spite of his "fragmented" and "unredeemable" experience. Galloway studies four authors who share Camus's belief in a "new secular humanism," in the "promise of rain to the fashionable wasteland." Also considers T. S. Eliot and James Joyce. Primary and secondary bibliography.

C74   Gardiner, Harold C. *Norms for the Novel.* New York: America Press, 1953. This study "tries to put before critic and reader of the modern American novel two sets of principles in the form of propositions." First, Gardiner "attempts to answer the question: do the norms of morality have any bearing on the novelist's art?" Second, he faces the question: "granting that these moral norms have been obtained in the novelist's art, what is that art designed to achieve?" Brief references to many novels written during the 1940s and the 1950s.

C75   ————, ed. *Fifty Years of the American Novel, 1900–1950: A Christian Appraisal.* New York: Scribner's, 1952. A collection of essays that indicates the opinions of academic critics who represent Catholic literary scholarship. Edith Wharton, Theodore Dreiser, Ellen Glasgow, Willa Cather, F. Scott Fitzgerald, John Dos Passos, William Faulkner, Ernest Hemingway, Thomas Wolfe, John Steinbeck, James T Farrell, Robert Penn Warren, and others. Primary bibliography.

C76   Gass, William H. *Fiction and the Figures of Life.* New York: Knopf, 1970. A collection of articles and reviews on the nature of fiction, literary figures, and the social significance of art. Gertrude Stein, Bertrand Russell, Vladimir Nabokov, Donald Barthelme, J. F. Powers, and others.

C77   Gayle, Addison, Jr. *The Way of the New World: The Black Novel in America.* Garden City, N.Y.: Anchor, 1975. Traces the history of the black novel and the sociological forces that shaped it. James Baldwin, Imamu Amiri Baraka (LeRoi Jones), William Wells Brown, Charles Waddell Chesnutt, W. E. B. Du Bois, Paul Laurence Dunbar, Ralph Ellison, Jessie Fauset, Rudolph Fisher, Henry Highland Garnet, Marcus Garvey, Chester Himes, Langston

Hughes, James Weldon Johnson, Claude McKay, Jean Toomer, Carl Van Vechten, Richard Wright, and others. Bibliography.

C78   Gelfant, Blanche Housman. *The American City Novel.* Norman: University of Oklahoma Press, 1954. Gelfant introduces a literary genre, "the twentieth century American city novel," defines the genre, suggests its social backgrounds, and discusses the relationship between the "social vision of the city and the aesthetics of the novel." Theodore Dreiser, Thomas Wolfe, Sherwood Anderson, Edith Wharton, John Dos Passos, James T. Farrell, Nelson Algren, Betty Smith, Leonard Bishop, Willard Motley, and others. Bibliography.

C79   Gibson, Walker. *Tough, Sweet and Stuffy: An Essay on Modern American Prose Styles.* Bloomington: Indiana University Press, 1966. Describes "three extreme but familiar styles in modern American prose": tough talk, in which the narrator-hero identifies himself as a hard man who has been around; sweet talk, or "the blandishments of advertising"; and stuffy talk, or "the hollow tones of officialese." Gibson studies the ways these styles create a specific character with a particular idiom. Saul Bellow, T. S. Eliot, William Faulkner, Ernest Hemingway, Wright Morris, Tom Wolfe, and others.

C80   Gindin, James. *Harvest of a Quiet Eye: The Novel of Compassion.* Bloomington: Indiana University Press, 1971. Gindin tries "to define a 'tradition of compassion,' a critical hypothesis based on an emotional attitude conveyed from author to reader," and to suggest a way into a subjective method of criticism. Traces this tradition from Anthony Trollope to Joyce Cary, Angus Wilson, Saul Bellow, Norman Mailer, Iris Murdoch, Philip Roth, and John Updike.

C81   ————. *Postwar British Fiction: New Accents and Attitudes.* Westport, Conn.: Greenwood, 1962. A humanistic, cultural, and social study of the contemporary novel in Britain. Individual chapters on Kingsley Amis, Doris Lessing, Alan Sillitoe, John Wain, Angus Wilson, Iris Murdoch, and William Golding; other writers covered in topical chapters are John Bowen, Shelagh Delaney, Nigel

Dennis, Lawrence Durrell, Margot Heinemann, Thomas Hinde, Bill Hopkins, Bernard Kops, Philip Larkin, Roger Longrigg, John Osborne, Harold Pinter, Andrew Sinclair, C. P. Snow, David Storey, Hugh Thomas, Honor Tracy, Keith Waterhouse, Arnold Wesker, and Colin Wilson.

C82   Gloster, Hugh M. *Negro Voices in American Fiction.* Chapel Hill: University of North Carolina Press, 1948. "With racial considerations motivating most of their work, they write chiefly about their status as a segregated, oppressed, ridiculed, and exploited minority in the American social order." Gloster's study is concerned with "racial expression" rather than "artistic evaluation." Traces the history of Negro literature from Reconstruction through Paul Dunbar, Langston Hughes, Thomas Nelson Page, Arna Bontemps, George Cable, Oscar Cargill, Charles Chesnutt, Countee Cullen, Richard Wright, and others. Bibliography.

C83   Gold, Herbert, ed. *First Person Singular: Essays for the Sixties.* New York: Dial, 1963. Essays by sixteen contemporary novelists on issues pertinent to the times. These novelists "have rediscovered something which a short recent tradition of novelists since Flaubert seemed to have given up . . . the joy of speaking out straight from the mind." Gore Vidal, Mary McCarthy, Arthur Miller, William Saroyan, William Styron, Harvey Swados, Nelson Algren, James Baldwin, Saul Bellow, George P. Elliott, Paul Goodman, Elizabeth Hardwick, Seymour Krim, and others.

C84   Gossett, Louise. *Violence in Recent Southern Fiction.* Durham, N.C.: Duke University Press, 1965. Gossett contends that "violence is part of the acute criticism to which Western writers in the twentieth century have subjected their culture." Studies physical and psychological violence in fiction since 1930. Thomas Wolfe, Erskine Caldwell, William Faulkner, Robert Penn Warren, Flannery O'Connor, Eudora Welty, William Styron, William Goyen, Truman Capote, Carson McCullers, and others.

C85   Greenblatt, Stephen Jay. *Three Modern Satirists: Waugh, Orwell, and Huxley.* New Haven: Yale University Press, 1965. Individual studies of each author's life and work. Using their mutual historical context as an objective standard, Greenblatt compares and contrasts the three satirists

129

and their responses to life. Through these combined approaches, he defines each writer's world view. Bibliography.

C86   Gross, Theodore L. *The Heroic Ideal in American Literature.* New York: Free Press, 1971. "Literary heroes dramatize the moral texture *of a country.* . . . This book considers some . . . heroes of American literature and their struggle with a conflict . . . between idealism and authority." This conflict is traced through "five heroic figures in American literature: the Emersonian hero; the Southern hero; the Black hero; the Disenchanted hero; the Quixotic hero." Does not offer a new definition of the hero, but argues that "the hero of American literature is the exceptional man who seeks to realize an ideal." Richard Wright, Ralph Ellison, James Baldwin, Ernest Hemingway, Saul Bellow, J. D. Salinger, and Norman Mailer.

C87   Gunn, James. *Alternate Worlds: The Illustrated History of Science Fiction.* Englewood Cliffs, N.J.: Prentice-Hall, 1975. An illustrated history that explains science fiction "in terms of the influences that created it and then affected its subsequent development." It defines science fiction and shows how it differs from other forms of narration. Gunn focuses upon writers, books, and magazines that influenced the science fiction tradition. Thirteen chapters chart the historical development of various movements. Appendix. Isaac Asimov, Ray Bradbury, Arthur C. Clarke, Harlan Ellison, Hugo Gernsback, James Gunn, Robert Heinlein, Sam Moskowitz, Theodore Sturgeon, A. E. Van Vogt, Kurt Vonnegut, Jr., and others.

C88   Hall, James. *The Lunatic Giant in the Drawing Room: The British and American Novel since 1930.* Bloomington: Indiana University Press, 1968. Hall studies six novelists "who have explored beyond the existing formulations of experience." He reports on a developing chronology of the novel and defines its main directions. Hall's aim is "to show what happens when a structure of feeling with a powerful hope and a compelling literature behind it meets new and not readily reconcilable aspirations." Establishes individual criteria for judgment on the six writers. Elizabeth Bowen, William Faulkner, Robert Penn Warren, Graham Greene, Saul Bellow, and Iris Murdoch. Bibliography.

C89 ————. *The Tragic Comedians: Seven Modern British Novelists.* Bloomington: Indiana University Press, 1963. "This book deals with novelists who make considerable use of what everyone can agree is comedy, but who so mix this with severer conflicts that the mixture becomes more important than either ingredient." E. M. Forster, Aldous Huxley, Evelyn Waugh, Henry Green, Joyce Cary, L. P. Hartley, and Anthony Powell. Bibliography.

C90 Handy, William J. *Modern Fiction: A Formalist Approach.* Carbondale: Southern Illinois University Press, 1971. A technical examination of six novels. Includes an introduction that stresses "meaning as well as technical development." James Joyce, Theodore Dreiser, William Faulkner, Ernest Hemingway, Saul Bellow, and Bernard Malamud.

C91 Hardy, John Edward. *Man in the Modern Novel.* Seattle: University of Washington Press, 1964. Hardy concentrates on the theme of self and the effort to know it as the central preoccupation of the twentieth century. Specifically, he demonstrates "the primary relevance of the theme to certain problems of *form* in the modern novel." Joseph Conrad, E. M. Forster, D. H. Lawrence, James Joyce, F. Scott Fitzgerald, Virginia Woolf, Ernest Hemingway, Evelyn Waugh, William Faulkner, Eudora Welty, and Robert Penn Warren.

C92 Harper, Howard M., Jr. *Desperate Faith: A Study of Bellow, Salinger, Mailer, Baldwin and Updike.* Chapel Hill: University of North Carolina Press, 1967. Contemporary fiction has the quality of "ultimate concern"—it deals with universal questions in unique and interesting ways. Harper's book is a study of the responses of five contemporary writers to these types of questions.

C93 Harper, Ralph. *The World of the Thriller.* Cleveland: Press of Case Western Reserve University, 1969. With the intention to suggest a phenomenology of reading thrillers, Harper explores existential themes in spy novels and the psychology of the reader's response. He discusses the world of the thriller, situational fiction, terror, danger, and violence. Graham Greene, Raymond Chandler, Ian Fleming, Dorothy Sayers, and others.

C94   Harris, Charles B. *Contemporary American Novelists of the Absurd.* New Haven, Conn.: College & University Press, 1971. Harris argues that the dominant theme in the American novel is the belief that we live in an absurd universe, chaotic and without meaning. He sees this theme reflected through the use of traditional novelistic devices in an ironic or farcical manner. This fusion of form and content becomes a metaphor for life. Harris also discusses camp and pop art as an extension of the absurdist technique. Joseph Heller, Kurt Vonnegut, Jr., Thomas Pynchon, John Barth, and others. Primary and secondary bibliography.

C95   Harrison, Gilbert A., ed. *The Critic as Artist: Essays on Books, 1920–1970.* New York: Liveright, 1972. H. L. Mencken's "The Critic's Motive" followed by sixty short essays on fiction. Philip Roth, Joseph Heller, James Thurber, James Joyce, Kurt Vonnegut, Jr., Katherine Anne Porter, James Bond, Saul Bellow, W. Somerset Maugham, Ernest Hemingway, Colette, Kay Boyle, Graham Geeene, Alan Sillitoe, and many others.

C96   Hartt, Julian N. *The Lost Image of Man.* Baton Rouge: Louisiana State University Press, 1963. The religious question in novels can be ignored but the human question cannot. Hartt states, "What a novelist says about the human condition in his novel can be discussed as a disclosure of human reality, and it reflects a moral conviction." William Faulkner, John Steinbeck, Ernest Hemingway, and others.

C97   Hassan, Ihab. *Radical Innocence: Studies in the Contemporary American Novel.* New York: Harper & Row, 1961. For Hassan, the contemporary American novel not only expresses our presence, but it "explores and enlarges the modalities of our *being.*" "Radical innocence" is the hero's desire to affirm "the human sense of life." Hassan writes, "It is the innocence of a self that refuses to accept the immitigable rule of reality, including death, an aboriginal Self the radical imperatives of whose freedom cannot be stifled." Studies three aspects of the American novel: the hero and the world, the forms of fiction, and the individual talent. William Styron, Harvey Swados, Norman Mailer, Frederick Buechner, Bernard Malamud, Ralph Ellison, Herbert Gold, John Cheever, J. P. Donleavy, Carson Mc-

Cullers, Truman Capote, J. D. Salinger, and Saul Bellow. Bibliography.

C98   Hauck, Richard Boyd. *A Cheerful Nihilism: Confidence and "The Absurd" in American Humorous Fiction.* Bloomington: Indiana University Press, 1971. This book is informed by Camus's essay on Sisyphus "because it concisely defines in modern terms the absurd sense as the sense of meaninglessness experienced by the man who has no abstract faith." Camus does not say "where a man gets the confidence to believe that his act of absurd creation does create meaning." The American authors "studied here have made the problem of confidence and absurd creation their primary humorous subject." Their reaction to meaninglessness has been nihilistic and cheerful. Their desire is "to create laughter out of absurdity." Traces "cheerful nihilism" from Jonathan Edwards, Benjamin Franklin, Herman Melville, and Mark Twain to William Faulkner and John Barth.

C99   Hays, Peter L. *The Limping Hero: Grotesques in Literature.* New York: New York University Press, 1971. Hays deals with novels that contain lame heroes—characters who are actually lame or symbolically so. This lameness is a literary symbol for a genital wound which symbolizes a social disability. Hays identifies the limping heroes as ancient fertility gods and discusses these figures as they appear in D. H. Lawrence, Tennessee Williams, Bernard Malamud, Saul Bellow, William Styron, and others. He, then, describes how these cripples express their author's view of life. Primary bibliography.

C100   Hemenway, Robert, ed. *The Black Novelist.* Columbus, Ohio: Merrill, 1970. "The essays in this book are intended (1) to suggest the historical tradition and esthetic worth of novels written by Black Americans; (2) to indicate the range of critical attitudes toward these novels; and (3) to permit the Black American novelist to speak for himself about his craft and his fellow craftsmen." The collection contains ten critical essays and nine theoretical essays by novelists. The book hopes to show how the black novelist has contributed to "American literary history." James Baldwin, Arna Bontemps, Ralph Ellison, William Gardner Smith, John A. Williams, Richard Wright, and Frank Yerby. Bibliography.

C101   Henderson, Harry B., III. *Versions of the Past: The Historical Imagination in American Fiction.* New York: Oxford University Press, 1974. Henderson studies the American historical novel and "compels us to reconsider the view that American writing has been deficient in a sense of history." He outlines two modes of historical thought and applies them to writers from James Fenimore Cooper to William Faulkner, John Barth, Ralph Ellison, and Norman Mailer.

C102   Hicks, Granville, assisted by Jack Alan Robbins. *Literary Horizons: A Quarter Century of American Fiction.* New York: New York University Press, 1970. Fifteen reviews published in the "Literary Horizons" column of the *Saturday Review* on the novels of writers who seem "representative" of the postwar period. Wright Morris, Saul Bellow, Bernard Malamud, James Baldwin, John Updike, Flannery O'Connor, Herbert Gold, Kurt Vonnegut, Jr., Louis Auchincloss, Vladimir Nabokov, Joseph Heller, Reynolds Price, Philip Roth, John Barth, and Norman Mailer.

C103   —————, ed. *The Living Novel: A Symposium.* New York: Macmillan, 1957. "This book is dedicated to the proposition that the novel is important, and is addressed to a skeptical world. That the contributors believe in the importance of the novel they have demonstrated in the best possible way—by learning how to write good novels and by writing them." Contributors discuss the lack of interest in the "serious novel." These writers submit evidence "that the novel is not dead and that it is not going to submit docilely to the murder that is plotted against it." Contributors include Saul Bellow, Paul Darcy Boles, John Brooks, Ralph Ellison, Herbert Gold, Mark Harris, Wright Morris, Flannery O'Connor, Harvey Swados, Jessamyn West, and Granville Hicks.

C104   Hillegas, Mark, ed. *Shadows of Imagination: The Fantasies of C. S. Lewis, J. R. R. Tolkien, and Charles Williams.* Carbondale: Southern Illinois University Press, 1969. Hillegas connects Lewis, Tolkien, and Williams to what he calls the "new era of post-realism." Their writing projects two trends: "the swing from realism and the end of the anti-rationalist movement." Looking ahead, Hillegas sees the coming of a "new fantasy," presenting what Lewis has called the ideas of the "other side." A collection of essays on the three authors.

C105   Hoffman, Frederick J. *The Art of Southern Fiction: A Study of Some Modern Novelists.* Carbondale: Southern Illinois University Press, 1967. Hoffman puts Faulkner aside to look at his contemporaries and explore the fiction of the South in terms of time and place. He discusses three categories of southern literature: those works that define the tradition without abstracting it, those that reveal the native particulars of a scene and time, and those that explore "the complex influence of a place as moral 'fable.'" Eudora Welty, Carson McCullers, James Agee, Flannery O'Connor, and William Styron.

C106   Hollister, Bernard C., and Deane C. Thompson. *Grokking the Future.* [Dayton, Ohio:] Pflaum/Standard, 1973. "This book has two objectives. One is to demonstrate how science fiction (SF) offers new insights into current social issues, and the other is to help students become more creative in their thinking about the future, thus increasing their options for tomorrow." Deals with many short stories and novels. Bibliography.

C107   Holman, C. Hugh. *The Roots of Southern Writing: Essays on the Literature of the American South.* Athens: University of Georgia Press, 1972. Holman's purpose is "to relate the work of southern writers to their physical, social, and moral environment and to the history of their region." His work is the response "of a southern student of the novel to certain aspects of his own culture viewed through the frames of idea or subject matter." Ellen Glasgow, Thomas Wolfe, William Faulkner, Flannery O'Connor, and earlier writers.

C108   Howe, Irving. *Politics and the Novel.* Greenwich, Conn.: Fawcett, 1967. Howe studies "what happens to the novel when it is subjected to the pressures of politics and political ideology." His primary emphasis is upon the nineteenth century, but he also includes a chapter on André Malraux, Ignazio Silone, Arthur Koestler, and George Orwell.

C109   Hoyt, Charles Alva, ed. *Minor American Novelists.* Carbondale: Southern Illinois University Press, 1970. "The major figure conceives of his preoccupation in terms of the whole world, while the minor can see the world only in terms of his preoccupation." A collection of essays on authors considered to be minor, ranging from Charles Brockden Brown to Flannery O'Connor and Edward Lewis Wallant.

C110   Hughes, Carl Milton, *pseud.* [John Milton Charles Hughes]. *The Negro Novelist: A Discussion of the Writings of American Negro Novelists, 1940–1950.* New York: Citadel, 1953. Hughes examines novels by Negro authors written between 1940 and 1950. He bases his argument on two assumptions: first, that there is one mainstream of American literature and, second, that various ethnic groups contribute to the mainstream. Out of the mainstream and ethnic groups emerges our national literature. Hughes analyzes the novel rather than the Negro. William Attaway, Chester Himes, Zora Neale Hurston, Willard Motley, Carl Oxford, Ann Petry, J. Saunders Redding, William Gardner Smith, Richard Wright, and Frank Yerby. Bibliography.

C111   Hugo, Howard E., ed. *Aspects of Fiction: A Handbook.* Boston: Little, Brown, 1962. This collection presents novelists on the craft of the novel. Forty-seven chronological essays by writers from Henry Fielding to Alain Robbe-Grillet, Jack Kerouac, Joyce Cary, William Faulkner, Elizabeth Bowen, and others.

C112   Iser, Wolfgang. *The Implied Reader: Patterns of Communication in Prose Fiction from Bunyan to Beckett.* Baltimore: Johns Hopkins University Press, 1974. "The present collection of essays is an attempt to lay the foundations for a theory of literary effects and responses based on the novel since that is the genre in which reader involvement coincides with meaning production." During the eighteenth century "the novel was concerned directly with social and historical norms that applied to a particular environment, and so it established an immediate link with the empirical reality familiar to its readers." The work's historical approach suggests that this involvement becomes more complex as the novel ages. William Faulkner, Ivy Compton-Burnett, Samuel Beckett, James Joyce, and others.

C113   Ishag, Saada, and Constance Denniston. *The American Novel:*

Two Studies. Emporia State Research Studies. Emporia: Kansas State Teachers College Press, 1965. Ishag writes on Melville; Denniston studies parody in James Purdy and Joseph Heller.

C114   Jameson, Storm. *Parthian Words.* New York: Harper & Row, 1970. Jameson's book is both "the moral autobiography of a writer as well as an essay in criticism." Includes chapters on the novel, language, whether the novel has gone into decline, the noveau roman, critics, and a new beginning for the novel.

C115   Johnson, Michael L. *The New Journalism: The Underground Press, the Artists of Nonfiction, and Changes in the Established Media.* Lawrence: University Press of Kansas, 1971. A history and analysis of the underground press, a study of three major nonfiction writers—Truman Capote, Tom Wolfe, and Norman Mailer—and an account of the new journalists' view of war, race, and radical scenes.

C116   Josipovici, Gabriel. *The World and the Book: A Study of Modern Fiction.* London: Macmillan, 1971. Calls for a reexamination of literary history "by using the insights of modernism to guide us through tradition." Modernism, states Josipovici, is "an insistence on the fact that what previous generations had taken for *the world* was only *the world seen through the spectacles of habit.*" To understand the anti-novel, then, we must grasp the premises of the traditional novel. Vladimir Nabokov, Saul Bellow, William Golding, and earlier writers.

C117   Kaplan, Harold. *The Passive Voice: An Approach to Modern Fiction.* Athens: Ohio University Press, 1966. Kaplan discusses the crisis of knowledge in modern intellectual history, the effects of solipsism and of moral passivity, the split consciousness which divides knowing and understanding, the perspectives of primitive naturalism and stoic naturalism, and the comic mood and tragedy. James Joyce, Ernest Hemingway, William Faulkner, and earlier writers.

C118   Kaplan, Sydney Janet. *Feminine Consciousness in the Modern British Novel.* Urbana: University of Illinois Press, 1975. During the first quarter of the twentieth century, two movements reached a climax: "experimentation with modes of consciousness in the novel" and the "feminist struggle for equality and independence." While the realistic novel dealt with social aspects of the feminist movement, women writers used the "novel of consciousness" to study psychological aspects. "They wanted to go beyond stereotypes." Kaplan states: The "feminine consciousness" is not a "particular sensibility among female writers. I am concerned with it as a literary device: a method of characterization of females in fiction." Her focus is upon "the ways in which the consciousnesses of women are organized in the novels of women writers." Kaplan examines five British novelists over seven decades to show women as physical beings, as social beings, and as thinking beings. Dorothy Richardson through Doris Lessing and Rosamond Lehmann.

C119   Karl, Frederick R. *A Reader's Guide to the Contemporary English Novel*. Rev. ed. New York: Octagon, 1975. (Appeared in 1962 as *The Contemporary English Novel*.) In 1930 a new generation of writers was established. Karl examines the differences between the writers before 1930 and those after. For Karl, the function of the novel is "the definition of man in his society." Thus, "the novelist must not detract from the pressures of the great world in favor of exclusive emphasis upon the small. Only then can the novel hope to fulfill itself." Samuel Beckett, Lawrence Durrell, C. P. Snow, Graham Greene, Elizabeth Bowen, Joyce Cary, George Orwell, Henry Green, Ivy Compton-Burnett, Anthony Powell, Angus Wilson, Nigel Dennis, William Golding, Iris Murdoch, Rex Warner, P. H. Newby, Doris Lessing, Alan Sillitoe, Muriel Spark, John Fowles, and Anthony Burgess.

C120   Karolides, Nicholas J. *The Pioneer in the American Novel, 1900–1950*. Norman: University of Oklahoma Press, 1967. Karolides discusses "the image of the frontier and the pioneer as presented to the reader's mind." His study is "an analysis of the conception of the pioneer in the novel to comprehend the way in which Americans see their past and how they see themselves in relation to their heritage." Alfred B. Guthrie, Jr., Zane Grey, Conrad Richter, Dale Van Every, and others.

C121   Kazin, Alfred. *Bright Book of Life: American Novelists and*

Storytellers from Hemingway to Mailer. Boston: Little, Brown, 1973. Discusses trends since World War II in the literature that conveys the "nature of our American experiences"; nine chapters: "A Dream of Order: Hemingway," "The Secret of the South: Faulkner to Percy," "The Decline of War: Mailer to Vonnegut," "Professional Observers: Cozzens to Updike," "The Earthly City of the Jews: Bellow to Singer," "Cassandras: Porter to Oates," "The Imagination of Fact: Capote to Mailer," "Absurdity as a Contemporary Style: Ellison to Pynchon," and "A Personal Sense of Time: Nabokov and Other Exiles." Also discusses James Baldwin, Jane Bowles, William Burroughs, John Cheever, Joan Didion, William Faulkner, William H. Gass, Bernard Malamud, Mary McCarthy, Carson McCullers, Flannery O'Connor, John O'Hara, J. F. Powers, Philip Roth, J. D. Salinger, Isaac Bashevis Singer, William Styron, Robert Penn Warren, and others.

C122   Kellogg, Gene. *The Vital Tradition: The Catholic Novel in a Period of Convergence.* Chicago: Loyola University Press, 1970. Kellogg studies only those novels in which the dramatic action depends on Roman Catholic theology, on the history of thought, or on the development of Roman Catholic "ideas." His aim is "to discover how the flowering of the Catholic novel began, what it achieved, and how it ended." He examines three Roman Catholic communities —French, English, and American. François Mauriac, Georges Bernanos, Evelyn Waugh, Graham Greene, J. F. Powers, and Flannery O'Connor. Bibliography.

C123   Kennard, Jean E. *Number and Nightmare: Forms of Fantasy in Contemporary Fiction.* Hamden, Conn.: Archon, 1975. Kennard's book is a study of the fantasy techniques of some British and American novelists who gained their reputation during the sixties. He examines these techniques in relation to the existential premises defined by Sartre and Camus. This study represents "an attempt to define two major forms of fantasy in contemporary fiction, *number* and *nightmare,* on the basis of the novelists' response to a Post-existential world view." Joseph Heller, John Barth, James Purdy, Kurt Vonnegut, Jr., Anthony Burgess, Iris Murdoch, and William Golding. Bibliography.

C124   Kennedy, Alan. *The Protean Self: Dramatic Action in Con-*
        temporary Fiction. New York: Columbia University Press,
        1974. "Modern literature like Sociology sets itself the task
        of accounting for the genesis of the Self." Kennedy argues
        that this "protean quality of language is the most telling
        reason why the concept of self which emerges from modern
        literature . . . is the concept of a protean self." He traces
        the heritage of romantic symbolism of the modern move-
        ment to the Miltonic conception of the self. The protean
        self is "evidence of a belief that there *is* a fundamental urge
        in man which is a dramatic or mimetic urge." Kennedy
        contends that contemporary criticism of the novel relies on
        "inadequate assumptions about the nature of Society and
        the relation of self, and literature, to Society." Joyce Cary,
        Muriel Spark, Christopher Isherwood, Graham Greene,
        John Fowles, and others.

C125   Ketterer, David. *New Worlds for Old: The Apocalyptic Imag-*
        ination, Science Fiction, and American Literature. Garden
        City, N.Y.: Anchor/Doubleday, 1974. For Ketterer, apoca-
        lyptic literature draws "upon surrealism, metaphysical po-
        etry, the pastoral tradition, Brecht's theory of estrangement,
        the work of Franz Kafka, the poetry of the romantics,
        particularly William Blake, and the phenomenological
        novel, among other possibilities." He sets apocalyptic sci-
        ence fiction against mainstream literature that treats the
        same theme in order to emphasize the concordance between
        the two. Ursula K. LeGuin, Kurt Vonnegut, Jr., Brian W.
        Aldiss, Stanislaw Lem, Ray Bradbury, Robert Heinlein,
        H. G. Wells, Edward Bellamy, Edgar Allan Poe, Jack Lon-
        don, Charles Brockden Brown, Mark Twain, Herman Mel-
        ville, and brief references to many others.

C126   Kiely, Benedict. *Modern Irish Fiction: A Critique.* Dublin:
        Golden Eagle, 1950. Kiely studies "modern Ireland through
        modern prose fiction" and "considers that fiction as a reve-
        lation of the Irish mind, of the way in which certain Irish
        eyes, smiling and otherwise, have in the last thirty years
        looked upon Ireland, Europe, the world, and the soul of
        man." Samuel Beckett, Elizabeth Bowen, William Carle-
        ton, Daniel Corkery, Graham Greene, James Joyce, Michael
        McLaverty, Francis MacManus, Flann O'Brian, Sean

O'Faoláin, James Stephens, and many others. Primary
bibliography.

C127   Klein, Marcus. *After Alienation: American Novels in Mid-
Century.* Freeport, N.Y.: Books for Libraries Press, 1970.
Klein discusses a period beginning about 1950. Since this
time, most serious novelists have been concerned with an
agony unknown to their predecessors. It is called, variously, "nihilism, poetic naturalism, radical innocence, the
death of dissidence, the age of accommodation. . . ." Klein
focuses upon the novel of accommodation in which "the
hero begins in freedom of the self and discovers that he is
isolated. He chooses community—he assumes radical obli-
gations, or declares himself a patriot, or he makes love—
and he discovers that he has sacrificed his identity, and his
adventures begin all over again." Saul Bellow, Ralph Ellison, James Baldwin, Wright Morris, and Bernard Malamud. Bibliography.

C128   ————, ed. *The American Novel since World War II.*
Greenwich, Conn.: Fawcett, 1969. A collection of essays in
four parts. Part 1—on class, values, and ideologies—includes essays by Philip Rahv, John Aldridge, William Bar-
rett, and Norman Mailer. In part 2, Lionel Trilling,
Herbert Gold, Alfred Kazin, Irving Howe, Philip Roth,
and Saul Bellow write on society and self. Part 3 is on the
underground; contributors include Lawrence Lipton, Paul
Goodman, Ihab Hassan, Benjamin DeMott, Burton Feldman, and Leslie Fiedler. Part 4—on shapes and language
in the novel—includes essays by John Hawkes, William
Phillips, William H. Gass, and John Barth.

C129   Klinkowitz, Jerome. *Literary Disruptions: The Making of a
Post-Contemporary American Fiction.* Urbana: University
of Illinois Press, 1975. The contemporary novelists who
have received the most critical attention are "in fact re-
gressive parodists, who by the Literature of Exhaustion
theory have confused the course of American fiction and
held back the critical (although not the popular) appreciation of Kurt Vonnegut, Jr., Donald Barthelme, Jerzy
Kosinsky, and the other writers surveyed in this book."
"Although the prologue studies fiction of the Sixties in
general, my real concern begins with the publishing season

of 1967–68, when for the first time in a long time a clear trend in literary history became evident." "The authors studied . . . are of a definite style and school: given to formal experimentation, a thematic interest in the imaginative transformation of reality, and a sometimes painful but often hilarious self-conscious artistry." Kurt Vonnegut, Jr., Donald Barthelme, Jerzy Kosinsky, LeRoi Jones (Imamu Amiri Baraka), James Park Sloan, Ronald Sukenick, Raymond Federman, Gilbert Sorrentino, and others. Bibliography.

C130 Knight, Damon. *In Search of Wonder: Essays on Modern Science Fiction.* Rev. and enl. ed. Chicago: Advent, 1967. A collection of critical notes and essays on the principal trends and authors of modern science fiction. Knight shows that science fiction is a field worth taking seriously. A. E. Van Vogt, Robert Heinlein, Isaac Asimov, Ray Bradbury, Henry Kuttner, Cyril Kornbluth, James Blish, Fletcher Pratt, Sam Moskowitz, and others. Bibliography.

C131 Kort, Wesley A. *Shriven Selves: Religious Problems in Recent American Fiction.* Philadelphia: Fortress, 1972. Kort examines the conflict between personal, religious, and public life. His aim is to expose this problem, its roots, its consequences, and its relation to literary elements of recent fiction by means of an examination of the characteristics of its predominantly confessional form. Peter de Vries, Bernard Malamud, J. F. Powers, William Styron, and John Updike.

C132 Kumar, Shiv K., ed. *Critical Approaches to Fiction.* New York: McGraw-Hill, 1968. A collection of modern critical essays on various aspects of fiction: plot, character, language, theme, and technique. The essays provide the student with a guide to "critical theory and practice." Contributors include Saul Bellow, Mary McCarthy, Eudora Welty, Mark Schorer, and others.

C133 Lebowitz, Naomi. *Humanism and the Absurd in the Modern Novel.* Evanston: Northwestern University Press, 1971. Lebowitz discusses two attitudes—"one associated with the 'old' humanist novel, the other with the 'new' absurdist fiction." She studies George Eliot, E. M. Forster, Fyodor

Dostoevsky, Saul Bellow, Albert Camus, Stanley Elkin, Gustave Flaubert, André Gide, and others.

C134   Lehan, Richard. *A Dangerous Crossing: French Literary Existentialism and the Modern American Novel.* Carbondale: Southern Illinois University Press, 1973. Argues that the postwar French novelists felt the influence of the American writers of the time. Lehan goes on to show that there was a reciprocal relationship and that the writers in both countries found their origins in similar situations and sources. Jean-Paul Sartre, Albert Camus, John Dos Passos, Ernest Hemingway, William Faulkner, Norman Mailer, Richard Wright, Saul Bellow, Ralph Ellison, Joseph Heller, John Barth, Thomas Pynchon, and others. Bibliographical essay.

C135   Lewis, R. W. B. *The Picaresque Saint: Representative Figures in Contemporary Fiction.* New York: Lippincott, 1959. Lewis's aim is "to describe a particular generation of novelists in Europe and America." The authors covered "suggest the varieties and . . . contradictions that the generation expresses." Lewis explores "the nature of the imaginative world [the generation] has succeeded in creating." The generation of James Joyce, Marcel Proust, and Thomas Mann was "artistic." This new generation is "human," and "the chief experience has been the discovery of what it means to be a human being and to be alive." Alberto Moravia, Albert Camus, Ignazio Silone, William Faulkner, Graham Greene, and André Malraux.

C136   Lindsay, Jack. *After the 'Thirties': The Novel in Britain, and Its Future.* London: Lawrence & Wishart, 1956. Lindsay studies the "postwar crisis in literature." He begins his study with the 1930s and "the break that occurred in 1939–1940." James Aldridge, Christopher Caudwell, Graham Greene, Ernest Hemingway, Storm Jameson, Doris Lessing, Wright Morris, and others.

C137   Litz, A. Walton, ed. *Modern American Fiction: Essays in Criticism.* New York: Oxford University Press, 1963. The aim of this collection is "to provide the reader with useful commentaries on the major writers of American fiction, from Stephen Crane to the present. William Faulkner, Ernest Hemingway, John Steinbeck, Robert Penn Warren, and others.

C138   Lodge, David. *The Novelist at the Crossroads and Other Essays on Fiction and Criticism.* Ithaca, N.Y.: Cornell University Press, 1971. A collection of essays of "considerable variation in form as well as matter." Lodge states, "I still hold unrepentantly to the primacy of language in literary matters." He advocates a critical pluralism to match the literary pluralism. The book is divided into four major categories: "Fiction and Criticism," "Fiction and Catholicism," "Fiction and Modernism," and "Fiction and Utopia." Graham Greene, Muriel Spark, William Burroughs, Samuel Beckett, Ernest Hemingway, John Updike, and others.

C139   Ludwig, Jack. *Recent American Novelists.* University of Minnesota Pamphlets on American Writers 22. Minneapolis: University of Minnesota Press, 1962. A monograph that treats Nelson Algren, James Baldwin, Saul Bellow, Ralph Ellison, Herbert Gold, James Jones, Jack Kerouac, Norman Mailer, Bernard Malamud, Wright Morris, Flannery O'Connor, J. D. Salinger, William Styron, Harvey Swados, John Updike, and others. Primary and secondary bibliography.

C140   Lundwall, Sam J. *Science Fiction: What It's All About.* New York: Ace Books, 1971. Translated from the Swedish by its author, the work presents a historical survey of the genre. He critically covers all aspects: "books, magazines, comics, fans and fandom, juvenilia, series characters, and literary giants." Brian Aldiss, Isaac Asimov, J. G. Ballard, Ray Bradbury, Frederic Brown, Harlan Ellison, Philip José Farmer, Hugo Gernsbach, Robert Heinlein, Robert Shockley, Theodore Sturgeon, and Kurt Vonnegut, Jr. Bibliography.

C141   Lutwack, Leonard. *Heroic Fiction: The Epic Tradition and American Novels of the Twentieth Century.* Carbondale: Southern Illinois University Press, 1971. Lutwack discusses recent American fiction in the light of the epic tradition. John Steinbeck, Ernest Hemingway, Saul Bellow, and Ralph Ellison. Bibliography.

C142   Lyons, John O. *The College Novel in America.* Carbondale: Southern Illinois University Press, 1962. Lyons traces the American college novel and American academic life from Nathaniel Hawthorne to Mary McCarthy, Randall Jarrell, Stringfellow Barr, and Carlos Baker. Bibliography.

C143 McCormack, Thomas, ed. *Afterwords: Novelists on Their Novels.* New York: Harper & Row, 1969. "After-the-fact prefaces" by novelists on their own work. They discuss how it began, what it looked like at various stages, problems, solutions, and how explicit the considerations of craft were. Louis Auchincloss, Wright Morris, Anthony Burgess, Robert Crichton, Mark Harris, Mary Renault, William Gass, Reynolds Price, George P. Elliott, Truman Capote, Ross MacDonald, John Fowles, Vance Bourjaily, and Norman Mailer.

C144 McCormick, John. *Catastrophe and Imagination: An Interpretation of the Recent English and American Novel.* London: Longmans, Green, 1957. A social, historical, and national study of the forces that have had a "tremendous weight in determining the balance of modern sensibility in the art-form of the novel." A survey treatment of Sherwood Anderson, John Dos Passos, William Faulkner, Ernest Hemingway, Aldous Huxley, Saul Bellow, Elizabeth Bowen, Joyce Cary, John Hawkes, Christopher Isherwood, Norman Mailer, John O'Hara, Anthony Powell, C. P. Snow, Robert Penn Warren, Evelyn Waugh, and others.

C145 McNelly, Willis E., ed. *Science Fiction: The Academic Awakening.* Shreveport, La.: College English Association, 1974. The purpose of this book is "*to aid teachers* of English, at whatever level, who might be approaching science fiction for the first time." It contains historical essays, subjective commentaries, bibliographies, personal statements, conjectural analyses, and objective descriptions.

C146 Madden, David, ed. *Rediscoveries: Informal Essays in Which Well-Known Novelists Rediscover Neglected Works of Fiction by One of Their Favorite Authors.* New York: Crown, 1971. Madden asked well-known novelists "to rediscover their own favorite neglected work of fiction." Harriette Arnow, Wolfgang Borchert, William Gaddis, Jean Giono, Caroline Gordon, William Goyen, Marianne Hauser, Walter M. Miller, Jr., Mario Puzo, Mary Lee Settle, Gertrude Stein, Richard Yates, and earlier writers. Bibliography.

C147 Malin, Irving. *New American Gothic.* Carbondale: Southern Illinois University Press, 1962. Malin studies the "tortuous inwardness" of six American gothic novelists. He charts their characteristics and tendencies; and then provides an evaluation of this group of writers. Truman Capote, James Purdy, Flannery O'Connor, John Hawkes, Carson McCullers, and J. D. Salinger.

C148 ————, ed. *Psychoanalysis and American Fiction*. New York: Dutton, 1965. Fifteen essays that approach American fiction from the psychoanalytical point of view. The essayists assume that our fiction holds "dark, unacknowledged truths about the national character." They explore themes, situations, styles, literary biography, and theories of culture. Frank Norris, William Faulkner, Erskine Caldwell, Saul Bellow, and earlier writers.

C149 Manlove, C. N. *Modern Fantasy: Five Studies*. Cambridge: Cambridge University Press, 1975. Manlove examines Charles Kingsley, George MacDonald, C. S. Lewis, J. R. R. Tolkien, and Mervyn Peake. Manlove defines fantasy and provides a literary analysis of the work of these five writers. Finally, he discusses the point at which a work fails to abide by its own laws and argues that this problem is typical of modern imaginative fantasy.

C150 May, John R. *Toward a New Earth: Apocalypse in the American Novel*. Notre Dame, Ind:. University of Notre Dame Press, 1972. May's purpose is "to derive from literary and theological sources a typology representing the various eschatological language traditions in their successive historical phases. Since apocalypse is the most poetic and imaginative form of eschatological writing, it will serve as the theological basis for the typology." William Faulkner, Flannery O'Connor, Nathanael West, Ralph Ellison, James Baldwin, Richard Wright, John Barth, Thomas Pynchon, Kurt Vonnegut, Jr., and some earlier writers.

C151 Meeter, Glenn. *Bernard Malamud and Philip Roth: A Critical Essay*. Contemporary Writers in Christian Perspective. Grand Rapids, Mich.: William B. Eerdmans, 1968. Meeter argues that Roth and Malamud "invite a particular response not only in religious but often in specifically Christian terms." He continues, "They deal again and again with the meeting of Judaism and Christianity—a meeting figured in their work by the plot devices of intermarriage and conversion, by the themes of law and grace, by images of blood and the cross." These two writers have set their task as the "reclothing" of religion. Bibliography.

C152   Miles, Rosalind. *The Fiction of Sex: Themes and Functions of Sex Difference in the Modern Novel.* Plymouth, Eng.: Vision Press, 1974. A study of the ways sex is treated in fiction and the fictional nature of sexual notions. Concerned with the sexual stereotypes and the nature of sex in literature and with woman writers in the twentieth century. Anthony Burgess, Ivy Compton-Burnett, Ernest Hemingway, Doris Lessing, Mary McCarthy, Carson McCullers, Katherine Mansfield, Iris Murdoch, and others. Bibliography.

C153   Miller, J. Hillis, ed. *Aspects of Narrative: Selected Papers from the English Institute.* New York: Columbia University Press, 1971. Papers that express "a concern for the interpretation of narrative." The collection includes "Indeterminacy and the Reader's Response in Prose Fiction," "Molestation and Authority in Narrative Fiction," "The Irrelevant Detail and the Emergence of Form," "Time and Narrative in *A la recherche du temps perdu,*" "Proust and the Art of Incompletion," "Autobiography and America," and "Witness and Testament: Two Contemporary Classics," *The Autobiography of Malcolm X* [Malcolm Little], and *The Armies of the Night* (Norman Mailer).

C154   Miller, Wayne Charles. *An Armed America: Its Face in Fiction—A History of the American Military Novel.* New York: New York University Press, 1970. A history of novelists who have reported and recreated their responses to war. Miller writes this history to provide "a better historical and cultural perspective from which the American military man and military machine may be understood and controlled." James Fenimore Cooper through Joseph Heller, John M. Haines, John P. Marquand, and James Gould Cozzens. Bibliography.

C155   Millgate, Michael. *American Social Fiction: James to Cozzens.* New York: Barnes & Noble, 1964. "The novelists discussed in this study are alike in that they set out deliberately to create an image of the society in which their characters move." The importance of their work lies in the social presentation they attempt. Millgate presents a hypothesis concerning the study of American social fiction: "It might be possible to obtain a different and richer impression of American social fiction, and hence of American fiction as a whole, by exploring the work of novelists other than those normally regarded as constituting the major tradition, and by considering this work in its relation, not to the literary achievements of the mid-nineteenth century, but to its own historical and social context. . . . " James Gould Cozzens, John Dos Passos, Norman Mailer, J. P. Marquand, C. P. Snow, and earlier writers.

C156   Millies, Suzanne. *Science Fiction Primer for Teachers.* Dayton, Ohio: Pflaum, 1975. Material is presented in outline form to help the teacher prepare a course in science fiction. Deals with definitions, history, major themes, and the value of science fiction. Ends with suggestions for classroom activities and an outline for a semester course. Bibliography.

C157   Milne, Gordon. *The American Political Novel.* Norman: University of Oklahoma Press, 1966. An examination of political issues in the novel. Milne analyzes the nature and the merits of this fictional form and indicates the link between literature and society. A chronological study from 1774 to Robert Penn Warren, Edwin O'Connor, and Allen Drury. Bibliography.

C158   Milton, John R. *Three West: Conversations with Vardis Fisher, Max Evans, Michael Straight.* Vermillion, N.D.: Dakota Press, 1970. These three writers discuss three different areas of the American western novel: the "regional novel," the "historical novel," and the "colloquial novel."

C159   Mizener, Arthur. *The Sense of Life in the Modern Novel.* Boston: Houghton Mifflin, 1963. Mizener studies "the relation of the represented life in the novel to 'nature,' and the effects of this relation on the novel's expression of values." James Gould Cozzens, John Dos Passos, William Faulkner, Ernest Hemingway, J. D. Salinger, John Updike, and nineteenth-century writers.

C160   —————. *Twelve Great American Novels.* New York: New American Library, 1967. A practical guide to reading twelve novels. Ernest Hemingway, William Faulkner, James Gould Cozzens, Robert Penn Warren, and earlier writers.

C161 Mooney, Harry J., Jr., and Thomas F. Staley, eds. *The Shapeless God: Essays on Modern Fiction.* Pittsburgh: University of Pittsburgh Press, 1968. A collection of essays seeking "to analyze specific components of what may be regarded as the religious awareness—a set of particular beliefs toward God and the question of man's relationship to Him—of the writer" whom the essayist is considering. Carlo Coccioli, Ignazio Silone, Graham Greene, Evelyn Waugh, J. F. Powers, Flannery O'Connor, Pär Lagerkvist, and Heinrich Böll. Includes a bibliography, "Religion and the Modern Novel," by Maralee Frampton.

C162 Moore, Harry T., ed. *Contemporary American Novelists.* Carbondale: Southern Illinois University Press, 1964. A collection of essays on a wide range of interests and authors. Eudora Welty, Carson McCullers, Mary McCarthy, Bernard Malamud, Saul Bellow, James Jones, Norman Mailer, Jack Kerouac, Joseph Heller, James Purdy, J. P. Donleavy, James Baldwin, Herbert Gold, Harvey Swados, John Hawkes, John Updike, William Styron, John Rechy, and Robert Gover.

C163 Morris, Robert K. *Continuance and Change: The Contemporary British Novel Sequence.* Carbondale: Southern Illinois University Press, 1972. A study of six British authors who have written novel sequences. Although each chapter focuses on an individual author, the chapters are unified by a common study of time and history in the novels. Doris Lessing, Olivia Manning, Lawrence Durrell, Anthony Burgess, and C. P. Snow.

C164 Morris, Wright. *About Fiction: Reverent Reflections on the Nature of Fiction with Irreverent Observations on Writers, Readers, and Other Abuses.* New York: Harper & Row, 1975. A fiction "primer" concerned with "what it's like or not like to be human." Morris defines fiction, studies the reading of fiction, the decline of fiction, and voice.

C165 Moskowitz, Sam. *Seekers of Tomorrow: Masters of Modern Science Fiction.* Cleveland: World, 1966. Takes up where *Explorers of the Infinite* left off; it is "a webwork history of science from then [1940] to 1965, told through the lives, works, and influences of more than a score of its most outstanding practitioners of the past twenty-five years." E. E.

Smith, John W. Campbell, Murray Leinster, Edmond Hamilton, Jack Williamson, John Wyndham, Eric Frank Russell, L. Sprague de Camp, Lester Del Ray, Robert A. Heinlein, A. E. Van Vogt, Theodore Sturgeon, Isaac Asimov, Clifford D. Simak, Fritz Leiber, C. L. Moore, Henry Kuttner, Robert Bloch, Ray Bradbury, Arthur C. Clarke, and Philip José Farmer.

C166   Mueller, William R. *Celebration of Life: Studies in Modern Fiction*. New York: Sheed & Ward, 1972. Mueller questions man's relationship to creation, his relationship to other human beings, his comprehension of God, and his relationship with God. Jean-Paul Sartre, Ralph Ellison, Albert Camus, Thomas Mann, George Orwell, François Mauriac, Herman Broch, and others. Bibliography.

C167   Nelson, Gerald B. *Ten Versions of America*. New York: Knopf, 1972. Presents views of America as experienced by characters created by Ernest Hemingway, F. Scott Fitzgerald, Kurt Vonnegut, Jr., Djuna Barnes, Joseph Heller, Philip Roth, Vladimir Nabokov, Saul Bellow, and Nathanael West. The biographies of these literary characters are informed by Nelson's understanding of Jonathan Edwards and of the American dream.

C168   Newby, P. H. *The Novel, 1945–1950*. London: Longmans, Green, 1951. A survey of the fiction "that has appeared in England since the end of the second world war." Elizabeth Bowen, Aldous Huxley, George Orwell, Evelyn Waugh, Ivy Compton-Burnett, Henry Green, Graham Greene, Joyce Cary, L. P. Hartley, and others. Primary bibliography.

C169   Nin, Anaïs. *The Novel of the Future*. New York: Macmillan, 1968. "The purpose of this book is to study the development and technique of the poetic novel." Nin evaluates writers who have integrated poetry and prose, centering her discussion on such trends as "expanded consciousness" or "psychedelic" experiences. Henry Miller, Marguerite Young, and brief references to other writers. Bibliography.

C170   Noble, David W. *The Eternal Adam and the New World Garden: The Central Myth in the American Novel since 1830*. New York: Braziller, 1968. Through a historical perspective, Noble finds that the reality of American history is that of "timeful change, timeful because change is always linked to the past and is always leading into the future." He links Frederick Jackson Turner's frontier hypothesis with "a theology of salvation for the American nation." James Fenimore Cooper through Ernest Hemingway, William Faulkner, Robert Penn Warren, James Gould Cozzens, Norman Mailer, James Baldwin, and Saul Bellow.

C171   O'Connor, William Van, ed. *Forms of Modern Fiction: Essays Collected in Honor of Joseph Warren Beach*. Minneapolis: University of Minnesota Press, 1948. Essays on techniques; individual authors; influences of myth, belief, manners or ideas; problems of tone; symbolism and philosophical position; the impact of the twentieth century; and "finding a basic criterion" for judging a novel. Ernest Hemingway, William Faulkner, Robert Penn Warren, and others.

C172   —————, ed. *Seven Modern American Novelists: An Introduction*. Minneapolis: University of Minnesota Press, 1964. "The seven essays which appear in this book were first published separately in the series of University of Minnesota Pamphlets on American Writers, and together with the other pamphlets in the series are intended as introductions to authors who have helped to shape American culture." William Faulkner, Ernest Hemingway, and earlier figures.

C173   Olderman, Raymond M. *Beyond the Wasteland: A Study of the American Novel in the Nineteen-Sixties*. New Haven: Yale University Press, 1972. Olderman concentrates "on trying to discover the essential vision of these particular writers writing at this particular time, hoping also to reveal something of the American consciousness in the sixties." He attempts "to isolate one set of characteristics, one configuration of themes, techniques, and visions, which is . . . the basis of a new aesthetic and thematic response to the ambiguities of human life." The problematic nature of reality has created the basis for a new romance, a new blend of fact and fiction. Ken Kesey, Stanley Elkin, John Barth, Joseph Heller, Thomas Pynchon, John Hawkes, Kurt Vonnegut, Jr., and Peter S. Beagle. Bibliography.

C174   Panichas, George A., ed. *The Politics of Twentieth-Century Novelists*. New York: Hawthorn, 1971. A sequel to *Mansions of the Spirit*. "Any cessation of interdisciplinary dialogue in the world of letters would inevitably signalize the triumph of the mechanical mind, belonging to the spirit of the time, over the creative mind belonging to the spirit of eternity." Panichas uses this thesis to discuss the relation between art and life for "a better understanding of literary-political problems." H. G. Wells, E. M. Forster, D. H. Lawrence, Wyndham Lewis, Aldous Huxley, George Orwell, Graham Greene, C. P. Snow, Theodore Dreiser, Sherwood Anderson, John Dos Passos, William Faulkner, John Steinbeck, Ralph Ellison, Norman Mailer, William Styron, and European novelists.

C175   Pearce, Richard. *Stages of the Clown: Perspectives on Modern Fiction from Dostoyevsky to Beckett.* Carbondale: Southern Illinois University Press, 1970. Pearce traces the historical antecedents of twentieth-century comic material and the comic view of life. Discusses the mingling of the comic and the tragic. Franz Kafka, William Faulkner, Flannery O'Connor, William Burroughs, Saul Bellow, John Hawkes, Ralph Ellison, Günter Grass, and Samuel Beckett. Selected bibliography.

C176   Peden, William. *The American Short Story: Continuity and Change, 1940–1975.* Boston: Houghton Mifflin, 1975. Peden suggests some of the directions that the American short story has taken since the beginning of our participation in World War II. Nelson Algren, James Baldwin, John Barth, Donald Barthelme, Paul Bowles, Richard Brautigan, Hortense Calisher, Truman Capote, John Cheever, Robert Creeley, Mary McCarthy, Bernard Malamud, Joyce Carol Oates, John O'Hara, J. D. Salinger, John Updike, and many others. Primary bibliography.

C177   ————. *The American Short Story: Front Line in the National Defense of Literature.* Boston: Houghton Mifflin, 1964. Surveys the short story in America since World War I. A form compatible with the temperament of our age, "the short story has become the literary mirror for reflecting an age in which the new tends to be obsolete by tomorrow." It is a form that asks questions rather than gives answers about specific facets of man's experience. John Cheever, William Goyen, James Purdy, Tennessee Williams, Jean Stafford, John Updike, Flannery O'Connor, John O'Hara, and Peter Taylor. Bibliography.

C178   Pendry, E. D. *The New Feminism of English Fiction: A Study of Contemporary Women-Novelists.* Tokyo: Kenkyusha, 1956. Asserts that the differences between men and women are more profound than mere biological differences. Argues that recently women have acquired "the sense of independence . . . necessary for the proper functioning of a culture." It attempts to assess "that change insofar as it has affected fiction." Begins with a survey of history before Virginia Woolf, who stands at the "cross-roads where men and women novelists part company." Numerous minor "women-novelists" are examined to establish "the basis for a tradition" followed by extensive discussions of Ivy Compton-Burnett, Elizabeth Bowen, Rosamond Lehmann, and Olivia Manning.

C179   Perkins, George, ed. *The Theory of the American Novel.* New York: Holt, Rinehart & Winston, 1970. A collection of novelists' writings on the novel. Contributors range from Charles Brockden Brown and James Fenimore Cooper to James T. Farrell, Robert Penn Warren, Richard Wright, Norman Mailer, Saul Bellow, and Vladimir Nabokov. Bibliography.

C180   Pinsker, Sanford. *The Schlemiel as Metaphor: Studies in the Yiddish and American Jewish Novel.* Carbondale: Southern Illinois University Press, 1971. Pinsker traces the origins of schlemiel characters and investigates the appearance of these characters in the novels of Isaac Bashevis Singer, Bernard Malamud, and Saul Bellow.

C181   Raban, Jonathan. *The Technique of Modern Fiction: Essays in Practical Criticism.* London: Edward Arnold, 1968. An application of practical criticism on fiction written in England and America since 1945. Divided into three sections (narrative, character, and style and language), it is a close reading of extracts from various fictions, illustrating this analysis of the traditional techniques of fiction.

C182   Rabinovitz, Rubin. *The Reaction against Experiment in the English Novel, 1950–1960.* New York: Columbia University Press, 1967. The decade of the fifties in England is marked by a rejection of the experimental novelists of the era from 1910 to 1940 and a "revival of enthusiasm for the Victorian novelists." Chapters on Kingsley Amis, Angus

Wilson, and C. P. Snow. Discussions of Lawrence Durrell, William Golding, Iris Murdoch, and others. Bibliography.

C183 Rajan, B., ed. *The Novelist as Thinker.* London: Dennis Dobson, 1967. A collection of essays on "theme," "message," and "ideas." Rajan writes: "The effect of a writer's beliefs on the structure of the novels which dramatize them, and in addition the power of certain beliefs to form and animate an artistic meaning are matters which demand to be seriously discussed." Aldous Huxley, Evelyn Waugh, Christopher Isherwood, L. H. Myers, Jean-Paul Sartre, and François Mauriac.

C184 Rand, Ayn. *The Romantic Manifesto: A Philosophy of Literature.* Cleveland: World, 1969. Rand explains her philosophy of "Romantic-realism." She states: "The motive and purpose of my writing is the *projection of an ideal* man. The portrayal of a moral idea, as my ultimate literary goal, as an end in itself—to which any didactic, intellectual or philosophical values contained in a novel are only the means."

C185 Ratcliffe, Michael. *The Novel Today.* London: Longmans, Green, 1968. A survey of novelists writing in English today, American writers excluded. A select reading list at the end of the survey provides a useful reference to the titles and publication dates of fiction published by over one hundred authors since 1950. Evelyn Waugh, C. P. Snow, Angus Wilson, Kingsley Amis, Doris Lessing, Anthony Burgress, Muriel Spark, William Golding, Graham Greene, Christopher Isherwood, and many others. Bibliography.

C186 Reinhardt, Kurt F. *The Theological Novel of Modern Europe: An Analysis of Masterpieces by Eight Authors.* New York: Ungar, 1969. Reinhardt's essays "offer a cross section which would be truly representative of the major problems with which the modern theological novel . . . has concerned itself." Graham Greene, Evelyn Waugh, and others.

C187 Richter, David H. *Fable's End: Completeness and Closure in Rhetorical Fiction.* Chicago: University of Chicago Press, 1974. A study of a subgenre of the contemporary novel—rhetorical fictions. The study focuses upon the structures of these novels, structures that are informed not by plot but by themes or theses. While rhetorical fictions appear to be "open-ended," they are complete and rounded works of art. Richter is concerned with the way the authors achieve this form and not with its effect upon a reader. Saul Bellow, Albert Camus, William Golding, Joseph Heller, and Thomas Pynchon. Bibliography.

C188   Rideout, Walter B. *The Radical Novel in the United States, 1900–1954: Some Interrelations of Literature and Society.* Cambridge, Mass.: Harvard University Press, 1956. A historical, social, and literary study. "I have attempted to conduct neither an attack nor a defense, but rather an examination, as objective an examination as possible, of a body of fiction . . . once praised in some quarters and now . . . categorically condemned." Norman Mailer, Willard Motley, Isidor Schneider, Howard Fast, and Nelson Algren. Bibliography.

C189   Rippier, Joseph S. *Some Postwar English Novelists.* Frankfurt/Main: Moritz Diesterweg, 1965. Though this period has not produced a Joyce or a Lawrence, it has produced good novels that may be studied under the leitmotifs, "search, sex, satire, . . . [and] savagery." While there is no major movement that unites the eight novelists discussed, Rippier evaluates them in terms of the following standards: their search for "some central quality or standard," their intentions, their "remarks" about fiction, and/or their sociological criticism. Angus Wilson, William Golding, Iris Murdoch, Lawrence Durrell, Kingsley Amis, John Wain, John Braine, and Alan Sillitoe. Bibliography.

C190   Robbe-Grillet, Alain. *For a New Novel: Essays on Fiction.* Translated by Richard Howard. New York: Grove Press, 1965. A collection of short articles written over a number of years, which outline Robbe-Grillet's view of the contemporary novel. Because the novel is alive, it must constantly free itself from social, economic, philosophical, and critical forces that would dictate its form and function. Each generation must write the new novel, and each novelist must invent his own form. Moving beyond existentialism, he bases his aesthetic ideas on the nature of things untouched by man's misconceptions.

C191   Rogers, Alva. *Astounding.* With editorial comments by Harry

Bates, F. Orlin Tremaine, and John W. Campbell. Chicago: Advent, 1964. A history of magazine science fiction from 1930 to 1960. Rogers's study is not a critical work, rather "it is a nostalgic excursion into the past, an attempt to recall my impressions and opinions of the magazine during most of that time." Rogers writes this book to convey "to later generations something of the color and excitement generated by pulp magazines." Isaac Asimov, John W. Campbell, L. Sprague de Camp, Robert A. Heinlein, Henry Kuttner, Hubert Rogers, A. E. Von Vogt, and many others.

C192   Rose, Lois and Stephen. *The Shattered Ring: Science Fiction and the Quest for Meaning.* Richmond, Va.: Knox, 1970. The authors discuss theology and science fiction, redefinitions of science fiction, H. G. Wells, man, nature, and history. Robert Heinlein, C. S. Lewis, Arthur C. Clarke, Walter M. Miller, Jr., Isaac Asimov, and others.

C193   Rosenblatt, Roger. *Black Fiction.* Cambridge, Mass.: Harvard University Press, 1974. Rosenblatt's emphasis is upon patterns that distinguish black fiction from modern literature. While a number of literary movements occurred in the nation during the past eighty years, black fiction "has continued to function within patterns peculiarly its own. It is the existence of the patterns, not simply of common external experiences, which makes the subject real." James Baldwin, Paul L. Dunbar, Ralph Ellison, Chester Himes, James Weldon Johnson, Claude McKay, Richard Wright, Ann Petry, and others. List of works cited.

C194   Rottensteiner, Franz. *The Science Fiction Book: An Illustrated History.* New York: Seabury, 1975. A history of science fiction in movies, comics, and novels. Discusses origins, contemporary practitioners, subgenres, science fiction of other lands, and strange characteristics (i.e., "why there is no sex in science fiction"). Isaac Asimov, George Orwell, Robert A. Heinlein, Ray Bradbury, Kurt Vonnegut, Jr., and others. Bibliography.

C195   Rubin, Louis D., Jr., *The Curious Death of the Novel: Essays in American Literature.* Baton Rouge: Louisiana State University Press, 1967. A collection of "miscellaneous critical writings" that studies the theme of the "writer's relationship with and alienation from his society" in the following writers: Karl Shapiro, Flannery O'Connor, William Faulkner, John Barth, Saul Bellow, Erskine Caldwell, Truman Capote, T. S. Eliot, Ernest Hemingway, Norman Mailer, Eugene O'Neill, Ezra Pound, Susan Sontag, William Styron, and Robert Penn Warren.

C196   ————, and John Rees Moore, eds. *The Idea of an American Novel.* New York: Crowell, 1961. Statements on the novel by writers, from James Fenimore Cooper to William Faulkner and Robert Penn Warren. Bibliography.

C197   Ruehlmann, William. *Saint with a Gun: The Unlawful American Private Eye.* New York: New York University Press, 1974. In the foreword, Aaron Marc Stein writes: "William Ruehlmann's perceptive examination of the heroes of American Private-Eye fiction reveals them for what they are: detectives only in part, if at all, but almost invariably avengers. The loners of the Old West who took justice into their own hands . . . now appear as the loners of the corrupt cities and they are represented as taking justice into their own hands because the legal machinery is not providing satisfactory vengeance." Mike Barry, Raymond Chandler, John Evans, Brett Halliday, Dashiell Hammett, James Jones, Henry Kane, Ross Macdonald, Peter McCurtain, Jon Messman, Don Pendleton, Mickey Spillane, Rex Stout, Donald E. Westlake, and others. Bibliography.

C198   Ruotolo, Lucio P. *Six Existential Heroes: The Politics of Faith.* Cambridge, Mass.: Harvard University Press, 1973. An existential study of the main characters of Virginia Woolf's *Mrs. Dalloway,* Graham Greene's *Brighton Rock,* William Faulkner's *The Bear,* Ralph Ellison's *Invisible Man,* William Golding's *Lord of the Flies,* and Bernard Malamud's *The Fixer.*

C199   Rupp, Richard H. *Celebration in Postwar American Fiction, 1945–1967.* Coral Gables, Fla.: University of Miami Press, 1970. "Current trends in criticism, stressing existentialism, despair, and desperate affirmation, tend to distort the fiction they explicate." Rupp's book "is a study of celebration in ten of the best American writers of fiction since the end of the Second World War." It is "affirmative, festive, and ultimately liturgical," stressing the "most significant work" of each writer and eschewing criticism. John Cheever, John

Updike, Eudora Welty, Flannery O'Connor, James Agee, J. D. Salinger, James Baldwin, Ralph Ellison, Bernard Malamud, and Saul Bellow.

C200   Samuelson, Davis. *Visions of Tomorrow: Six Journeys from Outer to Inner Space.* New York: Arno, 1975. Beginning with a historical and a theoretical overview, "this study is primarily an attempt to place and evaluate six novels representative of American and British science fiction in the period following World War II": Arthur C. Clarke's *Childhood's End,* Isaac Asimov's *The Caves of Steel,* Theodore Sturgeon's *More than Human,* Walter M. Miller's *A Canticle for Leibowitz,* Algis Budrys's *Rogue Moon,* and J. G. Ballard's *The Crystal World.* "For each book, the relation of the book to the author's other works is taken into account, as is the relation between his use of certain themes and techniques and the use made of them by other writers. The primary purpose of each examination, however, is a close reading which involves matters of form, style, imagery, symbolism, theme, and philosophical content as they relate to the success of this particular book, not merely to its representative quality." Bibliography.

C201   Sartre, Jean-Paul. *Literature and Existentialism.* Translated by Bernard Frechtman. New York: Citadel, 1969. A philosophical, historical, critical, pedagogical, and existential approach to the motives behind the literary act. The essays address the topics: "What is Writing?," "Why Write?," and "For Whom Does One Write?"

C202   Scholes, Robert. *The Fabulators.* New York: Oxford University Press, 1967. "It seems to me that the emergence of fabulation in recent fiction is not only an exciting development in itself; it also provides one answer to the great question of where fiction could go after the realistic novel." Scholes defines fabulation: "Fabulation . . . means a return to a more verbal kind of fiction. It also means a return to a more fictional kind. By this I mean a less realistic and more artistic kind of narrative: more shapely, more evocative; more concerned with ideas and ideals, less concerned with things." John Barth, Lawrence Durrell, John Hawkes, Iris Murdoch, Kurt Vonnegut, Jr., and Terry Southern.

C203   —————. *Structural Fabulation: An Essay on the Fiction of the Future.* Notre Dame, Ind.: University of Notre Dame Press, 1975. Four lectures that constitute "a kind of prolegomena to the serious reading of what we loosely call 'science fiction.'" In the first lecture, Scholes considers "the contemporary situation of fiction and its attendant literary criticism, arguing a case for fiction that concerns itself with the future." In the second, he offers "both a generic theory and a historical framework in which to consider contemporary works of fiction that insist on some radical discontinuity between the worlds they present to us and the world of our experience." The third lecture concerns varieties of modern science fiction and the fourth is about one writer, Ursula LeGuin. Select bibliography.

C204   Schorer, Mark. *The World We Imagine: Selected Essays.* New York: Farrar, Straus & Giroux, 1968. A collection of essays that includes "Technique as Discovery," "Fiction and the 'Analogical Matrix,'" "The World We Imagine," and "Notes on the Creative Act and Its Function." Also contains essays on Conrad Aiken, Katherine Anne Porter, Carson McCullers, Truman Capote, Ernest Hemingway, and earlier writers.

C205   Schraufnagel, Noel. *The Black American Novel: From Apology to Protest.* Deland, Fla.: Everett/Edwards, 1973. In 1940, Richard Wright's *Native Son* turned the course of the black novel toward a new trend in protest literature. "The evolution of this movement into the militant protest novel of the sixties, as well as the reaction of overt forms of social protest, is the subject of this study." Schraufnagel discusses the major novels of the period between 1940 and 1970. Richard Wright, James Baldwin, Chester Himes, William Gardner Smith, and others. Primary bibliography.

C206   Schulz, Max F. *Black Humor Fiction of the Sixties: A Pluralistic Definition of Man and His World.* Athens: Ohio University Press, 1973. "This study hopefully begins the establishment of guidelines preliminary to our coming to terms with the cultural and literary achievement represented by the Black Humor fiction of the Sixties." Schulz's primary aims are definition and the testing of the definition against the novels studied. He states that he "let the fiction itself" lead him to general concepts. Leonard Cohen, John

Barth, Kurt Vonnegut, Jr., Jorge Luis Borges, Thomas Berger, Thomas Pynchon, Robert Coover, Bruce Jay Friedman, and Charles Wright. Bibliography.

C207 —————. *Radical Sophistication: Studies in Contemporary Jewish-American Novels*. Athens: Ohio University Press, 1969. A study of some Jewish-American writers who, like the writers of black humor, departed from the tradition of "illusory optimism or the reactive pessimism" of America. These humanistic writers, "heirs both of an ancient social and religious ethic and of the modern existentialist temperament," settled between optimism and pessimism. They neither dropped out nor falsified experience; rather, they achieved a "radical sophistication." Isaac Bashevis Singer, Nathanael West, Bernard Malamud, Norman Mailer, Saul Bellow, Leslie A. Fiedler, Edward Lewis Wallant, Bruce Jay Friedman, and J. D. Salinger.

C208 Scott, Nathan A., Jr. *Craters of the Spirit: Studies in the Modern Novel*. Washington, D.C.: Corpus Books, 1968. Scott responds to Susan Sontag's *Against Interpretation* by arguing for the intellectual and cultural value and role of literature. While Scott does not see literature as a "surrogate for religion," he does see it as dealing with "how we live now, and how we ought to live." Early writers and Albert Camus, Samuel Beckett, Graham Greene, Saul Bellow, and Flannery O'Connor. Bibliography.

C209 —————. *Three American Moralists: Mailer, Bellow, Trilling*. Notre Dame, Ind.: University of Notre Dame Press, 1973. Explores the relationship among these three writers and the *Kulturkampf* that has lain upon the American scene since the early 1960s. Scott states that these writers are "at the absolute center of what is most deeply animating in American literature of the past and present."

C210 —————, ed. *Adversity and Grace: Studies in Recent American Literature*. Chicago: University of Chicago Press, 1968. This book is the fourth in a series of eight books being published under the general title "Essays in Divinity." The series is comprised of studies that realize the relationship between theology and other disciplines. "Theology and Literature represent the dialogue between Christian faith and culture in a special and almost unique way."

Saul Bellow, Bernard Malamud, Joseph Heller, Thomas Pynchon, J. D. Salinger, Flannery O'Connor, J. F. Powers, William Styron, and Norman Mailer.

C211 ————, ed. *Forms of Extremity in the Modern Novel.* Richmond, Va.: Knox, 1965. Modern literature is distinguished by its radicalism. No other tradition "has encouraged the artist to conceive his own cultural role so assertively." This literature is also characterized by fearlessness in formal experimentation and by a "lack of hesitance about improvising into existence *new* principles of meaning and *new* moral norms." Franz Kafka, Ernest Hemingway, Albert Camus, and Graham Greene. Selected bibliography.

C212 Seltzer, Alvin S. *Chaos in the Novel / The Novel in Chaos.* New York: Schocken, 1974. In the past, the novel was seen as a means for discovering truth. Most contemporary novelists, however, "see life as quintessentially chaotic" and, therefore, "wonder defeatedly if the novel can depict this chaotic vision." As Seltzer examines this tension between form and chaos, he writes: "Whereas form has too often seemed to shackle chaotic vision, that vision seems now to have shattered form, so that many experimental works, rather than impressing us as a different kind of novel, seem simply to be *less* of a *novel*." William Faulkner, Samuel Beckett, William S. Burroughs, Alain Robbe-Grillet, and others.

C213 Seward, William W., Jr. *Contrasts in Modern Writers: Some Aspects of British and American Fiction since Mid-Century.* New York: Fell, 1963. Over a hundred brief essays on books published during the 1950s constituting "a kind of informal journal of our literature in fiction at mid-century." Mainly covers British and American writers.

C214 Shapiro, Charles, ed. *Contemporary British Novelists.* Carbondale: Southern Illinois University Press, 1965. England has undergone "a rapid democratization and socialization since" World War II. These social changes have "created a lively literature." Shapiro collects essays by American critics on this literary scene. Kingsley Amis, Lawrence Durrell, William Golding, Doris Lessing, Iris Murdoch,

Anthony Powell, Alan Sillitoe, C. P. Snow, Muriel Spark, and Angus Wilson.

C215   Sherman, Bernard. *The Invention of the Jew: Jewish-American Education Novels (1916–1964)*. New York: Yoseloff, 1969. The lack of an accepted definition of Jewish-American literature presents a major problem for the historian. For the purposes of his study, Sherman states that "a Jewish-American novel will be considered such if it describes Jews experiencing the problems that were substantially, but not exclusively theirs." Specifically, Sherman examines the education novel in which the author describes "a youth outgrowing the protection of the home and encountering the beckoning life without." Saul Bellow, Abraham Cahan, Daniel Fuchs, Herbert Gold, Meyer Levin, Bernard Malamud, Isaac Rosenfeld, and others. Bibliography.

C216   Skaggs, Merrill Maguire. *The Folk of Southern Fiction*. Athens: University of Georgia Press, 1972. "This study of southern American local color fiction traces a literary tradition which heretofore has not been recognized as a part of the Southern heritage." Skaggs examines fictional representations of the "plain folk." The study traces this tradition from the nineteenth century to William Faulkner, Eudora Welty, and Flannery O'Connor. Selected bibliography of primary sources.

C217   Smith, Thelma, and Ward L. Miner. *Transatlantic Migration: The Contemporary American Novel in France*. Durham, N.C.: Duke University Press, 1955. "A study of the reception of the contemporary American novel in France." The authors also comment upon the influence of the American novel on French novelists. John Dos Passos, Ernest Hemingway, William Faulkner, Erskine Caldwell, and John Steinbeck. Bibliography.

C218   Solotaroff, Theodore. *The Red Hot Vacuum and Other Pieces on the Writing of the Sixties*. New York: Atheneum, 1970. A collection of essays and reviews. Includes "The Spirit of Isaac Rosenfeld," "Harry Golden and the American Audience," "Bernard Malamud: The Old Life and the New," "Irving Howe and the Socialist Imagination," "The Deadly James Purdy," "Alfred Chester: Daring and Doing," as well as essays on Flannery O'Connor, Jean-Paul Sartre, Paul

Goodman, R. D. Laing, William Burroughs, Paul Bowles, Susan Sontag, Saul Bellow, Philip Roth, and others.

C219   Spacks, Patricia Meyer. *The Female Imagination.* New York: Knopf, 1975. "Not a history of women's writing . . . but an examination of the ways the life of the imagination emerges in the world of women writing prose directly as women." It investigates "how women use their creativity to reveal and to combat" their shared difficulties. "Changing social conditions increase or diminish the opportunities for women's action and expression, but a special female self-awareness emerges through literature in every period. This book examines its continuities." Ivy Compton-Burnett, Lillian Hellman, Doris Lessing, Norman Mailer, Mary McCarthy, Sylvia Plath, and Eudora Welty. Bibliography.

C220   Spatz, Jonas. *Hollywood in Fiction: Some Versions of the American Myth.* The Hague: Mouton, 1969. Spatz writes: "In the fiction or drama I have selected, Hollywood or Southern California is more than a background; it is an important cultural phenomenon, an active and influential force in the imaginations and moral lives of its inhabitants. It is, in short, symbol rather than setting." John Dos Passos, Theodore Dreiser, James T. Farrell, William Faulkner, F. Scott Fitzgerald, Aldous Huxley, Norman Mailer, Budd Schulberg, John Steinbeck, Evelyn Waugh, Nathanael West, and others. Bibliography.

C221   Spencer, Sharon. *Space, Time and Structure in the Modern Novel.* New York: New York University Press, 1971. "A study of the genre from 1910 to the present, but only of those types of novels whose authors have designed them to be of this age, of the twentieth century, and who have sought to express those relationships in time and space and among characters that are distinctly 'modern.'" It attempts to rectify the general reader's rejection of experimental fiction "by describing the expressive aspirations that lie at the source of so many 'difficult' novels and by calling attention to vital relationships between experimental books and modern music and painting." Based on Einstein's theories, this book "studies books that embody approximations of time-space fusions achieved by various ingenious structural procedures." Composed of three parts, it studies the structures of the architectonic novel, the perspectives of the architectonic novel, and the spatialization of time. Bibliography.

C222   Springer, Mary Doyle. *Forms of the Modern Novella.* Chicago: University of Chicago Press, 1975. A generic study of the novella and its "relative purity of form." Springer provides an approach to the novella through her examination of plots and emphasis upon form. George Orwell, William Faulkner, Thomas Mann, Katherine Anne Porter, Alexander Solzhenitsyn, Kurt Vonnegut, Jr., and other writers. Bibliography.

C223   Stark, John O. *The Literature of Exhaustion: Borges, Nabokov, and Barth.* Durham, N.C.: Duke University Press, 1974. Writers of this group, in John Barth's words, "pretend that it is next to impossible to write an original." Literature is used up; therefore, writers should write about the present exhausted state of literature. Stark examines the techniques, themes, images, and characters in this type of literature and shows how the three writers relate closely to the basic assumptions of the literature of exhaustion. Bibliography.

C224   Starke, Catherine Juanita. *Black Portraiture in American Fiction: Stock Characters, Archetypes, and Individuals.* New York: Basic Books, 1971. Investigates cultural contexts, stock characters, archetypal patterns, and black individuals. Starke's investigation is based on two assumptions: first, "if cultural attitudes are changing, fictional symbols of black Americans may also be shifting from stereotyped to more individualized portraits; second, that if a trend toward individualization exists, it can be documented in popular fiction in the last century and a half." Primary and secondary bibliography.

C225   Stevenson, Lionel. *The History of the English Novel.* Vol. 11, *Yesterday and After.* New York: Barnes & Noble, 1967. The eleventh volume in Ernest Albert Baker's ten-volume series, *The History of the English Novel.* Stevenson wrote this literary history of writers and their novels to be read in conjunction with Baker's tenth volume. Samuel Beckett, Elizabeth Bowen, Joyce Cary, Ivy Compton-Burnett, Lawrence Durrell, Graham Greene, Aldous Huxley, George

Orwell, C. P. Snow, Evelyn Waugh, and many others. Bibliography.

C226   Steward, Douglas. *The Ark of God: Studies in Five Modern Novelists.* London: Carey Kingsgate, 1961. Five lectures on secular novelists who explore religious themes. James Joyce (apocalypticism), Aldous Huxley (mysticism), Graham Greene (Catholicism), Rose Macaulay (Anglicanism), and Joyce Cary (Protestantism).

C227   Strachey, John. *The Strangled Cry, and Other Unparliamentary Papers.* New York: Sloane, 1962. A collection of occasional writings on numerous topics by a British member of Parliament. The essays on literature are concerned with the political side of the works. Arthur Koestler, George Orwell, Whittaker Chambers, and Boris Pasternak.

C228   Stuckey, W. J. *The Pulitzer Prize Novels: A Critical Backward Look.* Norman: University of Oklahoma Press, 1966. "The main focus of this book is the prize novels themselves— their themes, ideas, sentiments, and especially their art and lack of art." Treats all of the novels to which Pulitzer prizes were awarded between 1917 and 1962. Stuckey's study attempts to answer this question: "How distinguished are Pulitzer prize novels?"

C229   Sullivan, Walter. *Death by Melancholy: Essays on Modern Southern Fiction.* Baton Rouge: Louisiana State University Press, 1972. Sullivan argues that the southern renascence is over. "Southern literature has declined because southern society more and more participates in the spiritual malaise that appears to be overwhelming all of western civilization. We suffer from a secular gnosticism. . . . " Allen Tate, William Faulkner, Flannery O'Connor, Robert Penn Warren, and Katherine Anne Porter.

C230   Sutherland, William, Jr., ed. *Six Contemporary Novels: Six Introductory Essays in Modern Fiction by Thomas Whitbread, William J. Handy, David Hagman, Richard Lehan, Ambrose Gordon, William Burford.* Austin: University of Texas, 1962. A collection of introductory essays. "Each takes a significant critical fact about a work of fiction and develops from it a critical statement." Lawrence Durrell, Boris Pasternak, C. P. Snow, Ernest Hemingway, William Faulkner, and Samuel Beckett.

C231   Swados, Harvey. *A Radical's America*. Boston: Little, Brown, 1962. Essays by Swados—a novelist, a Jew, and a Socialist —in which he writes about his America and "the creation of fiction."

C232   Symons, Julian. *Bloody Murder: From the Detective Story to the Crime Novel: A History*. London: Faber & Faber, 1972. Symons's historical survey of the detective story and the crime novel "is the result of the addiction, which started at the age of ten or eleven with Sherlock Holmes and Father Brown, and has survived the rigours of several years' reviewing of crime stories." His work is based "upon wide reading and rereading, but not an attempt to read the whole bulk of crime literature." Margery Allingham, Eric Ambler, John Buchan, John Dickson Carr, Raymond Chandler, G. K. Chesterton, Agatha Christie, Wilkie Collins, A. Conan Doyle, Emile Gaboriau, William Godwin, Dashiell Hammett, Howard Haycroft, Patricia Highsmith, Michael Innes, Monsignor Ronald Knox, John le Carre, Ellery Queen, Dorothy L. Sayers, Rex Stout, S. S. Van Dine, Willard Huntington Wright, and others.

C233   Tanner, Tony. *City of Words: American Fiction, 1950–1970*. New York: Harper & Row, 1971. Tanner's "primary aim is to try to *understand* the American imagination as it has expressed itself in fictional forms during this period." Essays on Vladimir Nabokov, Jorge Luis Borges, Ralph Ellison, Saul Bellow, Joseph Heller, James Purdy, William Burroughs, Thomas Pynchon, Kurt Vonnegut, Jr., John Hawkes, John Barth, Walker Percy, Sylvia Plath, Susan Sontag, William H. Gass, John Updike, Philip Roth, Frank Conroy, Bernard Malamud, Norman Mailer, Ken Kesey, William Gaddis, Donald Barthelme, and Richard Brautigan. Appendixes and bibliography.

C234   Tischler, Nancy M. *Black Masks: Negro Characters in Modern Southern Fiction*. University Park: Pennsylvania State University Press, 1969. "Whether or not there are Negro types in life, there certainly are in art, which is our stylized vision of life." For the southern writer the problem of classification of the individual is most acute when dealing with Negro characters. Tischler states the problem: "The artist has followed societal patterns by accepting the truth of the mask itself during the early years of our century gradually learning to perceive a diversity of masks, then a hint of another truth behind the masks, and finally to doubt that any truth lies in the mask at all." James Baldwin, Hamilton Basso, Erskine Caldwell, Ralph Ellison, William Faulkner, Ellen Glasgow, Carson McCullers, William Styron, Robert Penn Warren, Richard Wright, and others. Bibliography.

C235   Toliver, Harold. *Animate Illusions: Explorations of Narrative Structure*. Lincoln: University of Nebraska Press, 1974. A systematic study of fiction as an imaginative response to experience and of experience. Concentrates on the linear logic of narration. Discusses memory, history, fiction, modes, and conventions. Bibliography.

C236   Tuttleton, James W. *The Novels of Manners in America*. Chapel Hill: University of North Carolina Press, 1972. Tuttleton's aim is to define the "novel of manners" and to describe the "themes, styles, structures, character types, ideological postures, and the characteristic strategies by which the form is brought to life by our novelists." This description is "sociological, political, philosophical, economic, and historical as well as aesthetic." In addition, Tuttleton explores "the question of America's cultural diversity and the question of whether there could be a novel of manners in America." He studies the novels of James Fenimore Cooper through those of John O'Hara, John P. Marquand, Louis Auchincloss, James Gould Cozzens, John Hawkes, Vladimir Nabokov, James Purdy, and Paul Bowles.

C237   Umphlett, Wiley Lee. *The Sporting Myth and the American Experience: Studies in Contemporary Fiction*. Lewisburg, Pa.: Bucknell University Press, 1975. Organized thematically, this is not a historical nor a comprehensive survey; rather it is "a study of an archetypal figure familiar to American experience"—the sportsman. "How our writers of fiction have used the sporting experience to comment on our moral evolution as a people is what this book is about." Nelson Algren, Saul Bellow, John Cheever, William Faulkner, Leonard Gardner, Mark Harris, Ernest Hemingway, James Jones, Jeremy Larner, Bernard Malamud, Wright Morris, Howard Nemerov, Jay Neugeboren, J. F. Powers, Philip Roth, Budd Schulberg, and John Updike. Bibliography.

C238   Urang, Gunnar. *Shadows of Heaven: Religion and Fantasy in the Writing of C. S. Lewis, Charles Williams, and J. R. R. Tolkien.* Philadelphia: Pilgrim Press, 1971. In the first three chapters, Urang studies the relationship between each writer's religious belief and the "literary qualities" of his fiction. Then, in the concluding chapter, he asks, "Can the pattern of belief represented by the work be considered adequate to the experience and the developing consciousness of modern man?"

C239   Voss, Arthur. *The American Short Story: A Critical Survey.* Norman: University of Oklahoma Press, 1975. "This book presents a comprehensive survey of the American short story, its origins, its trends, and its creators." Historically organized, its final chapters deal with contemporary writers. Katherine Anne Porter, Eudora Welty, Mary McCarthy, Jean Stafford, J. F. Powers, J. D. Salinger, Bernard Malamud, Flannery O'Connor, and others. Bibliography.

C240   Walcutt, Charles Child. *Man's Changing Mask: Modes and Methods of Characterization in Fiction.* Minneapolis: University of Minnesota Press, 1966. Walcutt's aim is "to show how characterization depends upon plot, . . . how the significance of the plot reflects the social and moral values of a society and in turn determines the significance of the characters, and how the patterns of characterization established in fiction influence and affect the image of man that people 'recognize' in themselves." Shakespeare, Jane Austin, and Herman Melville through Ernest Hemingway, John O'Hara, J. D. Salinger, John Updike, Wright Morris, Anthony Powell, Samuel Beckett, Philip Roth, and Saul Bellow.

C241   Waldmeir, Joseph J. *American Novels of the Second World War.* 2nd ed. The Hague: Mouton, 1971. Waldmeir studies American novels "in which combat, actually or in retrospect, figures prominently." John Horne Burns, James Gould Cozzens, Alfred Hayes, Joseph Heller, Stefan Heym, William Hoffman, James Jones, John O. Killens, Norman Mailer, Anton Meyer, Irwin Shaw, Herman Wouk, and others. Bibliography.

C242 ————, ed. *Recent American Fiction: Some Critical Views.* Boston: Houghton Mifflin, 1963. This collection includes general statements on contemporary American fiction and essays "concerned in depth with a single novelist." Saul Bellow, Paul Bowles, Truman Capote, Ralph Ellison, Jack Kerouac, Norman Mailer, Bernard Malamud, Carson McCullers, Flannery O'Connor, James Purdy, J. D. Salinger, and William Styron. Bibliography.

C243 Walsh, Chad. *From Utopia to Nightmare.* New York: Harper & Row, 1962. Walsh's topic is "the gradual decline in our times of the utopian novel and its displacement by the 'dystopia' or 'inverted utopia.'" Edward Bellamy, Aldous Huxley, E. M. Forster, George Orwell, Vladimir Nabokov, C. S. Lewis, Ayn Rand, Kurt Vonnegut, Jr., Evelyn Waugh, and others. Bibliography.

C244 Watkins, Floyd C. *The Death of Art: Black and White in the Recent Southern Novel.* Athens: University of Georgia Press, 1970. "Modern Southern novels which treat the relationship between the black man and the white man are highly prejudiced against the white. It may be possible to defend this bias as historical, political, and social corrective; but as fiction the bias fails." A survey treatment in four categories: racism in fiction, the black, the white, and alienated novelists. Primary bibliography.

C245 Webster, Harvey Curtis. *After the Trauma: Representative British Novelists since 1920.* Lexington: University Press of Kentucky, 1970. An appreciative, not a critical, study of writers who matured generally after 1914. While these writers grew up in the ages of the wasteland and of anxiety, they provide a "chorus for survival." Rose Macaulay, Aldous Huxley, Ivy Compton-Burnett, Evelyn Waugh, Graham Greene, Joyce Cary, L. P. Hartley, and C. P. Snow.

C246 Weinberg, Helen. *The New Novel in America: The Kafkan Mode in Contemporary Fiction.* Ithaca, N.Y.: Cornell University Press, 1970. Weinberg examines the novels of "Americans whose writing in the 1950's and early 1960's represented a reaction against New Critical aestheticism and the self-protectively thin academic novel to which that aestheticism had brought the novel form." These writers "found their story in the self and its isolated, and therefore private and personal, search for meaningful human value." Weinberg's purpose is "to define and to distinguish between two types of contemporary novels, the absurdist and the activist, by reference to the novels of Franz Kafka." Saul Bellow, Norman Mailer, Bernard Malamud, Philip Roth, Herbert Gold, J. D. Salinger, Walker Percy, James Baldwin, Ralph Ellison, William Styron, and R. V. Cassill. Bibliography.

C247   Weinstein, Arnold L. *Vision and Response in Modern Fiction.* Ithaca, N.Y.: Cornell University Press, 1974. While most novels depict the education of their protagonists or narrators, they also "*constitute* an education" for a reader who "turns the pages in a sequential enterprise of progressive enlightenment, as the substance of the book becomes less opaque and more intelligible, and as its meaning emerges." In this sense, all novels "both describe and engender the acquisition of knowledge. The knowledge arrived at, and the itinerary taken, are usually divergent for reader and protagonist, and the joint educational process is variously informed by content, style, structure, and, of course, the reader's expectations. To analyze the ways in which specific novels achieve their meaning and posit their reality is the goal of this study." Mostly European or early English writers. John Barth, Samuel Beckett, William Faulkner, Jerzy Kosinski, Susan Sontag, and Wallace Stevens.

C248   Wescott, Glenway. *Images of Truth: Remembrances and Criticism.* New York: Harper & Row, 1962. "This volume consists of informal portraiture of two or three fellow writers near and dear to me, and of certain blessed elders and betters, with loving commentary on their production of stories and novels." Katherine Anne Porter, W. Somerset Maugham, Colette, Isak Dinesen, Thomas Mann, and Thornton Wilder.

C249   West, Paul. *The Modern Novel.* Vol. 1, *England and France.* Vol. 2, *The United States and Other Countries.* London: Hutchinson University Press, 1963. West is "primarily concerned with the novelist's effort to bring psychology back into proportion with manners, and to augment these two with a view of man in the abstract." According to West, the stream of consciousness was "a discovery which has been renewed in significance by novelists who have lost faith in society and therefore also in the novel as social portraiture." Kingsley Amis, Samuel Beckett, Erskine Caldwell, Truman Capote, Joyce Cary, Ivy Compton-Burnett, Lawrence Durrell, William Faulkner, Graham Greene, Ernest Hemingway, Aldous Huxley, Carson McCullers, Henry Miller, John O'Hara, Anthony Powell, C. P. Snow, Evelyn Waugh, Angus Wilson, and many others. Suggested readings.

C250 West, Ray B., Jr. *The Short Story in America, 1900–1950.* Chicago: Regnery, 1952. Surveys fifty years of the American short story, its background and history, the naturalists and the traditionalists. Ernest Hemingway, William Faulkner, Eudora Welty, Peter Taylor, J. F. Powers, Walter Van Tilburg Clark, Wallace Stegner, Lionel Trilling, and Truman Capote. Bibliography.

C251 Westbrook, Max, ed. *The Modern American Novel: Essays in Criticism.* New York: Random House, 1966. A collection of essays on the novel since 1914. Theodore Dreiser, Sherwood Anderson, Sinclair Lewis, F. Scott Fitzgerald, Thomas Wolfe, Ernest Hemingway, William Faulkner, John Steinbeck, Robert Penn Warren, J. D. Salinger, and Saul Bellow. Selected bibliography.

C252 White, John J. *Mythology in the Modern Novel: A Study of Prefigurative Techniques.* Princeton: Princeton University Press, 1971. "This study has two principal aims: to consider the main problems of interpretations raised by the use of myths in fiction, and to examine in detail various patterns of correspondences that contemporary novelists have chosen to establish between their subjects and classical prefigurations. The common goal of these two undertakings is a new way of looking at the role of mythology in the novel." White is concerned with American, English, and German novels. John Bowen, Anthony Burgess, John Hersey, James Joyce, Thomas Mann, Ann Quinn, John Updike, and others. Select bibliography.

C253 Wicker, Brian. *The Story-Shaped World: Fiction and Metaphysics: Some Variations on a Theme.* Notre Dame, Ind.: University of Notre Dame Press, 1975. Wicker states his purpose: "I have tried to explore the philosophical and theological implications of two main ideas: the idea that metaphor, especially as understood by linguists, is endemic in all communication since it is simply one of two 'poles' of language itself; and the idea that metaphor is never an 'innocent' figure but always implies a subterranean metaphysic." He, then, applies this theory to the novels of D. H. Lawrence, James Joyce, Evelyn Waugh, Samuel Beckett, Alain Robbe-Grillet, and Norman Mailer. Bibliography.

C254   Wisse, Ruth. *The Schlemiel as Modern Hero*. Chicago: University of Chicago Press, 1971. "A brief history of the literary schlemiel," from Eastern Europe to Saul Bellow, Bruce Jay Friedman, Bernard Malamud, Philip Roth, Isaac Bashevis Singer, Ernest Hemingway, Sholom Aleichem, and others. Bibliography.

C255   Witham, W. Tasker. *The Adolescent in the American Novel, 1920–1960*. New York: Ungar, 1964. This survey "begins with a rather short chapter sketching the literary and cultural background of the American novel of adolescence in the period discussed. The five following chapters present, in order of importance, the five areas in which adolescents face their most difficult problems of adjustment." Other chapters discuss more individual problems; and finally, Witham "ventures a prophecy as to future trends in novels of adolescence." Primary and secondary bibliography.

C256   Wollheim, Donald A. *The Universe Makers: Science Fiction Today*. New York: Harper & Row, 1971. With the atomic bomb, the world entered "into a science-fiction phase." Wollheim discusses a world that science fiction made and science fiction as a system of ideas. Robert Heinlein, C. M. Kornbluth, J. R. R. Tolkien, Olaf W. Stapleton, A. E. Van Vogt, Kurt Vonnegut, Jr., H. G. Wells, and others.

C257   Woodcock, George. *The Writer and Politics*. London: Porcupine, 1948. A collection of essays written from a social perspective on a variety of subjects, some literary ones. Woodcock's social impulse affirms the individual. Essays on George Orwell, Graham Greene, Ignazio Silone, Franz Kafka, and Rex Warner.

C258   Ziolkowski, Theodore. *Fictional Transfigurations of Jesus*. Princeton: Princeton University Press, 1972. Studies a group of modern novels that "pattern their modern action on the life of Jesus." Ziolkowski argues that "none of these works can be seen in the proper perspective if the shaping force of the fictional transfiguration is ignored or misunderstood." John Barth, Carlo Coccioli, Fyodor Dostoevsky, William Faulkner, Antonio Fogazzaro, Lars Görling, Günter Grass, Graham Greene, Herman Hesse. Nikos Kazantzakis, Arthur Koestler, Thomas Mann, John Steinbeck, Gore Vidal, and others. Selected bibliography.

D

Poetry

D1   Abbe, George. *You and Contemporary Poetry: An Aid-to-Appreciation.* Peterborough, N.H.: Noone House, 1968. Abbe discusses contemporary poetry by dividing his study into the following chapters: the modern idiom, image and diction, rhythm and sound, form, idea, poem and poet, and poem and reader. Abbe's investigation is "not a conventional schoolbook approach to poetry; historical or academic analysis is left to others." He focuses upon poems, not authors.

D2   Allen, Donald Merriam, and Warren Tallman, eds. *Poetics of the New American Poetry.* New York: Grove Press, 1973. Contemporary poetry is misunderstood because the pervasive influence of Cleanth Brooks's and Robert Penn Warren's *Understanding Poetry* is informed by the first wave of poetry in this century. The new poetry of Olson and his generation needs to be viewed from other perspectives that are set forth in these essays on poetry by poets. "The poets whose statements we include achieve spectacular fulfillments in our century of what Whitman was calling for in his." They all seek a new or renewed writing in hopes of a new or renewed world. The purpose of this book is to bring these lesser known statements to the attention of poetry readers. Essays by Walt Whitman, William Carlos Williams, Charles Olson, Robert Creeley, Allen Ginsberg, LeRoi Jones (Imamu Amiri Baraka), Gary Snyder, Lawrence Ferlinghetti, and others.

D3   Allen, Don Cameron, ed. *The Moment of Poetry.* Baltimore: Johns Hopkins University Press, 1962. Essays by John Holmes, May Sarton, Richard Eberhart, Richard Wilbur, and Randall Jarrell on poetry in general. They discuss such issues as the "poet's milieu," "how a poet works," and "will" and "psyche." Richard Wilbur and Randall Jarrell deal with specific works by A. E. Housman and Robert Frost.

D4   Alvarez, A. *Stewards of Excellence: Studies in Modern English and American Poets.* New York: Scribner's, 1958. (The British title is *The Shaping Spirit.*) Alvarez's study is not a "general guide to modern poetry"; instead, he deals with the differences between the English and American traditions and why "the great creative possibilities of modern poetry have come, in fact, to so little." Alvarez's answer is that "modernism" is an American concern. T. S. Eliot, Ezra Pound, William Empson, W. H. Auden, Wallace Stevens, and others.

D5   Baird, Martha, and Ellen Reiss, eds. *The Williams-Siegel Documentary.* New York: Definition Press, 1970. Letters by William Carlos Williams and Eli Siegel on aesthetic realism and the nature of poetry. Also other documents by Siegel on poetry. Concludes with a discussion of Allen Ginsberg, Wallace Stevens, W. H. Auden, Robert Frost, and Robert Lowell.

D6   Barker, George. *Essays.* London: MacGibbon & Kee, 1970. A series of essays on subjects from Shakespeare to Ezra Pound, affirming the value of poetry in the Western world. For Barker, poetry deals in the unknowns of existence and, at the same time, affirms the individual with an anarchic and perverse reaction to modern life. Frederico García Lorca, Dylan Thomas, Stephen Spender, Sydney Graham, Ezra Pound, Brian Higgins, and others.

D7   Bayley, John. *The Romantic Survival: A Study in Poetic Evolution.* London: Constable, 1964. Bayley shows "how romantic ideas, developing and proliferating over the course of more than a century, affected the writing and the reading of imaginative literature" by studying W. B. Yeats, W. H. Auden, and Dylan Thomas "in the context of romantic thought and theory."

D8   Bedient, Calvin. *Eight Contemporary Poets: Charles Tomlinson, Donald Davie, R. S. Thomas, Philip Larkin, Ted Hughes, Thomas Kinsella, Stevie Smith, W. S. Graham.* London: Oxford University Press, 1974. Postwar poetry in Britain and Ireland has proved increasingly robust and responsive to the times despite the dull plainness of the fifties. Because the poets are scattered in various schools, the formal English tradition is loosening and becoming more American. Bibliography.

D9   Berry, Francis. *Poetry and the Physical Voice.* London: Routledge & Kegan Paul, 1962. Sound, as well as grammar, is important to poetry. Berry applies his theory to Tennyson, Shelley, Milton, and Shakespeare and ends with a discussion of T. S. Eliot and W. H. Auden.

D10   Bewley, Marius. *Masks and Mirrors: Essays in Criticism.* New York: Atheneum, 1970. The last fourth of the collection deals with contemporary poetry. Essays on Wallace Stevens, T. S. Eliot, Ezra Pound; others are briefly mentioned.

D11   Blackburn, Thomas. *The Price of an Eye.* London: Longmans, Green, 1961. While he acknowledges the values of poetic technique, Blackburn says, "In this book I am going to concentrate on what poems say; it seems to me there has been rather too much picking about inside them to see how they function and are put together. The point is the work they do." Historical organization from Yeats to the fifties. W. B. Yeats, T. S. Eliot, Ezra Pound, Edwin Muir, Edith Sitwell, Robert Graves, Kathleen Raine, W. H. Auden, Stephen Spender, Cecil Day Lewis, Louis MacNeice, Dylan Thomas, George Barker, Vernon Watkins, W. S. Graham, and David Gascoyne. Bibliography.

D12   Blackmur, R. P. *Form and Value in Modern Poetry.* Garden City, N.Y.: Doubleday, 1952. A collection of essays on poets and poetry from Thomas Hardy to Ezra Pound, T. S. Eliot, Wallace Stevens, Marianne Moore, e. e. cummings, John Wheelwright, William Carlos Williams, Herbert Read, and others. Blackmur relates the "linguistic techniques" of the poems to their "intellectual and emotional form."

D13   ————. *Language as Gesture: Essays in Poetry.* New York: Harcourt, Brace, 1952. "When the language of words most succeeds it *becomes* gesture in its words." Blackmur studies the way language becomes gesture and provides insights into the nature of this process. Blackmur tries "to show in a series of varied and progressive examples how the symbol invests the actions in language with poetic actuality." Ezra Pound, T. S. Eliot, Wallace Stevens, Marianne Moore, Hart Crane, e. e. cummings, William Carlos Williams, and others.

D14   Bloom, Harold. *The Anxiety of Influence: A Theory of Poetry*. New York: Oxford University Press, 1973. "This book's main purpose is necessarily to present one reader's critical vision, in the context both of the criticism and poetry of his own generation, where their current crises most touch him, and in the context of his own anxieties of influence." Based on the premise that since Shakespeare "the anxiety of influence" is central to "poetic consciousness," the study aims to correct our idealized "accounts of how one poet helps to form another. Another aim, also corrective, is to try to provide a poetics that will foster a. more adequate practical criticism," since formalist, archetypal, and European imports have proven inadequate. The book studies six ways that major authors respond to influence and offers "A Manifesto for Antithetical Criticism."

D15   —————. *Kabbalah and Criticism*. New York: Seabury, 1975. The *Kabbalah* is a tradition of images, parables, and ideas pertaining to God. Three chapters that set forth the "primordial scheme" of the *Kabbalah*, relate this scheme "to a theory of reading poetry," and describe a "manifesto for antithetical"—or high romantic—criticism.

D16   —————. *A Map of Misreading*. New York: Oxford University Press, 1975. A further development of the theory of poetry set forth in *The Anxiety of Influence*. The first part of the study reaches back to the origins of poetry in order to discover a map of "misreading." The second part describes the map and applies it to Browning's *Childe Roland*. The final section applies the map to the Miltonian tradition in England and the Emersonian tradition in America. Wallace Stevens, Robert Penn Warren, A. R. Ammons, and John Ashbery.

D17   Bogan, Louise. *Achievement in American Poetry, 1900–1950*. Chicago: Regnery, 1951. A survey that discusses backgrounds and forerunners, the "American Renaissance," the avant-garde, postwar poetry, ideology and irrationalism, and poetry from 1939 to 1950. Ezra Pound, William Carlos Williams, T. S. Eliot, and W. H. Auden. Bibliography.

D18   ———. *A Poet's Alphabet: Reflections on the Literary Art and Vocation.* Edited by Robert Phelps and Ruth Limmer. New York: McGraw-Hill, 1970. It "includes the entire contents of . . . *Selected Criticism,* published in 1955; most of the articles, reviews, and miscellaneous critical pieces published since that date; and a few earlier pieces not previously published." Some of the reviews focus on contemporary issues and writers: anthologies of poems, W. H. Auden, T. S. Eliot, Robert Frost, Robert Graves, Philip Larkin, Robert Lowell, Ezra Pound, Karl Shapiro, Stephen Spender, and Richard Wilbur.

D19   Bowra, Cecil M. *Poetry and Politics, 1900–1960.* Cambridge: Cambridge University Press, 1966. Four lectures on public themes in poetry that Bowra delivered in May 1965 at Queens University, Belfast, on the invitation of the Wiles Foundation. T. S. Eliot, Ezra Pound, Edith Sitwell, and earlier figures.

D20   Boyers, Robert, ed. *Contemporary Poetry in America: Essays and Interviews.* New York: Schocken, 1974. Designed to serve the needs of teachers and students who wish "to develop a critical apparatus for dealing with the work of a variety of poets." The volume is a "representation of dominant urgings in our verse," taken from a special issue of *Salmagundi* magazine. Howard Nemerov, Stanley Kunitz, Robert Lowell, John Berryman, Randall Jarrell, Theodore Roethke, John Ashbery, Sylvia Plath, Adrienne Rich, W. D. Snodgrass, Charles Olson, Ben Belitt, Galway Kinnell, W. S. Merwin, James Wright, James Dickey, A. R. Ammons, Alan Dugan, Elizabeth Bishop, and David Wagoner.

D21   Brooks, Cleanth, and Robert Penn Warren. *Conversations on the Craft of Poetry with Robert Frost, John Crowe Ransom, Robert Lowell, Theodore Roethke.* New York: Holt, Rinehart & Winston, 1961. A transcript of the tape recording made to accompany the third edition of *Understanding Poetry.*

D22   Cambon, Glauco. *The Inclusive Flame: Studies in Modern*

American Poetry. Bloomington: Indiana University Press, 1965. An Italian's response to American poetry and life. Cambon states, "my work attempt[s] to probe into the recurrent American endeavor to grasp a totality of experience through poetry. . . . " Essays on "space, experiment, and prophesy," Edwin Arlington Robinson, Wallace Stevens, Hart Crane, William Carlos Williams, and Robert Lowell.

D23   ————. *Recent American Poetry.* University of Minnesota Pamphlets on American Writers, no. 16. Minneapolis: University of Minnesota Press, 1962. A monograph that surveys Robert Creeley, Robert Duncan, Lawrence Ferlinghetti, Allen Ginsberg, Anthony Hecht, Jack Hirschman, John Hollander, Randall Jarrell, X. J. Kennedy, Galway Kinnell, Stanley Kunitz, Denise Levertov, Robert Lowell, W. S. Merwin, Howard Nemerov, Kenneth Rexroth, Theodore Roethke, Karl Shapiro, W. D. Snodgrass, Richard Wilbur, and others. Primary and secondary bibliography.

D24   Cargas, Harry J. *Daniel Berrigan and Contemporary Protest Poetry.* New Haven, Conn.: College & University Press, 1972. While many modern writers, such as James Joyce, T. S. Eliot, Henry James, and Richard Wright, left their countries and lost the opportunity for "serious involvement in true issues," some contemporary poets believe that the artist's creativity should be rooted in "real" experiences. They feel that there should be a connection between the art and the life of the poet. Richard Eberhart, Karl Shapiro, Robert Lowell, Allen Ginsberg, LeRoi Jones (Imamu Amiri Baraka), and Daniel Berrigan.

D25   Carroll, Paul. *The Poem in Its Skin.* Chicago: Big Table, 1968. For Carroll, a poem is like a person; getting to know a poem, then, is like getting to know a person. Carroll argues that we must experience a poem in its own skin; we must make an effort to see each poem in its own existential reality, apart from preconceived critical dogmas. John Ashbery, Robert Creeley, James Dickey, Isabella Gardner, Allen Ginsberg, John Logan, W. S. Merwin, Frank O'Hara, W. D. Snodgrass, and James Wright.

D26   Charters, Samuel. *Some Poems / Poets: Studies in American Underground Poetry since 1945.* Berkeley, Calif.: Oyez,

1971. "What I've tried to do in these studies is to get down some of my own responses to writing that seem to have an importance in the growth of the new American poetry— with the intention that this kind of opening to an experience of the poem might lead someone to the poem itself." The inquiry concerns "underground" poets whose poetry is in "contrast to the 'visible' poetry of the academic writers." Charles Olson, Jack Spicer, Robert Duncan, Gary Snyder, Lew Welch, Allen Ginsberg, Lawrence Ferlinghetti, Robert Creeley, Brother Antoninus (William Everson), and Larry Eigner.

D27   Coblentz, Stanton. *The Generation That Forgot to Sing.* Mill Valley, Calif.: Wings, 1962. Seventeen short essays on aesthetics, poetry, and criticism.

D28   —————. *The Poetry Circus.* New York: Hawthorn, 1967. "Nonpoets and antipoets have taken over" in the modern period and still hold reign, Coblentz says. "The facts speak plainly and tell us that the pseudopoets possess the field. And since no general survey of these facts has ever been made, it has occurred to me to write the present book, not to advance any case of my own, but to serve as an advocate of poetry." Conrad Aiken, John Ashbery, W. H. Auden, John Berryman, Robert Creeley, e. e. cummings, T. S. Eliot, Allen Ginsberg, Randall Jarrell, Robert Lowell, Archibald MacLeish, Ezra Pound, Theodore Roethke, Karl Shapiro, Wallace Stevens, Allen Tate, Dylan Thomas, William Carlos Williams, and others. Bibliography.

D29   —————. *The Rise of Anti-Poets: Selected Editorials from Wings, A Quarterly of Verse.* Mill Valley, Calif.: Wings, 1955. Includes "What Are You Writing For?," "The Character of an Able Poet," "The Poet, the Politician, and the Press Agent," "The Rise of the Anti-Poets," "Is a Modern Wordsworth Possible?," "Is Poetry Important?," "Poetry in the Hour of Need," and others.

D30   Cohen, J. M. *Poetry of This Age, 1908–1958.* London: Hutchinson, 1962. Surveys the forty-eight most important poets of the six principal languages of Europe and America: English, French, German, Spanish, Italian, and Russian. Dylan Thomas, W. H. Auden, T. S. Eliot, Philip Larkin,

Robert Lowell, Edwin Muir, Ezra Pound, Wallace Stevens, Theodore Roethke, and others. Bibliography.

D31 Creeley, Robert. *Contexts of Poetry: Interviews 1961–1971.* Edited by Donald Allen. Bolinas, Calif.: Four Seasons Press, 1973. Creeley interviews David Ossman, Charles Tomlinson, Allen Ginsberg, John Sinclair, Robin Eichele, Linda Wagner, Brendan O'Gegan, Rony Allan, Lewis Mac-Adams, Douglas Flaherty, James Bradford, and Michael André.

D32 Davie, Donald. *Articulate Energy: An Inquiry into the Syntax of English Poetry.* New York: Harcourt, Brace, 1955. Davie examines three authorities in the field of poetic theory to study the nature of syntax in poetry. He discusses the ways syntax contributes to poetic effect and the ways a discrepancy between theory and practice can obstruct the reading and writing of poetry. Concerned mainly with earlier figures, but there is some attention paid to T. S. Eliot and Ezra Pound.

D33 Davy, Charles. *Words in the Mind: Exploring Some Effects of Poetry, English and French.* Cambridge, Mass.: Harvard University Press, 1965. Since poetry is no longer considered in our culture as "an inspiration from a god," its nature has been studied extensively by the symbolists and proponents of the "new poetry" and the "new criticism." Because no one has explained poetry, "I have tried, not to offer any final answer, but to approach [it] in the light of two rather neglected factors—the evolution of consciousness and the action of words on the mind."

D34 Dembo, L. S. *Conceptions of Reality in Modern American Poetry.* Berkeley: University of California Press, 1966. Dembo brings "to focus some of the important literary and philosophic issues raised in twentieth-century American poetry." He discusses "the involvement of poetry with epistemology and ontology." More specifically, Dembo examines "the problems of exotic perception when that world is one of 'objects,' and of psychological projection when that world is one of human affairs." William Carlos Williams, Wallace Stevens, Marianne Moore, e. e. cummings, Hart Crane, Ezra Pound, T. S. Eliot, Charles Olson, and Robert Duncan.

D35   Deutsch, Babette. *Poetry in Our Time*. New York: Columbia University Press, 1958. Deutsch discusses the rise and growth of modern English and American poetry to make it more accessible to the intelligent reader. She examines form and content in relation to the revolutions of the age in which the poems were composed. W. H. Auden, John Peale Bishop, e. e. cummings, T. S. Eliot, Robert Frost, John Masefield, John Crowe Ransom, Edith Sitwell, Wallace Stevens, Allen Tate, and William Carlos Williams.

D36   Dickey, James. *Babel to Byzantium: Poets and Poetry Now*. New York: Farrar, Straus & Giroux, 1968. Where poetry is concerned, "participation" is more important than judgment. "More often than not, our kind of education is likely to take us the other way, into systems of ranking poets and poems, into the now-familiar myopia of close-reading, into the sociology and history and psychology that surrounds poems, if you insist on looking at them in these particular ways, instead of into the bodily and often purely irrational experience of the poem." Over seventy short essays on Randall Jarrell, David Ignatow, Kenneth Burke, Gene Derwood, Howard Nemerov, W. S. Graham, Samuel French Morse, Reed Whittemore, Allen Ginsburg, Donald Drummond, John Ashbery, Rolph Humphries, Herbert Read, Katherine Hoskins, Philip Booth, Kenneth Patchen, May Sarton, William Jay Smith, Ted Hughes, and many others.

D37   ————. *Self-Interviews*. Recorded and edited by Barbara and James Reiss. Garden City, N.Y.: Doubleday, 1970. Tape-recorded interviews that "preserve the uninterrupted flow of a poet's spoken words about life and poetry." Dickey speaks about literary problems and his career.

D38   ————. *Sorties*. Garden City, N.Y.: Doubleday, 1971. Part 1 is Dickey's journal which includes everything from "meditations on the sublime to laundry lists." Part 2 contains the following essays: "The Self as Agent," "The Son, the Cave, and the Burning Bush," "Metaphor as Pure Adventure," "Spinning the Crystal Ball," "Edwin Arlington Robinson," and "The Greatest American Poet: Theodore Roethke."

D39   ————. *Spinning the Crystal Ball: Some Guesses at the Future of American Poetry*. Washington, D.C.: Library of

Congress, 1967. A pamphlet including a lecture delivered at the Library of Congress on April 24, 1967. Dickey offers these remarks from the vantage point of his "involvement in the situation from which the future must inevitably come." He speculates on the future and offers his hopes for American poetry.

D40   ————. *The Suspect in Poetry*. Madison, Minn.: Sixties Press, 1964. A collection of book reviews in which Dickey personally assesses twenty-four poets.

D41   Dodsworth, Martin, ed. *The Survival of Poetry: A Contemporary Survey*. London: Faber & Faber, 1970. Eight essays on poets "who can be said to have matured as poets only since about 1950." "No attempt has been made here at a uniformity of approach." The authors of these essays "speak as individuals, and not from some common point of view." Philip Larkin, Robert Lowell, John Berryman, Ted Hughes, Sylvia Plath, Thom Gunn, Charles Olson, Edward Dorn, and others. Bibliography.

D42   Donoghue, Denis. *Connoisseurs of Chaos: Ideas of Order in Modern American Poetry*. New York: Macmillan, 1965. Defines order and chaos in the work of Robert Lowell, Robert Frost, Wallace Stevens, and Theodore Roethke. Donoghue draws these definitions solely from these poets' work. Compares and contrasts them with earlier writers.

D43   ————, ed. *Seven American Poets from MacLeish to Nemerov: An Introduction*. Minneapolis: University of Minnesota Press, 1975. These reprints of the University of Minnesota Pamphlets on American Writers examine the ways in which a group of poets demonstrate being American. Archibald MacLeish, Richard Eberhart, Theodore Roethke, Randall Jarrell, John Berryman, Robert Lowell, and Howard Nemerov. Bibliography.

D44   Drew, Elizabeth. *Poetry: A Modern Guide to Its Understanding and Enjoyment*. New York: Norton, 1959. Emphasis upon the reading of poetry as an exploration. Includes chapters on basic verbal techniques, the subject matter of poetry as the communication of human experience, and the human themes in poetry. W. H. Auden, T. S. Eliot, Robert Frost, and earlier writers. Bibliography.

D45   Duncan, Robert. *As Testimony: The Poem and the Scene.* San Francisco: White Rabbit Press, 1964. A brief essay that began as a letter to George Stanley about meaning in poetry and life.

D46   Eckman, Frederick. *Cobras and Cockle Shells: Modes in Recent Poetry.* London: Sparrow Magazine, 1958. "This book surveys, on certain stylistic grounds, the poetry of . . . Americans under forty whose work has had magazine and book publication during the last decade." In his treatment of the poems of nearly fifty poets, Eckman finds three particular stylistic modes: "decorative," "substantive," and "kinetic."

D47   Ehrenpreis, Irvin, ed. *American Poetry.* Stratford-upon-Avon Studies 7. New York: St. Martin's, 1965. This volume is "a cooperative book" with essays collected "to present American poetry to readers on both sides of the Atlantic." Robert Frost, Marianne Moore, Ezra Pound, Wallace Stevens, e. e. cummings, T. S. Eliot, Robert Lowell, John Crowe Ransom, Allen Tate, Robert Penn Warren, William Carlos Williams, and earlier writers.

D48   Eliot, T. S. *On Poetry and Poets.* New York: Noonday, 1970. A collection of essays that includes "The Social Function of Poetry," "The Music of Poetry," "What is Minor Poetry?," "What is a Classic?," "Poetry and Drama," "The Three Voices of Poetry," "The Frontiers of Criticism," and others.

D49   —————. *The Three Voices of Poetry.* New York: Cambridge University Press, 1954. A short lecture on poetry. Eliot explains the "three voices": "The first is the voice of the poet talking to himself—or to nobody. The second is the voice of the poet addressing an audience, whether large or small. The third is the voice of the poet when he attempts to create a dramatic character speaking in verse; when he is saying, not what he would say in his own person, but only what he can say within the limits of one imaginary character addressing another imaginary character."

D50   Fairchild, Hoxie Neale. *Religious Trends in English Poetry.* Vol. 6, *1920–1965, Valley of Dry Bones.* New York: Columbia University Press, 1968. The final volume of Fairchild's extensive study of English poetry. This volume attempts to define the "spiritual temper" of the twentieth century as illustrated in its poetry. Rather than arranging his material by poets, Fairchild has substituted a "topic-by-topic treatment," focusing on such issues as war, science, eros, and death. In this volume, he has expanded his attention to American as well as English poetry. W. H. Auden, Gregory Corso, e. e. cummings, Robert Duncan, Lawrence Durrell, Richard Eberhart, T. S. Eliot, Allen Ginsberg, Robert Graves, C. S. Lewis, Robert Lowell, Louis MacNeice, Edwin Muir, Ezra Pound, Karl Shapiro, Edith Sitwell, Stephen Spender, Wallace Stevens, Dylan Thomas, William Carlos Williams, and many others. Bibliography.

D51   Feder, Lillian. *Ancient Myth in Modern Poetry*. Princeton: Princeton University Press, 1971. Feder's aim is twofold: "to develop a definition of myth as a continuous and evolving mode of expression, and to indicate how classical myth functions in modern English and American poetry as an aesthetic device which reaches into the deepest layers of personal, religious, social, and political life." Discusses Sigmund Freud, Northrop Frye, myth, the unconsciousness, ritual, and history in relation to W. B. Yeats, Ezra Pound, T. S. Eliot, W. H. Auden, and others.

D52   Fox, Hugh. *The Living Underground: A Critical Overview*. Troy, N.Y.: Whitston, 1970. In light of the multitude of slick and commercially attractive books, Fox sees evidence in poetry of the "media revolution" and less concentration on the "permanence" of art expression. Poetry is moving toward an annihilation of its definable nature into a new kind of "omni-art" or "synthesis of all sense and experience within the field of electronic expression." Brown Miller, Dick Higgins, Douglas Blazek, D. R. Wagner, Don Cauble, John Oliver Simon, Joel Deutsch, T. L. Kryss, Richard Krech, Richard Morris, Charles Potts, and others.

D53   Frankenberg, Lloyd. *Pleasure Dome: On Reading Modern Poetry*. Boston: Houghton Mifflin, 1949*; rpt. New York: Gordian, 1968. Frankenburg states: "I hope to provide a bridge to modern poetry for readers like myself, brought up on prose." Focuses on the relationship between sound and meaning in poetry. James Stephens, T. S. Eliot, Marianne Moore, e. e. cummings, Wallace Stevens, Ezra Pound, William Carlos Williams, Ogden Nash, W. H. Auden, Dylan Thomas, Robert Lowell, and Elizabeth Bishop. Primary bibliography.

D54   Fraser, G. S. *Vision and Rhetoric: Studies in Modern Poetry.* New York: Barnes & Noble, 1960. Essays on the theories enunciated by Sir Herbert Read, John Bayley, and Frank Kermode concerning the modern movement. Fraser also considers T. E. Hulme, the imagist movement, and the poetry of Ezra Pound and T. S. Eliot. In addition, Fraser examines the theory which defines a poem as being a mode of moral discourse and objects that this theory does not account for the personal experience of the poem. e. e. cummings, Robert Graves, W. H. Auden, Louis MacNeice, William Empson, Stephen Spender, and Dylan Thomas.

D55   Fuller, Roy. *Owls and Artificers: Oxford Lectures on Poetry.* New York: Library Press, 1971. Six lectures that look at the present and its poetry. I. A. Richards, W. H. Auden, Robert Bridges, T. S. Eliot, Marianne Moore, Wallace Stevens, and Dylan Thomas.

D56   Fussell, Edwin. *Lucifer in Harness: American Meter, Metaphor, and Diction.* Princeton: Princeton University Press, 1973. Fussell "attempts to explore the fundamental dilemma of American poetry as it appears in the three crucial fields of meter, metaphor, and poetic diction." Discusses the poet as he is harnessed to the English language and the English literary tradition. T. S. Eliot, William Carlos Williams, Wallace Stevens, and earlier writers.

D57   Gibson, Donald B., ed. *Modern Black Poets: A Collection of Critical Essays.* Englewood Cliffs, N.J.: Prentice-Hall, 1973. Essays arranged historically, beginning with a history of black poets. Essays on the twenties, the thirties, the forties, the fifties, Langston Hughes, and Countee Cullen. Contemporary poets: Melvin B. Tolson, Robert Hayden, Imamu Amiri Baraka (LeRoi Jones), Don L. Lee, Sonia Sanchez, Nikki Giovanni, and others.

D58   Ginestier, Paul. *The Poet and the Machine.* Translated by Martin B. Friedman. Chapel Hill: University of North Carolina Press, 1961. "The result of the application to the study of contemporary poetry of a method employed by the author in several volumes dealing with various branches of literature and whose general title is 'Toward a Science of Literature.'" Ginestier demonstrates "how frequently a poem can be illuminated by the discoveries of the pre-eminent modern sciences, psychoanalysis and sociology, in a study whose thematic unity—the influence upon poetry of the material progress of society"—offers evidence of the importance of his approach. Brief references to many poems. Some discussion of T. S. Eliot, Louis MacNeice, and Stephen Spender.

D59   Ginsberg, Allen. *Allen Verbation: Lectures on Poetry, Politics, Consciousness.* Edited by Gordon Ball. New York: McGraw-Hill, 1974. Lectures recorded during a cross-country college reading tour during the spring of 1971. Ginsberg's lectures cover such topics as "Gnostic" consciousness, "Political Opium," recent twentieth-century poetry, and the Vietnam War. Robert Duncan, Jack Kerouac, Ezra Pound, and others.

D60   Graves, Robert. *The Common Asphodel: Collected Essays on Poetry, 1922–1949.* London: Hamish Hamilton, 1949. A collection of reprinted essays that reveals Graves's attitudes toward poetry before and after the two world wars.

D61   ————. *The Crowning Privilege: Collected Essays on Poetry.* Freeport, N.Y.: Books for Libraries Press, 1970. Lectures on "Professional Standards in English Poetry." Also includes various essays on poets, such as e. e. cummings, Juana de Ashaje, and Ezra Pound, and essays from *The Common Asphodel.*

D62   ————. *On Poetry: Collected Talks and Essays.* New York: Doubleday, 1969. A collection that includes "Dr. Syntax and Mr. Pound," "Legitimate Criticism of Poetry," "Pulling a Poem Apart," "The Anti-Poet," "Techniques in Poetry," and twenty-five others. They represent Graves's thinking from 1954 to 1966.

D63   Gross, Harvey. *Sound and Form in Modern Poetry: A Study of Prosody from Thomas Hardy to Robert Lowell.* Ann Arbor: University of Michigan Press, 1965. Includes chapters on the nature of prosody and scansion, Thomas Hardy,

transitional figures, imagism, and contemporary poets. Ezra
Pound, T. S. Eliot, Hart Crane, William Carlos Williams,
e. e. cummings, Wallace Stevens, W. H. Auden, Stephen
Spender, Louis MacNeice, Dylan Thomas, William Empson, Vernon Watkins, Henry Reed, Stanley Kunitz, Theodore Roethke, and Robert Lowell.

D64　Hamburger, Michael. *The Truth of Poetry: Tensions in Modern Poetry from Baudelaire to the 1960's*. New York: Harcourt, Brace & World, 1969. Hamburger's premise is that
lyrical poetry changed dramatically and fundamentally after Baudelaire. In his study Hamburger concentrates on
"the tensions and conflicts apparent in the work of every
major poet, beginning with the work of Baudelaire." Guillaume Appollinaire, Charles Baudelaire, Gottfried Benn,
Bertolt Brecht, Tristan Corbière, T. S. Eliot, Helmut Heis-
senbütel, Frederico García Lorca, Stéphane Mallarmé,
Ezra Pound, Wallace Stevens, W. H. Auden, Robert Bly,
Robert Creeley, Robert Duncan, William Empson, George
Stefan, Robert Graves, Ted Hughes, Philip Larkin, William Carlos Williams, and others briefly mentioned.

D65　Hamilton, Ian. *A Poetry Chronicle: Essays and Reviews*. New
York: Barnes & Noble, 1973. A selection of poetry reviews
written for the *Observer* and the *TLS*. Includes essays on
the wasteland, Louis MacNeice, William Empson, the forties, Roy Fuller, Robert Lowell, John Berryman, the sixties' press, Philip Larkin, Donald Davie, and others.

D66　————, ed. *The Modern Poet*. New York: Horizon, 1969.
A selection of essays from the first fifteen issues of the
Review. Includes the dispute between A. Alvarez and Don-
ald Davie and interviews with William Empson and Robert
Lowell. Thom Gunn, Roy Fuller, Edwin Muir, Yvor Win-
ters, Sylvia Plath, Bernard Spenser, Philip Larkin, John
Berryman, Marianne Moore, Alun Lewis, and Randall
Jarrell.

D67　Highet, Gilbert. *The Powers of Poetry*. New York: Oxford
University Press, 1960. Essays on poetic techniques, character studies of individual poets, poems, and why anyone
writes poetry. Shakespeare through W. H. Auden, e. e.
cummings, T. S. Eliot, A. E. Housman, and Dylan Thomas.

D68   Hoffman, Daniel. *Barbarous Knowledge: Myth in the Poetry of Yeats, Graves, and Muir.* New York: Oxford University Press, 1967. Beginning with each author's roots in the ballad tradition, Hoffman demonstrates how these poets have worked toward the construction of myth.

D69   Hollander, John. *Modern Poetry: Essays in Criticism.* London: Oxford University Press, 1968. Hollander's purpose is to record the ways in which modern poetry has been read. Contributors include Ezra Pound, T. S. Eliot, F. R. Leavis, W. B. Yeats, Cleanth Brooks, Randall Jarrell, R. P. Blackmur, F. O. Matthiessen, Kenneth Burke, Yvor Winters, William Empson, Marius Bewley, Northrop Frye, A. Alvarez, Grover Smith, Frank Kermode, Louis L. Martz, Monroe K. Spears, Thomas R. Whitaker, Donald Davie, Helen Vendler, John F. Lynen, and Harold Bloom.

D70   —————. *Vision and Resonance: Two Senses of Poetic Form.* New York: Oxford University Press, 1975. A practical criticism, located between the tension of subject and object, which deals with the following issues: structural linguistics, music, and tradition. The twelve chapters move from discussions of aural qualities to visual ones. While examples are mainly from earlier periods, the following writers are discussed: W. H. Auden, Robert Bridges, T. S. Eliot, Robert Frost, Ezra Pound, Wallace Stevens, and William Carlos Williams.

D71   Holroyd, Stuart. *Emergence from Chaos.* Boston: Houghton Mifflin, 1957. Holroyd studies six poets representative of various types of religious experience, how they have reacted to spiritual chaos, and to what extent they have succeeded in emerging from chaos. This book is "an attack on humanism and a plea for the rediscovery of a religious standard of values." Walt Whitman, W. B. Yeats, Arthur Rimbaud, Dylan Thomas, T. S. Eliot, and others.

D72   Howard, Richard. *Alone with America: Essays on the Art of Poetry in the United States since 1950.* New York: Atheneum, 1969. A six-hundred-page "accounting" of American poets who have come into a "consequential identity" since the time of the Korean War. A. R. Ammons, John Ashbery, Robert Bly, Edgar Bowers, Gregory Corso, Robert Creeley, James Dickey, Alan Dugan, Irving Feldman, Edward Field, Donald Finkel, Allen Ginsberg, Paul Goodman, Anthony Hecht, Daryl Hine, Daniel Hoffman, John Hollander, Richard Hugo, Donald Justice, Galway Kinnell, Carolyn Kizer, Kenneth Koch, Denise Levertov, John Logan, William Meredith, James Merrill, W. S. Merwin, Howard Moss, Frank O'Hara, Sylvia Plath, Adrienne Rich, Anne Sexton, Louis Simpson, W. D. Snodgrass, Gary Snyder, William Stafford, Mark Strand, May Swenson, David Wagoner, Theodore Weiss, and James Wright.

D73 Hungerford, Edward, ed. *Poets in Progress: Critical Prefaces to Ten Contemporary Americans.* Evanston, Ill.: Northwestern University Press, 1962. Includes articles that first appeared in Northwestern University's *Tri-Quarterly*, critical analyses of separate poems, and prefaces. Theodore Roethke, Robert Lowell, Stanley Kunitz, Richard Wilbur, Richard Eberhart, W. D. Snodgrass, Howard Nemerov, J. V. Cunningham, Randall Jarrell, and W. S. Merwin. Primary bibliography.

D74 Hungerland, Isabel C. *Poetic Discourse.* Berkeley: University of California Press, 1958. An analytical study of the nature of language as poetic discourse, written for the scholar. Chapters on "Language and Poetry," "Literature as an Art: Poetry and Truth," "Literature as an Art: Appraisals of Literary Worth," "Figurative Language," "Symbols in Poetry," and "The Interpretation of Poetry." Among the many writers discussed are T. S. Eliot, Mary McCarthy, Robert Frost, Randall Jarrell, and Dylan Thomas.

D75 Jarrell, Randall. *Poetry and the Age.* New York: Knopf, 1953. Includes criticisms of the best and "a few of the worst American poets." Robert Frost, John Crowe Ransom, Wallace Stevens, Alex Comfort, Tristan Corbière, Muriel Rukeyser, R. P. Blackmur, William Carlos Williams, Robert Lowell, Richard Wilbur, and Marianne Moore.

D76 ————. *The Third Book of Criticism.* New York: Farrar, Straus & Giroux, 1965. The final collection of Jarrell's criticism with essays on six Russian short novels and on fifty years of American poetry. Brief discussions of many contemporary poets and essays on Wallace Stevens, Robert Graves, W. H. Auden, and Robert Frost.

D77   Jennings, Elizabeth. *Every Changing Shape.* Philadelphia: Dufour, 1962. Jennings's concerns are the making of poems, the nature of mystical experience, and the relationship between the two. T. S. Eliot, David Gascoyne, Wallace Stevens, Thomas Gilby, Henri Bremond, and many other earlier writers. Bibliography.

D78   ————. *Poetry To-day (1957–60).* London: Longmans, Green, 1961. A monograph that surveys poetry in Great Britain. Jennings states that the fifties "marked the rediscovery of elegance in poetry, elegance not as accretion or artifice but as a method of discerning and knowing." Kingsley Amis, Patricia Beer, Thomas Blackburn, Donald Davie, D. J. Enright, Roy Fuller, Robert Graves, Thom Gunn, John Holloway, Philip Larkin, Peter Levi, Norman MacGay, William Plomer, Anne Ridler, Quentin Stevenson, R. S. Thomas, Anthony Thwaite, Terence Tiller, Charles Tomlinson, and John Wain. Bibliography.

D79   Juhasz, Suzanne. *Metaphor and the Poetry of Williams, Pound, and Stevens.* Lewisburg, Pa.: Bucknell University Press, 1974. "William Carlos Williams, Ezra Pound, and Wallace Stevens are modern poets whose use of metaphor is fundamental to the structure of their poetry. The essays in this book closely examine each poet's characteristic use of metaphor and the function it fulfills in his work. . . ." Juhasz also studies the three poets as a group to discover "what their practices and their theories have in common." Bibliography.

D80   Kinneavy, Brother James Leo. *A Study of Three Contemporary Theories of Lyric Poetry.* Washington, D.C.: Catholic University of America Press, 1956. There are three "tendencies" in contemporary lyric theory: the lyric as choice, the lyric as conflict, and the lyric as emotion. Each tendency is represented by a discussion of a major critic: Elder Olson, Robert Petsch, and Henri Bonnet. In each category, "a brief historical survey of the position is outlined, then the views of the representative of the group are presented and evaluated, and finally the theory is applied to a particular poem. Thus there is a historical, theoretical, and critical treatment of each tendency." Bibliography.

D81   Kunitz, Stanley. *A Kind of Order, A Kind of Folly: Essays and*

Conversations. Boston: Little, Brown, 1975. "A collection
of critical and prose reflections" written between 1935 and
1975. Theodore Roethke, Robert Lowell, Conrad Aiken,
Louise Bogan, Kenneth Fearing, John Berryman, Marianne
Moore, Dylan Thomas, Wallace Stevens, Randall Jarrell,
John Crowe Ransom, Robert Frost, William Carlos Wil-
liams, James Wright, Jean Garrigue, Robert Graves,
Charles Olson, Robert Creeley, Ruth Pitter, Hugh Seid-
man, Peter Klappert, Michael Casey, Robert Hass, Michael
Ryan, and others.

D82 Lacey, Paul A. *The Inner War: Forms and Themes in Recent
American Poetry*. Philadelphia: Fortress, 1972. The poets
studied reflect "three emphases found widely in American
poetry in the 1960s: a preoccupation with the inner world
of the psyche and its relation to the world of everyday
existence; a reevaluation of the imagination as the faculty
of discovery and creation; and a blurring of lines which
have separated the poem from such other kinds of writing
as the notebook, diary, documentary, history, or confession." These poets declare "that we are in a new time,
with new themes and metaphors, new aesthetics, new attempts to speak of the world." Robert Bly, William Everson (Brother Antoninus), Denise Levertov, Anne Sexton,
and James Wright.

D83 Larrick, Nancy, ed. *Somebody Turned on a Tap in These Kids:
Poetry and Young People Today*. New York: Delacorte,
1971. This book "grew out of the Poetry Festival sponsored
by the School of Education of Lehigh University in the
spring of 1969. . . . Papers read during the festival and
talks and discussion taped that day make up the greater
part of the book." The focus is on poetry and young
people.

D84 Levertov, Denise. *The Poet in the World*. New York: New
Directions, 1973. A selection of Levertov's most important
critical statements: "some occasional, even impromptu in
nature—letters, manifestoes, advertisements—others, such
as lectures and essays, more formal in character." Includes
"Work and Inspiration," "Life at War," "The Untaught
Teacher," "Perhaps Fiction," and "Other Writers." They
all "bear directly upon topics of concern to writers today:

the poet's craft in an era that has abandoned conventional rules, the role of imagination in individual and social life, the writer as teacher and political activist."

D85   Lewis, C. Day. *The Poetic Image*. London: Jonathan Cape, 1947. A collection of the Clark Lectures delivered at Trinity College, Cambridge. Lewis studies the nature of the image, the field and the pattern of images. He addresses the problems of being a modern poet and the nature of modern poetry.

D86   Lindsay, Jack. *Meetings with Poets: Memories of Dylan Thomas, Edith Sitwell, Louis Aragon, Paul Eluard, Tristan Tzara*. London: Frederick Muller, 1968. Five literary portraits that represent "a comprehensive account of [Lindsay's] memories." Lindsay's method of relating these memories is determined by his "relations to the poet concerned."

D87   Ludwig, Richard M., ed. *Aspects of American Poetry*. Columbus: Ohio State University Press, 1962. Essays in honor of Howard Mumford Jones on Ezra Pound, Robert Frost, Wallace Stevens, Allen Tate, and others.

D88   McDowell, Frederick P. W., ed. *The Poet as Critic*. Evanston, Ill.: Northwestern University Press, 1967. Essayists discuss the reciprocal relations between the methods of creation and the methods of criticism and explore the use the poet makes of his critical faculties. Contributors include Murray Krieger, Elizabeth Sewell, Richard Ellmann, Ralph Freedman, Donald Hall, and René Wellek. They consider the work of T. S. Eliot, Wallace Stevens, John Crowe Ransom, and others.

D89   Maritain, Jacques. *Creative Intuition in Art and Poetry: The A. W. Mellon Lectures in the Fine Arts, 1952, National Gallery of Art, Washington*. New York: Pantheon, 1953. The purpose of this philosophic inquiry is "to try to make clear both the distinction and the indissoluble relationship" between art and poetry.

D90   Martz, Louis. *The Poem of the Mind: Essays on Poetry, English and American*. New York: Oxford University Press, 1966. "These essays deal with poetry of the interior life, where the mind, acutely aware of an outer world of drifting unstable forms, finds within itself the power to create coherence and significance." John Donne through T. S. Eliot, William Carlos Williams, Theodore Roethke, and Wallace Stevens.

D91 Mazzaro, Jerome, ed. *Modern American Poetry: Essays in Criticism.* New York: McKay, 1970. A collection of essays that deal with American poetry from a variety of points of view: biographical, sociological, aesthetical, new critical, psychoanalytical, phenomenological, stylistic, mythic, and impressionistic. Robert Frost, Wallace Stevens, William Carlos Williams, Ezra Pound, Marianne Moore, T. S. Eliot, e. e. cummings, Theodore Roethke, Robert Lowell, W. D. Snodgrass, and earlier writers.

D92 Meiners, R. K. *Everything to Be Endured: An Essay on Robert Lowell and Modern Poetry.* Columbia: University of Missouri Press, 1970. Meiners primarily discusses the relationship between Allen Tate and Robert Lowell and studies them against the backdrop of tradition. Through this study, Meiners evolves "an extreme statement of the conditions with which the modern poet has often seemed to have been faced, and the circumstances from which he has tried to break free."

D93 Mersmann, James F. *Out of the Vietnam Vortex: A Study of Poets and Poetry against the War.* Lawrence: University Press of Kansas, 1974. Mersmann's study is "a thematic analysis of the poetry written during the 1960s in protest of the American war in Vietnam." His approach studies: whether the war protest is legitimate; whether the experience of war has altered a poet's beliefs and practices; whether common themes and attitudes are tied to similar biographies and philosophic temper, or arise equally well from different backgrounds; whether protest is grounded in opportunism; and whether protest poetry is inferior to other types. Allen Ginsberg, Denise Levertov, Robert Bly, and Robert Duncan. Bibliography.

D94 Miller, James E., Jr.; Karl Shapiro; and Bernice Slote. *Start with the Sun: Studies in Cosmic Poetry.* Lincoln: University of Nebraska Press, 1960. An analysis of the Whitman tradition as it is advanced by D. H. Lawrence, Hart Crane, and Dylan Thomas. Also discussed are e. e. cummings,

T. S. Eliot, Allen Ginsberg, Robert Graves, Henry Miller, Ezra Pound, Wallace Stevens, and others.

D95   Miller, J. Hillis. *Poets of Reality: Six Twentieth-Century Writers.* Cambridge, Mass.: Harvard University Press, Belknap Press, 1965. Miller's study is based on the assumption that twentieth-century poetry is an extension of romanticism. He examines writers who have participated in romanticism and shows configurations of themes which permeate their work. Each chapter describes "one version of the journey beyond nihilism toward a poetry of reality." T. S. Eliot, Dylan Thomas, Wallace Stevens, William Carlos Williams, and earlier writers.

D96   Mills, Ralph J., Jr. *Contemporary American Poetry.* New York: Random House, 1966. Mills studies a group of American poets who began writing during the thirty-year period ruled by the "authority of T. S. Eliot and the new critics." Mills uses the word "contemporary" in the title rather than "modern" to "separate them from the pioneer modernists of Eliot's generation and the slightly later poets of the 1920's." These poets "have not enjoyed a mood of collective inspiration but, without the benefit of any shared aesthetic aim or revolutionary artistic goal, have had to cultivate voices on their own, making them distinctive by selecting for themselves models and guides both from earlier literature and from the pioneer modernists preceding them." Richard Eberhart, Stanley Kunitz, Theodore Roethke, Elizabeth Bishop, Brother Antoninus (William Everson), Karl Shapiro, Isabella Gardner, Robert Lowell, Richard Wilbur, Denise Levertov, James Wright, Anne Sexton. Primary and secondary bibliography.

D97   ——————. *Creation's Very Self: On the Personal Element in Recent American Poetry.* Fort Worth: Texas Christian University Press, 1969. Mills examines the movement of American poetry towards a dramatization of the poet's intimate psychological self. He studies the confessional poetry of Theodore Roethke, Frank O'Hara, Gary Snyder, Robert Lowell, Anne Sexton, Sylvia Plath, Denise Levertov, and others.

D98   ——————. *Cry of the Human: Essays on Contemporary American Poetry.* Urbana: University of Illinois Press,

1975. Mills collects essays that represent his critical interest since the 1960s. He studies poets who demonstrate how the American poetic imagination has met the challenge set by the character of life since mid century. This book includes "Creation's Very Self" and essays that stem from the considerations in it. David Ignatow, Galway Kinnell, Donald Hall, Philip Levine, and Theodore Roethke. Bibliography.

D99   Moore, Geoffrey. *Poetry To-Day*. London: Longmans, Green, 1958. A brief survey of British poetry from 1950 to 1957 that deals with poets who published a book during those years. Organized chronologically by Moore's estimation of when the authors matured—in the 1930s, 1940s, or 1950s—the study discusses the poetry the authors wrote in the 1950s. Treats many poets, especially T. S. Eliot and Edith Sitwell. Bibliography.

D100 Morgan, Kathleen E. *Christian Themes in Contemporary Poets: A Study of English Poetry of the Twentieth Century*. London: SCM Press, 1965. A study of poetry in a time antithetical to Christian faith. Each poet illustrates a different way of responding to this theme. The work concludes with a study of "images and form" in "these and other poets." Edwin Muir, David Gascoyne, Charles Williams, W. H. Auden, Norman Nicholson, and Anne Ridler. Bibliography.

D101 *National Poetry Festival Held in the Library of Congress, October 22–24, 1962: Proceedings*. Washington, D.C.: Library of Congress, 1964. Record of the panels, readings, and lectures at this conference. Lectures by Louise Bogan, Stanley Kunitz, Randall Jarrell, Babette Deutsch, Howard Nemerov, Karl Shapiro, Allen Tate, Léonie Adams, J. V. Cunningham, and Herbert Read.

D102 Nemerov, Howard. *Reflexions on Poetry and Poetics*. New Brunswick, N.J.: Rutgers University Press, 1972. Essays on poets, movements, unadmirable items on the scene, some lyric poems, and "self-poetizing." Thomas Mann, T. S. Eliot, Owen Barfield, Djuna Barnes, James Dickey, Kenneth Burke, Conrad Aiken, Randall Jarrell, and earlier writers.

D103 ————, ed. *Poets on Poetry*. New York: Basic Books, 1966. A collection of essays by poets on poetry. Contributors include Conrad Aiken, Ben Belitt, John Berryman, John Malcolm Brinnin, Gregory Corso, J. V. Cunningham, James Dickey, Robert Duncan, Richard Eberhart, Jack Gilbert, Barbara Howes, Vassar Miller, Marianne Moore, Howard Nemerov, William Jay Smith, May Swenson, Theodore Weiss, Reed Whittemore, and Richard Wilbur.

D104   Noon, William T., S.J. *Poetry and Prayer.* New Brunswick, N.J.: Rutgers University Press, 1967. Noon attempts "to discover what men of prayer and poets themselves are saying." In doing this, he formulates a "theory of poetry and prayer" which he tests with the work of Gerard Manley Hopkins, W. B. Yeats, Wallace Stevens, Robert Frost, and David Jones.

D105   Norris, Ruby Lee, ed. *The Turtle and the Teacher: A Dialogue between Poets and Students.* Richmond, Va.: Dietz Press, n.d. Represents "a partial record of the interaction between poets and children." Michael Mott, Dabney Stuart, and Sylvia Wilkinson acted as poets in residence. The book contains descriptions of inventive and meaningful techniques to get kids to read, along with the poems they wrote in response to the techniques.

D106   O'Connor, William Van. *Sense and Sensibility in Modern Poetry.* Chicago: University of Chicago Press, 1948. Explores these issues: "dissociation of sensibility"; the influence of symbolists, metaphysicals, and premodern Americans; the imagistic symbol, irony and structure; and the social and human dimension of this mode. Conrad Aiken, e. e. cummings, T. S. Eliot, Robert Frost, Robert Lowell, Archibald MacLeish, Ezra Pound, Delmore Schwartz, Karl Shapiro, Wallace Stevens, Allen Tate, and others. Bibliography.

D107   Olson, Charles. *Charles Olson and Ezra Pound: An Encounter at St. Elizabeths.* Edited by Catherine Seelye. New York: Grossman, 1975. Olson's notes concerning his encounter with Ezra Pound at St. Elizabeths hospital. The editor writes that Olson's chronicle is important as a "record of a personal and political encounter, the confrontation of a man of good conscience and a man of hate—the issue of politics as opposed to poetry. . . ."

D108 —————. *Human Universe and Other Essays.* Edited by Donald Allen. New York: Grove Press, 1967. Letters, reviews, and theoretical and critical essays, generally on contemporary poetry.

D109 Orr, Peter, ed. *The Poet Speaks: Interviews with Contemporary Poets Conducted by Hilary Morrish, Peter Orr, John Press, and Ian Scott-Kilvert.* New York: Barnes & Noble, 1966. Forty-five poets—some well-known, others not—talk about their own work. "Many of the poets whose interviews appear in this book can be heard reading their own poems in a recorded anthology on six long-playing records (RG 451-6) which I have edited for Argo." Few poets illustrate contemporary America's "confessional" or "projective" or avant-garde or "modern" or scholarly poetry. John Arden, Sylvia Plath, Herbert Read, Stephen Spender, Anthony Thwaite, Charles Tomlinson, and others.

D110 Ossman, David. *The Sullen Art: Interviews with Modern American Poets.* New York: Corinth Books, 1963. Fourteen interviews from the "The Sullen Art" radio series. An attempt to explain the "New York scene," and to demonstrate that the beat writers are not "a bunch of illiterate, barbaric, slightly criminal types." The collection is not a defense, but an attempt to "set the record straight." While the poets know each other, they do not constitute a school. Many of them have taught; many write critical articles; and many "would readily admit the talents of others who are called their opposition"—the academic poets. The interviews are not "manifestoes or essays," but informal statements about the poetry scene. Kenneth Rexroth, Paul Carroll, Paul Blackburn, Jerome Rothenberg, Robert Kelly, Robert Bly, John Logan, Gilbert Sorrentino, Robert Creeley, W. S. Merwin, Denise Levertov, LeRoi Jones (Imamu Amiri Baraka), Edward Dorn, and Allen Ginsberg.

D111 Ostroff, Anthony, ed. *The Contemporary Poet as Artist and Critic.* Boston: Little, Brown, 1964. Eight symposia: three poets write critiques of a poem by a contemporary, who then responds. "The poem, the three critiques, and the author's comment together constitute the finished symposium. . . . Disagreements among the critics expose limits or flaws in critical method as often as they expose limits in the poems being examined. The juxtapositions of essays in the symposia permit us to judge the relative efficacy of various critical approaches as well as their limits." Poets studied are Richard Wilbur, Theodore Roethke, Stanley Kunitz, Robert Lowell, John Crowe Ransom, Richard Eberhart, W. H. Auden, and Karl Shapiro. Bibliography.

D112 Owen, Gary, ed. *Modern American Poetry: Essays in Criticism.* Deland, Fla.: Everett/Edwards, 1972. A collection of essays on American poetry, reflecting the critical judgment of the early seventies. Taken together, the essays "should add up, so far as possible, to a complete history of what is significant in American poetry since World War I." This book is intended for an undergraduate or lay reader, not a specialist. Robert Frost, Wallace Stevens, William Carlos Williams, T. S. Eliot, e. e. cummings, Theodore Roethke, Robert Lowell, Richard Wilbur, James Dickey, and poets of the '60s.

D113 Packard, William, ed. *The Craft of Poetry: Interviews from the New York Quarterly.* Garden City, N.Y.: Doubleday, 1974. Interviews with W. H. Auden, Paul Blackburn, Anne Sexton, Stanley Kunitz, Jerome Rothenberg, Allen Ginsberg, Denise Levertov, Galway Kinnell, John Ashbery, James Dickey, Muriel Rukeyser, Richard Wilbur, Robert Creeley, Jackson MacLow, Howard Moss, Erica Jong, and Diane Wakoski. Includes a primary bibliography after each interview.

D114 Pearce, Roy Harvey. *The Continuity of American Poetry.* Princeton: Princeton University Press, 1961. Pearce is concerned with the history poems have made. His study is a cultural history, from the origins of American poetry to William Carlos Williams, Robert Frost, T. S. Eliot, John Crowe Ransom, Allen Tate, Conrad Aiken, e. e. cummings, Marianne Moore, and Wallace Stevens.

D115 *Poets at Work: Essays Based on the Modern Poetry Collection at the Lockwood Memorial Library, University of Buffalo,* by Rudolf Arnheim, W. H. Auden, Karl Shapiro, Donald A. Stauffer. New York: Harcourt, Brace, 1948. The four authors quickly assessed the large collection of published poems, worksheets, and letters. Their comments reflect the perspectives of the scholar (Stauffer), the poet (Shapiro), the psychologist (Arnheim), and the modern ethologist (Auden).

D116   Pratt, John Clark. *The Meaning of Modern Poetry*. Garden City, N.Y.: Doubleday, 1962. Not an ordinary book, but a tutor text. It is designed to lead a reader toward his own understanding of modern poetry through a series of questions and brief discussions of various possible answers to the questions. Covers all aspects of poetry. Designed for anyone who feels inadequate with a poem.

D117   Press, John. *The Chequer'd Shade: Reflections on Obscurity in Poetry*. London: Oxford University Press, 1958. Investigates "the nature of obscurity in poetry . . . to find out some of the reasons why certain poems are obscure." Press asks whether obscure poetry has always flourished, whether every variety of obscure poetry is undesirable, and whether an element of obscurity is found in all poetry. W. H. Auden, T. S. Eliot, Ezra Pound, and others. Bibliography.

D118   ————. *The Fire and the Fountain*. London: Oxford University Press, 1955. "The purpose of this book is to estimate the significance of this moment [of creation] for the poet, and to trace the way that a poem grows in his mind." Press discusses the characteristics of a true poet, the influence of sound and image upon creation, patterns of images, the value of meaning, and the value of formal patterns to structure the poem. W. H. Auden, T. S. Eliot, David Gascoyne, Robert Graves, W. R. Rodgers, Dylan Thomas, and others. Bibliography.

D119   ————. *The Lengthening Shadows*. London: Oxford University Press, 1971. Discusses "some of the reasons why the rise of puritan morality and of scientific rationalism tended to depress the status of poetry." Press articulates the conventional arguments against poetry: it is "immoral, trivial, and socially disruptive." He, then, makes an apology for poetry. W. H. Auden, Donald Davie, T. S. Eliot, Ezra Pound, and others. Bibliography.

D120   ————. *Rule and Energy: Trends in British Poetry since the Second World War*. London: Oxford University Press, 1963. Press surveys British poets since 1939 for an American audience. He argues that the period from 1939 to 1941 marked the end of an epoch in British poetry as the war cleared the way for a new generation of poets. His study is an analysis of this "revolution in poetic thought and sensibility." Kingsley Amis, W. H. Auden, Thomas Blackburn, Donald Davie, Lawrence Durrell, T. S. Eliot, Robert Graves, Thom Gunn, Ted Hughes, Philip Larkin, and Ezra Pound. Bibliography.

D121   Quinn, Sister M. Bernetta. *The Metamorphic Tradition in Modern Poetry: Essays on the Work of Ezra Pound, Wallace Stevens, William Carlos Williams, T. S. Eliot, Hart Crane, Randall Jarrell, and William Butler Yeats.* New York: Guardian Press, 1966. Metamorphosis, "man's desire and need to transcend the psychologically repressive conditions of his mechanized *milieu*," is an important theme. Metamorphic images occur in literature because (1) they become *personae* for the poet, (2) they "serve so well as verbal equations for contemporary emotional situations," (3) they serve as "descriptive" images "of the natural world and the way in which that world is known," and (4) they help discover the "unifying forces" in long poems, such as Crane's *The Bridge*. Bibliography.

D122   Rajan, B., ed. *Modern American Poetry.* London: Dennis Dobson, 1950. This volume is not meant "to be a handbook or a survey." It is based on separate studies of five writers whom the editor believes "many critics would include among the six most important of contemporary American poets." Also includes "A Little Anthology of Contemporary American Poetry." Allen Tate, John Crowe Ransom, Robert Penn Warren, Wallace Stevens, and e. e. cummings.

D123   Ransom, John Crowe; Delmore Schwartz; and John Hall Wheelock. *American Poetry at Mid-Century: Lectures Presented under the Auspices of the Gertrude Clarke Whittall Poetry and Literature Fund.* Washington, D.C.: Library of Congress, 1958. Includes "New Poets and Old Muses" by John Crowe Ransom, "The Present State of Poetry" by Delmore Schwartz, and "The Two Knowledges: An Essay on a Certain Resistance" by John Hall Wheelock.

D124   Rexroth, Kenneth. *The Alternative Society: Essays from the*

Other World. New York: Herder & Herder, 1970. Includes essays on the beat generation, black writers, poetry in 1965, poetry during the 1970s, and other topics.

D125 ————. *American Poetry in the Twentieth Century.* New York: Herder & Herder, 1971. A historical study of the roots and traditions of American poetry, moving decade by decade into the seventies. Connects poets to the cultural forces of their time by studying the relationships among poets and common ideas of the time, geography, and/or race group. Makes judgments about the immediate and long-range value of poets and their work. T. S. Eliot, Ezra Pound, Wallace Stevens, William Carlos Williams, e. e. cummings, Allen Ginsberg, others. Focuses on the poets of the seventies and on the following schools: Black Mountain, San Francisco, New York, midwestern, confessional, and black.

D126 Roethke, Theodore. *On the Poet and His Craft: Selected Prose of Theodore Roethke.* Edited by Ralph J. Mills, Jr. Seattle: University of Washington Press, 1965. Includes a paper Roethke wrote as a student at the University of Michigan, various essays on the craft of poetry, memoirs of Dylan Thomas and Richard Seilig, book reviews, and an essay on Louise Bogan.

D127 Rollins, Charlemae. *Famous American Negro Poets.* New York: Dodd, Mead, 1965. Brief essays on twelve "Negro poets who have particular appeal to young people." Biographical and bibliographical data and a sample of each poet's work make up each essay. Effie Lee Newsome, Arna Bontemps, Langston Hughes, Countee Cullen, Margaret Walker, Gwendolyn Brooks, and earlier figures. Bibliography.

D128 Rosenthal, M. L. *The Modern Poets: A Critical Introduction.* New York: Oxford University Press, 1960. Locates the problems readers have with modern poetry and attempts to remove the problems by describing the modern poetic tradition. "Without offering an exhaustive survey of *all* the modern poets and poetic currents, I have tried to plot a view that will suggest the range of our poetic landscape and its relation to the crisis of personality the modern mind has had to face." Ezra Pound, T. S. Eliot, Robert Frost,

William Carlos Williams, Wallace Stevens, W. H. Auden, Dylan Thomas, Robert Lowell, Karl Shapiro, Kenneth Rexroth, Charles Olson, and others. Bibliography.

D129 ————. *The New Poets: American and British Poetry since World War II.* New York: Oxford University Press, 1967. "My aim has been to identify a number of the crucial figures and poems and to suggest certain meaningful relationships among them in the light of the whole modern tradition" and "to examine certain key figures in such a way as to intimate the qualitative character of the whole scene as well as I am at this moment able to gauge it." Robert Lowell, Sylvia Plath, Allen Ginsberg, Theodore Roethke, John Berryman, Anne Sexton, Robert Creeley, Charles Olson, Robert Duncan, Ted Hughes, Philip Larkin, Thom Gunn, and others. Bibliography.

D130 ————. *Poetry and the Common Life.* New York: Oxford University Press, 1974. An attempt to help the lay reader experience poetry in such a way that he will see that poetry "counts," see "what connections it has with what we all really are and wish to be." "I hope these pages will help refresh the stream of modern thought about poetry by recalling that it is the poets, through their constant response to the touch of life, who are the truest spokesman for the wide human world in which they move and dream." W. H. Auden, Imamu Amiri Baraka (LeRoi Jones), John Berryman, Paul Blackburn, Robert Frost, Robert Lowell, William Carlos Williams, and others. Bibliography.

D131 Rukeyser, Muriel. *The Life of Poetry.* New York: Current Books, 1949*; rpt. New York: William Morrow, 1974. Rukeyser attempts to discover why people resist poetry. "I have tried to go behind the resistance, which is often a fear of poetry, and to show what might be ahead of this culture in conflict, with its background of strength and antagonism." Rukeyser suggests that poetry can be a meeting place for all kinds of imaginations.

D132 Sanford, Derek. *The Freedom of Poetry: Studies in Contemporary Verse.* London: Falcon, 1947. Written for the "humanist with a sense of crisis" and not for "the academic specialist" nor "for modern poets," these studies "suggest that the most satisfactory and stimulating works are those where harmonic and social significance [i.e., where aesthetics and relevance] come together in an equal degree." Sidney Kees, David Gascoyne, Alex Comfort, Lawrence Durrell, Nicholas Moore, Norman Nicholson, Wrey Gardiner, Kathleen Raine, and Anne Ridler. Bibliography.

D133   Schlauch, Margaret. *Modern English and American Poetry: Techniques and Ideologies.* London: Watts, 1956. Schlauch first "indicates to general readers how they may surmount the chief apparent difficulties in reading contemporary verse." Secondly, "the author has tried to give, for those more specifically interested in techniques, a fresh approach to the underlying problems of sound and rhythm." From her social perspective, Schlauch feels that the modern use of negative themes has diminished poetry. W. H. Auden, e. e. cummings, T. S. Eliot, Ezra Pound, Dylan Thomas, and others. Bibliography. Glossary of terms.

D134   Schmidt, Michael, and Grevel Lindop, eds. *British Poetry since 1960: A Critical Survey.* Oxford: Carcanet, 1972. This study traces the "most important movements," defends British poets from the attacks of American critics, and studies the various influences upon British poetry. Geoffrey Hill, Charles Tomlinson, Ian Hamilton, Donald Davie, Ted Hughes, Philip Larkin, Sylvia Plath, and others. List of poetry awards. Bibliography.

D135   Scott, Nathan A., Jr. *The Wild Prayer of Longing: Poetry and the Sacred.* New Haven: Yale University Press, 1971. "For those to whom the traditional language of liturgical theology is quite an alien tongue, the sacramental question remains a most pressing issue, the question as to what it is in the nature of reality that can be counted on finally to sanctify human existence." Scott attempts "to offer some indication of how a sacramental vision of the world may indeed define itself without resort to supernatural figuralism." These suggestions are informed by Erich Auerbach's *Mimesis* and the ideas of Martin Heidegger. Theodore Roethke, T. S. Eliot, Wallace Stevens, William Carlos Williams, and others.

D136   ————, ed. *Four Ways of Modern Poetry.* Richmond, Va.: John Knox, 1965. Scott gives a "Christian response" to modern poets. "The extraordinary richness and distinction of their work is in large part an affair of the radicalism with which they have faced into the 'boundary-situations' of human existence. . . . And though their 'stays against confusion' have not often been found in the great inherited traditions of religious belief, they do not for this reason lose authenticity of relevance to modern sensibilities: indeed, that authenticity may itself be proved by the audaciousness with which new terms for the sacred are conceived or with which the old terms are drastically reconceived." Wallace Stevens, Robert Frost, Dylan Thomas, and W. H. Auden. Selected bibliography.

D137 Scully, James, ed. *Modern Poetics*. New York: McGraw-Hill, 1965. Fifteen poets speak on their own work in letters, journal entries, or interviews. "The majority are concerned with poetry as a present and future activity, as a 'making' or strategy." Common themes are depersonalization and the emulation of the scientist. Work by Hart Crane, Gerard Manley Hopkins, W. B. Yeats, Ezra Pound, Robert Frost, T. S. Eliot, William Carlos Williams, e. e. cummings, Wallace Stevens, W. H. Auden, David Jones, Robert Lowell, John Crowe Ransom, Marianne Moore, and Dylan Thomas.

D138 Shapiro, Karl. *To Abolish Children and Other Essays*. Chicago: Quadrangle, 1968. Includes "To Abolish Children," "The Decolonization of American Literature," "Is Poetry an American Art?," "A Defense of Bad Poetry," "The Image of the Poet in America," "A Party in Milo," "The Death of Randall Jarrell," "To Revive Anarchism," and "A *Malebolge* of Fourteen Hundred Books."

D139 ——————. *Beyond Criticism: What the Poet Knows, the True Artificer, the Career of the Poem*. Lincoln: University of Nebraska Press, 1953. Shapiro sees literature as a battleground between the "poets of history" or those "who want to change the world" and "poets of myth" or "those to whom the world is not quite worthy of contemplation." Shapiro's aim is to "create an atmosphere of neutrality" to free the poet from these "ruinous" conventions.

D140 ——————. *English Prosody and Modern Poetry*. Baltimore: Johns Hopkins University Press, 1947*; rpt. Folcroft, Pa.: Folcroft Press, 1969. A brief study of "the emergence of a true English prosody and the accident of its eclipse by the new poetry."

D141   ———. *Essay on Rime.* New York: Reynal & Hitchcock, 1945. Three verse essays on confession in prosody, in language, and in belief. The stanzas are grouped into categories that touch on many aspects of modern poetry. Shapiro's side-by-side, running comments identify the context of some of the stanzas. T. S. Eliot, W. H. Auden, e. e. cummings, and William Carlos Williams.

D142   ———. *The Poetry Wreck: Selected Essays, 1950–1970.* New York: Random House, 1975. "These essays do not follow a chronology but describe roughly the military evolutions of modern poetry, the bastions of the Trio [Ezra Pound, T. S. Eliot, and W. B. Yeats], assaults upon the towers and their occupation, the comings and goings of the ambassador Auden, Dylan Thomas (the troubadour in the kitchen), the burning of Whitman at the stake, the Tom O'Bedlam antics of Henry Miller, the heroics of Williams, down through the witchcraft of the psychologists and the rise of the rabble poets. There are no conclusions, only praises and laments."

D143   ———, ed. *Prose Keys to Modern Poetry.* New York: Harper & Row, 1962. Shapiro argues that *"the key to understanding modern poetry lies not in the poems but in the prose foundation of the poems."* He collects these essays to "bring together most of the chief prose documents upon which modern poetry is based and without which the poetry is all but meaningless." Includes Edgar Allan Poe through T. S. Eliot, Wallace Stevens, W. H. Auden, William Carlos Williams, e. e. cummings, and Allen Tate.

D144   ———, and Robert Beum. *A Prosody Handbook.* New York: Harper & Row, 1965. A handbook designed to serve anyone who is interested in poetry or in poetic structure. Chapters on syllables, meter, rhythm, rhyme, stanza, stanza forms, and scansions. Glossary of prosodic terms. Bibliography.

D145   Shaw, Robert B., ed. *American Poetry since 1960: Some Critical Perspectives.* Chester Springs, Pa.: Dufour, 1974. Shaw selects descriptive essays of "many of the period's salient features of reputations inflated or deservedly attained, of achievements dubious or assured." These essays are concerned with '60s poetry in revolt against the "modernist school of poetics derived from [T. S.] Eliot and [Ezra] Pound and still ascendant in the 'fifties." Secondly, they deal with the trend "against impersonality" and, third, with the trend toward longer poems, the "epics of self." Finally, the essays describe the poet washing his hands of society "for primitivism." Robert Lowell, John Berryman, W. S. Merwin, John Ashbery, Frank O'Hara, Adrienne Rich, James Dickey, Sylvia Plath, James Tate, Sidney Goldfarb, Mark Strand, and others. Primary bibliography.

D146   Simpson, Louis. *Three on the Tower: The Lives and Works of Ezra Pound, T. S. Eliot and William Carlos Williams.* New York: William Morrow, 1975. A large study of the lives, ideas, and poetry of three men who greatly influenced the contemporary literary period.

D147   Skelton, Robin. *The Poetic Pattern.* Berkeley: University of California Press, 1956. An examination of the "nature of poetry." "I have discussed with poets the exact nature of the poetic process as they experienced it." In addition, Skelton studies the origins of poetry and its relationship to magic, science, truth, and the mind and its visions. W. H. Auden, T. S. Eliot, Robert Graves, Louis MacNeice, Ezra Pound, Kathleen Raine, Sir Herbert Read, Stephen Spender, and Dylan Thomas.

D148   Snyder, Gary. *Earth House Hold: Technical Notes and Queries to Fellow Dharma Revolutionaries.* New York: New Directions, 1969. Journal entries and essays on poetry.

D149   Southworth, James G. *More Modern American Poets.* Oxford: Blackwell, 1954*; rpt. Freeport, N.Y.: Books for Libraries Press, 1968. A collection of essays for the general reader which adds "light and shade" to the general impression created by *Some Modern American Poets.* "In the first volume the majority of the poets were content to work within the tradition; in the present one, eight of the twelve have attempted to alter and re-invigorate that tradition from various sources." William Carlos Williams, Ezra Pound, Elinor Wylie, John Crowe Ransom, Conrad Aiken,

Mark Van Doren, Robert Silliman Hillyer, Allen Tate, Laura Riding, Robert Penn Warren, and W. H. Auden.

D150   ————. *Some Modern American Poets.* Oxford: Blackwell, 1950*; rpt. Freeport, New York: Books for Libraries Press, 1968. A collection of essays for the general reader that attempts to "appraise the work of each poet as absolute poetry according to the tenets of classical criticism." Studies Emily Dickinson through Robert Frost, Wallace Stevens, Robinson Jeffers, Archibald MacLeish, e. e. cummings, Stephen Vincent Benét, and Hart Crane.

D151   Spears, Monroe K. *Dionysius and the City: Modernism in Twentieth-Century Poetry.* New York: Oxford University Press, 1970. "After attempting several kinds of definition against a broad background," Spears "focuses on British and American poetry and considers the emergence of modernism in the years 1909–14, the effect of rediscovering it upon a group of poets a decade later in the American South, and finally its relation to the second revolution of the mid-century in both criticism and poetry." W. H. Auden, Charles Baudelaire, Paul Cézanne, Hart Crane, James Dickey, T. S. Eliot, Northrop Frye, James Joyce, Robert Lowell, Ezra Pound, John Crowe Ransom, Theodore Roethke, Wallace Stevens, Allen Tate, William Carlos Williams, and others.

D152   Stanford, Derek. *Movements in English Poetry: 1900–1958.* Santiniketan, India: Santiniketan Press, 1959*; rpt. Folcroft, Pa.: Folcroft, 1969. A brief survey that provides "the reader with a background picture of changing thought in English poetry from the Great War to the present." It stresses group activity, not "personal performance."

D153   Stauffer, Donald Barlow. *A Short History of American Poetry.* New York: Dutton, 1974. A historical survey of American poetry ranging from 1765 to W. D. Snodgrass, Anne Sexton, Sylvia Plath, W. S. Merwin, James Dickey, Allen Ginsberg, Gary Snyder, Charles Olson, and others. Bibliography.

D154   Stepanchev, Stephen. *American Poetry since 1945: A Critical Survey.* New York: Harper & Row, 1965. American poetry since World War II "is authentically new . . . in that it chooses to live on the frontiers of language: it suggests, in word choice and metaphor, what the English language is becoming under the stresses and strains of American life." Stepanchev shows the lines of development of this poetry and examines Robert Lowell, Randall Jarrell, Karl Shapiro, Elizabeth Bishop, Richard Wilbur, Charles Olson, Robert Duncan, Robert Creeley, Robert Bly, LeRoi Jones (Imamu Amiri Baraka), May Swenson, and others. Primary bibliography.

D155 Stevens, Wallace. *The Necessary Angel: Essays on Reality and the Imagination.* New York: Vintage, 1951. Essays collected "to disclose definitions of poetry. In short, they are intended to be contributions to the theory of poetry." Neither another history nor a poetics, but an attempt to apprehend the "naked poem, the imagination manifesting itself in its domination of words." Contains statements on such practical matters as the metaphor and such theoretical issues as the nature of the imagination and its relationship to reality. Seven essays, one on Marianne Moore.

D156 Sutton, Walter. *American Free Verse: The Modern Revolution in Poetry.* New York: New Directions, 1973. Not a general discussion of American poetry, but a concentration "on the origins and growth of the modern free verse movement. . . . Of the first generation of modernists, Sutton devotes two chapters apiece to Ezra Pound and William Carlos Williams, who 'took upon themselves in a period of great disillusionment the role of epic spokesmen in the tradition of Whitman,' and gives special attention as well to e. e. cummings and Marianne Moore. The author then considers 'The Conservative Counterrevolution' of the New Critics and the 'Middle Generation.' And finally, with 'The Revolution Renewed,' he brings his discussion around to a wide-ranging appreciation of the 'Third Generation': Charles Olson's 'projective verse' and the 'Beat' movement, concretism and the poetry, among others, of Robert Creeley, Robert Duncan, Lawrence Ferlinghetti, Denise Levertov, Thomas Merton, Gary Snyder, and Kenneth Rexroth" (publisher's blurb).

D157 Tate, Allen, ed. *Six American Poets from Emily Dickinson to the Present: An Introduction.* Minneapolis: University of Minnesota Press, 1969. These reprints of the University of Minnesota Pamphlets on American Writers give "a somewhat longer perspective to modern American poetry than the rest of modernism around 1912 has led us to look for." Emily Dickinson, Edwin Arlington Robinson, Marianne Moore, Conrad Aiken, e. e. cummings, and Hart Crane. Bibliographies.

D158   Thurley, Geoffrey. *The Ironic Harvest: English Poetry in the Twentieth Century.* New York: St. Martin's, 1974. Defines modern poetry and clarifies the route poets took after the diminished reputation of the modernists. Describes the rise of the "intellectualist Puritan" and studies the contributions of the following poets: F. R. Leavis, William Empson, W. H. Auden, Stephen Spender, David Gascoyne, Dylan Thomas, Roy Fuller, Philip Larkin, Peter Porter, and Ted Hughes.

D159   Thwaite, Anthony. *Essays on Contemporary English Poetry: Hopkins to the Present Day.* Tokyo: Kenkyusha, 1957. (Rpt. with some revision in England as *Contemporary English Poetry: An Introduction* [London: Heineman, 1959].) Though written specifically for a Japanese audience, Western readers might find the book "interesting." Following a general discussion of twentieth-century poetry, the work focuses upon Gerard Manley Hopkins, W. B. Yeats, T. S. Eliot, W. H. Auden, Stephen Spender, Louis MacNeice, C. Day Lewis, Dylan Thomas, George Barker, Edwin Muir, Robert Graves, William Empson, and others. Bibliography.

D160   Unger, Leonard, ed. *Seven Modern American Poets: An Introduction.* Minneapolis: University of Minnesota Press, 1967. Reprints of the University of Minnesota Pamphlets on American Writers. "The seven poets discussed in this volume present a picture of the diversity which exists in modern American poetry to this day." The essays in this collection confront two questions: "Wherein are the poets modern? Wherein are the poets American?" Robert Frost, Wallace Stevens, William Carlos Williams, Ezra Pound, John Crowe Ransom, T. S. Eliot, and Allen Tate. Selected bibliographies.

D161   Waggoner, Hyatt Howe. *American Poets: From the Puritans to the Present.* Boston: Houghton Mifflin, 1968. Waggoner attempts "to see the poets as nearly as possible in their own terms, to see life with their eyes and feel it in terms of their values." His emphasis then is on "individual poets, their visions and their craft." From the Puritans through Theodore Roethke, Robert Lowell, Robert Creeley, and others. Bibliography.

D162 —————. *The Heel of Elohim: Science and Values in Modern American Poetry.* Norman: University of Oklahoma Press, 1950. Waggoner states that his book is "an essay in philosophical criticism—philosophical, not ideological. . . . But it is not a study of the beliefs of the poets as such. . . . Rather, I have tried always to see how belief is embodied in form and form is the substantial articulation of belief, to examine the work of certain poets against the background of modern science and philosophy on the assumption that ideally and ultimately 'content' and 'form' in poetry are one." Edwin Arlington Robinson, Robert Frost, T. S. Eliot, Robinson Jeffers, Archibald MacLeish, and Hart Crane.

D163 Wain, John. *Preliminary Essays.* London: Macmillan, 1957. Primarily concerns earlier topics but also contains essays on Ezra Pound, William Empson, and Dylan Thomas.

D164 Warren, Robert Penn. *Democracy and Poetry.* Cambridge, Mass.: Harvard University Press, 1975. Two essays, "America and the Diminished Self" and "Poetry and Selfhood," on the interrelationship between democracy and American poetry. All of art requires a free and responsible self, yet the self has decayed in American experience. Warren argues that poetry can rescue democracy and affirm the notion of the self.

D165 —————. *A Plea in Mitigation: Modern Poetry and the End of An Era.* Macon, Ga.: Wesleyan College, 1966. A lecture delivered at Wesleyan College in which Warren assesses modern poetry in terms of writers before, during, and after the modern age. Discusses the nature of modernity, new criticism, and the relationship of poet and society.

D166 Weatherhead, A. Kingsley. *The Edge of the Image: Marianne Moore, William Carlos Williams and Some Other Poets.* Seattle: University of Washington Press, 1967. Weatherhead brings Moore and Williams together because they both "represent objects and scenes clearly and preserve the hard contours of these representations against the kind of blurring and softening that they suffer in other kinds of poetry." His aim is "to tease out the essential principles which in each have determined the nature of the poetry." In addition, Weatherhead studies the beat poets who "throw light on the techniques and procedures of Williams and to a lesser extent of Miss Moore." Robert Duncan, Allen Ginsberg, Denise Levertov, Charles Olson, and others.

D167   Wells, Henry W. *Where Poetry Stands Now.* Toronto: Ryerson Press, 1948. A brief humanistic evaluation of trends in modern poetry. Its premise is that the needs of the individual and the needs of the community must both be met by poetry if it is to serve humanity. Chapters on the ascendancy of personalism and impersonalism, the reintegration of the two, and trends toward humanism. Scattered references to Ezra Pound, T. S. Eliot, Marianne Moore, Archibald MacLeish, William Carlos Williams, Robert Frost, and others.

D168   Wilder, Amos N. *Modern Poetry and the Christian Tradition: A Study in the Relation of Christianity to Culture.* New York: Scribner's, 1952. The premise of this study is that the imaginative arts reflect the nature of a society's spiritual crisis. The book studies the representative modern poets and interprets the importance of poetry to the age. It also supplies a discussion of the history necessary to understand the poetry and assess the strength of the Christian tradition. W. H. Auden, T. S. Eliot, Allen Tate, Wallace Stevens, Robert Lowell, and others.

D169   Winters, Yvor. *On Modern Poets.* New York: Meridian, 1959. Six essays on as many poets, based on critical principles articulated in Winters's other volumes. One of the main points here is that art must arouse our understanding and our emotions equally if it is to be successful. He finds the following six poets' work to be marred by romantic ideals: Wallace Stevens, T. S. Eliot, John Crowe Ransom, Hart Crane, Gerard Manley Hopkins, and Robert Frost.

D170   Woodcock, George. *British Poetry Today.* Vancouver: University of British Columbia, 1950. An address delivered to the students and public at the University of British Columbia on the state of poetry in 1950. Woodcock is concerned with the generation of poets after T. S. Eliot and Herbert Read and feels this generation is showing healthy signs of movement and growth.

D171   Woolmer, J. Howard. *A Catalogue of Imagist Poets.* With Essays by Wallace Martin and Ian Fletcher. New York: J. Howard Woolmer, 1966. Essays on the origins of imagism. Includes a catalogue of nearly three hundred entries.

E
Critical Theory

E1   Adams, Robert M. *Strains of Discord: Studies in Literary Openness.* Ithaca, N.Y.: Cornell University Books, 1958; rpt. Freeport, N.Y.: Books for Libraries Press, 1971. A study of literary forms as a structure of meaning, stressing "open forms" as a means for presenting unresolved conflicts. Classifies varieties of open-formed literary works and defines their effects. Considers criteria for judging open forms.

E2   Allen, Harold B., ed. *Readings in Applied Linguistics.* 2nd ed. New York: Appleton-Century-Crofts, 1964. A collection of articles designed "to meet the need for representation of current linguistic thought and applications." Allen asserts that "a knowledge of English linguistics is basic . . . even to the criticism of literature." The collection contains one section that deals with the relationship between linguistics and the study of literature.

E3   Bergonzi, Bernard, ed. *Innovations: Essays on Art and Ideas.* London: Macmillan, 1968. The purpose of this book is "to provide information and different points of view about a number of related cultural phenomena that are becoming increasingly noticeable in the modern world." The contributors to this collection raise questions in the areas of "aesthetic theory, artistic practice, psychological attitudes and social behavior." They are Leslie A. Fiedler, Frank Kermode, Ihab Hassan, Marshall McLuhan, Richard Kostelanetz, and others.

E4   Black, Edwin. *Rhetorical Criticism: A Study in Method.* New York: Macmillan, 1965. Writing for the advanced student, not the beginner, Black's orientation is methodological rather than historical. "This volume is an attempt to stimulate and expand the dialogue on rhetorical criticism. It has been written in the belief that variety is wanting in the methods of rhetoric, that the options available to the critic need to be multiplied, and above all, that the prevailing mode of rhetorical criticism is profoundly mistaken." It explains rhetorical criticism, relates it to general criticism and to Aristotle, and suggests "an alternative to neo-Aristotelianism."

E5   Blue, Ila Jacuith. *A Study of Literary Criticism by Some Negro Writers, 1900–1955*. Ann Arbor, Mich.: University Microfilms, 1971. A study of twenty-five Negro critics and a synthesis of their views on "Negro literature," art for art's sake, propaganda, "the function of literature, the nature and function of criticism, and the characteristics of poetry and fiction." Ralph Ellison, Gwendolyn Brooks, James Baldwin, Herman Dreer, and Arna Bontemps. Bibliography.

E6   Booth, Wayne C. *The Rhetoric of Fiction*. Chicago: University of Chicago Press, 1961. Booth's subject is "the technique of non-didactic fiction, viewed as the act of communicating with readers the rhetorical resources available to the writer of epic, novel, or short story as he tries, consciously or unconsciously, to impose his fictional work upon the reader." Booth studies the author's means of controlling his reader, the question of whether "rhetoric is compatible to art," the author's voice in fiction, impersonal narration, and the ways fiction communicates itself. Bibliography.

E7   ————. *A Rhetoric of Irony*. Chicago: University of Chicago Press, 1975. An extensive study of a rhetorical device that has become increasingly important since the nineteenth century. Moving from "stable" irony to "instable" irony, Booth studies the nature of irony, compares it to satire and parody, outlines ironic forms, and studies the ironic voice and taste in irony. Edward Albee, W. H. Auden, Samuel Beckett, Saul Bellow, T. S. Eliot, Flannery O'Connor, and brief references to others. Bibliography.

E8   Borden, Karen W., and Fauneil J. Rinn, eds. *Feminist Literary Criticism: A Symposium*. San Jose, Calif.: Diotima, 1974. This monograph of three brief essays and an introduction grew out of a research symposium at San Jose State University in 1974 on women's studies. The writers were all members of the English Department at that time and discuss in their articles the nature of feminist literary criticism. The essays are beginning attempts at analysis as well as personal statements.

E9   Bradbury, John M. *The Fugitives: A Critical Account.* Chapel Hill: University of North Carolina Press, 1958. A history of the "southern fugitives" that outlines the nature of their contribution to our literary heritage and employs some techniques of close textual analysis developed by this group. Bradbury contends that art must be judged not only on aesthetic terms, but also with social, philosophical, and metaphysical considerations. Certain of the "fugitives" ignore these factors and, thereby, distort the actual process of appreciation. John Crowe Ransom, Allen Tate, Cleanth Brooks, and Robert Penn Warren. Bibliography.

E10   Bradbury, Malcolm, and David Palmer, eds. *Contemporary Criticism.* Stratford-upon-Avon Studies 12. London: Edward Arnold, 1970. A collection of American and British critics who comment on and illustrate "the various methods of critical procedure that are now prevalent." But the editors say that "the volume also aspires to be an argument and a questioning—about where criticism has come to, where it is leading, and what kinds of growth and difficulty lie before it." Written for the professional or general reader, the essays suggest that the two limiting movements—academic professionalism and new criticism—are giving way to a new kind of formalism and to social concerns.

E11   Brecht, Bertolt. *Brecht on the Theatre: The Development of an Aesthetic.* Edited and translated by John Willet. New York: Hill & Wang, 1964. "This selection from Brecht's notes and theoretical writing is meant to give English-language readers the main texts and set these in chronological order so as to show how his ideas evolved, gradually forming into a quite personal aesthetic which applied to other spheres besides the theatre." A bibliography of other translations of individual theoretical texts.

E12   Brooke-Rose, Christine. *A Grammer of Metaphor.* London: Secker & Warburg, 1958. A grammatical approach to the study of metaphor. Brooke-Rose studies the ways in which "a metaphoric word reacts on other words to which it is syntactically and grammatically related." Her focus is how the metaphorical interaction varies depending upon the grammatical relationship.

E13   Brooks, Cleanth. *American Literature: Mirror, Lens, or Prism?* Leicester: Leicester University Press, 1967. The text of a Sir George Watson Lecture on the mimetic nature of literature. Using the topic of "poor white southerner," Brooks shows that literature does not literally mirror reality, but focuses it through a lens.

E14   ————. *A Shaping Joy: Studies in the Writer's Craft.* New York: Harcourt Brace Jovanovich, 1971. Out of three possible points of critical emphasis—the reader, the writing, and the writer—Brooks places emphasis upon the work itself. "Though experience is ultimately a seamless garment and everything is related to everything else, the form of the achieved work is properly distinguished from the process that went into its making and from the effects that it produces on a particular reader. . . ." T. S. Eliot, James Joyce, W. H. Auden, William Faulkner, A. E. Housman, and earlier writers.

E15   Brower, Reuben Arthur. *The Fields of Light: An Experiment in Critical Reading.* New York: Oxford University Press, 1951. An experiment in reading "to demonstrate some methods of reading analysis and to use them in discovering designs of imaginative organization in particular poems, plays, and novels."

E16   ————, and Richard Poirier, eds. *In Defense of Reading: A Reader's Approach to Literary Criticism.* New York: Dutton, 1962. These essays argue for "the necessity of confronting the work in all its particularity and life." Literary criticism must take into account history, respond to particular uses of language, pay close attention to style, and go beyond "close reading." The literary critic must describe what it is like to read a particular work within the relevant literary and historical contexts.

E17   Buckley, Vincent. *Poetry and Morality: Studies on the Criti-*

cism of Matthew Arnold, T. S. Eliot, and F. R. Leavis. London: Chatto & Windus, 1968. An analysis of some relevant writings of three modern critics whose contributions are important and influential from the perspective of Christianity. Buckley studies each of the critics in terms "of poetry and morality." He does not try to assess them as critics.

E18   Burke, Kenneth. *Language as Symbolic Action: Essays on Life, Literature, and Method.* Berkeley: University of California Press, 1968. Essays "concerned with the attempt to define and track down the implications of the term 'symbolic action,' and to show how the marvels of literature and language look when considered in that point of view." Burke's essays reflect a "theory of language, a philosophy of language based on that theory, and methods of analysis developed in accordance with the theory and the philosophy." Essentially, Burke offers a "symbol system."

E19   Burnshaw, Stanley. *The Seamless Web: Language-Thinking, Creature-Knowledge, Art-Experience.* New York: Braziller, 1970. The "poet" is the maker of art objects who is "concerned above all with keeping alive in his inner and outer worlds." "Poetry begins with the body and ends with the body." "My concern is . . . with the type of creature-mind developed by the human organism in its long movement through time out of the evolutionary shocks which gave birth to what we have named self-consciousness." Traces the movement of creation from the writer to the reader through biological and physiological premises. The discussion of creation occurs in the context of the basic problems of Western civilization and in the attempts to resolve these conflicts.

E20   Cary, Joyce. *Art and Reality: Ways of the Creative Process.* Vol. 20 of the World Perspectives Series. Edited by Ruth Nanda Anshen. New York: Harper & Bros., 1958. Cary's book is "an attempt to examine the relation of the artist with the world as it seems to him, and to see what he does with it." Out of confused, chaotic subject matter, the writer must find "some meaning in life before he gives it to us in a book." For Cary, the creative imagination is "in everlasting conflict with facts."

E21   Cary, Norman Reed. *Christian Criticism in the Twentieth Century: Theological Approaches to Literature.* Port Washington, N.Y.: Kennikat, 1975. Since Christians no longer find themselves in a majority, several critics in the last few decades have found it necessary to consciously introduce Christian ideas into their criticism to serve as a basis for evaluation. While these critics are varied in approach, they do form a school of Christian criticism. This study analyzes the background to this movement; the relationships between theology and art; the differences between sacrament, symbol and myth; and the nature of the tragic and the comic. Bibliography.

E22   Casey, John. *The Language of Criticism.* London: Methuen, 1966. Derives an outline of the nature of critical argument from the work of Susanne Langer, Clive Bell, Harold Osborne, T. S. Eliot, Middleton Murry, Yvor Winters, Northrop Frye, F. R. Leavis, and others. The topics under consideration are "the justification of critical judgments, the place of 'emotion' in our response to works of art and literature, the possibility of the systematic study of patterns of literacy symbolism, and the relations between critical and 'moral' judgment." Bibliography.

E23   Chadwick, Charles. *Symbolism.* London: Methuen, 1971. Takes the student beyond a compact definition of symbolism by discussing the theory of symbolism, Charles Baudelaire's "correspondences," Paul Verlaine's melodies, Arthur Rimbaud, Stéphane Mallarmé, Paul Valéry, and the repercussions of symbolism. Bibliography.

E24   Chase, Richard. *Quest for Myth.* Baton Rouge: Louisiana State University Press, 1949. A selective history of opinion about myth that argues that myth is "literature and therefore a matter of aesthetic experience and the imagination." Finally, Chase offers a theory of poetry as myth.

E25   Chatman, Seymour, ed. *Approaches to Poetics: Selected Papers from the English Institute.* New York: Columbia University Press, 1973. Six papers on structuralism, an approach to literature that argues that a poem or novel is not "primarily an art-object or an act of knowing or feeling." Rather it is a "significant language, signs used in a special way." Three essays deal with the two leading structuralists

—Roman Jakobson and Roland Barthes; and three essays deal with various aspects of structuralism.

E26   ————, and Samuel R. Levin, eds. *Essays on the Language of Literature.* Boston: Houghton Mifflin, 1967. Essays that try to "reconcile linguistics and literary history." The editors group the essays under five headings: "Sound Texture," "Metrics," "Grammar," "Literary Form and Meaning," and "Style and Stylistics."

E27   Cohen, Ralph, ed. *New Directions in Literary History.* Baltimore: Johns Hopkins University Press, 1974. Thirteen essays on a variety of topics, which first appeared in *New Literary History* and represent "new guides, maps, routes to old destinations." For these critics "the literary work is an 'event,' an 'action,' a relation established between reader and what he reads, audience and performance. This relationship is inevitably historical for some; for others it is historically indeterminate—but for all these critics the arguments for interpreting or justifying literary works as 'objects' are no longer adequate."

E28   Crane, Ronald S. *The Languages of Criticism and the Structure of Poetry.* Toronto: University of Toronto Press, 1953. Theorizes about the structure of poetry. Using Aristotle to inform his theory, Crane places importance not on ideas but on the "immediate causes" which have made things what they are and rendered them capable of affecting our minds as they do. He is also interested in "those cases which involve the efforts of human beings . . . to solve successfully the particular problems inherent" in the structure of poetry.

E29   Crews, Frederick, ed. *Psychoanalysis and the Literary Process.* Cambridge, Mass.: Winthrop Publishers, 1970. Crews "demonstrates the range and potential usefulness of psychoanalytic criticism" and "assists readers who are disposed to practice it themselves." This study includes the theoretical groundwork and essays on James Joyce and earlier writers. Bibliography.

E30   Culler, Jonathan. *Structuralist Poetics: Structuralism, Linguistics and the Study of Literature.* London: Routledge & Kegan Paul, 1975. Part 1 of Culler's book "considers the scope and the limitations of linguistic methods and reviews the various ways in which structuralists have attempted to apply linguistic models to the study of literature." Then, part 2 views linguistics "as a model which suggests how a poetics should be organized." Bibliography.

E31   Daiches, David. *Critical Approaches to Literature.* Englewood Cliffs, N.J.: Prentice-Hall, 1956. "To illuminate both the nature of literature and the nature of criticism, this book represents some of the more important ways in which literature has been discussed." Daiches addresses himself to three issues: the value of imaginative literature, the practical critic, and a definition of the nature of poetry.

E32   Damon, Phillip, ed. *Literary Criticism and Historical Understanding: Selected Papers from the English Institute.* New York: Columbia University Press, 1967. "Aesthetic wholeness and structural integrity are functions of larger systems of belief which define the concept of wholeness. . . . These systems need to be understood historically as something that gets *into* a work of art." In this light, Damon presents a collection of essays describing "the range within which historical reconstruction serves not simply to provide useful information but to complete one's own immediate experience of a text."

E33   de Man, Paul. *Blindness and Insight: Essays in the Rhetoric of Contemporary Criticism.* New York: Oxford University Press, 1971. Essays on contemporary literary theory: American new criticism, the role of the self, Georg Lukács's *Theory of the Novel,* the work of Maurice Blanchot, Georges Poulet, Jacques Derrida, and the nature of modernity.

E34   Dickie, George. *Aesthetics: An Introduction.* New York: Bobbs-Merrill, 1971. An introduction to aesthetics that includes a historical introduction, "the concept of the aesthetic," "contemporary philosophies, or conceptions, of art," related problems, and "the evaluation of art." Bibliography.

E35   Dolezel, Lubomír, and Richard W. Bailey, eds. *Statistics and Style.* New York: American Elsevier, 1969. An introductory collection of essays that explains the statistical analysis of style and illustrates it, generally on figures who wrote before 1945.

E36   Donovan, Josephine, ed. *Feminist Literary Criticism: Explorations in Theory*. Lexington: University Press of Kentucky, 1975. Donovan collects these essays "to present an interpretation, and in some sense a defense, of feminist literary criticism, which, like its mother movement, is already much misunderstood and maligned." Includes "American Feminist Literary Criticism: A Bibliographical Introduction"; "Subjectivities: A Theory of the Critical Process"; "Consciousness and Authenticity: Toward a Feminist Aesthetic"; "Virginia Woolf's Criticism"; and "Theories of Feminist Criticism." The essays provide "an overview of the existing body of feminist literary criticism," explain the issues that feminist critics are concerned with, and propose "a theoretical framework" for viewing feminist literary criticism.

E37   Duncan, Hugh Dalziel. *Language and Literature in Society: A Sociological Essay on Theory and Method in the Interpretation of Linguistic Symbols with a Bibliographical Guide to the Sociology of Literature*. Chicago: University of Chicago Press, 1953. "The purpose of this book is not to discuss how we can measure symbols but to analyze what kinds of ends can be achieved by what kind of symbols." Stresses the social implications of literature.

E38   Egri, Lajos. *The Art of Dramatic Writing: Its Basis in the Creative Interpretation of Human Motives*. New York: Simon & Schuster, 1946. "In this book we propose to show a new approach to writing in general, and to playwriting in particular. This approach is based on the natural law of dialectics." Egri argues that human character supplies the force to create rules for writing, for unifying plays, for making art. Directs this approach to authors, playwrights, and the general public.

E39   Eliot, T. S. *The Frontiers of Criticism: A Lecture Delivered at the University of Minnesota Williams Arena on April 30, 1956*. Minneapolis: University of Minnesota Press, 1956. Eliot says that current critical practices are more interpretative or explanatory than critical.

E40   Enright, D. J. *The Apothecary's Shop: Essays on Literature*. Philadelphia: Dufour Editions, 1957. "Since the great days of *The Sacred Wood* . . . criticism has gradually declined into a sophisticated grave"; Eliot's descendants lack his "*human* meaningfulness" in their "ingenious hunt for 'extra significance.'" Enright laments the loss of the "last great public theme in literature," the wasteland, and argues for a new "private theme that has public meaning."

E41   Foster, Richard. *The New Romantics: A Reappraisal of the New Criticism.* Bloomington: Indiana University Press, 1962. This book "is a study of the somewhat paradoxical nature of the New Criticism, and some of the prime attitudes, manners, and vocabularies, both conscious and unconscious, by means of which they achieved their successes." I. A. Richards, Eliseo Vivas, R. P. Blackmur, Allen Tate, and John Crowe Ransom.

E42   Fowler, Roger. *Style and Structure in Literature: Essays in the New Stylistics.* Ithaca, N.Y.: Cornell University Press, 1975. Fowler examines the diversity of research concerning the linguistic aspects of literature and applies this research to problems raised by the traditional tools of literary study. Written for the general reader.

E43   Fraiberg, Louis. *Psychoanalysis and American Literary Criticism.* Detroit: Wayne State University Press, 1960. A study that describes the ramifications of psychoanalysis and explains Freud's ideas on art. Following a study of Freud and his chief colleagues is an examination of six prominent American critics who used these or related ideas. Fraiberg's chief aims are, first, to clarify Freud's ideas and, second, to look for ways in which psychoanalysis can contribute to an understanding of literature.

E44   Frank, Joseph. *The Widening Gyre: Crisis and Mastery in Modern Literature.* New Brunswick, N.J.: Rutgers University Press, 1963. A collection of articles and reviews. Includes "Spatial Form in Modern Literature," "Reaction as Progress: Thomas Mann's *Dr. Faustus*," "The Dehumanization of Art," "Romanticism and Reality in Robert Penn Warren," "R. P. Blackmur," "Lionel Trilling and the Conservative Imagination," and others.

E45   Frye, Northrop. *Anatomy of Criticism: Four Essays.* Princeton: Princeton University Press, 1957. A theoretical book concerning the relationship of "myth," "symbol," "ritual," and "archetype" with criticism. Attempts to provide an over-view that unifies literary study into a coherent discipline. Includes four essays: "Historical Criticism: Theory of Modes"; "Ethical Criticism: Theory of Symbols"; "Arche-typal Criticism: Theory of Myths"; and "Rhetorical Criti-cism: Theory of Genres."

E46 ————. *The Critical Path: An Essay on the Social Context of Literary Criticism.* Bloomington: Indiana University Press, 1971. A monograph concerning "the relation of lit-erary criticism to communication theory" and the "social stereotypes of McLuhanism."

E47 Glicksberg, Charles I., ed. *American Literary Criticism, 1900–1950.* New York: Hendricks, 1951. Glicksberg collects a "cross-section of the critical ideas and methods employed by various eminent and representative critics during the past fifty years." This collection of expository and analyt-ical essays ranges from James Gibbons Huneker (1910) to Lionel Trilling (1950). Contributors include T. S. Eliot, Kenneth Burke, John Crowe Ransom, Joseph Krutch, Allen Tate, Edmund Wilson, Cleanth Brooks, Yvor Win-ters, and others.

E48 Goldberg, Gerald Jay, and Nancy Marmer Goldberg, eds. *The Modern Critical Spectrum.* Englewood Cliffs, N.J.: Pren-tice-Hall, 1962. The purpose of this collection is to clarify and categorize "dominant critical tendencies of our age." Each section of the book contains a theoretical statement and practical applications of the theory. Includes sections on formal criticisms, socio-cultural criticism, tradition, bi-ography, humanism, scholarship, psychology, and myth.

E49 Goodman, Paul. *Speaking and Language: Defense of Poetry.* New York: Random House, 1971. An analysis of oral and written language from the perspectives of the linguist, the artist, and the human. Fourteen chapters study language and literature as a human event. Topics covered are: speech as an action and a thing; speaking as a language, a sublanguage, and as a unique experience; constructed lan-guages; the literary process; style; and "communications." Goodman ends with a defense of literature.

E50 Gray, Bennison. *The Phenomenon of Literature.* The Hague:

Mouton, 1975. "In addition to analyzing the elements of fiction, this work argues that a fictional conception of literature is the most adequate one. . . . Viewed as a phenomenon, as an object of dispassionate study rather than as a source of values, literature is fiction." In developing the thesis that "literature is best defined and analyzed as fiction," Gray discusses the problems in literary study, the nature of fiction, the forms of literature, the elements and structure of narration, the interpretation of literature, and a theory of literature.

E51   Grebstein, Sheldon Norman, ed. *Perspectives in Contemporary Criticism: A Collection of Recent Essays by American, English, and European Literary Critics.* New York: Harper & Row, 1968. Includes sections on historical, formalistic, sociocultural, psychological, and mythopoeic criticism. Each section contains an introduction, selected bibliography, and at least five sample essays.

E52   Hall, Vernon, Jr. *A Short History of Literary Criticism.* New York: New York University Press, 1963. An introductory book on criticism from Plato to Bergson, Croce, Freudianism, I. A. Richards, T. S. Eliot, and the new criticism. Bibliography.

E53   Handy, William J. *Kant and the Southern New Critics.* Austin: University of Texas Press, 1963. Handy's study "shows the direct influence of the Kantian generative idea" upon the critical theories of John Crowe Ransom, Allen Tate, and Cleanth Brooks. Handy argues for the application of new criticism to fiction. Bibliography.

E54   ————, ed. *A Symposium on Formalist Criticism.* Austin: University of Texas Press, 1965. These papers study formalistic criticism from four perspectives: new criticism (John Crowe Ransom), the Chicago school (Elder Olson), psychological/mythic/archetypal criticism (Kenneth Burke), and representational symbolism (Eliseo Vivas).

E55   Harned, David Bailey. *Theology and the Arts.* Philadelphia: Westminster Press, 1966. "In order to clarify the fundamental options for a Christian interpretation of art and the wider human enterprise, I have dealt with Roman Catholic and Eastern Orthodox as well as Protestant theologians."

Harned's "essential concerns are with the way the man of letters serves our common welfare, and with some problems that beset Protestant theologians when they write of the world that God has made and of the venture in it that he has called man to pursue."

E56   Hartman, Geoffrey H. *Beyond Formalism: Literary Essays, 1958–1970*. New Haven: Yale University Press, 1970. Essays on the state of literary criticism, the novel, poetry, and literary history. Hartman's unifying concern is with the "mutuality of criticism and history"—with the combination of large speculative patterns and the daily, pragmatic effort of literary criticism. He argues that "an emphasis on words is discriminatory as well as discriminating unless it guides us to larger structures of the imagination." Essays on structuralism, modernism, Northrop Frye, Louis MacNeice, Robert Graves, and Robert Lowell.

E57   ————. *The Fate of Reading and Other Essays*. Chicago: University of Chicago Press, 1975. Essays that extend the concerns of *Beyond Formalism*. The purpose of these essays is "to broaden literary interpretation without leaving literature behind" and "to look inward toward the discipline of literary study itself." Hartman attempts "to gain an intrinsic mode of historical analysis—intrinsic to literature."

E58   Hassan, Ihab. *Paracriticisms: Seven Speculations of the Times*. Urbana: University of Illinois Press, 1975. Hassan's paracriticisms are "essays in language, traces of the times, fictions of the heart." They share a particular mode: "awareness of the age, engagement with certain ideas, certain dreams, love and exasperation mingling in [Hassan's] sense of literature, a desire to break out of criticism." Hassan writes about literary criticism, questions of culture and consciousness, and James Joyce and Samuel Beckett, whose work contains the extreme tensions of the contemporary imagination. At the center of Hassan's concerns lies the question: "What role will expanding human consciousness play in the universe?"

E59   Hernadi, Paul. *Beyond Genre: New Directions in Literary Classification*. Ithaca, N.Y.: Cornell University Press, 1972. "Genre concepts should be employed and transcended rather than ignored, codified, or rejected." The first and last chapters outline "a theory of literary classification that tries to avoid the customary pitfalls." The middle chapters survey around sixty modern theories of classification with lengthy studies on Georg Lukács and Northrop Frye.

E60   Hoffman, Frederick J. *Freudianism and the Literary Mind.* Rev. ed. New York: Grove Press, 1959. "An explanation of Freudian psychology as it relates to modern literature." Hoffman studies Freud's influence on literature in four chapters and applies Freud's ideas to James Joyce, D. H. Lawrence, Franz Kafka, Thomas Mann, Sherwood Anderson, Waldo Frank, F. Scott Fitzgerald, Conrad Aiken, Dylan Thomas, and Henry Miller. Bibliography.

E61   Holland, Norman. *The Dynamics of Literary Response.* New York: Oxford University Press, 1968. This book explores the "psychological assumptions" about the import of poetry and fiction on the mind and develops a "model for the interaction of literary works with the human mind." It deals with the following questions: "How do we willingly suspend disbelief? What is the role of plain statement as against poetic diction? How do we 'identify' with literary characters? What part does 'organic unity' play in our response? How does literature 'mean'? Can literature teach? Is the moral effect of literature good or bad—indeed, is there a moral effect at all?"

E62   Howe, Irving, ed. *Modern Literary Criticism: An Anthology.* Boston: Beacon Press, 1958. "Literary criticism has become fiercely professional, an 'institution' as well as a discipline." Howe presents "a sampling of modern American and British criticism" to the general public and students. He divides his study into four groups: "general literary discussions, studies of fiction, studies of poetry, and book reviews." Includes an introduction by Howe and essays by such critics as T. S. Eliot, Arnold Kettle, and Philip Rahv who practice their craft on figures from all of literature. Bibliography.

E63   Hyman, Stanley Edgar. *The Armed Vision: A Study in the Methods of Modern Literary Criticism.* New York: Knopf, 1952. Hyman's aims are threefold: to study the nature of modern critical method, to trace the ancestry of these techniques, and "to suggest some possibilities for an integrated and practical methodology that would combine and consolidate the best techniques of modern criticism." Critics examined include Edmund Wilson, Yvor Winters, T. S. Eliot, Van Wyck Brooks, Constance Rourke, Maud Bodkin, Christopher Caudwell, Caroline Spurgeon, R. P. Blackmur, William Empson, I. A. Richards, and Kenneth Burke. Bibliography.

E64   Inglis, Fred. *An Essential Discipline: An Introduction to Literary Criticism*. London: Methuen Educational, 1968. About his book for the general reader, Inglis writes: "I further hope that this book will serve to confirm or challenge some of the notions about literature held by full-time students of English in universities, where it would often seem that students are left to find out their own critical standards while their teachers are occupied with higher matters of research." For Inglis, the essential literary discipline is "fidelity to the text."

E65   International Federation for Modern Languages and Literature. *Literature and Science*. Oxford: Basil Blackwell, 1955. Essays collected under the headings: "Science and Literature," "Scientific Method and Literary Scholarship," and "Literary History and the History of Science."

E66   Jameson, Fredric. *Marxism and Form: Twentieth-Century Dialectical Theories of Literature*. Princeton: Princeton University Press, 1971. A new kind of Marxist criticism has taken over in recent years replacing that of the 1930s. This study summarizes the principal work of the theoreticians who created this Hegelian Marxism, creating a background for criticism. Concludes with a discussion of dialectical criticism. Bibliography.

E67   ————. *The Prison-House of Language: A Critical Account of Structuralism and Russian Formalism*. Princeton: Princeton University Press, 1972. An "introductory survey of these movements." It attempts to "clarify the relationships possible between the synchronic methods of Saussurean linguistics and the realities of time and history itself." Bibliography.

E68   Jennings, Edward M., ed. *Science and Literature: New Lenses for Criticism.* Garden City, N.Y.: Doubleday, 1970. These interdisciplinary essays aim "to invigorate the study of literature by gently modifying the teacher-scholar's attitude toward his subject." The materials in this collection are "potentially 'new knowledge' for the student and professor." Includes fourteen essays with brief headnotes that "point out how one might begin to develop their particular implications." Some common themes are the nature of language, the nature of structures, pattern-making, linguistics, and computers.

E69   Kermode, Frank. *The Sense of an Ending: Studies in the Theory of Fiction.* New York: Oxford University Press, 1967. Kermode's study is an attempt at "making sense of the ways we try to make sense of our lives." His concern is with "sense-making" or "fictions." Kermode examines the ways fictions can change the structure of time and the world. He offers a theory of literary fictions.

E70   Kirby, Michael. *The Art of Time.* New York: Dutton, 1969. Twelve essays focused upon the aesthetics of the avant-garde. Kirby rejects generic criticism to study art as "intellectual constructs that are helpful in describing experience." Includes essays on the theatre, dance, film, and sculpture.

E71   Krieger, Murray. *The Classic Vision: The Retreat from Extremity in Modern Literature.* Baltimore: Johns Hopkins University Press, 1971. For Krieger, modern literature begins in the eighteenth century. This work attempts to delineate the classic vision as one possible vision held by modern writers. By classic, Krieger means the ability to see extremity and "not to choose it." He studies this vision in the works of such early figures as Alexander Pope, Samuel Johnson, William Wordsworth, and Jonathan Swift. He ends with discussions of works by Robert Penn Warren, William Faulkner, and T. S. Eliot. Krieger uses a variety of critical approaches as he reduces each work to its "reductive metaphor."

E72   —————. *The New Apologists for Poetry.* Minneapolis: University of Minnesota Press, 1956. Krieger defends the "new critics," who are trying "to justify poetry by securing for it a unique function for which modern scientism cannot find a surrogate." The new critics, "by theorizing about what seems to them to be the difference between the nature and function of poetry and the nature and function of science, are collectively engaged in formulating a new 'apology' for poetry." Krieger analyzes the positions of critics contributing to this apology. T. E. Hulme, T. S. Eliot, I. A. Richards, Yvor Winters, John Crowe Ransom, Allen Tate, and Cleanth Brooks.

E73 ————, ed. *Northrop Frye in Modern Criticism: Selected Papers from the English Institute.* New York: Columbia University Press, 1966. An assessment of Frye's impact on modern criticism. Contains an introduction by Krieger, a checklist of works by and about Frye compiled by John E. Grant, three essays on Frye, and responses written by Frye.

E74 La Driére, James Craig. *Directions in Contemporary Criticism and Literary Scholarship.* Milwaukee: Brue, 1953. An "account of the current scene in criticism"—criticism of the "past fifty years or more that is still operative in or relevant to criticism today."

E75 Lane, Michael, ed. *Introduction to Structuralism.* New York: Basic Books, 1970. Structuralism is "a mode of thought common to disciplines as widely separated as mathematics and literary criticism." This collection tries to represent "the range and depth of structuralist activity." Includes one introduction for the specialist and another for the layman.

E76 Lang, Berel, and Forrest Williams, eds. *Marxism and Art: Writings in Aesthetics and Criticism.* New York: McKay, 1972. This collection reveals that many and diverse figures wrote on art from a Marxist perspective. The essays show how Marxism changed artistic thought about the Enlightenment. Topics considered are: theoretical concepts, art history and criticism, genres, and critical practice.

E77 Langer, Susanne K. *Feeling and Form: A Theory of Art.* New York: Scribner's, 1953. Based upon the theory of symbolism developed in *Philosophy in a New Key*, Langer examines the meaning of "expression, creation, symbol, import, intuition, vitality, and organic form." She studies the nature of art, feeling, communication, truths, and the cultural origins of various art forms. Her study is an attempt toward a theory of art based upon a theory of the symbol. Bibliography.

E78   ————. *Problems of Art: Ten Philosophical Lectures.* New York: Scribner's, 1957. A collection of lectures delivered to diverse audiences. All of the lectures deal with the nature of art—"what is created, what is expressed, what is experienced." Langer's topics are dance, expressiveness, creation, form, perception, relations among the arts, imitation in the arts, principles of art, symbols, and poetic creation.

E79   Laurenson, Diana, and Alan Swingewood. *The Sociology of Literature.* New York: Schocken, 1972. "In the English language there is no adequate guide to the social analysis of literature. . . . In this book we have attempted to fill this gap." The book discusses "literature as a social product," "examines social situations of the writer," and attempts "to relate theory to practice" with a "tentative analysis of proven literary texts." Bibliography.

E80   Lawall, Sarah N. *Critics of Consciousness: The Existential Structures of Literature.* Cambridge, Mass.: Harvard University Press, 1968. In contrast to traditional American critics, Lawall views literature as an "act, not an object." For Lawall, words are "nodes of energy." She looks for the same voice in a series of works by the same author and seeks "latent patterns of themes and impulses inside literature." She does not discuss "the symmetries and ambiguities of the formal text." Ontology is the root of this approach to criticism, and she argues that the author's "act of consciousness is the act of literature." "The critics of consciousness want to observe the writer's mind, to discover the patterns of perception embodied in his work, and to understand how these patterns of perception coordinate with the formal patterns of the text." Lawall centers her study upon "the Geneva schools."

E81   Leed, Jacob, ed. *The Computer and Literary Style: Introductory Essays and Studies.* Kent, Ohio: Kent State University Press, 1966. A collection of essays written for "scholars-at-large, rather than for specialists." The essays explain how to use the computer and the role of statistics in criticism.

They apply this new theory to Jonathan Swift, Hart Crane, the poetry of the seventeenth century, and Greek prose to study such problems as the ordering of prose, vocabulary analysis, indications of authorship, and literary analysis.

E82   Leeuw, Gerardus van der. *Sacred and Profane Beauty: The Holy in Art*. Translated by David E. Green. New York: Holt, Rinehart & Winston, 1963. Leeuw states: "Within this study I have tried to find paths and boundaries for anyone who says he understands something of the way God speaks through beauty." He argues that drama is the central, unified artistic religious expression. But art has been divided into genres; and in more recent times, each art has been separated into "*sacred* and *profane* forms." "The history of drama is a history of secularization." Leeuw describes secularization in each of the arts and attempts a "theological aesthetics." Bibliography.

E83   Lemon, Lee T. *The Partial Critics*. New York: Oxford University Press, 1965. Modern critics have become specialized. To determine their strengths and weaknesses, Lemon has "taken fairly common critical concepts—the value of semantic complexity in and for itself, for example—and isolated them, purified them, and traced them through the works of several critics." Lemon's focus is upon various psychological and social theories and upon the poem as a closed, open, and symbolic form. T. S. Eliot, Robert Frost, and others.

E84   Lerner, Laurence. *The Truest Poetry: An Essay on the Question "What Is Literature?"* New York: Horizon, 1964. "There are two types of literary theory, and two types of literature. One is constantly tugging literature in the direction of music. . . . The other is tugging literature towards ordinary human activity, and essentially toward speech." The pull is between perfection and "the fullness of the material." A theoretical study of literature that considers its relation to knowledge, expression, and rhetoric.

E85   Levin, Harry. *Symbolism and Fiction*. Charlottesville: University of Virginia Press, 1956. Levin argues this is the "age of ambiguity" and symbolic readings. His work is a brief history of symbolism and a study of the problems it creates for a reader. Because critics are "bedeviled by the ambiguous," they "long for the archetypal," thereby overlooking uniqueness and individuality in art. Levin uses *Moby Dick* as his major example.

E86 —————. *Why Literary Criticism Is Not an Exact Science.* Cambridge: Heffer & Sons, 1967. An analytical study of recent critical accomplishments. I. A. Richards, René Wellek, and Northrop Frye.

E87 Livingston, Ray. *The Traditional Theory of Literature.* Minneapolis: University of Minnesota Press, 1962. "An introduction to the Traditional doctrine of the nature and function of literature." Using Ananda Coomaraswamy as the "primary source of ideas here set forth," Livingston affirms the tradition of Western civilization and attacks its opponents. Discusses man, society, the role and function of art, and the process of judgment and criticism. Bibliography.

E88 McIntosh, Angus, and M. A. K. Halliday. *Patterns of Language: Papers in General, Descriptive and Applied Linguistics.* Bloomington: Indiana University Press, 1966. Essays on general linguistics, linguistics and English studies, descriptive linguistics in literary studies, style, graphology, typology, and patterns.

E89 Macksey, Richard, and Eugenio Donato, eds. *The Language of Criticism and the Science of Man: The Structuralist Controversy.* Baltimore: Johns Hopkins University Press, 1970. Structuralism is "a cross-discipline phenomenon." These essays are edited versions of thirty hours of lectures from the international symposium held at Johns Hopkins Humanities Center, where over one hundred humanists and social scientists gathered to "explore the impact of contemporary 'structuralist' thought on critical methods." Many of the essays are related to literary topics.

E90 Manheim, Leonard and Eleanor, eds. *Hidden Patterns: Studies in Psychoanalytic Literary Criticism.* New York: Macmillan, 1966. Essays informed by "ego psychology." Includes theoretical studies as well as essays on William Shakespeare, Nathaniel Hawthorne, Charles Dickens, Thomas Mann, Franz Kafka, William Faulkner, William Golding, and others.

E91   Matthiessen, F. O. *The Responsibilities of the Critic: Essays and Reviews.* Edited by John Rackliffe. New York: Oxford University Press, 1952. This book brings together Matthiessen's uncollected articles on "The Responsibilities of the Critic," critical appraisals of the artist, and new perspectives for the cultural historian. John Crowe Ransom, Wallace Stevens, Louis MacNeice, William Carlos Williams, Conrad Aiken, Allen Tate, and others.

E92   Meeker, Joseph W. *The Comedy of Survival: Studies in Literary Ecology.* New York: Scribner's, 1974. "Humanism" is incompatible with biological stability. Meeker's purpose is to identify those patterns in human art and thought which allow both a developed cultural life and a stable natural ecology to exist. His study is "an attempt to identify some adaptive and maladaptive postures in literary traditions of human culture and to enlist support for those which offer the prospect of a human future in closer agreement with the processes of nature than much of the human past has been." Bibliography.

E93   Miller, James E., Jr., ed. *Myth and Method: Modern Theories of Fiction.* Lincoln: University of Nebraska Press, 1960. Miller collects nine essays that suggest that the groundwork for mythic and archetypal criticism "was laid as far back as the late nineteenth century; and that the revolution early gained momentum and carried the day in the twentieth; and that currently, in mid-century, the revolutionary forces are being consolidated while radical, new campaigns are planned." Includes essays by Henry James, Joseph Conrad, Elizabeth Bowen, Percy Lubbock, Robert Humphrey, Mark Schorer, E. M. Forster, Richard Chase, and Northrop Frye. Bibliography.

E94   Nassar, Eugene Paul. *The Rape of Cinderella: Essays in Literary Continuity.* Bloomington: Indiana University Press, 1970. The fundamental critical act is "the probing for and the articulation of the unique and complex body of attitudes that impel and shape a work or body of literature, and an evaluation of the continuity or consistency of these central attitudes." Applies this critical approach to Wallace Stevens, T. S. Eliot, and earlier writers.

E95   Nelson, Cary. *The Incarnate Word: Literature as Verbal Space.*

Urbana: University of Illinois Press, 1973. Beginning with the *Pearl*, Nelson studies verbal space through William S. Burroughs. Nelson deals with one other contemporary author, William Carlos Williams, and ends with a statement of field theory, defining verbal space as "the locus of an interaction between the reader and the text." Bibliography.

E96 O'Connor, William Van. *An Age of Criticism, 1900–1950*. Chicago: Regnery, 1952. A history of American criticism that does not deal with scholarly or historical studies. "The job of such a literary history as this . . . is to describe the general character of various critical movements, to observe as far as possible the degree of success and failure engendered by specific methods." Bibliography.

E97 Olson, Charles. *Causal Mythology*. San Francisco: Four Seasons Foundation, 1969. A lecture delivered to the University of California Poetry Conference held at Berkeley, July 20, 1965. Olson discussed four issues—"The Earth," "The Image of the World," "The History or City," and "The Spirit of the World"—under the epigraph *"that which exists through itself is what is called meaning"* and read four poems in connection with these topics.

E98 ————. *Poetry and Truth: The Beloit Lectures and Poems*. Edited by George F. Butterick. San Francisco: Four Seasons Foundation, 1971. Three lectures containing Olson's poems. Discusses literary, historical, and philosophical issues.

E99 ————. *Projective Verse*. Brooklyn: Totem Press, 1959. A booklet in which Olson advocates open or projective verse and composition by field.

E100 ————. *Selected Writings*. Edited by Robert Creeley. New York: New Directions, 1967. Thirty-four essays by Charles Olson. Includes "The Resistance," "Projective Verse and Letter to Elaine Feinstein," "Human Universe," "Mayan Universe," and a bibliography of other works by Olson.

E101 Ortega y Gasset, José. *The Dehumanization of Art and Other Writings on Art and Culture*. Garden City, N.Y.: Doubleday, 1956. Five reprinted essays: "The Dehumanization of Art," "Notes on the Novel," "On Point of View in the

Arts," "In Search of Goethe from Within," and "The Self and the Other."

E102   Peckham, Morse. *Man's Rage for Chaos: Biology, Behavior, and the Arts.* New York: Chilton, 1965. Peckham studies the relationship of the arts and then proposes a "theory of the biological function of artistic behavior as a mode of adaptation of human organism to non-human environment." He applies the "game theory" to art, examines the sign or semantic function of art, and proposes a theory of perception. Bibliography.

E103   Philipson, Morris, ed. *Aesthetics Today.* Cleveland: World, 1961. Deals with the relations between the arts and cultural "relations between form and content with respect to the concept of style; problems involved in applying ideas of expression and communication to interpreting works of art; relations between art and the nature of knowledge; problems involved in the application of psychological and psychoanalytical hypotheses to the study of art; and lastly, issues currently under active consideration within aesthetics as a philosophic discipline."

E104   Phillips, William, ed. *Art and Psychoanalysis.* New York: Criterion, 1957. Phillips's purpose is "to make accessible in one volume some of the outstanding contributions" in psychoanalysis in the form of studies of single works of art or creative artists, theoretical essays, and literary pieces.

E105   Polletta, Gregory T., ed. *Issues in Contemporary Literary Criticism.* Boston: Little, Brown, 1973. An anthology of criticism to be used as a textbook. Its "purpose is to show the activity of literary criticism in contemporary performance." Contributors include Northrop Frye, R. P. Blackmur, Roland Barthes, Ihab Hassan, Susan Sontag, Mark Spilka, W. K. Wimsatt, M. H. Abrams, Donald Davie, F. W. Bateson, Kenneth Burke, Lionel Trilling, F. R. Leavis, A. Alvarez, Frank Kermode, Jorge Luis Borges, Erich Auerbach, and many others.

E106   Pritchard, John Paul. *Criticism in America: An Account of the Development of Critical Techniques from the Early Period of the Republic to the Middle Years of the Twentieth Century.* Norman: University of Oklahoma Press, 1956. A history that ranges from the nineteenth century to T. S. Eliot, Kenneth Burke, John Crowe Ransom, Allen Tate, Cleanth Brooks, R. P. Blackmur, Yvor Winters, T. K. Whipple, Edmund Wilson, Van Wyck Brooks, and the Chicago critics. Bibliographical notes.

E107 Ransom, John Crowe. *Beating the Bushes: Selected Essays 1941–1970*. New York: New Directions, 1972. Eleven essays on art and literature, in which Ransom deals with the main critical issues of the time.

E108 Rehder, Helmut, ed. *Literary Symbolism: A Symposium*. Austin: University of Texas Press, 1965. This symposium on symbolism was meant to study the symbol "as the sign which is the keystone of the life of the mind." Most of the examples in the book draw upon German literature.

E109 Richards, I. A. *Poetries: Their Media and Ends*. Edited by Trevor Eaton. The Hague: Mouton, 1974. A collection of essays, radio and television broadcasts, and lecture notes that "provide an up-to-date and unified account of [Richards's] poetics." Prepared for his eightieth birthday.

E110 Righter, William. *Myth and Literature*. London: Routledge & Kegan Paul, 1975. Examines the paradoxes of myth for writers and critics and the relationship of fiction to myth. Righter suggests "those affinities by which the literary mind has claimed the powers of its touchstone, and sought through its re-invention of myth its own imaginary and sense-making powers."

E111 Roberts, Thomas J. *When Is Something Fiction?* Carbondale: Southern Illinois University Press, 1972. Discusses eighteen "different ways in which critics use the term" *fiction*. These definitions operate "along four different axes of meaning." Roberts presents "a theory of the mind of the critic and of the laws that govern it" and is concerned with the "concept-structures" that fiction reflects. Bibliographical notes.

E112 Rooney, William Joseph. *The Problem of "Poetry and Belief" in Contemporary Criticism*. Washington, D.C.: Catholic University of America Press, 1949. A discussion of five "representative critics" who have "a more or less systematic theory concerning poetry and 'belief.'" The views of each have been "expounded" and "criticized," making the study "historical and critical at the same time." To I. A. Richards, poetry is "emotive language"; to Yvor Winters, John Crowe Ransom, and Allen Tate, it is "a kind of knowledge"; to T. S. Eliot, it is "in itself an object of contemplation." Bibliography.

E113   Rosenberg, Harold. *The Tradition of the New.* New York: Horizon, 1959. Essays on painting, poetry, the novel, drama, dancing, and recent American intellectual history. "The famous 'modern break with tradition' has lasted long enough to have produced its own tradition." This rejection of the immediate tradition has enabled man to discover other traditions, making self-creation necessary. "In these circumstances, criticism cannot divide itself into literary criticism, art criticism, social criticism, but must begin in establishing the terms of the conflict between the actual work or event and its illusory context."

E114   Scholes, Robert. *Structuralism in Literature: An Introduction.* New Haven: Yale University Press, 1974. Scholes's exclusive focus is the literary aspects of structuralism. He is "mainly concerned with the presentation of certain European critical thinking to an English-speaking audience" and with "the elaboration of certain principles of literary theory which emerge from this presentation." While Scholes emphasizes narrative literature, other aspects of structuralism may be located in the bibliographical appendix.

E115   —————, ed. *Learners and Discerners: A Newer Criticism.* Charlottesville: University Press of Virginia, 1964. Five Peters Rushton Seminars on modern literature by Harry Levin, John Frederick Nims, R. W. B. Lewis, Hugh Kenner, and Ihab Hassan. Professor Levin "calls for a new criticism which will combine the learning of historical scholarship with the discernment of the 'new criticism.' The essays . . . are all attempts . . . to provide this combination." Samuel Beckett, William Burroughs, T. S. Eliot, John Hawkes, Ernest Hemingway, Norman Mailer, Ezra Pound, Alain Robbe-Grillet, J. D. Salinger, and Wallace Stevens. Bibliography of Peters Rushton Seminar Lectures.

E116   —————, ed. *The Philosopher Critic.* Tulsa, Okla.: University of Tulsa Press, 1970. Five essays in which the authors

—Merle Brown, Eliseo Vivas, Robert Champigny, William H. Gass, and Thomas R. Whitaker—address themselves to the relationships between philosophy, literature, and criticism.

E117 Schorer, Mark; Josephine Miles; and Gordon McKenzie, eds. *Criticism: The Foundations of Modern Literary Judgment.* New York: Harcourt, Brace, 1948. A collection of critical essays concerning the "source," "form," and "end" of literary judgment. Contributors range from Plato, John Dryden, and Samuel Johnson to James T. Farrell, Herbert Read, W. H. Auden, Lionel Trilling, T. S. Eliot, William Empson, Cleanth Brooks, Robert Penn Warren, I. A. Richards, and others.

E118 Scott, Nathan A., Jr., ed. *The New Orpheus: Essays toward a Christian Poetic.* New York: Sheed & Ward, 1964. Scott presents a Christian theory of literature. This volume "concerns my desire to call the work of recent Christian critics and theorists to the attention of the general public (both within and outside the theological community) that 'keep up' with the best conversation going on in the literary criticism of our period." His essays are organized around five categories: "The Problem of a Christian Aesthetic"; "The Nature of the Christian Vision"; "Moorings for Theological Criticism"; "Belief and Form: The Problem of Correlation"; and "The 'Silence, Exile, and Cunning' and the Modern Imagination." Selected bibliography.

E119 Scott, Wilbur S., ed. *Five Approaches of Literary Criticism: An Arrangement of Contemporary Critical Essays.* New York: Collier, 1962. An introductory approach that includes illustrative essays and a bibliography for each of the five modes of literary criticism: moral, psychological, sociological, formalistic, and archetypal. The final essay by R. P. Blackmur acts as a synthesis. Bibliography.

E120 Shumaker, Wayne. *Elements of Critical Theory.* Berkeley: University of California Press, 1952. Explains what literary criticism is, its limitations, reference frames, the movement from analysis to evaluation, and evaluation as assumption. Shumaker states that "analysis and evaluation together make up the whole critical process." His study is a systematic view of a field often practiced intuitively and is a coherent beginning for the student.

E121   ——. *Literature and the Irrational: A Study in Anthropological Backgrounds.* Englewood Cliffs, N.J.: Prentice-Hall, 1960. Shumaker's basic question is: "Can an entire philosophy of literary form be based on the assumption that man yearns unknowingly for the unitary consciousness of the brute state?" He studies the awakening of the psyche during the creation process, the similarities "between primitive languages and the language of literature," the ways in which the story "substitutes for causal analysis in primitive thought and culture," and the literary types that are based in psychic habits from the past. This argument calls for the study of anthropology, depth psychology, and the rejection of current critical theories. Because our intellects are so highly trained, the artist must descend "to psychic levels too deep to have been affected by a highly conceptualized training." He must regress "to the mental potential in his own biological constitution and in that of his normal readers."

E122   Slatoff, Walter J. *With Respect to Readers: Dimensions of Literary Response.* Ithaca, N.Y.: Cornell University Press, 1970. "My purpose in the chapters that follow is to point out some inadequacies of our usual ways of studying and teaching literature, to insist that books exist primarily to be read and that they must be read by individual human beings, and to explore some of the questions which arise when we do seriously acknowledge that books require readers."

E123   Slote, Bernice, ed. *Myth and Symbol: Critical Approaches and Applications by Northrop Frye, L. C. Knights and Others.* Lincoln: University of Nebraska Press, 1963. An "experiment" in criticism that presents "definitions and illustrates forms of a comparatively new way of considering literature —a concentration on myth and symbol." The criticism included in this collection emphasizes the "doubleness of literature—that what is given in language and form is only the embodiment of something more that is not, that cannot be wholly stated." Secondly, the emphasis is upon the creative act. Includes essays on surrealism, Bertolt Brecht,

Archibald MacLeish, Katherine Anne Porter, William Faulkner, and others.

E124   Stallman, Robert Wooster, ed. *The Critic's Notebook.* Minneapolis: University of Minnesota Press, 1950. Notes collected in an attempt to "find out how—to quote F. R. Leavis's phrase—'how to talk to the point about poems, novels, and plays, and how to promote intelligent and profitable discussion of them.'" Stallman organizes three hundred quotations "into eight chapters dealing systematically with central concepts and problems of modern criticism," among them: "The Nature and Function of Criticism; Life and Art; Form; Poetic Meaning; and The Problem of Intentions." Draws on American and British criticism from 1920 to 1950. Bibliography.

E125   ————, ed. *Critiques and Essays in Criticism, 1920–1948, Representing the Achievement of Modern British and American Critics.* New York: Ronald, 1949. Designed as a textbook "for courses in modern criticism, aesthetics, and, as a correlative text, for courses offering a critical approach to recent American and British literature, particularly the poetry and the drama." Bibliography.

E126   Steiner, George. *Language and Silence: Essays on Language, Literature, and the Inhuman.* New York: Atheneum, 1967. "This is a book about language: about language and politics, language and the future of literature, about the pressures on language of totalitarian lies and cultural decay, about language and other codes of meaning (music, translation, mathematics), about language and silence." The underlying theme of each essay is "the life of language and of some of the complex energies of the word in our society and culture." Steiner considers the possibility that literary criticism "is no longer a very interesting or responsible exercise" and writes these essays to develop a philosophy of language that would place literature in the context of the larger structures of communication.

E127   Sutton, Walter. •*Modern American Criticism.* Englewood Cliffs, N.J.: Prentice-Hall, 1963. In this survey of American literary criticism, Sutton considers "five representative groups in a roughly chronological order: the New Humanists, psychological and myth critics, liberal and radical critics, New Critics, and neo-Aristotelians."

E128   Swallow, Alan. *An Editor's Essays of Two Decades.* Seattle: Experiment Press, 1962. Twenty-four essays written between 1939 and 1961. In the first two parts, "the essays treat critical theory, especially the relationships between general and philosophical ideas and any resultant literary methods. Two other parts vary from scholarly to critical essays upon English literature and contemporary literature." The last section examines the little magazine, book publishing, and teaching.

E129   Tate, Allen. *Essays of Four Decades.* Chicago: Swallow, 1968. Includes forty-two essays and six prefaces, many of which were published in earlier collections. The essays represent Tate's thought over the years.

E130   Tennyson, G. B., and Edward E. Ericson, Jr., eds. *Religion and Modern Literature: Essays in Theory and Criticism.* Grand Rapids, Mich.: William B. Eerdmans, 1975. A textbook anthology that examines relationships between religion and literature, the religious background of modern literature, and religious dimensions in modern literature.

E131   TeSelle, Sallie McFague. *Literature and the Christian Life.* New Haven: Yale University Press, 1966. TeSelle writes, "The sort of relationship between Christianity and literature that I propose to develop is one that not only protects their distinctive marks, but in fact emerges from the individuality of each." She looks at "the nature and function of literature and then at the Christian faith, in order to discover the relationship between them that emerges."

E132   Tindall, William York. *The Literary Symbol.* Bloomington: Indiana University Press, 1967. Tindall illustrates rather than surveys "symbolic parts and wholes." He begins "with an approach to definition and proceeds with history. Analysis of parts, such as image, action, and structure, occupies the center[,] and contemplation of form [occupies] the end."

E133   Tschumi, Raymond. *A Philosophy of Literature.* London: Linden, 1961. "This book is neither an introduction nor a theory of literature; it is a study of the relations between mind and facts, of the literary reality, of the creative way of looking at things, and of the continuity and wholeness of meaning." Literature serves as a link between facts and feelings, for it "creates its own reality and implies the continuity of time as well as the plenitude of life."

E134   Uitti, Karl D. *Linguistics and Literary Theory*. Englewood Cliffs, N.J.: Prentice-Hall, 1969. Written for "informed and interested readers" in other fields, this work explains the relationship of language and culture, examines the literary ramifications of linguistics, and studies the ways in which linguistics and literary theory interact.

E135   Van Kaam, Adrian, and Kathleen Healy. *The Demon and the Dove: Personality Growth through Literature*. Pittsburgh: Duquesne University Press, 1967. The work's premise is that "one of the tasks of the psychologist and the literary critic is to build a bridge between the science of human endeavor and the artistic expression of human experience in poetry, fiction, and drama." The first half of their study is written "from the point of view of a psychologist in dialogue with the criticism of literature which follows."

E136   Van Nostrand, Albert D., ed. *Literary Criticism in America*. New York: Liberal Arts Press, 1957. A collection of essays arranged to reveal the characteristics of American literary criticism. Selections by Walter Channing (1815) through George Santayana, Brander Matthews, T. S. Eliot, H. L. Mencken, Irving Babbitt, John Crowe Ransom, Robert Frost, Edmund Wilson, and R. P. Blackmur.

E137   Vickery, John B., ed. *Myth and Literature: Contemporary Theory and Practice*. Lincoln: University of Nebraska Press, 1966. This collection provides an introduction to the "theories, methods, and problems" of myth criticism. Includes essays by Joseph Campbell, Stanley Edgar Hyman, Northrop Frye, Philip Rahv, Joseph L. Blotner, Harry Slochower, and others.

E138   Vivas, Eliseo. *The Artistic Transaction and Essays on Theory of Literature*. Columbus: Ohio State University Press, 1963. Vivas's essays emphasize the fact that "our relationship to art is a 'trans-action.'" To Vivas, "Art is an object of culture, or better yet, an object of and in culture, having what status in being may be claimed for it because it functions at the mental plane. It is art only for men capable of inter-acting with a consciously *made,* physical stimulus in some medium or other." For Vivas, art is "an objective affair sharable by those who share the symbolic system that makes it what it is."

E139 ————. *Creation and Discovery: Essays in Criticism and Aesthetics.* New York: Noonday, 1955. Vivas says, "My dominant interest in the manner in which art informs culture has controlled my literary criticism." He explores "the meanings and values embodied in some poems" which gave him "an insight into the modern world." Through these poems, he works toward his own theory of aesthetics.

E140 Watson, George. *The Study of Literature.* London: Penguin, 1969. The first part of the book affirms literary history as a valuable intellectual discipline in the face of the apparent success of the formalists, mythologists, and structural linguists. Watson argues that "Western literature does not derive its significance from the ways in which it may chance to bear upon present problems." He feels that the value of the past is that it is "different from the present." He outlines the historical approach to criticism. In the second part, he discusses "certain humane disciplines largely outside literature" and how they have misdirected literary study. They are linguistics, psychoanalysis, sociology, the history of ideas, and the idea of cultural history. Bibliography.

E141 Wellek, René. *Concepts of Criticism.* Edited by Stephen G. Nichols, Jr. New Haven: Yale University Press, 1963. Wellek is concerned with "the *methods* of studying literary works." His purpose is "to secure a firm base for the task of achieving a full understanding of imaginative literature." To accomplish this, he uses the methods developed in *Theory of Literature.*

E142 ————. *Discriminations: Further Concepts of Criticism.* New Haven: Yale University Press, 1970. Published after *Concepts of Criticism, Discriminations* indicates Wellek's concern "for clarity, coherence, and definiteness in one's thinking about literature. The volume begins with theoretical statements about comparative literature, moves on to studies of two period concepts—classicism and symbolism . . . —and then proceeds to discuss individual problems and issues in a roughly chronological order." Includes "A Bibliography of the Writings of René Wellek from January 1, 1963, to December 31, 1969."

E1. ————, and Austin Warren. *Theory of Literature.* New York: Harcourt, Brace, 1949. A theoretical study concerning extrinsic and intrinsic approaches to literary study. Attempts to create an overview for the student of literature by uniting poetics, criticism, scholarship, and literary history. Bibliography.

E144 West, Ray B., Jr., ed. *Essays in Modern Literary Criticism.* New York: Rinehart, 1952. An anthology that includes "The Backgrounds of Modern Criticism," "Modern Critical Theory," "The Practice of Criticism," and "Biographies and Bibliographies." Contributors include Ezra Pound, T. S. Eliot, Allen Tate, R. P. Blackmur, I. A. Richards, W. K. Wimsatt, Jr., Monroe C. Beardsley, Mark Schorer, Yvor Winters, John Crowe Ransom, Robert Penn Warren, Cleanth Brooks, F. R. Leavis, Percy Lubbock, and others.

E145 Wheelwright, Philip. *Metaphor and Reality.* Bloomington: Indiana University Press, 1962. Concerned with writing "that is radically perspectival. All writing, to be sure, is perspectival in the most general sense; for even the most banal cliché or the most plainly factual report is formulated from a certain standpoint, and represents a certain trend of associations and expectations." Wheelright differentiates between "the perspectival and the universal. . . . The difference is between perspectives that have become standardized and perspectives that are freshly born and individual." He studies the role of language in all ontological inquiries, the distinction between "stereotyped language" and "language that is alive," the emergence of symbols, man's tendency to create myths and "the relation of this tendency to his metaphoric and symbolic modes of language and of thought," and the relationship between reality and expressive language.

E146 Wimsatt, W. K., Jr. *The Verbal Icon: Studies in the Meaning of Poetry.* Lexington: University of Kentucky Press, 1954. Includes essays on the intentional fallacy, on Wimsatt's objections to the "neo-Aristotelianism expounded by a group of critics at Chicago," on the responsibilities of the critic who is "willing to defend literature as knowledge," on the problems of verbal style, and on the relation of literature to other values.

E147 —————, ed. *Explication as Criticism: Selected Papers from the English Institute, 1941–1952.* New York: Columbia University Press, 1963. Wimsatt "asserts that explication *is* criticism; it *is* the evaluative account of the poem." Wimsatt's introductory essay is followed by applications of this theory to writers who did their major creative work before 1945.

E148 Winters, Yvor. *The Function of Criticism: Problems and Exercises.* Denver: Alan Swallow, 1957. While Winters applies his critical ideas to early writers, his response to modernism and to formalism is distinguished by an interest in human experience as it is manifested in literary language. He begins this work with a discussion of the problems facing the modern critic.

F
Studies Published after 1975

F1   *Ackroyd, Peter. *Notes for a New Culture: An Essay on Modernism.* London: Vision, 1976.

F2   *Adams, Robert Martin. *After Joyce: Studies in Fiction after Ulysses.* New York: Oxford University Press, 1977.

F3   Allen, Mary. *The Necessary Blankness: Women in Major American Fiction of the Sixties.* Urbana: University of Illinois Press, 1976.

F4   *American Literary Scholarship: An Annual/1976.* Edited by J. Albert Robbins. Durham, N.C.: Duke University Press, 1978.

F5   Arata, Ester Spring, and Nicholas John Rotoli. *Black American Playwrights, 1800 to the Present: A Bibliography.* Metuchen, N.J.: Scarecrow, 1976.

F6   Ash, Brian. *Who's Who in Science Fiction.* New York: Taplinger, 1976.

F7   Atkins, John. *Six Novelists Look at Society: An Inquiry into the Social Views of Elizabeth Bowen, L. P. Hartley, Rosamond Lehmann, Christopher Isherwood, Nancy Mitford, C. P. Snow.* London: Calder, 1977.

F8   Austen, Roger. *Playing the Game: The Homosexual Novel in America.* Indianapolis: Bobbs-Merrill, 1977.

F9   Berghahn, Marion. *Images of Africa in Black American Literature.* Totowa, N.J.: Rowman & Littlefield, 1977.

F10   Berryman, John. *The Freedom of the Poet: Collected Essays.* New York: Farrar, Straus & Giroux, 1976.

F11   Bloom, Harold. *Figures of Capable Imagination.* New York: Seabury, 1976.

F12 *————. *Poetry and Repression: Revisionism from Blake to Stevens.* New Haven: Yale University Press, 1976.

F13 *Bold, Alan. *Thom Gunn and Ted Hughes.* Edinburgh: Oliver & Boyd, 1976.

F14 *Books in Series in the United States, 1966–1975.* New York: Bowker, 1977.

F15 Borklund, Elmer. *Contemporary Literary Critics.* New York: St. Martin's, 1977.

F16 *Bradbury, Malcolm, ed. *The Novel Today: Contemporary Writers' Modern Fiction.* Totowa, N.J.: Rowman & Littlefield, 1977.

F17 Bretnor, Reginald, ed. *The Craft of Science Fiction.* New York: Harper & Row, 1976.

F18 *Calinescu, Matei. *Faces of Modernity: Avant-Garde, Decadence, Kitsch.* Bloomington: Indiana University Press, 1977.

F19 Callow, James T., and Robert J. Reilly. *Guide to American Literature from Emily Dickinson to the Present.* New York: Barnes & Noble, 1977.

F20 Cannady, Joan. *Black Images in American Literature.* Rochelle Park, N.J.: Hayden, 1977.

F21 *Carter, Everett. *The American Idea: The Literary Response to American Optimism.* Chapel Hill: University of North Carolina Press, 1977.

F22 Carter, Paul A. *The Creation of Tomorrow: Fifty Years of Magazine Science Fiction.* New York: Columbia University Press, 1977.

F23 Cassis, A. F. *The Twentieth-Century English Novel: An Annotated Bibliography of General Criticism.* New York: Garland, 1977.

F24 *Clareson, Thomas D. *Many Futures, Many Worlds: Theme and Form in Science Fiction.* Kent, Ohio: Kent State University Press, 1977.

F25 *Contemporary Literary Critics.* New York: St. Martin's, 1977.

F26 Dettelbach, Cynthia Golomb. *In the Driver's Seat: The Auto-*

mobile in American Literature and Popular Culture. Westport, Conn.: Greenwood, 1976.

F27 *Diamond, Arlyn, and Lee Edwards. *The Authority of Experience: Essays in Feminist Criticism.* Amherst: University of Massachusetts Press, 1977.

F28 *Dickstein, Morris. *Gates of Eden: American Culture in the Sixties.* New York: Basic Books, 1977.

F29 *A Directory of American Fiction Writers: 1976 Edition.* New York: Poets & Writers, 1976.

F30 Dolan, Paul J. *Of War and War's Alarms: Fiction and Politics in the Modern World.* New York: Free Press, 1976.

F31 Edmiston, Susan, and Linda D. Cirino. *Literary New York: A History and Guide.* Boston: Houghton Mifflin, 1976.

F32 *Esslin, Martin. *An Anatomy of Drama.* London: Smith, 1976.

F33 Farrell, James T. *Literary Essays, 1954–1974.* Edited by Jack Alan Robbins. Port Washington, N.Y.: Kennikat, 1976.

F34 *Faulkner, Peter. *Humanism in the English Novel.* New York: Barnes & Noble, 1976.

F35 Fidell, Estelle, ed. *Fiction Catalog.* 9th ed. New York: Wilson, 1976.

F36 *Fisher, Dexter, ed. *Minority Language and Literature: Retrospective and Perspective.* New York: MLA, 1977.

F37 *Fowler, Roger. *Linguistics and the Novel.* Totowa, N.J.: Rowman & Littlefield, 1977.

F38 Fraser, George. *Essays on Twentieth-Century Poets.* Totowa, N.J.: Rowman & Littlefield, 1977.

F39 *Frye, Northrop. *Spiritus Mundi: Essays on Literature, Myth, and Society.* Bloomington: Indiana University Press, 1976.

F40 Fulton, Len. *Small Press Record of Books in Print.* 6th ed. Paradise, Calif.: Dustbooks, 1977.

F41 Garvin, Harry R., ed. *Makers of the Twentieth-Century Novel.* Lewisburg, Pa.: Bucknell University Press, 1977.

F42 *———, ed. *Twentieth-Century Poetry, Fiction, Theory.* Lewisburg, Pa.: Bucknell University Press, 1977.

F43   Geduld, Harry M., and Ronald Gottesman, eds. *Robots, Robots.* Boston: New York Graphic Society, 1978.

F44   Gershator, Phillis. *A Bibliographic Guide to the Literature of Contemporary American Poetry, 1970–1975.* Metuchen, N.J.: Scarecrow, 1976.

F45   *Gohdes, Clarence. *Bibliographical Guide to the Study of the Literature of the U.S.A.* 4th ed. Durham, N.C.: Duke University Press, 1976.

F46   *Gordon, David J. *Literary Art and the Unconscious.* Baton Rouge: Louisiana State University Press, 1976.

F47   *Granger's Index to Poetry, 1970–1977.* Edited by William James. New York: Columbia University Press, 1978.

F48   Gray, Richard. *The Literature of Memory: Modern Writers of the American South.* Baltimore: Johns Hopkins University Press, 1977.

F49   *Hayman, Ronald. *Artaud and After.* New York: Oxford University Press, 1977.

F50   *Heiserman, Arthur. *The Novel before the Novel.* Chicago: University of Chicago Press, 1977.

F51   Hendin, Josephine. *Vulnerable People: A View of American Fiction since 1945.* New York: Oxford University Press, 1978.

F52   *Henn, T. R. *Last Essays Mainly on Anglo-Irish Literature.* New York: Harper & Row, 1976.

F53   Heyen, William, ed. *American Poets in 1976.* Indianapolis: Bobbs-Merrill, 1976.

F54   *Hiatt, Mary. *The Way Women Write.* New York: Teachers College Press, 1977.

F55   Higdon, David Leon. *Time and English Fiction.* Totowa, N.J.: Rowman & Littlefield, 1977.

F56   Hipkiss, Robert A. *Jack Kerouac, Prophet of the New Romanticism: A Critical Study of the Published Works of Kerouac and a Comparison of Them to Those of J. D. Salinger, James Purdy, John Knowles, and Ken Kesey.* Lawrence: Regents Press of Kansas, 1976.

F57 *Holbrook, David. *Lost Bearings in English Poetry.* New York: Harper & Row, 1977.

F58 *Hollowell, John. *Fact and Fiction: The New Journalism and the Nonfiction Novel.* Chapel Hill: University of North Carolina Press, 1977.

F59 Hughes, Catharine. *American Playwrights, 1945–75.* London: Pitman, 1976.

F60 Hughson, Lois. *Thresholds of Reality: George Santayana and Modernist Poetics.* Port Washington, N.Y.: Kennikat, 1976.

F61 *The International Authors and Writers Who's Who.* 7th ed. Edited by Ernest Kay. Cambridge: Melrose, 1976.

F62 *Jackson, Blyden. *The Waiting Years: Essays on American Negro Literature.* Baton Rouge: Louisiana State University Press, 1977.

F63 *Jennings, Elizabeth. *Seven Men of Vision: An Appreciation.* New York: Harper & Row, 1977.

F64 Jones, Peter G. *War and the Novelist: Appraising the American War Novel.* Columbia: University of Missouri Press, 1976.

F65 *Josipovici, Gabriel. *The Lessons of Modernism.* Totowa, N.J.: Rowman & Littlefield, 1977.

F66 *——————. *The Modern English Novel: The Reader, the Writer and the Work.* London: Open Books, 1976.

F67 Juhasz, Suzanne. *Naked and Fiery Forms: Modern American Poetry by Women: A New Tradition.* New York: Harper & Row, 1976.

F68 *Kalstone, David. *Five Temperaments: Elizabeth Bishop, Robert Lowell, James Merrill, Adrienne Rich, John Ashbery.* New York: Oxford University Press, 1977.

F69 Kauffman, Stanley. *Persons of the Drama: Theater Criticism and Comment.* New York: Harper & Row, 1976.

F70 *Kegan, Robert. *The Sweeter Welcome: Voices for a Vision of Affirmation: Bellow, Malamud and Martin Buber.* Needham Heights, Mass.: Humanitas Press, 1977.

F71   Kiell, Norman. *Varieties of Sexual Experience: Psychosexuality in Literature.* New York: International Universities Press, 1976.

F72   King, Kimball. *Twenty Modern British Playwrights: A Bibliography, 1956 to 1976.* New York: Garland, 1977.

F73   *Kirkpatrick, Daniel, ed. *Twentieth Century Children's Writers.* New York: St. Martin's, 1977.

F74   Klinkowitz, Jerome, with graphics by Roy R. Behrens. *The Life of Fiction.* Urbana: University of Illinois Press, 1977.

F75   *Klotman, Phyllis Rauch. *Another Man Gone: The Black Runner in Contemporary Afro-American Literature.* Port Washington, N.Y.: Kennikat, 1976.

F76   Knight, Damon. *Turning Points: Essays on the Art of Science Fiction.* New York: Harper & Row, 1977.

F77   Krieger, Murray. *Theory of Criticism: A Tradition and Its System.* Baltimore: Johns Hopkins University Press, 1976.

F78   *————, and L. S. Dembo. *Directions for Criticism: Structuralism and Its Alternatives.* Madison: University of Wisconsin Press, 1977.

F79   Lambert, Gavin. *The Dangerous Edge: An Inquiry into the Lives of Nine Masters of Suspense.* New York: Grossman, 1976.

F80   *Langbaum, Robert. *The Mysteries of Identity: A Theme in Modern Literature.* New York: Oxford University Press, 1977.

F81   Larson, Charles R. *American Indian Fiction.* Albuquerque: University of New Mexico Press, 1978.

F82   *Leary, Lewis. *American Literature: A Study and Research Guide.* New York: St. Martin's, 1976.

F83   Lensing, George S., and Ronald Moran. *Four Poets and the Emotive Imagination: Robert Bly, James Wright, Louis Simpson, and William Stafford.* Baton Rouge: Louisiana State University Press, 1976.

F84   Lepper, Gary M. *A Bibliographical Introduction to Seventy-five*

Modern American Authors. Berkeley, Calif.: Serendipity Books, 1976.

F85   *Lieberman, Laurence. *Unassigned Frequencies: American Poetry in Review, 1964–77.* Urbana: University of Illinois Press, 1977.

F86   MacAdam, Alfred J. *Modern Latin American Narratives: The Dreams of Reason.* Chicago: University of Chicago Press, 1977.

F87   *McConnell, Frank D. *Four Postwar American Novelists: Bellow, Mailer, Barth, and Pynchon.* Chicago: University of Chicago Press, 1977.

F88   *McGrory, Kathleen, and John Unterecker, eds. *Yeats, Joyce, and Beckett: New Light on Three Modern Irish Writers.* Lewisburg, Pa.: Bucknell University Press, 1977.

F89   Magill, Frank N. *Masterplots: 2,010 Plot Stories & Essay Reviews from the World's Fine Literature.* Rev. ed. Englewood Cliffs, N.J.: Salem Press, 1976.

F90   ————, ed. *Magill's Literary Annual: Essay-Reviews of 200 Outstanding Books Published in the United States.* Englewood Cliffs, N.J.: Salem Press, 1977–. (The annuals for 1976 pick up where the *Survey of Contemporary Literature* ends.)

F91   ————, ed. *Masterpieces of World Literature in Digest Form.* 12 vols. Rev. ed. New York: Harper, 1976.

F92   ————, ed. *Survey of Contemporary Literature; Updated Reprints of 2,300 Essay-Reviews from Masterplot Annuals, 1954–1976, and Survey of Contemporary Literature Supplement with 3,300 Bibliographical Reference Sources.* 12 vols. Rev. ed. Englewood Cliffs, N.J.: Salem Press, 1977.

F93   *Malkoff, Karl. *Escape from the Self: A Study in Contemporary Poetry and Poetics.* New York: Columbia University Press, 1978.

F94   Matthews, J. H. *Toward the Poetics of Surrealism.* Syracuse: Syracuse University Press, 1976.

F95   *May, Charles E. *Short Story Theories.* Athens: Ohio University Press, 1976.

F96   May, Keith M. *Out of the Maelstrom: Psychology and the Novel in the Twentieth Century.* New York: St. Martin's, 1977.

F97   Mellown, Elgin W. *A Descriptive Catalogue of the Bibliographies of Twentieth Century British Poets, Novelists, and Dramatists.* 2nd ed., rev. and enl. Troy, N.Y.: Whitston, 1978.

F98   Mikhail, E. H. *Contemporary British Drama, 1950–1976: An Annotated Critical Bibliography.* Totowa, N.J.: Rowman & Littlefield, 1976.

F99   Miller, Wayne Charles. *A Handbook of American Minorities.* New York: New York University Press, 1976.

F100   ————; Faye Vowell; et al. *A Comprehensive Bibliography for the Study of American Minorities.* New York: New York University Press, 1976.

F101   Moers, Ellen. *Literary Women.* Garden City, N.Y.: Doubleday, 1976.

F102   Moskowitz, Sam. *Strange Horizons: The Spectrum of Science Fiction.* New York: Scribner's, 1976.

F103   Myers, Carol Fairbanks. *Women in Literature: Criticism of the Seventies.* Metuchen, N.J.: Scarecrow, 1976.

F104   Nagel, James, ed. *American Fiction: Historical and Critical Essays.* Boston: Northeastern University Press & Twayne, 1977.

F105   *Oberg, Arthur. *Modern American Lyric: Lowell, Berryman, Creeley, Plath.* New Brunswick, N.J.: Rutgers University Press, 1977.

F106   *Olson, Elder. *On Value Judgments in the Arts and Other Essays.* Chicago: University of Chicago Press, 1976.

F107   Orr, John. *Tragic Realism and Modern Society: Studies in the Sociology of the Modern Novel.* Pittsburgh: University of Pittsburgh Press, 1978.

F108   *Partridge, A. C. *The Language of Modern Poetry: Yeats, Eliot, Auden.* New York: Academic Press, 1976.

F109   Patterson, Margaret C. *Literary Research Guide: An Evaluative, Annotated Bibliography of Important Reference*

Books and Periodicals on American and English Literature, of the Most Useful Sources for Research in Other National Literatures, and of More Than 300 Reference Books in Literature-Related Subject Areas. Detroit: Gale, 1976.

F110 Paul, Sherman. *Repossessing and Renewing: Essays in the Green American Tradition.* Baton Rouge: Louisiana State University Press, 1976.

F111 *Perkins, David. *A History of Modern Poetry from the 1890's to the High Modernist Mode.* Cambridge, Mass.: Harvard University Press, 1976.

F112 Perkins, Michael. *The Secret Record: Modern Erotic Literature.* New York: William Morrow, 1976.

F113 *Pescatello, Ann M., ed. *Old Roots in New Lands: Historical and Anthropological Perspectives on Black Experiences in the Americas.* Westport, Conn.: Greenwood, 1977.

F114 *Pinksy, Robert. *The Situation of Poetry: Contemporary Poetry and Its Traditions.* Princeton: Princeton University Press, 1977.

F115 *Primeau, Ronald, ed. *Influx: Essays on Literary Influence.* Port Washington, N.Y.: Kennikat, 1976.

F116 *The Publication of Poetry and Fiction: A Conference Held at the Library of Congress, October 20 and 21, 1975.* Washington, D.C.: Library of Congress, 1977.

F117 *Purdy, Strother B. *The Hole in the Fabric: Science, Contemporary Literature, and Henry James.* Pittsburgh: University of Pittsburgh, 1977.

F118 Rabkin, Eric S. *The Fantastic in Literature.* Princeton: Princeton University Press, 1976.

F119 Ramchand, Kenneth. *The West Indian Novel and Its Background.* London: Faber & Faber, 1976.

F120 * *The Reader's Adviser: A Layman's Guide to Literature, 1974–1977.* 3 vols. 12th ed. General editor, Sarah L. Prakken. New York: Bowker, 1977.

F121 *Redmond, Eugene B. *Drumvoices: The Mission of Afro-American Poetry.* New York: Doubleday, 1976.

F122   Resnick, Michael. *The Official Guide to Fantastic Literature.* Florence, Ala.: House of Collectibles, 1976.

F123   Ries, Lawrence W. *Wolf Masks: Violence in Contemporary Poetry.* Port Washington, N.Y.: Kennikat, 1977.

F124   Rosa, Alfred F., and Paul A. Eschholz. *Contemporary Fiction in America and England, 1950–1970: A Guide to Information Sources.* Vol. 10 in the American Literature, English Literature, and World Literatures in English Information Guide Series. Detroit: Gale, 1976.

F125   Rose, Alan Henry. *Demonic Vision: Racial Fantasy and Southern Fiction.* Hamden, Conn.: Archon, 1976.

F126   *Rose, Mark, ed. *Science Fiction: A Collection of Critical Essays.* Englewood Cliffs, N.J.: Prentice-Hall, 1976.

F127   *Rubin, Louis D., Jr. *Four Fugitives: A Study of Poetry and the South.* Baton Rouge: Louisiana State University Press, 1978.

F128   Russell, John. *Style in Modern British Fiction: Studies in Joyce, Lawrence, Forster, Lewis, and Green.* Baltimore: Johns Hopkins University Press, 1977.

F129   *Sarotte, Georges-Michel. *Like a Brother, Like a Lover: Male Homosexuality in the American Novel and Theatre from Herman Melville to James Baldwin.* New York: Doubleday, 1978.

F130   *Schiff, Hilda. *Contemporary Approaches to English Studies.* New York: Barnes & Noble, 1976.

F131   Scholes, Robert, and Eric S. Rabkin. *Science Fiction: History, Science, Vision.* New York: Oxford University Press, 1977.

F132   Schwartz, Narda Lacey. *Articles on Women Writers, 1960–1975: A Bibliography.* Santa Barbara, Calif.: American Bibliographical Center, 1977.

F133   Schwarz, Alfred. *From Buchner to Beckett: Dramatic Theory and the Modes of Tragic Drama.* Athens: Ohio University Press, 1978.

F134   *Seymour-Smith, Martin. *Who's Who in Twentieth-Century Literature.* New York: Holt, Rinehart & Winston, 1976.

F135   *Showalter, Elaine. *A Literature of Their Own: British Women from Brontë to Lessing.* Princeton: Princeton University Press, 1977.

F136   Smith, Roger N. *Paperbook Parnassus: The Birth, The Development, The Pending Crisis . . . of the Modern American Paperbound Book.* Boulder, Colo.: Westview Press, 1976.

F137   *Spacks, Patricia M. *Imagining a Self.* Cambridge, Mass.: Harvard University Press, 1976.

F138   ————, ed. *Contemporary Women Novelists.* Englewood Cliffs, N.J.: Prentice-Hall, 1977.

F139   *Spiegel, Alan. *Fiction and the Camera Eye: Visual Consciousness in Film and the Modern Novel.* Charlottesville: University Press of Virginia, 1976.

F140   Spilka, Mark, ed. *Towards a Poetics of Fiction: Essays from Novel, A Forum on Fiction, 1967–1976.* Bloomington: Indiana University Press, 1977.

F141   *Spiller, Robert E. *Milestones in American Literary History.* Westport, Conn.: Greenwood, 1977.

F142   Stade, George, ed. *Six Contemporary British Novelists.* New York: Columbia University Press, 1976.

F143   Steinbrunner, Chris; Otto Penzler; et al. *Encyclopedia of Mystery and Detection.* New York: McGraw-Hill, 1976.

F144   Sternberg, Meir. *Expositional Modes and Temporal Ordering in Fiction.* Baltimore: Johns Hopkins University Press, 1977.

F145   *Thurley, Geoffrey. *The American Moment: American Poetry in the Mid-Century.* New York: St. Martin's, 1978.

F146   Thwaite, Anthony. *Twentieth-Century English Poetry: An Introduction.* New York: Barnes & Noble, 1978.

F147   Tilton, John W. *Cosmic Satire in the Contemporary Novel.* Lewisburg, Pa.: Bucknell University Press, 1977.

F148   Trimmer, Joseph F. *The National Book Awards for Fiction: An Index to the First Twenty-five Years.* Boston: G. K. Hall, 1978.

F149   Turner, Alberta T., ed. *Fifty Contemporary Poets: The Creative Process.* New York: McKay, 1977.

F150   *Twentieth Century Literary Criticism.* Edited by Dedria Bryfonski and Phyllis Carmel Mendelson. Detroit: Gale, 1978.

F151   Tytell, John. *Naked Angels: The Lives and Literature of the Beat Generation.* New York: McGraw-Hill, 1976.

F152   Updike, John. *Picked-Up Pieces.* New York: Knopf, 1976.

F153   Vidal, Gore. *Matters of Fact and of Fiction: Essays, 1973–1976.* New York: Random House, 1977.

F154   *Vinson, James. *Contemporary Dramatists.* 2nd ed. New York: St. Martin's, 1977.

F155   *Watson, George. *Politics and Literature in Modern Britain.* Totowa, N.J.: Rowman & Littlefield, 1977.

F156   *Weimann, Robert. *Structure and Society in Literary History.* Charlottesville: University Press of Virginia, 1976.

F157   West, Thomas Reed. *Nature, Community and Will: A Study in Literary and Social Thought.* Columbia: University of Missouri Press, 1976.

F158   *Whitaker, Thomas R. *Fields of Play in Modern Drama.* Princeton: Princeton University Press, 1977.

F159   *Williams, Harry. *"The Edge Is What I Have": Theodore Roethke and After.* Lewisburg, Pa.: Bucknell University Press, 1977.

F160   *Wimsatt, W. K. *Day of the Leopards: Essays in Defense of Poems.* New Haven: Yale University Press, 1976.

F161   *Writers at Work: The Paris Review Interviews.* Fourth Series. Edited by George Plimpton. New York: Viking, 1976.

F162   *Young, Thomas Daniel, ed. *The New Criticism and After.* Charlottesville: University Press of Virginia, 1976.

Part 2
Study Guides

G

Abstract, Summary, and Excerpt Collections

G1   *Abstracts of English Studies.* Boulder, Colo.: National Council of Teachers of English, 1958– (monthly).

G2   *American Literary Scholarship: An Annual.* See H30.

G3   **American Literature Abstracts: A Review of Current Scholarship in the Field of American Literature.* San Jose: California State Colleges, 1967– (semi-annually).

G4   *Book Review Digest.* New York: Wilson, 1905–.

G5   *Contemporary Literary Criticism: Excerpts from Criticism of the Works of Today's Novelists, Poets, Playwrights, and Other Creative Writers.* Edited by Carolyn Riley. Detroit: Gale, 1973–76.

G6   Curley, Dorothy Nyren. *Library of Literary Criticism: Modern American Literature.* 3 vols. 4th ed. New York: Ungar, 1973.

G7   ————; Maurice Kramer; and Elaine Fialka. *Modern American Literature.* 4 vols. 4th enl. ed. New York: Ungar, 1969–76.

G8   *Dissertations Abstracts International.* Ann Arbor, Mich.: University Microfilms, 1938–. (Formerly *Microfilm Abstracts and Dissertation Abstracts.*)

G9   Magill, Frank Northern, ed. *Masterplots Annual: Magill's Literary Annual: Essay-Reviews of 100 Outstanding Books Published in the United States.* New York: Salem, 1970–. (The annuals for 1970 pick up where the *Survey of Contemporary Literature* ends.)

G10   ————, ed. *Survey of Contemporary Literature; Updated*

Reprints of 1500 Essay-Reviews from Masterplots Annuals, 1954–1969. 7 vols. New York: Salem, 1971.

G11   *Masters Abstracts: Abstracts of Selected Masters Theses on Microfilm.* Ann Arbor, Mich.: University Microfilms, 1962–.

 G12   *MLA Abstracts of Articles in Scholarly Journals.* New York: Modern Language Association, 1972–. (Series begins with 1970.)

G13   Nyren, Dorothy. *A Library of Literary Criticism: Modern American Literature with Index to Critics and Supplement.* See H93.

G14   Temple, Ruth Z., and Martin Tucker. *A Library of Literary Criticism: Modern British Literature.* See H101.

H

Bibliographies and Indexes

BIBLIOGRAPHIES OF BIBLIOGRAPHIES

H1   Altick, Richard D., and Andrew Wright. *Selective Bibliography for the Study of English and American Literature.* 5th ed. New York: Macmillan, 1975.

H2   Bell, Inglis F., and Jennifer Gallup. *A Reference Guide to English, American and Canadian Literature: An Annotated Checklist of Bibliographical and Other Reference Materials.* Vancouver: University of British Columbia Press, 1971.

H3   Besterman, Theodore. *Literature, English and American: A Bibliography of Bibliographies.* Totowa, N.J.: Rowman & Littlefield, 1971.

H4   ————. *A World Bibliography of Bibliographies and of Bibliographical Catalogues, Calendars, Abstracts, Digests, Indexes, and the Like.* 5 vols. 4th ed. Lausanne: Societas Bibliographica, 1965–66.

H5   *The Bibliographical Index: A Cumulative Bibliography of Bibliographies.* New York: Wilson, 1938–.

H6   *Bibliotheck: A Scottish Journal of Bibliography and Allied Topics.* Stirling, Scotland: University Library, 1956–.

H7   Bond, Donald F. *A Reference Guide to English Studies.* 2nd ed. Chicago: University of Chicago Press, 1971.

H8   *Bulletin of Bibliography and Magazine Notes.* Westwood, Mass.: Faxon, 1897–.

H9   Cross, Tom. *Bibliographical Guide to English Studies.* 10th ed. Chicago: University of Chicago Press, 1951.

H10   Eager, Alan R. *A Guide to Irish Bibliographical Material.* London: Chaucer House, 1964.

H11   *Gray, Richard A. *Serial Bibliographies in the Humanities and Social Sciences.* Assistance by Dorothy Villmow. Ann Arbor, Mich.: Pierian, 1969.

H12   Havlice, Patricia P. *Index to American Author Bibliographies.* Metuchen, N.J.: Scarecrow, 1971.

H13   *Howard-Hill, Trevor Howard. *Bibliography of British Literary Bibliographies.* Oxford: Clarendon, 1969.

H14   *Hutchins, Margaret. *Syllabus for the Study of Bibliography and Reference for Use in Connection with Library Service 262.* 4th ed. New York: School of Library Service at Columbia University, 1947.

H15   Kehler, Dorothea. *Problems in Literary Research: A Guide to Selected Reference Works.* Metuchen, N.J.: Scarecrow, 1975.

H16   Kennedy, Arthur G., and Donald B. Sands. *A Concise Bibliography for Students of English.* 5th ed. Revised by William E. Colburn. Stanford, Calif.: Stanford University Press, 1972.

H17   Mellown, Elgin W. *A Descriptive Catalogue of the Bibliographies of 20 Century British Writers.* Troy, N.Y.: Whitson, 1972.

H18   Nilon, Charles H. *Bibliography of Bibliographies in American Literature.* New York: Bowker, 1970.

H19   Patterson, Margaret C. *Literary Research Guide.* See F109.

H20   Platt, Peter, comp. *A Guide to Book Lists and Bibliographies for the Use of Schools.* Oxford: School Library Association, 1975.

H21   Ryder, Dorothy E. *Canadian Reference Sources: A Selective Guide.* Ottawa: Canadian Library Association, 1973.

H22   "A Selective Checklist of Bibliographical Scholarship." *Studies in Bibliography,* 1950–69; "Check List of Bibliographical Scholarship," 1970–73.

H23   Virginia University Bibliographical Society. *Studies in Bibliography.* Vols. 16, 17. Charlottesville: The Bibliographical Society, 1963–64.

H24   Walsh, S. Padraig. *Anglo-American General Encyclopedias: A*

BIBLIOGRAPHIES AND INDEXES

Historical Bibliography, 1703–1967. New York: Bowker, 1968.

H25   Winchell, Constance M. *Guide to Reference Books.* 8th ed. Chicago: American Library Association, 1967.

H26   Wright, Andrew. *A Reader's Guide to English and American Literature.* Glenview, Ill.: Scott, Foresman, 1970.

H27   Wynar, Bohdan S. *Reference Books in Paperback: An Annotated Guide.* Littleton, Colo.: Libraries Unlimited, 1972.

GENERAL BIBLIOGRAPHIES

H28   **Adirondack Bibliography: A List of Books, Pamphlets and Periodical Articles Published through the Year 1955.* Gabriels, N.Y.: Adirondack Mountain Club, 1958.

H29   *American Doctoral Dissertations, 1963/64–.* Ann Arbor, Mich.: University Microfilms, 1965–. See H68.

H30   *American Literary Scholarship: An Annual.* Edited by James Woodress (1963–67); J. Albert Robbins (1968–). Durham, N.C.: Duke University Press, 1963–.

H31   **American Literature Abstracts: A Review of Current Scholarship in the Field of American Literature.* See G3.

H32   *Annals of English Literature, 1475–1950: The Principal Publications of Each Year Together with an Alphabetical Index of Authors with Their Works.* 2nd ed. revised and updated by Robert W. Chapman. Oxford: Clarendon, 1961.

H33   "Annual Bibliography of Comparative Literature, 1949–69." *Yearbook of Comparative and General Literature,* 1952–70.

H34   *Annual Bibliography of English Language and Literature.* Cambridge: Modern Humanities Research Association, 1920–.

H35   "Articles on American Literature Appearing in Current Periodicals." *American Literature,* 1929–.

H36   Bateson, Frederick W., and George Watson, eds. *The Cambridge Bibliography of English Literature.* See H48.

H37 Blanck, Jacob. *Bibliography of American Literature.* 6 vols. to date. New Haven: Yale University Press, 1955–.

H38 *Book Review Index.* Detroit: Gale, 1965–.

H39 *Books in Print: An Author-Title-Series Index to the Publishers' Trade List Annual.* New York: Bowker, 1948–.

H40 *British Books in Print.* London: Whitaker, 1874–.

H41 *British Humanities Index.* London: Library Association, 1962–.

H42 The British Museum. *General Catalogue of Printed Books to 1955. Supplements.* London: Trustees of the British Museum, 1965–.

H43 ——————. *Subject Index of Modern Books Acquired.* London: Trustees of the British Museum, 1902–.

H44 *British National Bibliography.* Edited by A. J. Wells. London: Council of the British National Bibliography, 1950–.

H45 Bryer, Jackson R. *Fifteen Modern American Authors: A Survey of Research and Criticism.* Durham, N.C.: Duke University Press, 1969.

H46 *——————. Sixteen Modern American Authors: A Survey of Research and Criticism.* New York: Norton, 1973.

H47 Burke, W. J., and Will D. Howe. *American Authors and Books: 1640 to the Present Day.* 3rd. rev. ed. Revised by Irving and Ann Weiss. New York: Crown, 1972.

H48 *The Cambridge Bibliography of English Literature.* Edited by Frederick W. Bateson and George Watson. 5 vols. Cambridge: Cambridge University Press, 1940–57.

H49 Cheshire, David. *Theatre: History, Criticism and Reference.* London: Clive Bingley, 1967.

H50 Cohen, Henning. *Articles in American Studies, 1954–1968: A Cumulation of the Annual Bibliographies from American Quarterly.* 2 vols. Ann Arbor, Mich.: Pierian, 1972.

H51 Combs, Richard E. *Authors: Critical and Biographical References.* See I4.

H52 *Comprehensive Dissertation Index, 1861–1972.* 37 vols. and supplements. Vols. 29–30, *Language and Literature.* Ann Arbor, Mich.: Xerox University Microfilms, 1973.

BIBLIOGRAPHIES AND INDEXES

H53   *The Concise Cambridge Bibliography of English Literature, 600–1950.* Edited by George Watson. 2nd ed. Cambridge: Cambridge University Press, 1965.

H54   *Contemporary Authors: A Bio-Bibliographical Guide to Current Authors and Their Works.* Detroit: Gale, 1962–.

H55   *Cumulative Book Index.* New York: Wilson, 1928–.

H56   "Current Bibliography." *Twentieth-Century Literature,* 1955–.

H57   Eastwood, Wilfred, and John T. Good. *Signposts: A Guide to Modern English Literature.* See J4.

H58   *Essay and General Literature Index.* New York: Wilson, 1900–.

H59   Fleischmann, Wolfgang Bernard. *Encyclopedia of World Literature in the 20th Century.* See J6.

H60   Fulton, Len, ed. *Small Press Record of Books.* 4th ed. Paradise, Calif.: Dustbooks, 1975.

H61   *Gibian, George. *Soviet Russian Literature in English: A Checklist Bibliography of Soviet Russian Literary Works in English and of Articles and Books in English About Soviet Russian Literature.* Ithaca: New York Center for International Studies, Cornell University, 1967.

H62   Gohdes, Clarence. *Bibliographical Guide to the Study of the Literature of the U.S.A.* See F45.

H63   *Granger's Index to Poetry: Indexing Anthologies Published through December 31, 1970.* 6th ed. Edited by William James Smith. New York: Columbia University Press, 1973.

H64   Gray, Richard A. *A Guide to Book Review Citations: A Bibliography of Sources.* Columbus: Ohio State University Press, 1969.

H65   Harmon, Maurice. *Modern Irish Literature, 1800–1967: A Reader's Guide.* Chester Springs, Pa.: Dufour, 1968.

H66   *Harvard University Library. *American Literature.* Cambridge, Mass.: Harvard University Press, 1970.

H67   Hoffman, Hester R. *The Reader's Adviser.* 9th ed. New York: Bowker, 1960. (Previously *Bessie Graham's Bookman's Manual Guide to Literature.*)

H68   *Index to American Doctoral Dissertations, 1955/56–1962/63.* Ann Arbor, Mich.: University Microfilms, 1957–63. See H29.

H69   *An Index to Book Reviews in the Humanities.* (Quarterly.) Williamston, Mich.: Phillip Thomson, 1960–.

H70   **Index to Theses Accepted for Higher Degrees in the Universities of Great Britain and Ireland, 1950/1–.* London: Whitrow & Paterson, 1953–.

H71   *Jones, Brynmor. *A Bibliography of Anglo-Welsh Literature, 1900–1965.* Swansea, Wales: Library Association of Wales and Monmouthshire, 1970.

H72   Jones, Howard Mumford, and Richard M. Ludwig. *Guide to American Literature and Its Backgrounds since 1890.* 4th ed. rev. and enl. Cambridge, Mass.: Harvard University Press, 1972.

H73   Koehmstedt, Carol L. *Plot Summary Index.* Metuchen, N.J.: Scarecrow, 1973.

H74   Leary, Lewis. *American Literature: A Study and Research Guide.* See F82.

H75   ————. *Articles on American Literature, 1900–1950.* Durham, N.C.: Duke University Press, 1954.

H76   ————. *Articles on American Literature, 1950–1967.* Durham, N.C.: Duke University Press, 1970.

H77   ————, ed. *Contemporary Literary Scholarship: A Critical Review.* See A182.

H78   *Library of Congress and National Union Catalog Author Lists, 1942–1962: A Master Cumulation.* 152 vols. to date. Detroit: Gale, 1969–.

H79   *Library of Congress Catalog, Books: Subjects, 1950–1954.* 20 vols. with annual cumulations. Ann Arbor, Mich.: Edwards, 1955.

H80   *Literary History of the United States.* Vol. 2, *Bibliography.* Edited by Robert E. Spiller, et al. 4th ed., rev. New York: Macmillan, 1974.

H81   McNamee, Lawrence F. *Dissertations in English and American*

Literature: Theses Accepted by American, British and German Universities, 1865–1964. New York: Bowker, 1968. *Supplement One, 1964–1968,* 1969.

H82 *Marshall, Thomas F. *An Analytical Index to "American Literature": Volumes I-XXX, March 1929–January 1959.* Durham, N.C.: Duke University Press, 1963.

H83 *Masters Abstracts.* See G11.

H84 Modern Humanities Research Association. *Annual Bibliography of English Language and Literature.* See H34.

H85 *MLA International Bibliography of Books and Articles on the Modern Languages and Literature.* New York: Modern Language Association, 1921–.

H86 *National Union Catalog: Pre–1956 Imprints.* London: Mansell, 1968–.

H87 *National Union Catalog: A Cumulative Author List, 1965–.* Washington, D.C.: Library of Congress, 1958–.

H88 *The New Cambridge Bibliography of English Literature.* Edited by George Watson. New York: Cambridge University Press, 1969–.

H89 *New Cambridge Bibliography of English Literature.* Edited by Ian Willison. Vol. 4, *1900–1950.* New York: Cambridge University Press, 1973.

H90 *Newspaper Index.* Wooster, Ohio: Micropublishers, 1972–.

H91 *The New York Times Book Review Index, October 10, 1896–.* New York: Arno, 1968–.

H92 *New York Times Index.* New York: New York Times, 1913–.

H93 Nyren, Dorothy. *A Library of Literary Criticism: Modern American Literature with Index to Critics and Supplement.* 3rd ed. New York: Ungar, 1964.

H94 Pownall, David E. *Articles on Twentieth Century Literature: An Annotated Bibliography, 1954–1970: An Expanded Cumulation of "Current Bibliography" in the Journal Twentieth-Century Literature. Volume One to Volume Sixteen, 1955 to 1970.* New York: Kraus-Thompson Organization, 1973.

H95   *Publishers' Trade List Annual.* 6 vols. New York: Bowker, 1872–.

H96   **Quarterly Checklist of Literary History: English, American, French, German: An International Index of Current Books, Monographs, Brochures, and Separates.* Vol. 1 (Oct. 1958)–.

H97   *Readers' Guide to Periodical Literature: An Author and Subject Index.* New York: Wilson, 1900–.

H98   *Social Science and Humanities Index.* New York: Wilson, 1907–74.

H99   Spiller, Robert E., et al., eds. *Literary History of the United States.* Vol. 2, *Bibliography.* See H80.

H100   *Subject Guide to Books in Print: An Index to The Publishers' Trade List Annual.* 2 vols. New York: Bowker, 1957–.

H101   Temple, Ruth Z., and Martin Tucker. *A Library of Literary Criticism: Modern British Literature.* 3 vols. New York: Ungar, 1966.

H102   ————, and Martin Tucker. *Modern British Literature: A Reference Guide and Bibliography.* New York: Ungar, 1975.

H103   Tucker, Martin. *The Critical Temper: A Survey of Modern Criticism on English and American Literature from the Beginnings to the Twentieth Century.* New York: Ungar, 1969.

H104   Val Baker, Denys, ed. *Writers of To-Day.* See A297.

H105   ————, ed. *Writers of To-Day: 2.* See A298.

H106   Watson, George, ed. *The Concise Cambridge Bibliography of English Literature, 600–1950.* See H53.

H107   Winterich, John T. *Writers in America 1842–1967.* Jersey City, N.J.: Davey, 1968.

H108   Woodress, James, ed. *American Literary Scholarship: An Annual.* See H30.

H109   ————, and Marian Koritz. *Dissertations in American Literature, 1891–1966.* Rev. and enl. ed. Durham, N.C.: Duke University Press, 1968.

BIBLIOGRAPHIES AND INDEXES

H110   *The Writers' and Artists' Yearbook: A Directory for Writers, Artists, Playwrights, Writers for Film, Radio, and Television, Photographers and Composers.* London: Black, 1906–.

H111   *Yearbook of Comparative and General Literature, 1962.* Bloomington: Indiana University Press, 1962.

H112   *The Yearbook of English Studies.* Cambridge: Modern Humanities Research Association, 1971–.

H113   *The Year's Work in English Studies: 1919–.* London: Oxford University Press, 1921–.

H114   *The Year's Work in Modern Language Studies.* Edited for the Modern Humanities Research Association. London: Oxford University Press, 1957–.

DRAMA BIBLIOGRAPHIES

H115   Adelman, Irving, and Rita Dworkin. *Modern Drama: A Checklist of Critical Literature on 20th Century Plays.* Metuchen, N.J.: Scarecrow, 1967.

H116   Baker, Blanche M. *The Theater and Allied Arts: A Guide to Books Dealing with the History, Criticism, and Technique of the Drama and Theater, and Related Arts and Crafts.* New York: Wilson, 1952.

H117   Bonin, Jane F. *Prize-Winning American Drama: A Bibliographic and Descriptive Guide.* Metuchen, N.J.: Scarecrow, 1973.

H118   Breed, Paul F., and Florence M. Sniderman. *Dramatic Criticism Index: A Bibliography of Commentaries on Playwrights from Ibsen to the Avant-Garde.* Detroit: Gale, 1972.

H119   Chicorel, Marietta, ed. *Chicorel Bibliography to the Performing Arts.* New York: Chicorel Library, 1972.

H120   ————. *Chicorel Index to Plays in Periodicals.* New York: Chicorel Library, 1973.

H121   ————. *Chicorel Index to the Spoken Arts on Discs, Tapes, and Cassettes.* New York: Chicorel Library, 1973.

H122 —————. *Chicorel Theater Index to Plays for Young People in Periodicals, Anthologies, and Collections.* New York: Chicorel Library, 1974.

H123 —————. *Chicorel Theater Index to Plays in Anthologies, Periodicals, Discs, and Tapes.* 3 vols. New York: Chicorel Library, 1970–72.

H124 Coleman, Arthur, and Gary R. Tyler. *Drama Criticism.* Vol. 1, *A Checklist of Interpretation since 1940 of English and American Plays.* Denver, Colo.: Swallow, 1966.

H125 Conner, John M. and Billie M. *Ottemiller's Index to Plays in Collections: An Author and Title Index to Plays Appearing in Collections Published between 1900 and Mid–1970.* 5th ed., rev. and enl. Metuchen, N.J.: Scarecrow, 1970.

H126 **Cumulated Dramatic Index, 1909–1949.* 2 vols. Boston: Faxon, 1965.

H127 Gohdes, Clarence. *Literature and Theater of the States and Regions of the U.S.A.: An Historical Bibliography.* Durham, N.C.: Duke University Press, 1967.

H128 Guernsey, Otis L. *Directory of the American Theater, 1894–1971, Indexed to the Complete Series of Best Plays in Theater Yearbooks: Titles, Authors, and Composers of Broadway, Off-Broadway, and Off-off-Broadway Shows and Their Sources.* New York: Dodd, Mead, 1971.

H129 *Guide to the Performing Arts.* Edited by Sara Y. Belknap. Metuchen, N.J.: Scarecrow, 1957–67.

H130 Hunter, Frederick J. *Drama Bibliography: A Short-Title Guide to Extended Reading in Dramatic Art for the English-Speaking Audience and Students in the Theatre.* Boston: G. K. Hall, 1971.

H131 Ireland, Norma O. *Index to Full Length Plays, 1944–1964.* Boston: Faxon, 1965.

H132 Keller, Dean H. *Index to Plays in Periodicals.* Metuchen, N.J.: Scarecrow, 1971. (Supplement, 1973.)

H133 Litto, Frederick M. *American Dissertations on the Drama and the Theatre: A Bibliography.* Kent, Ohio: Kent State University Press, 1969.

H134   Long, Eugene Hudson. *American Drama from Its Beginnings to the Present.* New York: Appleton-Century-Crofts, 1970.

H135   McCarty, Clifford. *Published Screenplays: A Checklist, No. 18 of the Serif Series: Bibliographies and Checklists.* General editor, William White. Kent, Ohio: Kent State University Press, 1971.

H136   Melnitz, William W. *Theatre Arts Publications in the United States, 1947–1952: A Five Year Bibliography.* Dubuque, Iowa: American Educational Theatre Association, 1959.

H137   Mersand, Joseph. *Index to Plays, with Suggestions for Teaching.* New York: Scarecrow, 1966.

H138   Mikhail, E. H. *A Bibliography of Modern Irish Drama.* Seattle: University of Washington Press, 1972.

H139   *"Modern Drama: A Selective Bibliography of Works Published in English."* (Annually, 1959–.) *Modern Drama,* 1960–.

H140   National Council of Teachers of English, Committee on Playlists. *Guide to Play Selection.* 2nd ed. New York: Appleton-Century-Crofts, 1958.

H141   *The New York Times Directory of the Theatre.* New York: Arno, 1973.

H142   Ottemiller, John H. *Index to Plays in Collections: An Author and Title Index to Plays Appearing in Collections between 1900 and 1962.* 4th ed., rev. and enl. New York: Scarecrow, 1964.

H143   Palmer, Helen H., and Anne Jane Dyson. *American Drama Criticism: Interpretations, 1890–1965 Inclusive, of American Drama since the First Play Produced in America.* Hamden, Conn.: Shoe String, 1967 (Supplement I, 1970).

H144   Patterson, Charlotte A. *Plays in Periodicals: An Index to English Language Scripts in Twentieth Century Journals.* Boston: G. K. Hall, 1970.

H145   *Play Index.* New York: Wilson, 1949–72.

H146   Ryan, Pat M. *American Drama Bibliography: A Checklist of Publications in English.* Fort Wayne, Ind.: Fort Wayne Publishing Library, 1969.

H147   Salem, James M. *Drury's Guide to Best Plays.* 2nd ed. Metuchen, N.J.: Scarecrow, 1969.

H148   ————. *A Guide to Critical Reviews.* Part 1, *American Drama from O'Neill to Albee;* Part 2, *Musicals from Rodgers-and-Hart to Lerner-and-Lowe;* Part 3, *British and Continental Drama from Ibsen to Pinter;* Part 4, *Screenplays from "The Jazz Singer" to "Dr. Strangelove."* 2 vols. Metuchen, N.J.: Scarecrow, 1966–71.

H149   Samples, Gordon. *The Drama Scholars' Index to Plays and Filmscripts: A Guide to Plays and Filmscrips in Selected Anthologies, Series, and Periodicals.* Metuchen, N.J.: Scarecrow, 1974.

H150   Stratman, Carl J. *American Theatrical Periodicals, 1798–1967: A Bibliographical Guide.* Durham, N.C.: Duke University Press, 1970.

H151   ————. *Bibliography of the American Theatre Excluding New York City.* Chicago: Loyola University Press, 1965.

H152   ————. *Britain's Theatrical Periodicals, 1720–1967: A Bibliography.* New York: New York Public Library, 1972. (Titled *A Bibliography of British Dramatic Periodicals, 1720–1960* in the 1962 edition.)

H153   *Theatre Books in Print: An Annotated Guide to the Literature of the Theatre, the Technical Arts of the Theatre, Motion Pictures, Television and Radio.* Edited by A. E. Santaniello. 2nd ed. New York: Drama Book Shop, 1966.

H154   Vinson, James. *Contemporary Dramatists.* See I40.

H155   Vowles, Richard B. *Dramatic Theory: A Bibliography.* New York: New York Public Library, 1956.

H156   West, Dorothy Herbert, and Dorothy Margaret Peake. *Play Index, 1949–.* New York: Wilson, 1953–.

H157   Wilson, Sheila. *The Theatre of the 'Fifties.* London: Library Association, 1963.

H158   *Young, William C. *American Theatrical Arts: A Guide to Manuscripts and Special Collections in the United States and Canada.* Chicago: American Library Association, 1971.

BIBLIOGRAPHIES AND INDEXES

Fiction Bibliographies

H159   Adelman, Irving, and Rita Dworkin. *The Contemporary Novel: A Checklist of Critical Literature on the British and American Novel since 1945.* Metuchen, N.J.: Scarecrow, 1972.

H160   "Annual Bibliography of Short Fiction Interpretation." *Studies in Short Fiction*, 1964–.

H161   Bell, Inglis, and Donald Baird. *The English Novel 1578–1956: A Checklist of Twentieth-Century Criticism.* Denver, Colo.: Swallow, 1958.

H162   Bufkin, E. C. *The Twentieth Century Novel in English: A Checklist.* Athens: University of Georgia Press, 1967.

H163   Coan, Otis W., and Richard G. Lillard. *America in Fiction: An Annotated List of Novels That Interpret Life in the United States.* 4th ed. Stanford, Calif.: Stanford University Press, 1956.

H164   Cook, Dorothy Elizabeth, and Isabel S. Monro. *Short Story Index: An Index to 60,000 Stories in 4,320 Collections.* New York: Wilson, 1953.

H165   Cotton, Gerald, and Hilda Mary McGill. *Fiction Guides General: British and American.* Hamden, Conn.: Archon, 1967.

H166   *————, and Alan Glencross. *Fiction Index.* London: Association of Assistant Librarians, 1953.

H167   Dickinson, A. T. *American Historical Fiction.* 3rd ed. Metuchen, N.J.: Scarecrow, 1971.

H168   *Fiction Catalog.* 9th ed. New York: Wilson, 1908–.

H169   Gerstenberger, Donna, and George Hendrick. *The American Novel: A Checklist of Twentieth-Century Criticism.* 2 vols. Denver, Colo.: Swallow, 1961–70.

H170   Harper, Howard. "General Studies of Recent American Fiction: A Selected Checklist." *Modern Fiction Studies* 19 (Spring 1973): 127–33.

H171   Kearney, E. I., and L. S. Fitzgerald. *The Continental Novel:*

A Checklist of Criticism in English, 1900–1966. Metuchen, N.J.: Scarecrow, 1968.

H172 Kerr, Elizabeth. *Bibliography of the Sequence Novel.* Minneapolis, Minn.: University of Minnesota Press, 1950.

H173 *Leclaire, Lucien. *A General Analytic Bibliography of the Regional Novelists of the British Isles, 1800–1950.* Paris: G. de Bussac, 1954.

H174 Logasa, Hannah. *McKinley Bibliographies.* Vol. 1, *Historical Fiction: Guide for Junior and Senior High Schools and the General Reader.* 10th rev. and enl. ed. Compiled by Leonard B. Irwin. Brooklawn, N.J.: McKinley, 1968.

H175 McGarry, Daniel D., and Sara H. White. *World Historical Fiction Guide: An Annotated, Chronological, Geographical and Topical List of Selected Historical Novels.* 2nd ed. Metuchen, N.J.: Scarecrow, 1973.

H176 Nevius, Blake. *The American Novel: Sinclair Lewis to the Present.* New York : Appleton-Century-Crofts, 1970.

H177 Palmer, Helen H., and Anne Jane Dyson. *English Novel Explication: Criticism to 1972.* Hamden, Conn.: Shoe String, 1973.

H178 Thurston, Jarvis, et al. *Short Fiction Criticism: A Checklist of Interpretation since 1925 of Stories and Novelettes (American, British, and Continental), 1800–1958.* Denver, Colo.: Swallow, 1960.

H179 Vinson, James. *Contemporary Novelists.* See I41.

H180 Walker, Warren. *Twentieth Century Short Story Explication: Interpretations, 1900–1966.* Hamden, Conn.: Shoe String, 1967. (Supplement I [1967–69], 1970).

H181 Wiley, Paul L. *The British Novel: Conrad to the Present.* Northbrook, Ill.: AHM Publishing, 1973.

H182 Woodress, James. *American Fiction, 1900–1950: A Guide to Information Sources.* Detroit: Gale, 1974.

H183 *Wright, Robert Glenn. *Author Bibliography of English Language Fiction in the Library of Congress through 1950.* Boston: G. K. Hall, 1973.

BIBLIOGRAPHIES AND INDEXES

Poetry Bibliographies

H184   *The Bibliography of Contemporary Poets: A Comprehensive International Index of Today's Writers of Poetry. London: Regency, 1970.

H185   Chicorel, Marietta, ed. Chicorel Index to Poetry in Anthologies and Collections in Print. 4 vols. New York: Chicorel Library, 1974.

H186   *————, ed. Chicorel Index to Poetry in Anthologies and Collections—Retrospective. 4 vols. New York: Chicorel Library, 1975.

H187   *————, ed. Chicorel Index to Poetry in Collections in Print, on Discs and Tapes: Poetry on Discs, Tapes, and Cassettes. New York: Chicorel Library, 1972.

H188   Cline, Gloria S., and Jeffrey A. Baker. Index to Criticisms of British and American Poetry. Metuchen, N.J.: Scarecrow, 1973.

H189   Davis, Floyd M. Contemporary American Poetry: A Checklist. Metuchen, N.J.: Scarecrow, 1975.

H190   Dyson, Anthony E. English Poetry: Select Bibliographical Guides. London: Oxford University Press, 1971.

H191   Kherdian, David. Six Poets of the San Francisco Renaissance: Portraits and Checklists. Fresno, Calif.: Giligia, 1967.

H192   Kuntz, Joseph. Poetry Explication: A Checklist of Interpretation since 1925 of British and American Poems Past and Present. Rev. ed. Denver, Colo.: Swallow, 1962.

H193   Murphy, Rosalie, and James Vinson. Contemporary Poets of the English Language. Chicago: St. James, 1970. See also I42.

H194   Rollins, Charlemae. Famous American Negro Poets. See D127.

H195   Shapiro, Karl. A Bibliography of Modern Prosody. Baltimore: Johns Hopkins University Press, 1948.

H196   Vinson, James, and D. L. Kirkpatrick. Contemporary Poets. See I42.

H197   Woolmer, J. Howard. A Catalogue of Imagist Poets. With Essays by Wallace Martin and Ian Fletcher. See D171.

H198 Zulauf, Sander W., and Irwin H. Weiser. *Index of American Periodical Verse, 1971–*. Metuchen, N.J.: Scarecrow, 1973–.

Bibliographies by Topic

Specialized Bibliographies

H199 *Anderson, David L., with George S. Maas and Diane-Marie Savoye. *Symbolism: A Bibliography of Symbolism as an International and Multi-Disciplinary Movement.* New York: New York University Press, 1975.

H200 Anderson, Robert Roland. *Spanish American Modernism: A Selected Bibliography.* Tucson: University of Arizona Press, 1970.

H201 *Astrinsky, Aviva. *A Bibliography of South African English Novels, 1930–1960.* Cape Town, South Africa: University of Cape Town Libraries, 1965; rpt. 1970.

H202 *Bailey, Richard W., and Delores M. Burton. *English Stylistics: A Bibliography.* Cambridge, Mass.: M.I.T. Press, 1968.

H203 *Baldensperger, Fernand, and Werner P. Friederich. *Bibliography of Comparative Literature.* Chapel Hill: University of North Carolina Press, 1950.

H204 Barnes, Melvin. *Best Detective Fiction: A Guide from Godwin to the Present.* Hamden, Conn.: Linnet, 1975.

H205 *Biography Index: A Cumulative Index to Biographical Material in Books and Magazines.* New York: Wilson, 1945–.

H206 Boyd, George N., and Lois Boyd. *Religion in Contemporary Fiction: Criticism from 1945 to the Present.* San Antonio, Tex.: Trinity University Press, 1973.

H207 Carter, Paul J., and George K. Smart, eds. *Literature and Society, 1961–1965: A Selective Bibliography.* Coral Gables, Fla.: University of Miami Press, 1967.

H208 Coleman, Arthur. *Epic and Romance Criticism.* Vol. 1, *A Checklist of Interpretations, 1940–1972, of English and American Epics and Metrical Romances.* New York: Watermill, 1973.

H209   Czechoslovak P.E.N. Club. *American Literature in Czechoslovakia, 1945–1965.* New York: Czechoslovak P.E.N., 1966.

H210   *Durham, Philip, and Tauno F. Mustanoja. *American Fiction in Finland: An Essay and Bibliography.* Helsinki, Finland: Société Néophilogique, 1960.

H211   *Griffin, E. G. *Bibliography of Literature and Religion.* Alberta, Canada: University of Alberta Department of English, 1969.

H212   Hackett, Alice Payne. *Seventy Years of Best Sellers, 1895–1965.* New York: Bowker, 1967.

H213   Hagen, Ordean A. *Who Done It? A Guide to Detective, Mystery, and Suspense Fiction.* New York: Bowker, 1969.

H214   Hatzfeld, Helmut. *A Critical Bibliography of the New Stylistics Applied to the Romance Literatures.* Chapel Hill: University of North Carolina Press, 1953.

H215   Hoffman, Frank. *Analytical Survey of Anglo-American Traditional Erotica.* Bowling Green, Ohio: Bowling Green University Popular Press, 1973.

H216   Johnson, Merle D. *American First Editions.* 4th ed. Revised and enlarged by Jacob Blanck. Waltham, Mass.: Mark, 1965.

H217   Kaplan, Louis. *A Bibliography of American Autobiographies.* Madison: University of Wisconsin Press, 1961.

H218   Kiell, Norman. *Psychoanalyses, Psychology and Literature: A Bibliography.* Madison: University of Wisconsin Press, 1963.

H219   Libman, Valentina A. *Russian Studies of American Literature: A Bibliography.* Translated by Robert V. Allen. Edited by Clarence Gohdes. Chapel Hill.: University of North Carolina Press, 1969.

H220   *Marshall, Thomas, and George Smart, eds. *Literature and Society, 1956–1960.* Coral Gables, Fla.: University of Miami Press, 1962.

H221   ————; George K. Smart; and Louis J. Budd, eds. *Literature and Society, 1950–1955: A Selective Bibliography.* Coral Gables, Fla.: University of Miami Press, 1956.

H222   *Matthews, William. *American Diaries in Manuscript, 1580–1954: A Descriptive Bibliography.* Athens: University of Georgia Press, 1973.

H223   ————. *British Autobiographies: An Annotated Bibliography of British Autobiographies Published or Written before 1951.* Berkeley: University of California Press, 1955.

H224   Miles, Louis Tonko. *Style and Stylistics: An Analytical Bibliography.* New York: Free Press, 1967.

H225   Palmer, Helen H., and Anne Jane Dyson. *European Drama Criticism, 1960–1966.* Hamden, Conn.: Shoe String, 1968. (Supplement I [to January 1970], 1970.)

H226   Shapiro, Nat. *Popular Music: An Annotated Index of American Popular Songs, 1920–1964.* 6 vols. 2nd ed. New York: Adrian Press, 1967–.

H227   Shibles, Warren A. *Metaphor: An Annotated Bibliography and History.* Whitewater, Wisc.: Language Press, 1971.

H228   Young, William C. *Documents of American Theater History.* Chicago: American Library Association, 1973–.

Minority Bibliographies

H229   Abrash, Barbara. *Black American Literature in English since 1952: Works and Criticism.* New York: Johnson Reprint, 1967.

H230   Arata, Ester Spring, and Nicholas John Rotoli. *Black American Playwrights, 1800 to the Present: A Bibliography.* See F5.

H231   *Brasch, Ila Wales, and Walter Milton Brash. *A Comprehensive Annotated Bibliography of American Black English.* Baton Rouge: Louisiana State University Press, 1974.

H232   *Chapman, Abraham. *The Negro in American Literature and a Bibliography of Literature by and about Negro Americans.* Oshkosh: Wisconsin Council of Teachers of English, 1960.

H233   Chapman, Dorothy H. *Index to Black Poetry.* Boston: G. K. Hall, 1974.

H234   *Deodene, Frank, and William P. French. *Black American*

Fiction since 1952: A Preliminary Checklist. Chatham, N.J.: Chatham Bookseller, 1970.

H235 Hatch, James V. *Black Image on the American Stage: A Bibliography of Plays and Musicals, 1770–1970.* New York: DBS Publications, 1970.

H236 *Hirschfelder, Arlene B. *American Indian Authors: A Representative Bibliography.* New York: Association of American Indian Affairs, 1970.

H237 *Homer, Dorothy R. *The Negro in the United States: A List of Significant Books.* 9th ed., rev. New York: New York City Public Library, 1965.

H238 *————, and Ann M. Swarthout. *Books about the Negro: An Annotated Bibliography.* New York: Praeger, 1966.

H239 Kaiser, Ernest. "Recent Books." *Freedomways: A Quarterly Review of the Negro Freedom Movement*, 1961–.

H240 Leffall, Dolores C. *Bibliographic Survey: The Negro in Print, Five Year Subject Index, 1965–1970.* Washington, D.C.: Negro Bibliographic and Research Center, 1971.

H241 Miller, Elizabeth W. *The Negro in America: A Bibliography.* 2nd ed., rev. and enl. Compiled by Mary L. Fisher. Cambridge, Mass.: Harvard University Press, 1970.

H242 Miller, Wayne Charles; Faye Vowell; et al. *A Comprehensive Bibliography for the Study of American Minorities.* See F100.

H243 *The Negro: A List of Significant Books.* 9th ed., rev. New York: New York Public Library, 1965.

H244 Porter, Dorothy B. *The Negro in the United States: A Selected Bibliography.* Washington, D.C.: Library of Congress, 1970.

H245 ————. A *Working Bibliography on the Negro in the United States.* Ann Arbor, Mich.: University Microfilms, 1969.

H246 Reardon, William R., and Thomas D. Pawley. *The Black Teacher and the Dramatic Arts: A Dialogue, Bibliography, and Anthology.* Westport, Conn.: Negro Universities Press, 1970.

H247   Rollins, Charlemae. *We Build Together: A Reader's Guide to Negro Life and Literature for Elementary and High School Use.* Rev. ed. Champaign, Ill.: National Council of Teachers of English, 1967.

H248   Turner, Darwin T. *Afro-American Writers.* Goldentree Bibliographies in Language and Literature. New York: Appleton-Century-Crofts, 1970.

H249   Welsch, Erwin K. *The Negro in the United States: A Research Guide.* Bloomington: Indiana University Press, 1965.

H250   *Whiteman, Maxwell. *A Century of Fiction by American Negroes, 1853–1952: A Descriptive Bibliography.* Philadelphia: Albert Saifer, 1955.

Regional Bibliographies

H251   Boger, Lorise C. *The Southern Mountaineer in Literature: An Annotated Bibliography.* Morgantown: West Virginia University Library, 1964.

H252   Coyle, William. *Ohio Authors and Their Books: Biographical Data and Selective Bibliographies for Ohio Authors, Native and Resident, 1796–1950.* Cleveland, Ohio: World, 1962.

H253   Dobie, J. Frank. *Guide to Life and Literature of the Southwest.* Rev. and enl. ed. Dallas: Southern Methodist University Press, 1952.

H254   Fuson, Ben W. *Centennial Bibliography of Kansas Literature, 1854–1961.* Salina: Kansas Wesleyan University, 1961.

H255   *McMillan, James B. *Annotated Bibliography of Southern American English.* Coral Gables, Fla.: University of Miami Press, 1971.

H256   Major, Mabel; Rebecca W. Smith; and T. M. Pearce. *Southwest Heritage: A Literary History with Bibliography.* Rev. ed. Albuquerque: University of New Mexico Press, 1948.

H257   Powell, William S. *North Carolina Fiction, 1734–1957: An Annotated Bibliography.* Chapel Hill: University of North Carolina Library, 1958.

H258   Rubin, Louis D. *A Bibliographical Guide to the Study of Southern Literature.* With an appendix containing 68 ad-

15 April 1980

Professor Pemberton:

I understand from my colleague the language
and literature editor Ken McIntock that
CHOICE owes you a good book to review in
atonement for the last assignment. I do
sincerely hope this is better, BUT, I check
titles in my favorite sub-sub-genre, detect
fiction, and found that the best bibliograf
(Jacques Barzun and W.H. Taylor's) is missi
Hope this is the exception, not the rule.

                              Virginia Clark
                    reference & humaniti
                              editor

100 Riverview Center
Middletown, Connecticut 06457
(203) 347-6933

15 April 1980

Professor Pemberton:

I understand from my colleague the language
and literature editor Ken McLintock that
CHOICE owes you a good book to review in
atonement for the last assignment. I do
sincerely hope this is better, BUT, I check
titles in my favorite sub-sub-genre, detect
fiction, and found that the best*bibliograp
(Jacques Barzun and W.H. Taylor's) is missi
Hope this is the exception, not the rule.

J. Clark

Virginia Clark
reference & humaniti
editor

* published in time to be included. Hubin
massive new one is too new — but they
should have known it was underway.

ditional writers of the colonial South by J. A. Leo Lemay. Baton Rouge: Louisiana State University Press, 1969.

H259　Stroup, Thomas B. *Humanistic Scholarship in the South: A Survey of Work in Progress.* Chapel Hill: University of North Carolina Press, 1948.

H260　*Thompson, Lawrence S., and Algernon D. Thompson. *The Kentucky Novel.* Lexington: University of Kentucky Press, 1953.

H261　Thornton, Mary Lindsay. *A Bibliography of North Carolina, 1589–1956.* Chapel Hill: University of North Carolina Press, 1958.

Science Fiction Bibliographies

H262　*Bleiler, Everett F. *The Checklist of Fantastic Literature: A Bibliography of Fantasy, Weird, and Science Fiction Books Published in the English Language.* Chicago: Shasta, 1948.

H263　Briney, Robert E., and Edward Wood. *SF Bibliographies: An Annotated Bibliography of Bibliographical Works on SF and Fantasy Fiction.* Chicago: Advent, 1972.

H264　Clareson, Thomas. *Science Fiction Criticism: An Annotated Checklist.* Kent, Ohio: Kent State University Press, 1972.

H265　*Clarke, I. F. *The Tale of the Future: From the Beginning to the Present Day, a Checklist.* London: Library Association, 1961.

H266　*Crawford, J. H. *333: A Bibliography of the Science-Fantasy Novel.* Providence, R.I.: Grandon, 1953.

H267　Day, Bradford M. *The Checklist of Fantastic Literature in Paperbound Books.* New York: Arno, 1975.

H268　*————. *The Supplemental Checklist of Fantastic Literature.* New York: Science-Fiction & Fantasy Publications, 1963.

H269　Day, Donald B. *Index to the Science Fiction Magazines, 1926–1950.* Portland, Ore.: Perri, 1952.

H270　Hall, H. W. *Science Fiction Book Review Index, 1923–1973.* Detroit: Gale, 1975.

H271   Hutchison, Tom. *British Science Fiction and Fantasy.* N.p. National Book League in Association with the British Council, 1975.

H272   *Index to the Science Fiction Magazine, 1966–1970.* West Hanover, Mass.: New England Science Fiction Association, 1971.

H273   *Metcalf, Norman. *The Index of Science Fiction Magazines, 1951–1965.* New York: Stark, 1968.

H274   Pfeiffer, John R. *Fantasy and Science Fiction: A Critical Guide.* Palmer Lake, Colo.: Filter, 1971.

H275   Siemon, Frederick. *Science Fiction Story Index, 1950–1968.* Chicago: American Library Association, 1971.

H276   Strauss, Edwin S. *The MIT Science Fiction Society's Index to the S-F Magazines, 1951–1965.* Cambridge, Mass.: MIT Science Fiction Society, 1966.

H277   Tuck, Donald H. *The Encyclopedia of Science Fiction and Fantasy through 1968: A Bibliographic Survey of the Fields of Science Fiction, Fantasy, and Weird Fiction through 1968.* Vol. 1, *Who's Who, A-L.* Chicago: Advent, 1974. (Volumes 2 and 3 in progress.)

I

Biographical Guides and Directories

I1 *Authors and Writer's Who's Who.* Edited by L. G. Pine. 4th ed. London: Burke's Peerage, 1960.

I2 Browning, David C. *Everyman's Dictionary of Literary Biography: English and American.* London: Dent, 1958.

I3 Burke, W. J., and Will D. Howe. *American Authors and Books: 1640 to the Present Day.* See H47.

I4 Combs, Richard E. *Authors: Critical and Biographical References: A Guide to 4,700 Critical and Biographical Passages in Books.* Metuchen, N.J.: Scarecrow, 1971.

I5 *Contemporary Authors: A Bio-Bibliographical Guide to Current Authors and Their Works.* See H54.

I6 *Current Biography Yearbook.* New York: Wilson, 1940–. (Formerly *Current Biography: Who's News and Why.*)

I7 Delke, Bernard. *Profiles of Modern American Authors.* Rutland, Vt.: Tuttle, 1969.

I8 *A Directory of American Fiction Writers: 1976 Edition.* See F29.

I9 *A Directory of American Poets: Names and Addresses of More Than 1500 Contemporary Poets Whose Work Has Been Published in the United States.* 1975 ed. New York: Publishing Center for Cultural Resources, 1974.

I10 Fleischmann, Wolfgang Bernard. *Encyclopedia of World Literature in the 20th Century.* See J6.

I11 Garraty, John Arthur. *Encyclopedia of American Biography.* New York: Harper & Row, 1974.

I12 Gaye, Freda. *Who's Who in the Theater: A Biographical Record of the Contemporary Stage.* 14th ed. London: Pitman, 1967.

I13 Handley-Taylor, Geoffrey. *The International Who's Who in Poetry*. 2 vols. London: Cranbrook Tower, 1958.

I14 Hargreaves-Mawdsley, W. N. *Everyman's Dictionary of European Writers*. New York: Dutton, 1968.

I15 Harte, Barbara, and Carolyn Riley. *200 Contemporary Authors: Bio-bibliographies of Selected Leading Writers of Today with Critical and Personal Sidelights*. Detroit: Gale, 1969.

I16 Havlice, Patricia Pate. *Index to Literary Biography*. 2 vols. Metuchen, N.J.: Scarecrow, 1975.

I17 Hetherington, John. *Forty-Two Faces*. Melbourne: F. W. Cheshire, 1962.

I18 Hoehn, Mathew. *Catholic Authors: Contemporary Biographical Sketches 1930–1952*. 2 vols. Newark, N.J.: St. Mary's Abbey, 1948–52.

I19 *The International Authors and Writers Who's Who.* See F61.

I20 Kay, Ernest. *International Who's Who in Poetry, 1974–75*. 4th ed. Totowa, N.J.: Rowman, 1974.

I21 Kunitz, Stanley J. *Twentieth Century Authors: A Biographical Dictionary of Modern Literature*. New York: Wilson, 1955.

I22 Longaker, Mark, and Edwin C. Bolles. *Contemporary English Literature*. New York: Appleton-Century-Crofts, 1953.

I23 *McGraw-Hill Encyclopedia of World Biography*. 12 vols. New York: McGraw-Hill, 1973.

I24 Magill, Frank N., et. al. *Cyclopedia of World Authors*. 3 vols. Rev. ed. Englewood Cliffs, N.J.: Salem Press, 1974.

I25 *New Century Cyclopedia of Names*. 3 vols. New York: Appleton-Century-Crofts, 1954.

I26 Parker, John. *Who's Who in the Theater: A Biographical Record of the Contemporary Stage*. 15th ed. London: Pitman, 1972.

I27 Reginald, R. *Contemporary Science Fiction Authors*. New York: Arno, 1975.

I28 Rigdon, Walter. *The Biographical Encyclopedia and Who's Who of the American Theater*. New York: Heineman, 1966.

129   Rollins, Charlemae. *Famous American Negro Poets.* See D127.

130   Romig, Walter. *The Guide to Catholic Literature.* 5 vols. Grosse Point, Mich.: Walter Romig, n.d.

131   Rush, Theressa Gunnels; Carol Fairbanks Myers; and Esther Spring Arata. *Black American Writers Past and Present: A Biographical Dictionary.* 2 vols. Metuchin, N.J.: Scarecrow, 1975.

132   *Seymour-Smith, Martin. *Who's Who in Twentieth-Century Literature.* See F134.

133   Shockley, Ann Allen, and Sue P. Chandler. *Living Black American Authors: A Biographical Directory.* New York: Bowker, 1973.

134   Spender, Stephen, and Donald Hall. *The Concise Encyclopedia of English and American Poets and Poetry.* New York: Hawthorn, 1963.

135   Tuck, Donald H. *The Encyclopedia of Science Fiction and Fantasy through 1968.* See H277.

136   Unger, Leonard. *American Writers: A Collection of Literary Biographies.* 4 vols. New York: Scribner's, 1974.

137   Untermeyer, Louis. *Lives of the Poets.* New York: Simon & Schuster, 1959.

138   Val Baker, Denys, ed. *Writers of To-Day.* See A297.

139   ————, ed. *Writers of To-Day: 2.* See A298.

140   Vinson, James. *Contemporary Dramatists.* London: St. James, 1973.

141   ————. *Contemporary Novelists.* New York: St. Martin's, 1972.

142   ————, and D. L. Kirkpatrick. *Contemporary Poets.* 2nd ed. London: St. James, 1975. See also H193.

143   Wakeman, John. *World Authors, 1950–1970: A Companion Volume to Twentieth Century Authors.* New York: Wilson, 1975.

144   Warfel, Harry R. *American Novelists of Today.* New York: American Books, 1951.

STUDY GUIDES

I45   Winterich, John T. *Writers in America 1842–1967*. See H107.

I46   *The Writer's Directory: 1974–76*. New York: St. Martin's, 1973.

J

Handbooks and Guides

J1   Anderson, Michael; Jacques Guicharnard; Kristin Morrison; Jack D. Zippes, et al. *Crowell's Handbook of Contemporary Drama*. New York: Crowell, 1971.

J2   *Bergonzi, Bernard. *The History of Literature in the English Language*. Vol. 7, *The Twentieth Century*. London: Barrie & Jenkins, 1970.

J3   Calkins, Elizabeth, and Barry McGhan. *Teaching Tomorrow: A Handbook of Science Fiction for Teachers*. Dayton, Ohio: Pflaum/Standard, 1972.

J4   Eastwood, Wilfred, and John T. Good. *Signposts: A Guide to Modern English Literature*. Cambridge: National Book League at the University Press, 1960.

J5   Elton, William. *A Glossary of the New Criticism*. Chicago: Modern Poetry Association, 1948. (Revised in 1949 as *A Guide to the New Criticism*.)

J6   Fleischmann, Wolfgang Bernard. *Encyclopedia of World Literature in the 20th Century*. 4 vols. New York: Ungar, 1967–.

J7   Fowler, Roger. *A Dictionary of Modern Critical Terms*. London: Routledge & Kegan Paul, 1973.

J8   Goldberg, Gerald J., and Nancy Marmer Goldberg. *The Modern Critical Spectrum: The Major Schools of Modern Literary Criticism Explained and Illustrated for Today's Reader*. Englewood Cliffs, N.J.: Prentice-Hall, 1962.

J9   Green, Elizabeth A. *The Negro in Contemporary American Literature: An Outline for Individual and Group Study*. College Park, Md.: McGrath, 1968.

J10   Grigson, Geoffrey. *The Concise Encyclopaedia of Modern World Literature*. New York: Hawthorn, 1973.

STUDY GUIDES

J11   Hassan, Ihab. *Contemporary American Literature, 1945–1972: An Introduction.* See A138.

J12   Malkoff, Karl. *Crowell's Handbook of Contemporary American Poetry.* New York: Crowell, 1973.

J13   Matlaw, Myron. *Modern World Drama: An Encyclopedia.* New York: Dutton, 1972.

J14   Melchinger, Siegfried. *The Concise Encyclopedia of Modern Drama.* Edited by Henry Popkin. Translated by George Wellwarth. New York: Horizon Press, 1964.

J15   Richardson, Kenneth. *Twentieth Century Writing: A Reader's Guide to Contemporary Literature.* London: Newnes Books, 1969.

J16   Rosenthal, T. G. *American Fiction since 1900.* Reader's Guides, Fourth Series, no. 8. Cambridge: Cambridge University Press for the National Book League, 1961.

J17   Scott, Arthur F. *Current Literary Terms: A Concise Dictionary of Their Origin and Use.* New York: St. Martin's, 1965.

J18   Seymour-Smith, Martin. *Funk and Wagnalls Guide to Modern World Literature.* New York: Funk & Wagnalls, 1973.

J19   Ward, A. C. *Longman Companion to Twentieth Century Literature.* 2nd ed. London: Longman, 1975.

Index

Abbe, George, D1
Abbs, Peter, A1
Abrams, M. H., E105
Abramson, Doris E., B1
Abrash, Barbara, H229
absurdity, B57, B62, B66, B93, B95, B106, C94, C98, C133
Achebe, Chinua: mentioned in C52
Ackroyd, Peter, F1
Adamov, Arthur: mentioned in B21, B31, B57, B107
Adams, Henry: mentioned in A325
Adams, Léonie, D101
Adams, Robert M., E1, F2
Adelman, Irving, H115, H159
adolescence, C255
aesthetic realism, D5
affirmation, A50, A125, C73, C166, C199, C214, C245, D6
Agee, James: mentioned in A68, A99, A166, A176, A260, A269, C70, C105, C199
Agnon, S. Y.: mentioned in A6
Aichinger, Ilse: mentioned in A180
Aichinger, Peter, C1
Aiken, Conrad, A2, A26, D103; mentioned in C204, D28, D81, D102, D106, D114, D149, D157, E60, E91
Albee, Edward, A322, B64, B148; mentioned in A16, A55, A88, A138, A143, A290, A303, A311, B9, B16, B21, B23, B26, B30–31, B33–35, B46, B48–49, B53–55, B57, B61–62, B66, B76, B77, B85, B88, B90, B91, B93, B95, B99, B101, B105, B112, B114, B123–24, B134, B142, B150–152, E7
Aldiss, Brian W., C2, C47; mentioned in C30, C125, C140
Aldridge, John W., C3–7, C128; mentioned in C71, C136

Aleichem, Sholom: mentioned in A153, C254
Algren, Nelson, A26, A320; mentioned in A10, A49, A100, A112, A166, C61, C78, C83, C139, C176, C188, C237
alienation, A1, A50, A125, A280, B16, B50, B147, C22, C36, C71, C98, C123, C127, C229. See also hero and anti-hero
aliterature, A210, C116, C223. See also experiments in literature
Allan, Rony, D31
allegory, B22. See also surveys
Allen, Donald, A51, D2, D31
Allen, Don Cameron, D3
Allen, Harold B., E2
Allen, L. David, C8, C9
Allen, Mary, F3
Allen, Ralph G., B74
Allen, Robert V., H219
Allen, Walter, A3, A289, C10–12
Allen, Woody: mentioned in B99–100
Allingham, Margery: mentioned in C232
Allsop, Kenneth, A4–5
Alter, Robert, A6, C13–14
Altick, Richard D., H1
Alvarez, A[lfred], A7–8, D4, D69, E105; mentioned in D66
Ambler, Eric: mentioned in C232
America, A3, A13–14, A19, A25, A39, A43, A55, A83, A93, A105, A123, A138, A178, A200, A228, A281, A302, B124, C65, C86, C167, C170, C233, C236–237, D4, D22, D43, F21, H163
Amis, Kingsley, A89, A91, C15; mentioned in A4, A9, A229, C12, C27, C30, C42, C81, C182, C185, C189, C214, C249, D78, D120
Ammons, A. R., D20; mentioned in D16, D72

293

INDEX

Anand, Mulk Raj: mentioned in A298
Anderson, David, A9
Anderson, David L., H199
Anderson, Lindsay, A208
Anderson, Maxwell, B64; mentioned in A281, B23, B46, B50, B117, B123, B142, B147
Anderson, Michael, J1
Anderson, Poul: mentioned in C29–30, C45
Anderson, Robert: mentioned in B21
Anderson, Robert Roland, H200
Anderson, Sherwood: mentioned in A120, A167, C36, C78, C144, C174, C251, E60
André, Michael, D31
Andreyev, Leonid: mentioned in A317
Angelou, Maya: mentioned in C43
anger, A4, B92, B139
Anouilh, Jean: mentioned in B8, B18, B21, B31, B33–34, B42, B67, B71
Ansorge, Peter, B2
Antin, Mary: mentioned in A133
antithetical criticism, D14–16
Antoninus, Brother (William Everson): mentioned in A48, D26, D82, D96
apocalypse, C150
Appollinaire, Guillaume: mentioned in D64
Aragon, Louis: mentioned in D86
Arata, Ester Spring, F5, H230, I31
Arden, John, B110, B148, D109; mentioned in B2–3, B21, B24–25, B27–28, B31, B37, B55, B87, B102, B111, B127, B139, B152, B155
Armstrong, William A., B3
Arnheim, Rudolf, D115
Arnow, Harriette: mentioned in A226, C146
Arrabal, Fernando: mentioned in B21, B34, B93
Artaud, Antonin: mentioned in A210, B4, B15, B20–21, B34–35, B39, B54, B93, F49
Ash, Brian, C16, F6
Ashbery, John, D20, D113; mentioned in A55, D16, D25, D28, D36, D72, D145, F68
Asher, Don: mentioned in C67
Ashton, Winifred (Clemence Dane), B40
Asimov, Isaac, C38; mentioned in C2, C8–9, C29, C87, C130, C140, C165, C191–192, C194, C200
Astrinsky, Aviva, H201
Atheling, William, Jr. (James Blish), C29–30, C47; mentioned in C130
Atkins, John, A10, F7
Atkinson, J. Brooks, B5–7

Attaway, William: mentioned in A205, C110
Auchincloss, Louis, A224, C17, C143; mentioned in C102, C236
Auden, W. H., A11, A215, A289, D111, D113, D115, E117; mentioned in A7, A21, A58, A71, A73, A75, A78, A81, A94, A98, A148–149, A159, A183, A204, A206, A255, A262, A268, A296, A298, A308, A318, B43, B60, D4–5, D7, D9, D11, D17–18, D28, D30, D35, D44, D50–51, D53–55, D63–64, D67, D70, D76, D100, D117–120, D128, D130, D133, D136, D141–143, D147, D149, D151, D158–159, D168, E7, E14
Audiberti, Jacques: mentioned in B21
Auerbach, Erich, E105; mentioned in D135
Austen, Roger, F8
Austin, Mary: mentioned in A132
automobile, F26
Axthelm, Peter, C18
Ayckbourn, Alan: mentioned in B140
Aylen, Leo, B8

Babbitt, Irving, E136
Babel, Isaac: mentioned in A159
background, A76, A147, A166, A281, B20, B47, C41, C144, D143, E3
Bader, A. L., A12
Bailey, J. O., C19
Bailey, Richard W., E35, H202
Baird, Donald, H161
Baird, Martha, D5
Baker, Blanche M., H116
Baker, Carlos, A199; mentioned in C142
Baker, Elliott: mentioned in C41
Baker, Ernest Albert: mentioned in C225
Baker, Jeffrey A., H188
Baker, Paul, B138
Balakian, Nona, C20
Balch, Marson, B65
Baldensperger, Fernand, H203
Baldwin, James, A31, A111; mentioned in A10, A17, A55, A62, A64, A68, A85, A88, A113, A129, A146, A159, A166, A172, A191, A201, A205, A238, A269, A292–293, A312, B1, B16, B33, B142, C20, C41, C43, C52, C54, C77, C83, C86, C92, C100, C102, C121, C127, C139, C150, C162, C170, C176, C193, C199, C205, C234, C246, E5, F129
Baldwin, Kenneth H., C21
Baldwin, Michael, A323

INDEX

INDEX

Berger, Thomas: mentioned in A132, A324, C206

Berghahn, Marion, F9

Bergman, Ingmar: mentioned in A274

Bergonzi, Bernard, C27, E3, J2

Bergson, Henri: mentioned in C46, E52

Berlin, Isaiah, A235

Berman, Ed: mentioned in B2

Bermel, Albert, B15

Bernanos, Georges: mentioned in A53, C122

Berrigan, Daniel: mentioned in B86, D24

Berry, Francis, D9

Berry, Thomas Elliot, C28

Berryman, John, D20, D103, F10, F105; mentioned in A7–8, A55, A138, A275, D28, D41, D43, D65–66, D81, D129–130, D145

Berthoff, Warner, A13–14

Bester, Alfred, C56; mentioned in C8–9

Besterman, Theodore, H3–4

Betjeman, John: mentioned in A5

Betti, Ugo, B38; mentioned in B21, B37

Betts, Doris, A40

Beum, Robert, D144

Bewley, Marius, A15, D10, D69

Bier, Jesse, A16

Bigsby, C. W. E., A17, B16

Billetdoux, François: mentioned in B21

biography and bibliography, A5, A36, A68, A141, A155, A297–298, A319, B53, C248, D86, D146, F23, F29, F40, F44, F47, F61, F72, F82, F84, F89–92, F97–98, F109, F134, F154. *See also* sections G and H

biology, E19, E92, E102

Bishop, Elizabeth, D20; mentioned in A21, D53, D96, D154, F68

Bishop, John Peale: mentioned in A318, D35

Bishop, Leonard: mentioned in C78

Black, Edwin, E4

Blackburn, Paul, D110, D113; mentioned in D130

Blackburn, Thomas, D11; mentioned in D78, D120

black humor, C206. *See also* surveys

Blackmur, R. P., D12–13, D69, E105, E119, E136, E144; mentioned in A262, A304, D75, E41, E44, E63, E106

black writers, A17, A62, A99, A110–111, A113, A129, A146, A191–192, A201, A205, A292–294, A312, B1, C34, C43, C52, C77, C82, C100, C110, C193, C205, C224, C234, C244, D57, D124, D127, E5, F5,

F9, F20, F36, F62, F75, F99, F100, F113, F121, F125, H194, H229–235, H237–241, H243–250, I29, I31, I33, J9

Blanchot, Maurice: mentioned in E33

Blanck, Jacob, H37, H216

Blau, Herbert, B17

Blau, Léon: mentioned in A53

Blazek, Douglas: mentioned in D52

Bleiler, Everett F., H262

Blish, James, C29–30, C47; mentioned in C130

Bloch, Robert, C56; mentioned in C165

Bloom, Harold, D14–16, D69, F11–12

Blotner, Joseph, C31–32, E137

Blue, Ila Jacuith, E5

Bluefarb, Sam, C33

Bly, Robert, D110; mentioned in A55, D64, D72, D82, D93, D154, F83

Bode, Carl, A18–20

Bodkin, Maud: mentioned in E63

Bogan, Louise, A21, D17–18, D101; mentioned in D81, D126

Bogard, Travis, B18

Boger, Lorise C., H251

bohemianism. *See* beat generation

Bold, Alan, F13

Boles, Paul Darcy, C103

Böll, Heinrich: mentioned in A180, C161

Bolles, Edwin C., 122

Bolt, Robert, B110; mentioned in B3, B21, B27, B33, B49, B55

Bond, Donald, H7

Bond, Edward: mentioned in B2, B140

Bond, James: mentioned in C95

Bone, Robert A., C34

Bonham-Carter, Victor, A89

Bonin, Jane F., H117

Bonnet, Henri: mentioned in D80

Bontemps, Arna, A111, A227; mentioned in C82, C100, D127, E5

Booth, Philip: mentioned in D36

Booth, Wayne C., E6–7

Borchert, Wolfgang: mentioned in C146

Borden, Karen W., E8

Borges, Jorge Luis, A63, E105; mentioned in C206, C223, C233

Borklund, Elmer, F15

Bottomly, Gordon: mentioned in B137

Boucher, Anthony, C38; mentioned in C29

Bourjaily, Vance, A91, A199, C143; mentioned in A104, C3

Bourne, Randolph, A147

Bova, Ben, C35, C39

Bowden, Edwin T., C36

Bowen, Elizabeth, A22, A26, A31, C111,

INDEX

E93; mentioned in A37, A44, C11, C42, C88, C119, C126, C144, C168, C178, C225, F7

Bowen, John, A323; mentioned in C81, C252

Bowers, Edgar: mentioned in D72

Bowles, Jane: mentioned in C121

Bowles, Paul: mentioned in C3, C61, C176, C218, C236, C242

Bowra, Cecil M., D19

Boyd, George N., H206

Boyd, Lois, H206

Boyers, Robert, A34, D20

Boyle, Kay, A199; mentioned in C95

Bradbury, John M., A23, E9

Bradbury, Malcolm, C37, E10, F16

Bradbury, Ray, A26; mentioned in A131, C2, C15, C29–30, C87, C125, C130, C140, C165, C194

Bradford, James, D31

Brady, Frank, A24

Braine, John: mentioned in A4, C189

Brasch, Ila Wales, H231

Brash, Walter Milton, H231

Brashers, Howard C., A25

Brautigan, Richard: mentioned in A48, C176, C233

Brecht, Bertolt, B36, B38, E11; mentioned in A208, A315, B4, B15, B18, B20, B27, B31, B33, B37, B48, B54, B56, B59, B63, B67, B71, B76, B79, B91, B96, B107, B111, B132, B134, B155, C125, D64, E123

Bree, Germaine, A270

Breed, Paul F., H118

Breit, Harvey, A26

Bremond, Henri: mentioned in D77

Brenton, Howard: mentioned in B2, B140

Bretnor, Reginald, C38–39, F17

Bridges, Robert: mentioned in D55, D70

Bridie, James: mentioned in B143

Briney, Robert E., H263

Brinnin, John Malcolm, D103

Broadway, A99, B5, B30, B47, B72, B78, B99, B115, B125, B154

Broch, Herman: mentioned in C166

Brockett, Oscar G., B19–21

Brodbeck, May, A27

Brodtkorb, Paul, Jr., A83

Broes, Arthur T., C40

Brook, Peter: mentioned in B39

Brooke-Rose, Christine, E12

Brooks, Cleanth, A28, D21, D69, E13–14, E47, E117, E144; mentioned in D2, E9, E53, E72, E106

Brooks, Gwendolyn, A63, A223; mentioned in A17, A62, A312, D127, E5

Brooks, John, C103

Brooks, Van Wyck, A26, A29; mentioned in E63, E106

Brophy, Brigid, A30

Brother Antoninus (William Everson): mentioned in A48, D26, D82, D96

Broussard, Louis, B22

Brower, Reuben Arthur, E15–16

Brown, Francis, A31

Brown, Frank London: mentioned in A201

Brown, Frederic: mentioned in C140

Brown, Gilmor, B138

Brown, John Mason, A32, B23

Brown, John Russell, B24–27

Brown, Kenneth: mentioned in B16

Brown, Merle, E116

Brown, Norman O., A34

Brown, Trisha: mentioned in B94

Brown, William Wells: mentioned in C77

Browne, Wynyard: mentioned in B145

Browning, David C., I2

Bruns, Gerald L., A33

Brustein, Robert, A34, A91, B28–30; mentioned in B85, B132

Bryant, Jerry H., C41

Bryer, Jackson R., C69, H45–46

Bryfonski, Dedria, F150

Buchan, John: mentioned in C232

Buchen, Irving, A34

Buck, Pearl: mentioned in A101, A143

Buckley, Vincent, E17

Budd, Louis J., H221

Budry, Algis: mentioned in C200

Buechner, Frederick: mentioned in C3, C97

Buero Vallejo, Antonion: mentioned in B21

Bufkin, E. C., H162

Bullins, Ed: mentioned in B21

Burford, William, C230

Burgess, Anthony, A34–35, C42, C143; mentioned in A104, C27, C119, C123, C152, C163, C185, C252

Burke, Kenneth, A147, D69, E18, E105; mentioned in A15, B59, D36, D102, E54, E63, E106

Burke, W. J., H47, I3

Burns, Alan, A89

Burns, John Horne: mentioned in C241

Burnshaw, Stanley, E19

Burroughs, William S., A322; mentioned in A5, A16, A48, A98, A131, A139, A195, A233, A266, A272, A300, C41, C63, C121, C138, C175, C212, C218, C233, E95, E115

INDEX

Burrows, David L., A36
Burton, Delores M., H202
Butor, Michel, C47
Butterfield, Stephen, C43
Buzzati, Dino: mentioned in B57

Cable, George W.: mentioned in A258, C82
Cage, John: mentioned in A66, B97
Cahan, Abraham: mentioned in A133, A200, C215
Cahill, Susan, A37
Cahill, Thomas, A37
Caillois, Roger: mentioned in A210
Cain, George: mentioned in A201
Calder, Jenni, C44
Calder, John, A89
Caldwell, Erskine, A38, A224; mentioned in A18, A49, A259–260, C53, C70, C84, C148, C195, C217, C234, C249
Calinescu, Matei, F18
Calisher, Hortense: mentioned in C176
Calkins, Elizabeth, J3
Callahan, Patrick J., C47
Callard, Maurice, A89
Callow, James T., F19
Cambell, Roy: mentioned in A73
Cambon, Glauco, D22–23
Campbell, John W., Jr., C38, C191; mentioned in C29–30, C62, C165
Campbell, Joseph, E137
Campton, David: mentioned in B139
Camus, Albert: mentioned in A9, A69, A88, A103, A172, A180, A208, A210, A231–232, A273, A278, A315, B21, B33, B71, C18, C41, C73, C98, C133–135, C166, C187, C208, C211
Cannady, Joan, F20
Cannan, Denis: mentioned in B139
Capote, Truman, A26, A224, A320, C143; mentioned in A49, A100, A138, A143, A159, A260, B117, C3, C20, C61, C84, C97, C115, C121, C147, C176, C195, C204, C242, C249, C250
Cargas, Harry J., D24
Cargill, Oscar: mentioned in C82
Carleton, William: mentioned in C126
Carpenter, Frederic I., A39
Carr, John, A40
Carr, John Dickson: mentioned in C232
Carroll, Paul, D25, D110; mentioned in A48
Carson, Rachel, A223
Carter, Arthur: mentioned in B117

Carter, Everett, F21
Carter, Lin, C45
Carter, Paul A., F22
Carter, Paul J., H207
Cary, Joyce, A26, A320, C111, E20; mentioned in C11–12, C14, C32, C42, C80, C89, C119, C124, C144, C168, C225–226, C245, C249
Cary, Norman Reed, E21
Casey, John, E22
Casey, Michael, D81
Cassady, Neal: mentioned in A48
Cassill, R. V., A109; mentioned in C246
Cassis, A. F., F23
Castaneda, Carlos: mentioned in A324
Catholic writers, A53, A122, A127, A231, B49, C69, C122, I30
Cauble, Don: mentioned in D52
Caudwell, Christopher, A147; mentioned in C136, E63
Caute, David: mentioned in B140
Cavafy, Constantine: mentioned in A277
Céline, Louis-Ferdinand, A322; mentioned in A152–153
Cendrars, Blaise, A322
Chadwick, Charles, E23
Chaiken, Joseph: mentioned in B39, B99
Chambers, Whittaker: mentioned in C227
Champigny, Robert, E116
Chandler, Raymond: mentioned in A5, C93, C197, C232
Chandler, Sue P., I33
Chapman, Abraham, H232
Chapman, Dorothy H., H233
Chapman, Robert W., H32
Chappell, Fred, A40, A109
characterization. See literary craft and theory
Charters, Samuel, D26
Chase, Mary: mentioned in B117, B133
Chase, Richard, E24, E93
Chassman, Neil A., A41
Chatman, Seymour, E25–26
Chayefsky, Paddy: mentioned in B26–27, B53, B105
Cheek, Leslie, Jr., B138
Cheever, John: mentioned in A64, C6, C97, C121, C176–177, C199, C237
Chekhov, Anton, B36; mentioned in A278, B16, B37, B48, B62–63, B91, B100
Cheshire, David, H49
Chesnutt, Charles Waddell: mentioned in A17, A205, C77, C82
Chester, Alfred: mentioned in C218

INDEX

INDEX

Cotton, Gerald, H165–166

Coward, Noel, A26; mentioned in B21, B41, B83, B145

Cowley, Malcolm, A12, A26, A49, A320; mentioned in C5

Cox, C. B., A50

Coyle, William, H252

Cozzens, James Gould, A221; mentioned in A112, A181, A282, A311, C57, C61, C121, C154–155, C159–160, C170, C236, C241

Crane, Hart, A147, D137; mentioned in D13, D22, D34, D63, D94, D121, D150–151, D157, D162, D169, E81

Crane, Ronald S., E28

Crawford, J. H., H266

creativity, A148, A185, A226, A274, A317, B48, C22, C88, C117, C129, C135, C169, C204, C233, D33, D82, D88–90, D98, D104, D118, D147, D155, E19–20, E56, E58, E80, E102, E133

Creeley, Robert, A51, D2, D31, D110, D113, E100; mentioned in A41, A48, A55, A66, C176, D23, D25–26, D28, D64, D72, D81, D129, D154, D156, D161, F105

Cregan, David: mentioned in B140

Crews, Frederick, E29

Crichton, Robert, C143

Cronin, Anthony, A52

Cross, Tom, H9

Croyden, Margaret, B39

Cruise O'Brien, Conor, A53–54; mentioned in B86

Cruse, Harold: mentioned in A17

Cruz, Victor Hernandez: mentioned in A201

Cullen, Countee: mentioned in A205, C82, D57, D127

Culler, Jonathan, E30

culture. See humanism; society

cummings, e. e., A26, D137; mentioned in A16, A18–19, A46, A55, A167, A186, A198, A308, B43, C1, D12–13, D28, D34–35, D47, D50, D53–54, D61, D63, D67, D91, D94, D106, D112, D114, D122, D125, D133, D141, D143, D150, D156–157

Cunliffe, Marcus, A55

Cunningham, J. V., D101, D103; mentioned in D73

Curley, Dorothy N., G6, G7

Dabney, Lewis M., A36

Dada. See absurdity; modernism

Dahlberg, Edward, A56; mentioned in A66

Daiches, David, A57–58, E31

Damon, Phillip, E32

Dane, Clemence, B40

Davenport, Basil, C55–56

Davenport, F. Garvin, A59

Davidson, Donald, A60; mentioned in A260

Davie, Donald, D32, D69, E105; mentioned in D8, D65–66, D78, D119–120, D134

Davies, Horton, C57

Davies, Robertson, A61

Davis, Arthur P., A62

Davis, Floyd M., H189

Davis, Ossie: mentioned in A17, A312, B1

Davy, Charles, D33

Day, Bradford M., H267–268

Day, Donald B., H269

Deane, Peter, A236

de Ashaje, Juana: mentioned in D61

de Camp, L. Sprague, C38; mentioned in C30, C45, C62, C165, C191

Delaney, Shelagh: mentioned in B33, B111, B139, B152, C81

Delany, Samuel R., C47

Delke, Bernard, 17

Del Ray, Lester: mentioned in C165

de Man, Paul, E33

Dembo, L. S., A63, D34, F78

Demby, William, A227; mentioned in A205, C34

DeMott, Benjamin, A34, C128

Dennis, Nigel, B41; mentioned in B152, C27, C81, C119

Denniston, Constance, C113

Deodene, Frank, H234

d'Errico, Ezio: mentioned in B57

Derrida, Jacques: mentioned in E33

Derwood, Gene: mentioned in D36

detective fiction, C93, C197, C232, F79, F143, H204, H213

Dettelbach, Cynthia Golomb, F26

Detweiler, Robert, C58

Deutsch, Babette, D35, D101

Deutsch, Joel: mentioned in D52

Devlin, Denis: mentioned in A218

de Vries, Peter: mentioned in C57, C131

Dewey, Ken: mentioned in B97

dialogue. See literary craft and theory

Diamond, Arlyn, F27

Dickey, James, A109, D20, D36–40, D103, D113; mentioned in A226, A300, D25, D72, D102, D112, D145, D151, D153

Dickie, George, E34

Dickinson, A. T., H167

Dickinson, Hugh, B42

INDEX

Dickson, Gordon R., C39
Dickstein, Morris, F28
Diderot, Denis: mentioned in A164, C13
Didion, Joan: mentioned in C121
Dillard, R. H. W., A64, A109
Dinesen, Isak: mentioned in C248
Dobie, J. Frank, H253
Dodson, Owen, A227; mentioned in C34
Dodsworth, Martin, D41
Dolan, Paul J., F30
Dolezel, Lubomír, E35
Donato, Eugenio, E89
Donleavy, J. P.: mentioned in A10, A37, A64, C41, C97, C162
Donoghue, Denis, A65, B43, D42–43
Donovan, Josephine, E36
Dorn, Edward, D110; mentioned in D41
Dos Passos, John, A26, A199, C72; mentioned in A3, A88, A112, A262, A277, A301, C3, C61, C70, C75, C78, C134, C144, C155, C159, C174, C217, C220
Dostoevsky, Fyodor: mentioned in A127, A180, A231, A271, A296, C18, C133, C175, D258
Douglas, Lloyd: mentioned in A18
Downer, Alan S., B44–47
Downs, Lenthiel H., A143
Drabble, Margaret, A89
drama of confrontation, B16
Dreer, Herman: mentioned in E5
Drew, Elizabeth, D44
Driver, Tom F., B48
Drummond, Donald: mentioned in D36
Drury, Allen: mentioned in C157
Duberman, Martin, A66
Du Bois, W. E. B.: mentioned in A62, A205, C77
Dugan, Alan, D20; mentioned in D72
du Gard, Martin: mentioned in A152
Dujardin, Edouard: mentioned in C60
Dunbar, Paul Laurence: mentioned in A17, A205, C77, C82, C193
Duncan, Hugh Dalziel, E37
Duncan, Robert, A67, D45, D103; mentioned in A48, A55, A66, D23, D26, D34, D50, D59, D64, D93, D129, D154, D156, D166
Duncan, Ronald: mentioned in B137
Dunsany, Lord: mentioned in C45
Dupee, F. W., A68
Duprey, Richard A., B49
Durant, Ariel, A69
Durant, Will, A69
Durham, Philip, H210
Durr, R. A., A70

Durrell, Lawrence, A31, A321; mentioned in A10, A78, A119, A166, A170, A192, A249, C24, C60, C68, C81, C119, C163, C182, C189, C202, C214, C225, C230, C249, D50, D120, D132
Dürrenmatt, Friedrich, B36, B148; mentioned in A301, B21, B56, B63
Dusenbury, Winifred L. [Frazer], B50
Dworkin, Rita, H115, H159
Dyson, A. E., A50, C59, H190
Dyson, Anne Jane, H143, H177, H225

Eager, Alan R., H10
Eagleton, Terence, A71
Eastlake, William: mentioned in A324
Eastwood, Wilfred, H57, J4
Eaton, Trevor, E109
Eberhart, Richard, D3, D103, D111; mentioned in A7, A64, A99, B43, D24, D43, D50, D73, D96
Eckman, Frederick, D46
ecology, A173, E92
economics. See politics and economics
Eddison, E. R.: mentioned in C45
Edel, Leon, C60
Edgar, David: mentioned in B2
Edmiston, Susan, F31
Edwards, Lee, F27
Egri, Lajos, E38
Ehrenpreis, Irvin, D47
Ehrmann, Jacques, C63
Eichele, Robin, D31
Eigner, Larry: mentioned in D26
Eiseley, Loren: mentioned in A141
Eisinger, Chester E., C61
Elder, Lonne, III: mentioned in A17
Eliot, T. S., A26, A147, A215, A321, B36, B51–52, D48–49, D69, D137, E39, E47, E62, E117, E136, E144; mentioned in A1, A8–9, A15, A21, A24, A28, A42, A44, A49, A55–56, A58, A60, A65, A69–71, A73, A75, A78, A81, A88, A96, A101, A103–104, A106, A118, A122, A127, A145, A149, A154, A179, A183, A185–186, A198, A206, A208, A211, A214, A216–217, A219, A225, A228, A232, A244–247, A252, A255, A262–266, A268, A275, A278, A286, A296–297, A300, A303–304, A306, A314–315, A318, B3, B8–9, B21–23, B26–28, B31, B34, B41–43, B48–49, B55, B59–61, B63, B67, B71, B73, B80–83, B85, B87, B101, B104, B106–107, B112–113, B121–124, B126–127, B137, B143, B145, B155–156, C73, C79, C195, D4,

INDEX

Feldman, Burton, C128

Feldman, Irving: mentioned in D72

Fergusson, Francis, B59; mentioned in B8

Ferlinghetti, Lawrence, D2; mentioned in A48, A131, A189, A233, A277, B132, D23, D26, D156

Ferril, Thomas Hornsby: mentioned in A43

Fialka, Elaine, G7

fiction as consciousness, E6, E50, E69, E85, E93, E111. *See also* self-consciousness

Fidell, Estelle, F35

Fiedler, Leslie A., A84–87, C64–65, C128, E3; mentioned in A202–203, A251, A256, C207

Field, Edward: mentioned in D72

Fielding, Gabriel: mentioned in A130

fifties, the, A4, A6, A41, A49–50, A99, A112, A238, A257, A318, B24, B111, B117, B136, B144–145, B156, B158, C182, C213, D99, D170, H157

Findlater, Richard, B60

Findlay, Robert R., B21

Finkel, Donald: mentioned in D72

Finkelstein, Sidney, A88

Firbank, Ronald: mentioned in A7

Firchow, Peter, A89

Fisch, Harold, A90

Fischer, John, A91

Fisher, Dexter, F36

Fisher, Mary L., H241

Fisher, Rudolph: mentioned in C77

Fisher, Vardis, C158

Fishman, Soloman, A92

Fitzgerald, F. Scott: mentioned in A20, A120, A192, A308, C3, C75, C91, C167, C220, C251, E60

Fitzgerald, L. S., H171

Fitzgerald, Robert: mentioned in A21

Fitzmaurice, George: mentioned in B84

Flaherty, Douglas, D31

Fleischmann, Wolfgang Bernard, H59, J6

Fleming, Ian: mentioned in C93

Fletcher, Ian, D171

Foerster, Norman, A93, A147

Fogazzaro, Antonio: mentioned in C258

Folsom, James K., C66

Foote, Shelby, A40, A109; mentioned in A260

Ford, Boris, A94

Ford, Ford Madox: mentioned in A168

Ford, Jesse Hill, A40

Foreman, Richard: mentioned in B94

Forester, C. S., A26; mentioned in A5

formalism, A50, A83, A186, A232, A247, A268, B24, C7, C90, C181, C204, E9–10, E14–15, E28, E41, E54, E67, E115, E127, E146–147, F162, J5

forties, the, A100, A112, A257, B143, B158, C61, C168, D65

Forster, E. M., A26, A320, E93; mentioned in A291, A297, C7, C89, C91, C133, C174, C243, F128

Foster, Joseph R., A95

Foster, Paul: mentioned in B21

Foster, Richard, E41

Fowler, Roger, E42, F37, J7

Fowles, John, C48, C143; mentioned in A141, C13, C37, C119, C124

Fowlie, Wallace, F96

Fox, Hugh, D52

Fraiberg, Louis, E43

Frampton, Maralee, C161

Frank, Joseph, E44

Frank, Waldo: mentioned in E60

Frankenberg, Lloyd, D53

Fraser, George, F38

Fraser, G. S., A97, D54

Frazer, John, A98

Freed, Donald: mentioned in B86

Freedman, Morris, B61–63

Freedman, Ralph, D88

French, Warren, A99–101, C67

French, William P., H234

Frenz, Horst, A102, B64

Freud, Sigmund, B38; mentioned in A166, B133, D51, E43, E52, E60

Friederich, Werner P., H203

Friedman, Alan Warren, C68

Friedman, Bruce Jay: mentioned in A203, C206–207, C254

Friedman, Maurice, A103

Friedman, Melvin J., A104, C69

Frisch, Max: mentioned in B56, B79, B92, B107

Frohock, W. M., A105, C70

frontier. *See* west

Frost, Robert, A26, A321, D21, D137, E136; mentioned in A11, A16, A36, A43, A55, A60, A70, A106, A123, A153, A179, A228, A279–280, A286, A288, A305, D3, D5, D18, D35, D42, D44, D47, D70, D74–76, D81, D87, D91, D104, D106, D112, D114, D128, D130, D136, D150, D160, D162, D167, D169, E83

Fry, Christopher, B36, B38; mentioned in A58, A106, A145, A211, B3, B21, B27, B31, B43, B48, B60, B63, B71, B80, B82–83, B113, B117, B127, B137, B143, B145, B155–156

INDEX

Frye, Northrop, D69, E45–46, E73, E93, E105, E123, E137, F39; mentioned in A169–170, D51, D151, E22, E56, E59, E86
Frye, Roland Mushat, A106
Fuchs, Daniel: mentioned in C215
Fuller, Edmund, A107, C71
Fuller, Hoyt W., A110
Fuller, Roy, A89, D55; mentioned in D65–66, D78, D158
Fulton, Len, F40, H60
Fuson, Ben W., H254
Fussell, Edwin, D56

Gaboriau, Emile: mentioned in C232
Gaddis, William: mentioned in C146, C233
Gado, Frank, C72
Gaines, Ernest J., A227; mentioned in A201
Gallo, Richard: mentioned in B94
Galloway, David D., C73
Gallup, Jennifer, H2
Gard, Robert E., B65, B138
Gardiner, Harold C., A108, C74–75
Gardiner, Wrey: mentioned in D132
Gardner, Isabella: mentioned in D25, D96
Gardner, John, C25
Gardner, Leonard: mentioned in C237
Gardner, R. H., B66
Garnet, Henry Highland: mentioned in C77
Garraty, John Arthur, I11
Garrett, George, A40, A64, A109; mentioned in A260
Garrigue, Jean: mentioned in D81
Garvey, Marcus: mentioned in C77
Garvin, Harry R., F41–42
Gascar, Pierre: mentioned in A180
Gascoigne, Bamber, B67
Gascoyne, David: mentioned in A232, D11, D77, D100, D118, D132, D158
Gass, William H., C25, C76, C128, C143, E116; mentioned in C121, C233
Gassner, John, A12, B38, B68–74
Gaye, Freda, I12
Gayle, Addison, Jr., A110–111, C77; mentioned in A201
Geduld, Harry M., F43
Geismar, Maxwell, A112, A224
Gelber, Jack: mentioned in A164, B16, B48, B57, B93, B152
Gelfant, Blanche Housman, C78
Genet, Jean: mentioned in A30, A139, A177, A192, A232, B18, B21, B33–34, B48–49, B54, B57, B61, B90, B93, B107, B111–112
genres. *See* literary craft and theory
Gernsback, Hugo: mentioned in C87, C140
Gershator, Phillis, F44
Gerstenberger, Donna, H169
Ghéon, Henri: mentioned in B8
Gibian, George, H61
Gibson, Donald B., A113, D57
Gibson, Walker, C79
Gide, André: mentioned in A69, A103, A119, A262, A297, B8, B42, C18, C133
Gierow, Karl Ragnar, A114
Gilbert, Jack, D103
Gilby, Thomas: mentioned in D77
Gilman, Richard, A115, B75
Gindin, James, C80–81
Ginestier, Paul, D58
Ginsberg, Allen, A322, D2, D31, D59, D110, D113; mentioned in A3, A48, A55, A131, A133–134, A138, A189, A233, A251, A307, D5, D23–26, D28, D36, D50, D72, D93–94, D125, D129, D153, D166
Giono, Jean: mentioned in C146
Giovanni, Nikki: mentioned in A312, D57
Giraudoux, Jean, B36; mentioned in B8, B18, B33, B42, B67, B71, B107
Glencross, Alan, H166
Glicksberg, Charles I., A116–120, E47
Glicksohn, Susan, C47
Gloster, Hugh M., A111, C82
Godard, Jean Luc: mentioned in A266, A274
Gohdes, Clarence, F45, H62, H127, H219
Gold, Herbert, A224, C83, C103, C128; mentioned in C97, C102, C139, C162, C215, C246
Gold, Michael, A147
Goldberg, Gerald Jay, E48, J8
Goldberg, Nancy Marmer, E48, J8
Golden, Harry: mentioned in A272, C218
Goldfarb, Sidney: mentioned in D145
Golding, William: mentioned in A64, A81, A159, A170, A177, A197, A231, A237, A251, A269, A311, C18, C24, C40, C81, C116, C119, C123, C182, C185, C187, C189, C198, C214, E90
Goldman, William: mentioned in C67
Good, John T., H57, J4
Goodman, Paul, A121, C128, E49; mentioned in A133, A259, C83, C218, D72
Gordon, Ambrose, C230
Gordon, Caroline: mentioned in A228, C61, C146
Gordon, David: mentioned in B94

INDEX

B73, B81, B107, B112, B134, B155
Ignatow, David: mentioned in D36, D98
imagination. *See* creativity
Indians. *See* West, the
Inge, William, A224, B64, B148; mentioned in B26, B50, B66, B77, B88, B90, B105, B108, B117, B123, B133
Inglis, Fred, E64
Innes, Michael: mentioned in C232
international issues, A71, A95, A114, A117, A130, A144, A176, A178, A187, A212, A241, A246, A253, A275, A277, A303, B27, B32, B34, B58, B78, B90, B94, B146, C134, C217, D30, H61, H96, H203
interviews and statements, A22, A26, A38, A40, A63, A67, A89, A102, A109, A160, A184, A199, A209, A213, A215, A221, A223–224, A227, A230, A239, A249–250, A271, A286, A289, A320, A321–323, B36, B55, B64, B110, B138, B148, C25, C72, C103, C111, C143, C158, C179, D20–21, D31, D37–39, D45, D48–49, D59–62, D66, D75, D81, D84, D101–103, D107–111, D113, D123, D126, D137–138, D147–148, E11, E39, E97–99, E107, E109, E129, F161
Ionesco, Eugène, A213, B36, B38, B148; mentioned in A5, A119, A172, A273, B4, B21, B31, B33–34, B41–42, B49, B56–57, B66, B74, B91–93, B96, B107, B111, B126, B155
Ireland, Norma O., H131
Irish literature, A37, B84, B136, C126, D8, F52, F88, H10, H65
irony, C59, E7
Iser, Wolfgang, C112
Ishag, Saada, C113
Isherwood, Christopher, A26; mentioned in A5, A170, A183, A257, C124, C144, C183, C185, F7
Israel, Robert: mentioned in B94
Ivask, Ivar, A161
Izenour, George C., B138

Jackson, Blyden, F62
Jackson, Charles, A26
Jacobs, Robert D., A260
Jaffe, Rona, A223
Jakobson, Roman: mentioned in E25
James, Clive, A162
James, Henry, E93; mentioned in A15, A56, A94, A244, A275, A279, A308, C40, C60, C155, D24
James, William, F47
Jameson, Fredric, E66–67

Jameson, Storm, A163, C114; mentioned in C136
Jarrell, Randall, D3, D20, D69, D75–76, D101; mentioned in A55, A260, A268, C142, D23, D28, D36, D43, D66, D73–74, D81, D102, D121, D138, D154
Jeffers, Robinson, B64; mentioned in A39, A43, A69, A117, B42, D150, D162
Jellicoe, Ann: mentioned in B33, B139
Jennings, Edward M., E68
Jennings, Elizabeth, D77–78, F63
Jewish writers, A6, A87, A90, A99, A133, A190, A202–203, C10, C64, C151, C180, C207, C215, C254, F70
Johnson, James Weldon: mentioned in A205, C77, C193
Johnson, Merle D., H216
Johnson, Michael L., C115
Johnson, Pamela Hansford, A89
Johnston, Denis: mentioned in A309, B84
Jonas, Joan: mentioned in B94
Jones, Brynmor, H71
Jones, David, D137; mentioned in A170, D104
Jones, David Michael: mentioned in C40
Jones, Howard Mumford, H72
Jones, James, A26, A224, A322; mentioned in A49, A112, A120, A269, C1, C20, C41, C139, C162, C197, C237, C241
Jones, LeRoi. *See* Baraka, Imamu Amiri
Jones, Margo, B138
Jones, Peter G., F64
Jong, Erica, D113
Jordan, June: mentioned in A201
Josipovici, Gabriel, C116, F65–66
Joyce, James: mentioned in A21, A33, A42, A46, A52, A56, A58, A69, A75, A127, A170, A186, A277, A297, B59, C4, C10, C13, C24, C46, C60, C68, C71, C73, C90–91, C95, C112, C117, C126, C135, C226, C252–53, D24, D151, E14, E29, E58, E60, F2, F88, F128
Juhasz, Suzanne, D79, F67
Justice, Donald: mentioned in D72

Kafka, Franz: mentioned in A6, A69, A85, A119, A139, A180, A197, A208, A210, A231, A244, A266, B112, C46, C125, C175, C211, C246, C257, E60, E90
Kagarlitski, Julius, C47
Kaiser, Ernest, H239
Kalstone, David, F68
Kampf, Louis, A164
Kane, Henry: mentioned in C197

INDEX

Kaplan, Charles, A165
Kaplan, Harold, C117
Kaplan, Louis, H217
Kaplan, Sydney Janet, C118
Kaprow, Allen: mentioned in B97
Karl, Frederick R., C119
Karolides, Nicholas J., C120
Kauffman, Stanley, F69
Kaufman, George S.: mentioned in B85, B117
Kay, Ernest, F61, I20
Kazan, Elia: mentioned in C67
Kazantzakis, Nikos: mentioned in A69, C258
Kazin, Alfred, A12, A91, A166, A167, C121, C128
Keane, John B.: mentioned in B84
Kearney, E. I., H171
Kees, Sidney: mentioned in D132
Kees, Weldon, A221
Kegan, Robert, F70
Kehler, Dorothea, H15
Keller, Dean H., H132
Kellogg, Gene, C122
Kelly, Robert, D110
Kennard, Jean E., C123
Kennedy, Adrienne: mentioned in B1
Kennedy, Alan, C124
Kennedy, Andrew K., B87
Kennedy, Arthur: mentioned in B48
Kennedy, Arthur G., H16
Kennedy, X. J.: mentioned in D23
Kenner, Hugh, A168, E115
Kermode, Frank, A169–170, D69, E3, E69, E105; mentioned in D54
Kernan, Alvin B., B88
Kerouac, Jack, C111; mentioned in A48, A105, A116, A120, A131–132, A181, A189, A233, A254, A307, C20, C40, C41, C71, C139, C162, C242, D59, F56
Kerr, Elizabeth, H172
Kerr, Walter, B89–91
Kershaw, John, B92
Kesey, Ken: mentioned in A86, A324, C173, C233, F56
Ketterer, David, C48, C125
Kettle, Arnold, E62
Keyes, Francis Parkinson, A26
Kherdian, David, H191
Kidd, Walter E., A101
Kiell, Norman, F71, H218
Kiely, Benedict, C126
Kierkegaard, Søren: mentioned in A69, A88, A119
Killens, John O.: mentioned in A293, C241

Killinger, John, A171–172, B93
King, Kimball, F72
King, Larry L., A40
King, Martin Luther, Jr.: mentioned in A59
Kingsley, Charles: mentioned in C149
Kinneavy, Brother James Leo, D80
Kinnell, Galway, D20, D113; mentioned in D23, D72, D98
Kinsella, Thomas: mentioned in D8
Kipphardt, Heinar: mentioned in B86
Kirby, David K., C21
Kirby, Michael, B94, E70
Kirkpatrick, Daniel, F73
Kirkpatrick, D. L., H196, I42
Kitchen, Laurence, B95–96
Kizer, Carolyn: mentioned in D72
Klappert, Peter: mentioned in D81
Klein, Marcus, C63, C127–128
Klinkowitz, Jerome, C63, C129, F74
Klotman, Phyllis Rauch, F75
Knight, Damon, C130, F76; mentioned in C29–30
Knights, L. C., E123
Knott, Frederick: mentioned in B117
Knowles, John, A31; mentioned in F56
Knox, Monsignor Ronald: mentioned in C232
Koch, Kenneth: mentioned in A68, D72
Koehmstedt, Carol L., H73
Koestler, Arthur, A26; mentioned in A35, A103, A219, A244, A297, C18, C32, C44, C108, C227, C258
Kolodny, Annette, A173
Kopit, Arthur: mentioned in B21, B86, B99, B101, B152
Kops, Bernard: mentioned in B139, B152, C81
Koritz, Marian, H109
Kornbluth, Cyril M., C56; mentioned in C15, C29, C130, C256
Kort, Wesley A., C131
Kosinski, Jerzy, C25; mentioned in A180, C129, C247
Kostelanetz, Richard, A174–176, B97, C63, E3
Kramer, Maurice, G7
Kramm, Joseph: mentioned in B117
Krech, Richard: mentioned in D52
Krieger, Murray, D88, E71–73, F77–78
Krim, Seymour: mentioned in A272, C83
Kronenberger, Louis, B98
Krutch, Joseph Wood, A147, E47
Kryss, T. L.: mentioned in D52
Kumar, Shiv K., C132

INDEX

INDEX

Lewis, R. W. B., C135, E115
Lewis, Sinclair: mentioned in A20, A101, A112, A123, C57, C251
Lewis, Wyndham: mentioned in A73, A168, A283, C11, C174
Lewisohn, Ludwig: mentioned in A133
Libman, Valentina A., H219
Lidman, Sara, A63
Lieberman, Laurence, F85
Lillard, Richard G., H163
Limmer, Ruth, D18
Lindop, Grevel, D134
Lindsay, Jack, C136, D86
Lingner, Erika, A188
Lipton, Lawrence, A34, A189, C128
Liptzin, Sol, A190
literary craft and theory, A12, A14, A24, A73, A92, A197, A276, A288, B15, B20, B22, B35–36, B38, B40, B43, B63, B67, B69–70, B72–73, B87, B94, B116, B121–122, B142, C14, C37, C50, C59, C76, C83, C85, C111–113, C132, C135, C141, C147, C163, C190, C196, C201, C222, C235, C240, C247, D1, D5, D8–9, D11, D14–16, D27–29, D53, D80, D88, D115, D117, D119, D131, D155, E3, E11, E13, E31, E50, E59, E72, E84, E111, E117, E128, E138–139, E141–143
literary life, the, A12, A22, A29, A38, A58, A68, A74, A82, A92, A121, A124, A141, A156, A163, A174, A193, A236, A261, B60, B73, B76, B89, B102, B116, B128, B154, C195
literature of exhaustion, C129, C223
Little, Malcolm (Malcolm X): mentioned in A205, C153
Littlejohn, David, A191–192
Littlewood, Joan: mentioned in B111, B132, B139
Litto, Frederick M., H133
Litvinoff, Emanual, A323
Litz, A. Walton, C137
Livings, Henry: mentioned in B139
Livingston, Ray, E87
Locke, Alain, A110–111
Lodge, David, C138
Logan, John, D110; mentioned in D25, D72
Logasa, Hannah, H174
loneliness. *See* alienation
Long, Eugene Hudson, H134
Longaker, Mark, I22
Longrigg, Roger: mentioned in C81
Lorca, Federico García, B36; mentioned in A297, B18, D6, D64

love, A96
Lovecraft, H. P.: mentioned in A317, C45
Lowell, Robert, A321, D20–21, D66, D111, D137; mentioned in A7–8, A21, A36, A47, A55, A64, A68, A81, A128, A166, A275, B33, B150, D5, D18, D22–24, D28, D30, D41–43, D47, D50, D53, D63, D65, D73, D75, D81, D91–92, D96–97, D106, D112, D128–130, D145, D151, D154, D161, D168, E56, F68, F105
Lowry, Malcolm: mentioned in A100, C37
Lubbock, Percy, E93, E144
Ludwig, Jack, C139
Ludwig, Richard M., D87, H72
Lukács, Georg: mentioned in A273, E33, E59
Lumley, Frederick, B107
Lundwall, Sam J., C140
Lutwack, Leonard, C141
Lynen, John F., D69
Lyons, John O., C142
lyric, D80. *See also* surveys
Lytle, Andrew Nelson: mentioned in A260, C61

Maas, George S., H199
MacAdam, Alfred J., F86
MacAdams, Lewis, D31
McCaffrey, Anne, C39
McCarthy, Mary, A194–195, A289, A321, B108, C132; mentioned in A10, A78, A99, A137, A238, A283, C4, C6, C17, C20, C61, C83, C121, C142, C152, C162, C176, C219, C239, D74
McCarty, Clifford, H135
Macaulay, Rose: mentioned in C226, C245
McClure, Michael: mentioned in A48, A189, A233
McConnell, Frederic, B138
McCormack, Thomas, C143
McCormick, John, C144
McCullers, Carson: mentioned in A100, A143, A198, A260, A283, A301, B50, B142, C5, C10, C17, C20, C33, C61, C84, C97, C105, C121, C147, C152, C162, C204, C234, C242, C249
McCurtain, Peter: mentioned in C197
MacDiarmid, Hugh: mentioned in A7
MacDonald, George: mentioned in C149
MacDonald, Ross, C143; mentioned in C197
McDonnell, Frank D., F87
McDowell, Frederick P. W., D88
McGarry, Daniel D., H175

311

INDEX

MacGay, Norman: mentioned in D78
McGhan, Barry, J3
McGill, Hilde Mary, H165
McGinley, Phyllis, A26
McGrath, John: mentioned in B2
McGrory, Kathleen, F88
Machen, Arthur: mentioned in A283
MacInnes, Helen, A26
McIntosh, Angus, E88
MacIver, R. M., F196
McKay, Claude: mentioned in A205, C77, C193
McKenzie, Gordon, E117
Macksey, Richard, E89
McLaverty, Michael: mentioned in C126
MacLeish, Archibald, A12, A91, B64; mentioned in A99, B9, B22, B26, B43, B49, B53, B124, B147, D28, D43, D106, D150, D162, D167, E123
MacLow, Jackson, D113
McLuhan, Marshall, E3; mentioned in A115, E46
MacManus, Francis: mentioned in C126
McMillan, James B., H255
McNamee, Lawrence F., H81
MacNeice, Louis, A197; mentioned in A7, A46, A64, D11, D50, D54, D58, D63, D65, D147, D159, E56, E91
McNeir, Waldo, A198
McNelly, Willis E., C145
McRobbie, Kenneth, C49
Madden, Charles, A199
Madden, David, A200, C146
Maeterlinck, Maurice, B36
Magie, Nanneska N., C69
Magill, Frank N., F89, F90, F91, F92, G9, G10
Mailer, Norman, A26, A147, A322, C128, C143, C179; mentioned in A3, A7–8, A10, A14, A16, A34, A48–49, A55, A84, A88, A99, A112, A115, A120, A131, A133, A138, A141, A153, A159, A166, A176, A179, A200, A203, A219, A226, A238, A245–246, A269, A290, A301, A319, B132, C1, C3–4, C6, C20, C32, C64, C80, C86, C92, C97, C101–102, C115, C121, C134, C139, C144, C153, C155, C162, C170, C174, C188, C195, C207, C209–210, C219–220, C233, C241–242, C246, C253, E115, F87
Major, Clarence, A201, A227
Major, Mabel, H256
Malamud, Bernard: mentioned in A6, A16, A36, A50, A68, A84–85, A99, A138, A157, A159, A166, A169, A202–203, A219,

A245, A259, A269, A272, C10, C20, C22, C49, C64, C90, C97, C99, C102, C121, C127, C131, C139, C151, C162, C176, C180, C198–199, C207, C210, C215, C218, C233, C237, C239, C242, C246, C254, F70
Malcolm X: mentioned in A205, C153
Malin, Irving, A202–203, C147, C148
Malkoff, Karl, F93, J12
Mallarmé, Stéphane: mentioned in A33, D64, E23
Malraux, André: mentioned in C108, C135
Manchester, William, A109
Mander, John, A204
Manheim, Eleanor, E90
Manheim, Leonard, E90
Manlove, C. N., C149
Mann, Thomas, A221; mentioned in A68–69, A154, A298, A310, C14, C46, C135, C166, C222, C248, C252, C258, D102, E44, E60, E90
manners, novel of, C236. See also society
Manning, Olivia: mentioned in C163, C178
Mansfield, Katherine: mentioned in A30, C152
Margolies, Edward, A205
Maritain, Jacques, D89
Marowitz, Charles, B109–111; mentioned in B2
Marquand, John P., A26; mentioned in A112, C1, C154–155, C236
Marshall, Thomas F., H82, H220–221
Martin, F. David, A206
Martin, Wallace, D171
Martz, Louis, D69, D90
Maschler, Thomas Michael, A89
Maschler, Tom, A207
Mascolo, Dionys: mentioned in A210
Masefield, John: mentioned in A145, A232, B137, B145, D35
Matlaw, Myron, J13
Matthews, Brander, E136
Matthews, Honor, A208, B112
Matthews, J. H., F94
Matthews, William, H222–223
Matthiessen, F. O., D69, E91
Maugham, W. Somerset, A26, A209; mentioned in A5, A69, A131, A298, B60, B83, B98, C95, C248
Mauriac, Claude, A210
Mauriac, François, A320, C69; mentioned in A53, C12, C122, C166, C183
May, Charles E., F95
May, John R., C150
May, Keith M., F96
Mayfield, Julian, A227; mentioned in A62

INDEX

INDEX

INDEX

Peake, Mervyn: mentioned in C149
Pearce, Richard, C175
Pearce, Roy Harvey, A234, D114
Pearce, T. M., H256
Peckham, Morse, E102
Peden, Margaret Sayers, A109
Peden, William, A109, C176–177
Péguy, Charles: mentioned in A53
Pendleton, Don: mentioned in C197
Pendry, E. D., C178
Penzler, Otto, F143
Percy, Walker, A40; mentioned in A259, A269, C121, C233, C246
Perelman, S. J., A321
Peretz, I. L.: mentioned in A85
Perkins, David, F111
Perkins, George, C179
Perkins, Michael, F112
Perreault, John: mentioned in B94
Pescatello, Ann M., F113
pessimism. *See* alienation
Petry, Ann, A227; mentioned in A62, C34, C110, C193
Petsch, Robert: mentioned in D80
Pfeiffer, John R., H274
Phelps, Robert, A236, D18
phenomenological novel, C125. *See also* experimental literature
Philipson, Morris, E103
Phillips, Elizabeth C., B123
Phillips, William, A34, C128, E104
philosophy, A47, C117, C183, C184, C253, D34, D162, E78, E94, E116
picaresque, C14, C135
Pine, L. G., I1
Pinner, David: mentioned in B140
Pinsker, Sanford, C180
Pinsky, Robert, F114
Pinter, Harold, A322, B110, B148; mentioned in A176, A197, B2–4, B15, B21, B24–27, B31, B33–34, B41, B54, B57, B62, B75–76, B87, B90–93, B96, B100–102, B111–112, B126–127, B139, B152, B155, C81
Pirandello, Luigi, B36; mentioned in A119, B18, B48, B56, B63, B67, B73–74, B107
Pitt, Valerie, A237
Pitter, Ruth: mentioned in D81
places as setting and influence, A131, A240, A254, A308, C78, C142, C220
Plater, Alan: mentioned in B140
Plath, Sylvia, A323, D20, D109; mentioned in A7–8, A136, A151, A266, C54, C219, C233, D41, D66, D72, D97, D129, D134, D145, D153, F105

Platt, Peter, H20
Plimpton, George, A34, A321–322, F161
Plomer, William: mentioned in D78
plot. *See* literary craft and theory
Plummer, Christopher: mentioned in B76
Podhoretz, Norman, A238; mentioned in A64
poetic plays and novels, B27, B43, B51–52, C169
Pohl, Frederik, C39; mentioned in C15
Poirier, Richard, E16
politics and economics, A43, A54, A114, A121, A151, A153, A187–188, A301, B11, B16–17, B86, B99, B115, B131, B152, C5, C31–32, C44, C108, C128, C157, C174, C188, C227, C231, C257, D19, D24, D93, E66, E76, F30, F155
Polletta, Gregory T., E105
Pondrom, Cyrena N., A63
pop art, A18, A242, A273, A295, B28, B103, C94, H212, H226
Popkin, Henry, J14
pornography. *See* eroticism
Porter, Dorothy B., H244–245
Porter, Katherine Anne, A223, A239, A321; mentioned in A18, A120, A131, A218, A254, A260, A272, A305, A310, C6–7, C17, C95, C121, C204, C222, C229, C239, C248, E123
Porter, Peter: mentioned in D158
Porter, Thomas E., B124
post-modernism, A55, A229, C4, C68, C73, C117, C123, C127, C129, C173, C190, C202, C246, D8, D52, D82, D96, D139, D142, D145, D170, E58, E69, E92
Potts, Charles: mentioned in D52
Poulet, Georges: mentioned in E33
Pound, Ezra, A147, A215, A321, D69, D107, D137, E144; mentioned in A1, A21, A46, A51, A55–56, A65–66, A69, A75, A100, A105, A143, A151, A168, A183, A252, A262, A264–266, A268, A275, A277, A310, A316, A325, B43, C195, D4, D6, D10–13, D17–19, D28, D30, D32, D34, D47, D50–51, D53–54, D59, D61–64, D70, D79, D87, D91, D94, D106, D117, D119–121, D125, D128, D133, D142, D145–147, D149, D151, D156, D160, D163, D167, E115
Powell, Anthony: mentioned in A170, A283, C27, C42, C89, C119, C144, C214, C240, C249
Powell, Dawn: mentioned in A318
Powell, Grosvenor E., A36
Powell, Lawrence Clark, A240
Powell, William S., H257

INDEX

INDEX

Reznikoff, Charles, A63
rhetorical criticism and fiction, C187, E4, E6–7
Rice, Elmer, B64; mentioned in B22, B50, B77, B117, B147
Rich, Adrienne, D20; mentioned in D72, D145, F68
Richards, Frank: mentioned in A5
Richards, I. A., A147, E109, E117, E144; mentioned in D55, E41, E52, E63, E72, E86, E112
Richardson, Jack: mentioned in B152
Richardson, Kenneth, J15
Richardson, Robert, A252
Richman, Robert, A253
Richter, Conrad: mentioned in C120
Richter, David H., C187
Rideout, Walter B., C188
Riding, Laura: mentioned in D149
Ridler, Anne: mentioned in B137, D78, D100, D132
Ries, Lawrence, F123
Riesman, David: mentioned in A137
Rigdon, Walter, I28
Riggs, Lynn: mentioned in B147
Righter, William, E110
Riley, Carolyn, G5, I15
Rimbaud, Arthur: mentioned in D71, E23
Rinehart, Mary Roberts, A26
Rinn, Fauneil, J., E8
Rippier, Joseph S., C189
Robbe-Grillet, Alain, C111, C190; mentioned in A139, A172, A176, A185, A210, A252, A266, A277, A300, A317, C212, C253, E115
Robbins, Jack Alan, C102, F34
Robbins, J. Albert, F4, H30
Robert, Martha: mentioned in C13
Roberts, Patrick, B126
Roberts, Thomas J., E111
Robinson, Cecil, A254
Robinson, Edwin Arlington: mentioned in D22, D38, D157, D162
Robson, W. W., A255
Rodgers, Richard: mentioned in A100, B76, B133
Rodgers, W. R.: mentioned in D118
Roethke, Theodore, A12, A221, D20–21, D111, D126; mentioned in A55, A99, A138, A143, A179, A234, A271, A300, D23, D28, D30, D38, D42–43, D63, D73, D81, D90–91, D96–98, D112, D129, D135, D151, D161
Rogers, Alva, C191
Rogers, David, B123

Rogers, Hubert: mentioned in C191
Rogers, Robert, A256
Rollins, Charlemae, D127, H194, H247, I29
romanticism, A299, B106, C51, D7, D95. *See also* surveys
Romig, Walter, I30
Rooney, William Joseph, E112
Rosa, Alfred F., F124
Rose, Alan Henry, F125
Rose, Lois, C192
Rose, Mark, F126
Rose, Stephen, C192
Rosenberg, Harold, E113; mentioned in A219
Rosenblatt, Roger, C193
Rosenfeld, Isaac, A257; mentioned in A202, A272, C215, C218
Rosenthal, M. L., A31, D128–130
Rosenthal, T. G., J16
Ross, Lillian, A224
Rostand, Edmond: mentioned in B116
Rostand, Jean: mentioned in A210
Roth, Philip, C128; mentioned in A34, A84, A133, A151, A159, A166, A202–203, A219, A238, A272, C58, C80, C95, C102, C121, C151, C167, C218, C233, C237, C240, C246, C254
Rothenberg, Jerome, D110, D113; mentioned in A55
Rotoli, Nicholas John, F5, H230
Rottensteiner, Franz, C194
Rourke, Constance: mentioned in E63
Rowse, A. L., A235
Roy, Emil, B127
Rubin, Louis D., Jr., A258–260, C195–196, F127, H258
Rudkin, David: mentioned in B139
Ruehlmann, William, C197
Rukeyser, Muriel, A199, D113, D131; mentioned in D75
Ruotolo, Lucio P., C198
Rupp, Richard H., C199
Rush, Theressa Gunnels, I31
Russell, Bertrand, A235; mentioned in C76
Russell, Eric Frank: mentioned in C165
Russell, John, F128
Ryan, Michael: mentioned in D81
Ryan, Pat M., H146
Ryder, Dorothy E., H21

Sackler, Howard: mentioned in B99
Sagan, Françoise, A320
Sainer, Arthur, B128–129
Salem, James M., H147–148

318

INDEX

INDEX

D18, D23–24, D28, D50, D96, D106, D128, D154
Shapiro, Nat, H226
Shaw, George Bernard, B36; mentioned in A30, A37, A44, A106, A149, A183, A219, A263, A270, A301, A318, B9–10, B15, B18, B27–28, B41, B48–49, B62–63, B71, B73, B75, B81, B83, B87, B98, B106–108, B116–117, B122, B127, B143, B145, B156–157
Shaw, Irwin: mentioned in C3, C61, C64, C241
Shaw, Robert: mentioned in B86, B140
Shaw, Robert B., D145
Sheed, Wilfred, A269
Shepard, Sam: mentioned in B2, B28, B100
Sherman, Bernard, C215
Sherwood, Robert E., A26; mentioned in A106, B22, B147
Shibles, Warren A., H227
Shockley, Ann Allen, I33
Shockley, Robert: mentioned in C140
Sholokov, Mikhail: mentioned in A69
short stories, C23, C176–177, C239, C250, F95, H164, H178, H180
Showalter, Elaine, F135
Shumaker, Wayne, E120–121
Siegel, Eli, D5
Siemon, Frederick, H275
Sievers, W. David, B133
silence, A139–140, A274, E126
Sillitoe, Alan: mentioned in A5, A169, A188, C6, C10, C81, C95, C119, C189, C214
Silone, Ignazio: mentioned in A5, A152, A298, C108, C135, C161, C257
Silvers, Robert B., A91
Simak, Clifford D.: mentioned in C165
Simenon, Georges, A320; mentioned in A210
Simmons, Charles, C20
Simmons, Pip: mentioned in B2
Simon, John, B134–135
Simon, John Oliver: mentioned in D52
Simon, Neil: mentioned in B21, B99–100
Simpson, Alan, B136
Simpson, Louis, D146; mentioned in D72, F83
Simpson, Norman Frederick: mentioned in B3, B21, B41, B57, B111, B139, B152
Sinclair, Andrew: mentioned in C81
Sinclair, John, D31
Singer, Isaac Bashevis, A63; mentioned in

A152, A203, A251, A259, C121, C180, C207, C254
Sitwell, Edith, A235; mentioned in A5, A7, A46, A297, D11, D19, D35, D50, D86, D99
sixties, the, A6, A41, A55, A121, A130, A272, A282, A318, B25, B37, B39, B65, B69, B75, B95, B101, B105, B111, B129, B131, B134–135, B140, B143, B150, C67, C83, C123, C129, C173, C206, C218, D25, D65, D82, D93, D124, D145, F28
Skaggs, Merrill Maguire, C216
Skelton, Robin, D147
Slatoff, Walter J., E122
Slavitt, David, A109
Sloan, James Park: mentioned in C129
Slochower, Harry, E137
Slote, Bernice, A270, D94, E123
Smart, George K., H207, H220–221
Smith, Betty: mentioned in C78
Smith, Clark Ashton: mentioned in C45
Smith, Edward E.: mentioned in C62, C165
Smith, Grover, D69
Smith, Herbert: mentioned in A188
Smith, Rebecca W., H256
Smith, Roger N., F136
Smith, Stevie: mentioned in D8
Smith, Thelma, C217
Smith, William Gardner: mentioned in C34, C100, C110, C205
Smith, William James, H63
Smith, William Jay, D103; mentioned in D36
Sniderman, Florence M., H118
Snodgrass, W. D., A271, D20; mentioned in D23, D25, D72–73, D91, D153
Snow, C. P., A91, A224; mentioned in A5, A78, A107, A116, A126, A170, A283, C12, C27, C37, C42, C49, C60, C81, C119, C144, C155, C163, C174, C182, C185, C214, C225, C230, C245, C249, F7
Snyder, Gary, D2, D148; mentioned in A48, A55, A189, A233, A307, D26, D72, D97, D153, D156
society, A18, A54, A71, A83, A92, A105, A108, A118, A136, A148, A150–152, A169, A188, A207–208, A213, A220, A229, A270, A273, A290–291, B7, B16–17, B25, B28, B30, B56, B61, B105–106, B124, C3–5, C10, C21–22, C27, C65, C76, C127–128, C155, C159, C189, C236, C249, C257, D58, D133, D164, D167, E10, E37, E46, E79, E91, E103, E126, E139, F7, F107, F156–157, H207, H220–221

INDEX

Solotaroff, Theodore, A272, C218

Solzhenitsyn, Alexander: mentioned in A69, C222

Sontag, Susan, A273–274, C25, E105; mentioned in A115, A272, C195, C208, C218, C233, C247

Sorrentino, Gilbert, D110: mentioned in C129

Southern, Terry: mentioned in C202

Southern writers, A23, A59–60, A178, A258, A260, C10, C53, C84, C105, C107, C216, C229, C244, D151, E9, E53, F48, F127, H251, H255, H258–259

Southworth, James G., D149–150

space and time, C46, C163, C221, E44, E69, E95

Spacks, Patricia M., C219, F137–138

Spanos, William V., B137

Spark, Muriel, C69; mentioned in A169, A237, A277, C37, C119, C124, C138, C185, C214

Spatz, Jonas, C220

Spears, Monroe K., D69, D151

Speight, Johnny: mentioned in B139

Spencer, Sharon, C221

Spender, Stephen, A12, A31, A275, D109, I34; mentioned in D6, D11, D18, D50, D54, D58, D63, D147, D158–159

Spenser, Bernard: mentioned in D66

Spenser, Colin: mentioned in B140

Spenser, Elizabeth: mentioned in A99, A260

Sperr, Martin: mentioned in B21

Spicer, Jack: mentioned in A48, D26

Spiegel, Alan, F139

Spilka, Mark, E105, F140

Spillane, Mickey: mentioned in A49, C197

Spiller, Robert E., A276, F141, H80, H99

sports, C237

Springer, Mary Doyle, C222

Spurgeon, Caroline: mentioned in E63

Stade, George, F142

Stafford, Jean, A26; mentioned in C17, C61, C177, C239

Stafford, William: mentioned in D72, F83

Staley, Thomas F., C161

Stallman, Robert Wooster, E124–125

Stanford, Barbara Dodds, A294

Stanford, Derek, D152

Stanford, Donald E., A277

Stapleton, Olaf W.: mentioned in C256

Stark, John O., C223

Starke, Catherine Juanita, C224

Stauffer, Donald A., D115

Stauffer, Donald Barlow, D153

Stead, Christine: mentioned in A137

Steele, Wilbur Daniel, A26

Stefan, George: mentioned in D64

Stegner, Wallace: mentioned in C61, C250

Stein, Aaron Marc, C197

Stein, Gertrude: mentioned in A80, C76, C146

Stein, Walter, A278

Steinbeck, John: mentioned in A3, A20, A39, A69, A99, A101, A103, A112, A116, A158, A254, A297, C10, C33, C36, C70, C75, C96, C137, C141, C174, C217, C220, C251, C258

Steinbrunner, Chris, F143

Steiner, George, E126; mentioned in B8

Stepanchev, Stephen, D154

Stephens, James: mentioned in C126, D53

Sterling, E. F., C48

Sternberg, Meir, F144

Stevens, David H., B138

Stevens, Wallace, A215, A221, D137, D155; mentioned in A14–15, A19, A24, A33, A36, A43, A55, A65, A99–100, A149, A153–154, A169, A178–179, A185, A228, A234, A252, A262, A266, A275, A288, A300, B43, C247, D4–5, D10, D12–13, D16, D22, D28, D30, D34–35, D42, D47, D50, D53, D55–56, D63–64, D70, D75–77, D79, D81, D87–88, D90–91, D94–95, D104, D106, D112, D114, D121–122, D125, D128, D135–136, D143, D150–151, D160, D168–169, E91, E94, E115, F12

Stevenson, Lionel, C47, C225

Stevenson, Quentin: mentioned in D78

Stevick, Philip, C48

Steward, Douglas, C226

Stone, Edward, A279–280

Stone, Irving: mentioned in A5

Stoppard, Tom: mentioned in B21, B102, B140

Storey, David, A323; mentioned in B140, C10, C81

Stout, Rex: mentioned in C197, C232

Strachey, John, C227

Strachey, Lytton: mentioned in A128, C59

Straight, Michael, C158

Strand, Mark: mentioned in D72, D145

Stratman, Carl J., H150–152

Straumann, Heinrich, A281–282

Strauss, Edwin S., A276

Street, James Hawck: mentioned in C57

Strider, Marjorie: mentioned in B94

Strindberg, August, B36; mentioned in A115, A315, A317, B15, B37, B112

Strong, Patience: mentioned in A5

INDEX

Strong, Thomas B., A259
structuralism, E25, E30, E67, E75, E89, E114, F78
Stuart, Aimée: mentioned in B117
Stuart, Dabney: mentioned in D105
Stubbs, Harry C. (Hal Clement), C39; mentioned in C8–9
Stuckey, W. J., C228
Sturgeon, Theodore: mentioned in C29–30, C87, C140, C165, C200
Styron, William, A320; mentioned in A64, A88, A112, A138, A141, A219, A258, A260, A264, A269, C1, C4–6, C20, C22, C24, C53, C58, C73, C83–84, C97, C99, C105, C121, C131, C139, C162, C174, C195, C210, C234, C242, C246
suicide, A8
Sukenick, Ronald, C25, C63; mentioned in C129
Sullivan, Walter, C229
Sundman, Per Olof, A63
surfiction, C63
surrealism, A154, C125, F91. *See also* surveys
surveys, A25, A35, A42, A44, A57–58, A69, A93–94, A97, A124, A138–139, A142–143, A161, A175, A212, A263, A287, B19, B21, B31, B44–45, B48, B67–71, B74, B77, B83, B85, B98, B102, B107, B114–115, B123, B128, B141, B149, B155, B157, C10–11, C20, C37, C42, C48, C119, C121, C139, C185, C225, C230, C233, D17, D23, D30, D45, D72, D76, D78, D81, D96, D99, D112, D120, D129, D134, D152–154, D156, D159, D161, E34, E52, E63–64, E74, E83, E86, E106, E120, E124, E127, E135, E143
Susann, Jacqueline, A223
Sutherland, William, Jr., C230
Sutton, Walter, D156, E127
Swados, Harvey, C103, C231; mentioned in C83, C97, C139, C162
Swallow, Alan, E128
Swarthout, Ann M., H238
Swenson, May, D103; mentioned in D72, D154
Swingewood, Alan, E79
symbolism, A96, A154, B106, C171, D13, D106, E18, E23, E45, E77, E85, E108, E123, E132, E142, H199. *See also* surveys
Symons, Julian, A283, C232
Synge, J. M.: mentioned in B127
Synge, William, B36; mentioned in B73–74, B81, B98

Sypher, Wylie, A284–285; mentioned in C26

Taffel, Norman: mentioned in B94
Taine, John: mentioned in C62
Tallman, Warren, D2
Tanner, Tony, C233
Tardieu, Jean: mentioned in B21, B57
Tate, Allen, A286, D101, D157, E47, E129, E144; mentioned in A149, A169–170, A247, A258, A262, A264–265, A277, C229, D28, D35, D47, D87, D92, D106, D114, D122, D143, D149, D151, D160, D168, E9, E41, E53, E72, E91, E106, E112
Tate, James: mentioned in D145
Taylor, Cecil P.: mentioned in B140
Taylor, Henry, A109
Taylor, John Russell, B139–140
Taylor, Karen Malpede, B141
Taylor, Peter: mentioned in A260, C61, C177, C250
Taylor, William E., B142
teaching and learning, A148, A150, A182, A193, A268, A294, C145, C156, C160, C247, D20, D36, D44, D83, D105, D116, E122, E128, H140, H174, H246–247
Tempkin, Pauline B., B65
Temple, Ruth Z., G14, H101–102
Tennyson, G. B., E130
Terry, Megan: mentioned in B131
Terson, Peter: mentioned in B21, B140
TeSelle, Sallie McFague, E131
theater of cruelty, B34. *See also* experimental literature
theater of mixed means, B97
theology. *See* Catholic writers; Christian issues; Jewish writers; religion
Thirkell, Angela, A26
Thomas, Dylan, A26, D137; mentioned in A78, A94, A137, A176, A211, A218, A232, A268, D6–7, D11, D28, D30, D50, D53, D54–55, D63, D67, D71, D74, D81, D86, D94–95, D118, D126, D128, D133, D136, D142, D147, D158–159, D163, E60
Thomas, Hugh: mentioned in A4, C81
Thomas, R. S.: mentioned in D8, D78
Thompson, Algernon D., H260
Thompson, Deane C., C106
Thompson, Lawrence S., H260
Thornton, Mary Lindsay, H261
Thorp, Willard, A287
Thurber, James, A26, A320; mentioned in A5, A16, C95
Thurley, Geoffrey, D158, F145

322

INDEX

INDEX

C129, C140, C150, C167, C173, C194, C202, C206, C222, C233, C243, C256
Von Szeliski, John, B147
von Wilpert, Gero, A161
Voss, Arthur, C239
Vowell, Faye, F100, H242
Vowles, Richard B., H155

Wager, Walter, B148
Wager, Willis, A303
Waggoner, Hyatt Howe, D161–162
Wagner, D. R.: mentioned in D52
Wagner, Linda, D31
Wagoner, David, D20; mentioned in D72
Wain, John, A89, A147, A207, A304, D163; mentioned in A4, A229, C81, C189, D78
Wakeman, John, I43
Wakoski, Diane, D113
Walcutt, Charles Child, C240
Waldmeir, Joseph J., C241–242
Walker, Alice, A227
Walker, Margaret: mentioned in A62, D127
Walker, Warren, H180
Wallace, Irving, A223
Wallant, Edward Lewis: mentioned in A203, C22, C109, C207
Walsh, Chad, C243
Walsh, S. Padraig, H24
war and violence, A58, A98, A180, B7, B55, B95, C1, C3, C10, C70, C84, C136, C154, C241, D93, F30, F64, F123
Ward, A. C., J19
Ward, Douglas Turner: mentioned in A17
Warfel, Harry R., I144
Warner, Rex: mentioned in C119, C257
Warren, Austin, E143
Warren, Robert Penn, A26, A31, A223, A305, A320, C72, C179, C196, D21, D164–165, E117, E144; mentioned in A21, A28, A59–60, A84–85, A100, A176, A247, A258, A260, A264–265, A280, A283, A301, A319, C7, C22, C53, C61, C70, C75, C84, C88, C91, C121, C137, C144, C157, C160, C170–171, C195, C229, C234, C251, D2, D16, D47, D122, D149, E9, E44, E71
Waterhouse, Keith: mentioned in B3, C10, C81
Watkins, Floyd C., A306, C244
Watkins, Vernon: mentioned in D11, D63
Watson, George, E140, F155, H36, H48, H53, H88, H106
Watts, Alan W., A307

Waugh, Evelyn, A26, A322, C69: mentioned in A5, A30, A35, A53, A71, A170, A247, A283, A298, A317, C11, C27, C42, C50, C59, C85, C89, C91, C122, C144, C161, C168, C183, C185–186, C220, C225, C243, C245, C249, C253
Weales, Gerald, B149–151
Weatherhead, A. Kingsley, D166
Webster, Harvey Curtis, C245
Wedgwood, C. V., A235
Weidlé, Vladimir: mentioned in A210
Weil, Simone: mentioned in A273
Weimann, Robert, F156
Weimer, David R., A308
Weinberg, Helen, C246
Weinstein, Arnold L., C247
Weiser, Irwin H., H198
Weiss, Ann, H47
Weiss, Irving, H47
Weiss, Peter, B148; mentioned in A130, B21, B33–34, B56, B86, B107, B126
Weiss, Theodore, D103; mentioned in D72
Welch, Denton: mentioned in A46
Welch, Lew: mentioned in D26
Wellek, René, D88, E141–143; mentioned in E86
Wells, A. J., H44
Wells, Henry W., D167
Wells, H. G.: mentioned in A317, C8–9, C30, C125, C174, C192, C256
Wells, Ida: mentioned in C43
Wellwarth, George, B152, J14
Welsch, Erwin K., H249
Welty, Eudora, C132; mentioned in A100, A129, A258–260, A305, A310, C20, C61, C84, C91, C105, C162, C199, C216, C219, C239, C250
Wescott, Glenway, C72, C248; mentioned in A218
Wesker, Arnold, B110, B148; mentioned in A188, A204, B2–3, B24–25, B27, B31, B92, B111, B127, B139, B152, C81
Wesley, Richard: mentioned in B86
west, the, A43, A86–87, A132, A240, A303, A324, C66, C120, C158, F81, H236, H253, H256
West, Anthony, A309
West, Dorothy: mentioned in C34
West, Dorothy Herbert, H156
West, Jessamyn, C103
West, Nathanael: mentioned in A177, A238, A283, A311, A317, C150, C167, C207, C220
West, Paul, C249
West, Ray B., Jr., A310, C250, E144

INDEX

West, Rebecca, A323
West, Thomas Reed, F157
Westbrook, Max, C251
Westlake, Donald E.: mentioned in C197
Weston, Christine, A26
Whalen, Philip: mentioned in A48, A233, A251, A307
Wharton, Edith: mentioned in A153, A290, C75, C78
Wheelock, John Hall, D123
Wheelwright, John: mentioned in D12
Wheelwright, Philip, E145
Whipple, T. K.: mentioned in E106
Whitaker, Thomas R., D69, E116, F158
Whitbread, Thomas B., A311, C230
White, E. B.: mentioned in A16
White, John J., C252
White, Patrick: mentioned in A7
White, Sara H., H175
White, William, H135
Whitehead, James, A40, A109
Whiteman, Maxwell, H250
Whiting, John, B110, B153; mentioned in B3, B31, B127, B139, B155, B156
Whitlow, Roger, A312
Whitman, Robert: mentioned in B97
Whitman, Walt, D2; mentioned in A18–20, A134, A308, D71, D94, D142, D156
Whittemore, Reed, A221, D103; mentioned in D36
Wicker, Brian, C253
Wickham, Glynne, B154
Wideman, John, A227
Wieners, John: mentioned in A233
Wiesel, Elie: mentioned in A6
Wilbur, Richard, A109, A199, D3, D103, D111, D113; mentioned in A21, A55, A99, A179, A303, D18, D23, D73, D75, D96, D112, D154
Wilde, Oscar: mentioned in A75, A317, B63, B127
Wilder, Amos N., A313, D168
Wilder, Thornton, A320, B36, B64; mentioned in A100, A107, A281, B18, B22–23, B26, B37, B48–49, B53, B59, B63, B66, B77, B80, B85, B88, B105, B108, B114, C67, C248
Wiley, Paul L., H181
Wilkinson, Chris: mentioned in B2
Wilkinson, Sylvia, A109; mentioned in D105
Williams, Charles: mentioned in A81, A107, A216–217, A248, B137, C104, C238, D100
Williams, Duncan, A314

Williams, Forrest, E76
Williams, Harry, F159
Williams, Heathcote: mentioned in B2, B100, B140
Williams, John A., A227; mentioned in A201, A312, C100
Williams, Raymond, A315, B155; mentioned in A188
Williams, Tennessee, B36, B64, B148; mentioned in A5, A16, A100, A106, A131, A138, A143, A177, A181, A260, A281, A315, B9–10, B18, B21–23, B26, B31, B33–35, B41–42, B46, B48–49, B53–54, B58, B60–63, B66–67, B71, B73–74, B76–77, B79–80, B85, B88, B90–91, B96, B104–106, B108, B114, B116, B123–124, B133, B142, B147, B150, B157, C99, C177
Williams, William Carlos, A26, A215, A316, A322, D2, D5, D137; mentioned in A3, A33, A36, A48, A51, A55, A65–66, A104, A131, A168, A189, A244–245, A247, A249, A251–252, A254, A264, A268, A299, A308, A325, D12–13, D17, D22, D28, D34–35, D47, D50, D53, D56, D63–64, D70, D75, D79, D81, D90–91, D95, D112, D114, D121, D125, D128, D130, D135, D141–143, D146, D149, D151, D156, D160, D166–167, E91, E95
Williamson, Audrey, B156
Williamson, Jack, C39; mentioned in C62, C165
Willison, Ian, H89
Wilson, Angus, A31, A89, A320; mentioned in A204, A237, C27, C37, C80–81, C119, C182, C185, C189, C214, C249
Wilson, Colin, A207, A317; mentioned in A4, A64, A122, C81
Wilson, Edmund, A26, A318, E47, E136; mentioned in A36, A153, A169–170, A262, A283, A291, A304, E63, E106
Wilson, Garff, B157
Wilson, Robert: mentioned in B94
Wilson, Sheila, H157
Wilson, Snoo: mentioned in B2
Wimsatt, W. K., Jr., E105, E144, E146–147, F160
Winchell, Constance M., H25
Winterich, John T., H107
Winters, Yvor, A147, A221, D69, D169, E47, E144, E148; mentioned in A55, A262, A277, D66, E22, E63, E72, E106, E112
Wisse, Ruth, C254
Witham, W. Tasker, C255
Wittgenstein, Ludwig: mentioned in A69

INDEX

Wodehouse, P. G., A223; mentioned in C6
Wolfe, Thomas: mentioned in A39, A112, A200, A231, A258, A305, C24, C40, C46, C53, C70, C75, C78, C84, C107, C251
Wolfe, Tom, C25; mentioned in A148, C79, C115
Wollheim, Donald A., C256
women, A136–137, A173, C17, C54, C118, C152, C178, C219, E8, E36, F3, F54, F67, F101, F103, F132, F135, F138
Wood, Charles: mentioned in B140
Wood, Edward, H263
Woodcock, George, C257, D170
Woodham-Smith, Cecil, A26
Woodress, James, H30, H108–109, H182
Woolf, Virginia: mentioned in A42, A136, A244, A290, A298, C7, C12, C24, C46, C60, C68, C91, C178, C198, E36
Woolmer, J. Howard, D171, H197
Worsley, T. C., B158
Wouk, Herman: mentioned in C64, C241
Wright, Andrew, H1, H26
Wright, Charles, A227; mentioned in C206
Wright, George T., A319
Wright, James, D20; mentioned in D25, D72, D81–82, D96, F83
Wright, Richard, A110–111, C179; mentioned in A17, A62, A113, A129, A143, A146, A172, A191, A201, A205, A257, A312, B1, C33–34, C43, C52, C77, C82, C86, C100, C110, C134, C150, C193, C205, C234, D24
Wright, Robert Glenn, H183

Wright, Willard Huntington: mentioned in C232
Wylie, Elinor: mentioned in D149
Wylie, Philip, C38; mentioned in C1, C15
Wynar, Bohdan S., H27
Wyndham, John: mentioned in C165

Yates, Richard: mentioned in C146
Yeats, William Butler, B36, D69, D137; mentioned in A28, A44, A75, A127, A154, A168, A266, A268, A278, A317, B127, B155, D7, D11, D51, D68, D71, D104, D121, D142, D159, F88
Yerby, Frank, A26, A91; mentioned in C100, C110
Yevtushenko, Yevgeni: mentioned in A69
Young, Al, A227
Young, LaMonte: mentioned in B97
Young, Marguerite: mentioned in C169
Young, Stanley: mentioned in B117
Young, Stark: mentioned in B10
Young, Thomas Daniel, F162
Young, Wayland, A34
Young, William C., H158, H228

Zebrowski, George, C39
Ziolkowski, Theodore, C258
Zippes, Jack D., J1
Zola, Emile, B36; mentioned in A291
Zolla, Elémire, A324
Zukofsky, Louis, A63, A325; mentioned in A51
Zulauf, Sander W., H198